Hitler and the
Forgotten Nazis

Bruce F.
Pauley

**Hitler and
the Forgotten
Nazis**

A History of Austrian National Socialism

The University of North Carolina Press   Chapel Hill

© 1981 The University of North Carolina Press

All rights reserved

Manufactured in the United States of America

ISBN 0-8078-1456-3

Library of Congress Catalog Card Number 80-17006

Library of Congress Cataloging in Publication Data

Pauley, Bruce F
   Hitler and the forgotten Nazis.

   Bibliography: p.
   Includes index.
   1. Austria—Politics and government—1918–1938.
2. Nazionalsozialistische Deutsche Arbeiterpartei in Österreich. 3. Hitler, Adolf, 1889
–1945. I. Title.
DB97.P38   943.6'051   80-17006
ISBN 0-8078-1456-3

For my mother,

Mark, and Glenn

Contents

The Fatherland Front. The July Agreement. The
Austrian Nazis and the Agreement. The July
Agreement: Its Impact on the Austrian Economy and
the Fatherland Front.

List of Illustrations

The intense interest in Hitler that has been sweeping Europe and America the last few years appears to have no end. The popularity of the biographies by John Toland, Joachim Fest, Werner Maser, and Alan Bullock attest to the fascination which Adolf Hitler still has for the public more than thirty years after his death. With so many books and articles already written on the Nazi dictator the reader may ask how still another work about Hitler and National Socialism can be justified. The answer is that until now the Austrian manifestations of National Socialism have been neglected. This focus hardly needs explanation as it was in Germany, after all, where Hitler and his Nazi party first attained power in 1933.

Yet the exclusive attention devoted to German National Socialism has led to enormous historical omissions. It should never be forgotten that Hitler was Austrian, as were many other prominent Nazis, such as Adolf Eichmann, Ernst Kaltenbrunner, and Arthur Seyss-Inquart. In fact, National Socialism began, not in Germany, but in the Austrian Empire—long before the party, which Hitler joined in September 1919, was founded. Moreover, Austrian Nazis manned some of the most notorious concentration camps, one of which —Mauthausen—was in Austria itself. In fact, outrages committed against Austrian Jews by Austrian Nazis during and after 1938 were on the whole worse than those perpetrated by German Nazis against the Jews of Germany.

The Austrian Nazi movement is also interesting because it was filled with incredible contradictions. Many of its members were inspired by a very real, if in our view perverted, idealism whose ends they were willing to realize through violence. They loudly proclaimed their support of the *Führerprinzip* (leadership principle), but could never agree on which of their own leaders to follow. They proudly asserted their allegiance to one large German *Volk*, but jealously guarded the autonomy of the Austrian Nazi party and the Austrian state, viewing Germans from the *Altreich* as "outsiders." They sought to bring the Austrian people together in a single mass movement, but denounced compromise and left the country more divided than ever.

In this day of international terrorism waged by militant minorities the Austrian Nazis stand as an early example of how a small, fanatical band, supplied in part by smuggled weapons and fueled by propaganda, can infiltrate legitimate institutions, undermine governments, and destabilize society itself. Likewise, the Austrian Nazi challenge illustrates how a threatened government will often acquire some of the characteristics of its hated opposition.

The Austrian Nazis also played an important, albeit not widely recognized, role in the German seizure of Austria—the famous Anschluss of March 1938. This event marked the Third Reich's first takeover of a sovereign state and is therefore an important milestone on the road to the Second World War.

Yet the Nazis of Austria have virtually been forgotten. Not only were they neglected by their contemporaries in Germany, they have also suffered the same fate at the hands of historians. The Austrians have had little incentive to discuss their contributions to the history of National Socialism. When the Allies declared at the Moscow Conference in November 1943 that Austria was the "first victim of German aggression," the Austrians were only too willing to agree. For the Allies the declaration was a useful pretext to reduce German territory. For the Austrians it was a heaven-sent alibi, an admission by the Allies themselves that Austria played only a passive role in the Anschluss drama of 1938.

During the ten long years of postwar Allied occupation the Austrians were anxious to avoid raising any issues that might be used by the Allies to prolong their stay. Thus, when a former prominent Austrian Nazi, Alfred Persche, wrote an excellent account of the party's activities between 1936 and 1938,[1] the Austrian chancellor and leader of the conservative (People's) party, Alfons Gorbach, recommended that it not be published. Although Gorbach admitted that the book had "many new and highly interesting details," the author's claim that 80 percent of the Austrian people had been Nazis would "certainly be exploited by the Soviet Union, the Communists, and the Socialists." Persche's book "would only arouse a violent controversy over the years 1934–38."[2] Consequently, it remains unpublished to this day.

For personal reasons too, a curtain of silence has been drawn across the history of Austrian National Socialism. Until 1949 the Allied Control Commission in Austria indiscriminately applied denazification laws to all former Nazis thus excluding them from the franchise and discriminating against them in all areas of public and private life. Under these circumstances former Nazis would obviously not discuss their past political activities voluntarily. Former party members are not eager to tell their children or grandchildren about their past activities or motivations for joining. The younger generation, they fear, growing up in completely different and happier times, would never understand the anxieties, frustrations, and hopes that governed their actions four decades earlier.

Adolf Hitler himself contributed substantially to the ignorance surrounding the Austrian Nazis. Although he was born in Austria and grew to manhood in Vienna at the very moment National Socialism was gathering strength, he would not admit to being influenced by any Austrian nationalist except Georg von Schönerer, who was safely dead and therefore not a potential rival. For Hitler, the Nazi movement began in 1920, when he announced the party's Twenty-five Point program. To confess that the party had Austrian predecessors would only diminish his prestige and "genius."

Once in control of the German Nazi party, Hitler showed surprisingly little interest in the Austrian Nazis for many years. His first ambition was to seize power in Germany. When that was accomplished he would rebuild the German armed forces. Only then would he turn his attention to the German-speaking people of Austria.

But the Austrian Nazis had aspirations of their own. They could not forget their origins or the separate existence of their country, whose autonomy, if not independence, they wished to preserve. Although the Austrian Nazis had a variety of leaders, some relatively moderate, others more radical, they all strove to play roles free from German dictation. And however much Hitler might wish to forget them, the pretentions of the Austrian *Parteigenossen* kept reminding him of their existence, often in most embarrassing ways.

After World War II, while the world's attention was riveted on the Nuremberg trials and the denazification of German Nazis, the Nazis of Austria were once again largely forgotten. And so it has remained for the past thirty years. During a period when the West Germans have taken a long and agonizing look at their Nazi heritage, the Austrians have tried hard to convince themselves that National Socialism was a strictly foreign phenomenon. So whereas hundreds of books have been written about German Nazism, no book in any language has appeared to date which concentrates exclusively on the Nazis of Austria.

The term *fascism* is used frequently throughout this book; consequently it would be helpful to define this word. I am painfully well aware of the long-standing debate among scholars concerning the word's definition and even whether or not the term should still be employed.[3] Admittedly, the term is ambiguous at best and is defined in somewhat different ways by nearly everyone using it. Nevertheless, the similarities between certain movements and political parties in interwar Europe in general, and Austria in particular, are so striking that it seems to me helpful to give them a common label. In so doing I do not mean to imply that fascist groups did not have their own unique historical developments and separate identities. Nor can any definition perfectly apply to all of them.

Some of the most frequently cited characteristics of fascist movements include the following: first, they were decidedly negative in their ideology. Thus they were opposed to "Marxism" (i.e., socialism and communism), liberalism, and usually (though not always) to Judaism. They generally favored such vague and nonspecific ideas as a " 'new world,' love of power, and the dramatic appeal of youth, elite consciousness and mass influence, revolutionary order and veneration of tradition."[4] They were ultranationalistic and hoped to reunite their socially divided people into "people's communities."[5] In common with many nonfascist regimes they limited civil liberties and tolerated the existence of only one, all-encompassing political party.[6] They stressed emotion and sentiment over reason, action instead of words, and violence in place of peace. Perhaps above all they believed in the necessity of dictatorial leadership, the famous Führerprinzip, to help bring about a national regeneration.[7]

The Austrian Nazis, or at least those who remained loyal to Hitler, fit neatly into this definition of fascism. Yet they were by no means the only group in Austria to do so. Indeed, it was the widespread nature of many of these concepts that for many years diluted the Nazis' appeal and limited their growth.

Acknowledgments

A host of individuals and institutions have given me invaluable assistance during the many years I have been studying Austrian Nazism and fascism. My initial research trip to Austria in 1963–64 was made possible by the Fulbright-Hays fellowship program. Subsequent research since 1972 has been supported by stipends from the National Endowment for the Humanities and the American Philosophical Society. Additional financial assistance has come from faculty development grants from Florida Atlantic University (in cooperation with Robert Schwarz) and the University of Central Florida. The latter institution also generously provided me with released time from teaching and a sabbatical leave.

I was able to broaden my knowledge of international fascism in 1974 by attending a conference on Comparative European Nazism and Fascism sponsored by the Department of Sociology at the University of Bergen, Norway. Equally valuable was an eight-week seminar at Vanderbilt University in 1976, "Europe in the Age of Fascism, 1919–1945: A Historical Re-examination," supported by the National Endowment for the Humanities and directed by Professor Charles F. Delzell, who also read portions of my manuscript.

In Europe my studies were greatly aided by Anton Porhansl of the Fulbright Commission in Vienna, and Gerhard Jagschitz and the late Ludwig Jedlicka of the Institut für Zeitgeschichte. Numerous librarians and archivists assisted me at the Austrian Nationalbibliothek and at the *Tagblatt* Archive of the Arbeiterkammer, both also in Vienna. Professor Walter Goldinger permitted me to use the resources of the Allgemeines Verwaltungsarchiv. The late Friedrich Vogl, and Dr. Herbert Steiner were especially accommodating at the Dokumentationsarchiv des österreichischen Widerstandes. Daniel P. Simon, the director of the Berlin Document Center, facilitated my use of the records of the Nazi party. The staff of the Bundesarchiv in Koblenz, West Germany, was extremely efficient in helping me to utilize the Schumacher Collection of

Austrian Nazi correspondence. In this country, Robert Wolfe, the chief of the Modern Military Branch of the Military Archives Division of the National Archives provided me with copies of the Nuremberg interrogations.

Dr. Gerhard Botz of the Institut für Neuere Geschichte und Zeitgeschichte of the Johannes-Kepler University in Linz on several occasions sent me valuable documents and recent publications. Professors Andrew G. Whiteside of Queens College of the City University of New York, John Haag of the University of Georgia, Ronald Smelser of the University of Utah, Maurice Williams of Okanagan College, British Columbia, and Robert Schwarz of Florida Atlantic University all read the manuscript with critical insight and provided me with many useful suggestions. Professor Richard Adicks of the University of Central Florida added helpful comments on the book's style. Needless to say, I alone bear responsibility for any errors of fact or judgment that may remain in the text.

I would also like to thank Professor Gerald Kleinfeld, editor of *German Studies Review*, for allowing me to republish here portions of my article "From Splinter Party to Mass Movement: The Austrian Nazi Breakthrough" (February 1979, pp. 7–29). Likewise, I am indebted to Professor Douglas Unfug, editor of *Central European History*, for his permission to republish sections of my article entitled "Fascism and the *Führerprinzip*: The Austrian Example" (September 1979, pp. 272–96).

Wava Raffensparger and Laurie Hodge of the UCF interlibrary loan office, devoted many hours to obtaining rare books and microfilm from other institutions. Mrs. Karen Morgan of Oviedo, Florida, along with my two young sons, Mark and Glenn, saved me much tedious labor by typing literally thousands of note cards. Finally, a special debt of gratitude is owed my wife, Marianne, who proofread much of the manuscript and who for years patiently sacrificed countless family excursions so that this project could be brought to completion.

Oviedo, Florida   *Bruce F. Pauley*
31 March 1980

The following acronymns and abbreviations are used in the notes and, where marked by a single asterisk, also in the text. Two asterisks indicate use in the Bibliography.

AA	Auswärtiges Amt; German Foreign Ministry, Berlin
Abw.	Abwehr; Intelligence
AVA	Allgemeines Verwaltungsarchiv; General Administrative Archive, Vienna
A-Z	*Arbeiter-Zeitung*, Vienna
BDC	Berlin Document Center
CSP*	Christlichsoziale Partei; Christian Social party of Austria
DAP*	Deutsche Arbeiterpartei; German Workers' party of Austria
DAP	*Deutsche Arbeiter-Presse*, Vienna
DBFP	*Documents on British Foreign Policy, 1919–1939*
DGFP	*Documents on German Foreign Policy, 1918–1945*
DNSAP	Deutsche Nationalsozialistische Arbeiterpartei; German National Socialist Workers' party. Name adopted by the Austrian Nazis in May 1918
DÖW	Dokumentationsarchiv des österreichischen Widerstandsbewegung; Documentation Archive of the Austrian Resistance Movement, Vienna
FRUS	*Papers Relating to the Foreign Relations of the United States*
GVP*	Grossdeutsche Volkspartei; Greater German People's party of Austria
HB*	Hitler Bewegung; Hitler Movement (of the Austrian National Socialist German Workers' party)
HI, NS-HA	Hoover Institution, Stanford University, NSDAP Hauptarchiv; Central Archive of the Nazi party (microfilm collection)

HJ*	Hitler Jugend; Hitler Youth
HW*	Heimwehr; Home Guard
H-Z	*Heimatschutz-Zeitung*, Vienna
IdVF	*Informationsdiensthder Vaterländische Front*, Vienna
IMT	International Military Tribunal. *Trials of the Major War Criminals before the International Military Tribunal*
K.	Karton; carton
LL	Landesleitung; State Directorship
"Ministries Case"	*Trials of the War Criminals before the Nuremberg Military Tribunals*, Case 11
MLB	Monatliche Lageberichte des BKA/General Direktion für die öffentliche Sicherheit, Vienna; Monthly situation reports of the Austrian Security Directorate, DOW, #6184a.
NA	National Archives, Washington, D.C.
NCA	*Nazi Conspiracy and Aggression*
n.d.	no date
NG	Nazi Government Ministries Series (Nuremberg documents)
NI	Nuremberg Interrogations; *Records of the United States War Crimes Trials Interrogations, 1946–1949*
NS	Nationalsozialistische; National Socialist
NSDAP*	Nationalsozialistische Deutsche Arbeiterpartei; National Socialist German Workers' party or Nazi party
NSM	*Nationalsozialistische Monatshefte*
ÖB	*Österreichischer Beobachter*
OH-Z	*Österreichische Heimatschutz-Zeitung*, Vienna
PA	Personalakten; Personnel documents of the Nazi party, Berlin Document Center
PAAA	Politisches Archiv des Auswärtiges Amt; Political Archives of the German Foreign Ministry, Bonn
PK	Parteikanzlei-korrespondenz; Nazi party correspondence in the Berlin Document Center
-PS	Paris Storey Series (Nuremberg trial documents)
R.	reel number
RL	Reichsleitung; Imperial Directorship of the Nazi party, Munich
SA	Sturmabteilung; Storm Division or Storm Troopers of the NSDAP
Schmidt-Prozess	*Der Hochverratsprozess gegen Dr. Guido Schmidt vor dem Wiener Volksgericht*
SDP*	Sozialdemokratische Partei; Social Democratic party of Austria

Slg. Sch.	Sammlung Schumacher; Schumacher collection of Austrian Nazi correspondence in the Bundesarchiv of Koblenz, West Germany
SS	Schützstaffeln; elite guards of the NSDAP
T-	microfilm series number; National Archives, Captured German Documents
TA	*Tagblatt* Archive in the Arbeiterkammer, Vienna
Tgb	*Der Tagblatt*, Graz
USCHLA	Untersuchungs- und Schlichtungsausschuss; Investigation and Conciliation Committee of the NSDAP
VF*	Vaterländische Front; Fatherland Front
Vkst	*Volksstimme*, Linz
Wissenschaft- liche Kom- mission**	Wissenschaftliche Kommission des Theodor-Körner Stiftungsfonds und des Leopold-Kunschak-Preises zur Erforschung der österreichischen Geschichte der Jahre 1927 bis 1938
#	document number

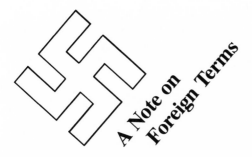

A Note on Foreign Terms

A study of Austrian National Socialism involves many German words for which no commonly accepted English equivalents exist. In such cases the original German form has been used in this book for both the singular and the plural. Except when being defined, singular terms are in Roman letters, e.g.: Gauleiter, Heimwehr, Landesleiter, and Parteigenosse. To distinguish plurals, italics are employed, e.g.: *Gauleiter*, *Heimwehren*, *Landesleiter*, and *Parteigenossen*.

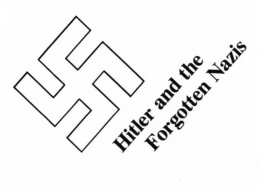

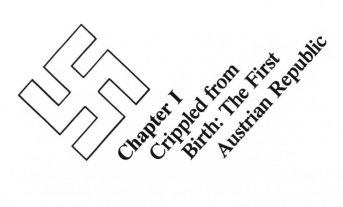

Chapter I
Crippled from
Birth: The First
Austrian Republic

In the history of European fascism between the two world wars one fact stands out: nowhere did fascists enjoy the majority support of their countrymen before coming to power. Therefore, whatever success the fascists had cannot be understood apart from the weaknesses and divisions of their opponents and the internal problems of the states in which they arose. This fundamental truth is just as valid for the Nazis of Austria as it is for the German Nazis in the Weimar Republic and the Fascists of pre-1922 Italy.

Nazism, and European fascism in general, did not arise in a vacuum. If the new Republic of Austria, which was founded in 1918, had had a long democratic tradition, a prosperous economy, and, perhaps above all, a citizenry with a burning desire for independence, the Nazis, or any other fascist group, would hardly have attracted more than a handful of supporters. But such conditions did not exist in Austria. Although having some democratic elements, the fallen Austrian Empire had been essentially authoritarian. Worse yet, the political parties of postwar Austria regarded each other as enemies rather than as fellow citizens having honest if differing viewpoints.

The division of the Austro-Hungarian Monarchy into a patchwork of Successor States also left the Austrian economy so shattered that it would not recover until after the Second World War. So, far from greeting their new state and constitution with joy and optimism, most Austrians were convinced that their country could survive economically and politically only if joined to its great German neighbor in a so-called Anschluss. It should surprise no one, therefore, that parties arose in Austria demanding the abolition of democracy and the independence of the state.

Austria at the Paris Peace Conference

The German-speaking people of the Austrian Empire were undoubtedly the monarchy's most loyal subjects. Only with considerable misgivings was a republic proclaimed by the German remnant of the Imperial Austrian Parliament on 12 November 1918. Although the new state bore a faint resemblance to the medieval crownlands that belonged to the Habsburgs before 1526, it was in reality a new and, to most of its citizens, an unwelcome creation. For the German-Austrians their state represented not liberation but punishment for losing the war. That the German-Austrians were regarded by the victorious Western powers as a vanquished fragment of the Austro-Hungarian Monarchy was only too apparent from their treatment at the Paris Peace Conference.

The Austrian delegation was housed—or perhaps more accurately, "imprisoned"—in the Château of Saint-Germain in the suburbs of Paris. Like other enemy delegations, they were literally locked up, and their correspondence with the outside world was censored.[1] By the time the Austrians reached the French capital there was little left to decide. Disputed border areas had already been militarily occupied by Austria's neighbors; and those countries' territorial claims, for the most part, had already been recognized by the "Big Four" (the United States, Britain, France, and Italy). Lacking the military power of its neighbors, and cut off by them from vitally needed food supplies, Austria prudently asked only for the German-speaking areas of the old monarchy. But even this request was denied.

The final terms of the Treaty of Saint Germain, signed on 12 September 1919, awarded to other states not only the more remote German-speaking areas, such as northern Bohemia, Austrian Silesia, and northern Moravia, (ceded to Czechoslovakia), but also contiguous regions with solid German majorities. Thus, southern Bohemia and southern Moravia, with 357,000 Germans and 18,500 Czechs were given to Czechoslovakia for "historical" reasons.[2] The Drau (Drava) River valley of southern Styria, which afforded Austria its best rail link between its eastern and western provinces, was assigned to Yugoslavia without a plebiscite, even though it had a German-speaking majority. And most brutally of all, the beloved South Tyrol, with 225,000 German-Austrians and next to no Italians, was turned over to Italy so that the 38 million Italians could have a strategic frontier against 6.5 million Austrians. Only in German West Hungary (later called the Burgenland), with 285,000 people, and in southern Carinthia, were boundary decisions made which benefited Austria.

Assets and Liabilities of the New Republic

With little more than 32,000 square miles the Austrian Republic had only 23 percent of the territory and 26 percent of the population of just the Austrian half of the fallen Dual Monarchy.[3] No less than a third of Imperial Austria's German-speaking subjects had been placed under alien rule. Nevertheless, the country was not entirely without assets. About 96 percent of its population now spoke German, making the country by far the most linguistically homogeneous of the Successor States. Only 10 percent of its land was totally unproductive; 38 percent was covered with forests, and 22 percent was arable.[4] Austria also possessed considerable quantities of iron ore, great water-power potential, and many skilled workers. The country's majestic mountains and baroque cities had long attracted tourists. Moreover, being astride several Alpine passes and the middle Danube, it was at the junction of several important trade routes.

But the negative side of the ledger was more important, at least initially. In many instances the new boundaries had separated Austria's factories from their natural resources and from allied industries. Styrian iron- and steelworks and the textile factories of Vorarlberg had been powered by coal from Austrian Silesia and Bohemia, now part of Czechoslovakia, whereas petroleum had come from Galicia, which was given to Poland. Nor were the Successor States, which eagerly sought to build up their infant industries, anxious to trade with Austria. Austrian industries, previously having sold their goods in a free-trade area of 54 million people, now had a domestic market only one-eighth the size of the monarchy and had few opportunities for export.[5]

The draconian reduction in Austria's size naturally also created a serious shortage of food, all the more so because the country was now largely mountainous. As a result of the peace treaty, Austria was able to produce only two-thirds of its wheat demands in 1919, one-fifth of the necessary rye, one-third of the barley, and one-fifth of its oats. In meat and dairy products the country was considerably better off but still not self-sufficient.[6] In succeeding years Austria's food situation gradually improved. More intensified farming methods and tariffs raised production enough that by 1937 the country was approaching self-sufficiency in certain basic foodstuffs. But the agricultural gains were paid for in higher prices to consumers.[7]

Even though nearly every Austrian was adversely affected by the breakup of the Habsburg Monarchy, the middle class was by far the hardest-hit social group. The bourgeoisie was traditionally the most thrifty of all the segments of Central European society. As a consequence, it was the group most devastated by the inflation that affected Austria during and especially after the World War. A savings account which before the war would have been enough to buy a small house was worth only a postage stamp by 1922. As late as 1919, sixteen Austrian crowns could purchase a dollar. It took 177 crowns for the same transaction in January 1921, and a fantastic 83,000 in August 1922. During the same period the cost of living increased 2,645-fold.[8] Rent control, which began during the war and has lasted to the present day in Vienna, also hurt middle-class landlords by making their rent receipts practically worthless.

Even more important, the passing of the old monarchy left unemployed many middle-class German Austrians, who had made up the largest proportion of civil servants in the empire. An administrative personnel, which had been too large even for the 30 million people living in just the Austrian half of the Dual Monarchy, now served a state with only a fraction of its previous population. There were no fewer than 233,000 civil servants in Austria in 1919–20 or 615,000 counting their dependents.[9] Another 120,000 citizens were state pensioners.[10]

Thus, one of the major ingredients of a successful democracy—a strong, prosperous, and self-confident middle class—was missing in Austria between the world wars. The proletarianization of the middle class, or at least the fear of dropping down into the proletariat, made the Austrian bourgeoisie vulnerable to political extremism, including fascism.

Although Austria's economy was slow to recover from the ravages of war and partition, some progress was made between early 1919 and 1921 with the help of food and medicine supplied by Herbert Hoover's American Relief Administration.[11] More substantial assistance ultimately came in 1922 from the League of Nations. In the so-called Geneva Protocols the British, French, Italian, and Czechoslovakian governments guaranteed a twenty-year loan equal to $126 million. The loan did not come without strings. Austria had to agree to a program of financial austerity involving the dismissal of thousands of civil servants. It also had to balance its budget, accept a commissioner general appointed by the League and, most important of all, promise not to give up its independence for the duration of the loan.[12]

Economically the Geneva Protocols were a moderate success. The loan enabled the government to electrify the railways the next year and also contributed to the development of water power. Likewise, the authorities began a comprehensive highway building program. In 1924 a new currency, the Austrian schilling, was introduced, equal to ten thousand of the old paper crowns and about fourteen American cents. By 1928 and 1929 the government came close to balancing the budget for the first time. The recovery reached a peak in these same two years when the gross national product was 105 percent of the prewar level (for the same area) and private consumption was 117 percent of the 1913 level. Only industrial production still lagged slightly behind the prewar standard.

Despite the gradual improvement in the Austrian economy after 1924, serious doubts about the country's *Lebensfähigkeit* (viability) remained widespread. Even in the most prosperous years there was a troublesome surplus of imports over exports. In an age of autarky only self-sufficient countries were considered viable. For Austrians, their self-doubt became a self-fulfilling prophecy. Foreigners, impressed by the Austrians' pessimism about their future, were reluctant to invest in a dying state. Consequently, Austrian industries were constantly short of the capital they needed to expand. In turn, this shortage left unsolved the chronic unemployment rate, which rarely fell below 10 percent of the work force.[13]

The Anschluss Movement

Difficult as its economic problems were, an even worse dilemma for the young Austrian Republic was the repudiation of its very existence by the majority of its citizens. It was this rejection, more than any other single factor, that aided the Nazis' cause. The heart and soul of the Austrian Nazis' program was their desire for an Anschluss, or union, with Germany. Far from creating the issue, however, or even monopolizing it, the Nazis merely succeeded in exploiting it more effectively than any other Austrian party.

Although their country's desperate economic circumstances in 1918–19 intensified the Austrians' yearning for an Anschluss, the ambition long antedated the end of the First World War. From the beginning of the Holy Roman Empire until Austria's expulsion from the German Confederation in 1866, the lands that later comprised the Austrian Republic had always been a part of Germany. Thereafter the Austrians continued to look enviously at the German Empire's higher standard of living. Although for the most part loyal subjects of the Habsburgs, the German-Austrians felt emotionally, linguistically, culturally, and historically closer to the people of Germany than they did to the non-Germans of the Dual Monarchy.

Even though relations between the German and Austro-Hungarian empires were far from untroubled during the First World War,[14] propaganda and a shared danger held the alliance together. The war greatly heightened nationalism in each of the belligerent countries. Whereas the ideology had a disruptive effect on the multinational Habsburg Monarchy, it tended to strengthen spiritual ties between German-speaking people on either side of the Inn River. When nationalism and the war threatened to destroy the Habsburg Monarchy, union with Germany appeared to be the only practical alternative for the ten million Germans of the Austrian Empire.

The defeat of Austria-Hungary and the disintegration of the Dual Monarchy did have one apparent advantage for the German Austrians: it seemed to settle the question that had been troubling them since 1848: whether they were really Austrians or Germans. Now all divisions of loyalty were temporarily swept away. The Austrian Republic was seen by most of its citizens as a mere remnant of the old Empire, a totally artificial creation. "Threatened by new neighbors which only yesterday had been her subject peoples, she was lamenting her present, questioning her past, and doubtful of her future. Union with Germany seemed thus to many Austrians the only solution to her staggering problems."[15] The Anschluss represented the possibility of regaining both Austria's former prosperity and its lost prestige.

The Anschluss movement was led in the early postwar years by the Austrian Social Democratic party (SDP), supported by various traditionally pan-German groups. Until at least the beginning of 1918 the Socialists had supported the Austro-Hungarian Monarchy, believing that the economic development of the industrial proletariat would be enhanced by a large free-trade area. When the November Revolution toppled the Hohenzollern dynasty in Germany and replaced it with a Socialist government, the Austrian SDP pushed for a union of the two countries.

But pro-Anschluss opinion was not unanimous in Austria. Even traditional pan-German groups, whose roots stretched back far beyond 1919, were repelled at the thought of joining a Socialist Germany. And the conservative Christian Social party (CSP) paid at best lip service to the Anschluss idea when not actively opposing it.[16] This fear was especially strong among industrialists and financiers who feared German competition. As Catholics, the Christian Socials showed little enthusiasm for Protestant Germany. If they officially supported the Anschluss program it was mainly to appease their coalition partners in the Austrian government.

Most Austrians in late 1918 innocently if naively believed that their Anschluss aspirations would be realized. President Woodrow Wilson had favored national self-determination as one of his famous Fourteen Points. When he arrived at the Paris Peace Conference he had still not made up his mind whether to exclude German Austria from this principle.[17]

But Wilson gradually came to agree with Georges Clemenceau, the French premier, that Germany could not be rewarded for losing the war by being given more territory than it would lose. Thus, it was the American president who suggested the compromise formula, incorporated in the treaties of Saint-Germain and Versailles, that Austria could "not alienate its independence" without the unanimous approval of the Council of the League of Nations. But France alone, as a permanent member of the Council, could veto such a move. By leaving alive the hope of a possible future union, the Allies could avoid the odium of flagrantly violating their own principle of self-determination.[18]

Yet, this very hope helped to keep the Anschluss movement active in both Austria and Germany. A less ambiguous stand, along with territorial concessions to Austria in the South Tyrol, and perhaps along the Czechoslovak border, might well have thwarted the Anschluss drive from the beginning.

Charles Seymour, one of the American experts at Paris, noted in a private letter that "everything that has been done in Paris has tended to force Austria into the arms of Germany. A little more tact and diplomatic skill and Austria could have been kept absolutely free from German influence. . . . A really wise policy would have been to place German Austria on the same plane as Jugoslavia and Czechoslovakia—not regarding it as an enemy state."[19]

The anti-Anschluss provisions of the Paris Peace Treaties had an unexpected consequence. Pro-Anschluss sentiment in Austria had been at a peak during the winter of 1918–19 just after the fall of the monarchy. But the Bolshevik revolution in Bavaria in April 1919 and Spartacist activities elsewhere in Germany dampened prounion enthusiasm, especially among already skeptical bourgeois circles. Christian Social newspapers editorialized that by renouncing the Anschluss Austria would improve its chance of retaining disputed German-speaking districts in the South Tyrol, Bohemia, Moravia, Silesia, Styria, and Carinthia. This hope, of course, proved to be in vain, as the Treaty of Saint-Germain denied Austria *both* the Anschluss and the contested territories. The Austrians therefore felt doubly betrayed, and pro-Anschluss feelings quickly revived.[20]

The renewed strength of pro-Anschluss sentiment was revealed two years later in two local plebiscites. In April 1921, 90 percent of the eligible voters in the Tyrol cast 145,302 ballots in favor of the province's joining Germany whereas only 1,805 opposed the proposition. The next month a plebiscite in the province of Salzburg resulted in over 98,000 voting for an Anschluss whereas only 877 opposed the issue out of a total electorate of 126,482.[21] A similar vote in Styria was prevented in June only by pressure from the Allies, who threatened to resolve the Burgenland dispute in Hungary's favor if the plebiscite were not canceled.[22]

In subsequent years Anschluss passions in Austria cooled but never died completely. The departure of the Social Democrats from the German government in 1923 and the election of the ultraconservative Paul von Hindenburg as president in 1925 made Germany far less attractive to the Austrian Socialists, but far more appealing to the bourgeoisie. Consequently, the years between 1925 and 1929 continued to be filled with Anschluss demonstrations, including one in Vienna in 1928, which drew some 200,000 participants. A year later a questionnaire distributed to members of the Austrian National Assembly revealed that two-thirds of its delegates still backed the union with Germany.[23]

The Anschluss remained almost the single goal of Austria's foreign policy until 1933.[24] The Great Depression served only to solidify the conviction that a union with Germany was the one hope for recovery. With its extreme dependence on foreign trade, Austria was harder hit by the Depression than perhaps any other industrialized country in the world. But to imagine that a merger with Germany could cure Austria's economic ills was wishful thinking. Except for the period 1925–29, Germany was as impoverished as Austria. At best an Anschluss could have produced temporary political and psychological gains for the German and Austrian governments.

The latter two goals were in fact exactly what the Austrian chancellor, Johannes Schober, had in mind when he secretly negotiated a customs union with Germany in 1930. No other governments had been consulted when the project was suddenly publicized in March 1931. The result was predictable. Although Britain and the United States were sympathetic, France, and the so-called Little Entente countries of Czechoslovakia, Yugoslavia, and Rumania were bitterly opposed, seeing in the plan a thinly disguised Anschluss. France's opposition was decisive. Only it had the financial resources to supply Austria with another desperately needed loan; but its price was the cancellation of the customs-union project. The upshot was a diplomatic victory for France and a humiliating defeat for the German and Austrian governments. Moderates in the two German-speaking countries suffered another setback. Only the Nazis benefited. The Austrians, denied the forbidden fruit once again, wanted it more than ever. Not until the Nazis rose to power in Germany would some Austrians begin to reconsider their Anschluss ambitions.

The Austrian Constitution and Parliament

Adding to the problems of the Austrian Republic were flaws in its constitution. Of course, not even the most perfect constitution can guarantee the success of democracy. In the case of Austria, however, the constitution tended to accentuate already existing political problems.

Before the war the Austrian people had felt a sense of loyalty to their emperor, their German nationality, and their province. When the object of their first devotion disappeared, the German Austrians fell back on the other two. After the war the new Austrian constitution of 1920 accorded the nine provinces (Upper and Lower Austria, Burgenland, Styria, Salzburg, Carinthia, Tyrol, Vorarlberg, and Vienna) a wide degree of local autonomy. Vienna, which had been the capital of Lower Austria as well as the Austrian Empire, was made into a separate province. The Socialists took advantage of Vienna's new autonomy to push through Western Europe's most advanced social welfare program. Including such things as subsidized housing, health care, and adult education, the costly program was largely paid for by the taxes of Vienna's middle and upper classes.

The decentralizing character of the Austrian constitution could also be seen in the role of the president. His functions were mostly decorative; unlike the German president, he had no emergency powers.[25] Most observers now believe that the reaction against the relatively centralized rule of the Habsburgs went much too far. Parliament, the least experienced and least responsible branch of government, secured the most authority, whereas the executive, the most experienced branch of government, retained the least power, at least during the 1920s.

Although the Imperial Austrian Parliament had performed some useful services before the war, it had never overcome the reputation established by the disgraceful behavior of its deputies during the "Badeni crisis" just before the turn of the century. In order to prevent the passage of a language law supported by the Czechs and Premier Kasimir Badeni, the German delegates had resorted to all manner of wild antics, which were later imitated by the non-German representatives. Parliament consequently became the butt of innumerable jokes, which were still being repeated in the Republic.[26]

Unfortunately, the behavior of the parliamentarians did not greatly improve after the war. The worst offenders this time were the Social Democrats. Although they had cooperated with the Imperial Parliament, they became obstructionists in the Republic in order to block legislation they disliked. The strongest proponents of parliamentarianism thus became the worst offenders against parliamentary decorum. Party rivalries were such that legislation was judged, not on its intrinsic merits, but on how its passage would affect the various political parties. Obstructionism thus ultimately served to discredit democracy itself.

Austrian democracy, like that of Germany, was also hampered by the system of proportional representation. Of course proportional representation did not make democracy impossible, as was seen in Switzerland. Under this arrangement, a given party's candidates for Parliament were selected by the party secretary. The concomitant "closed list" system required the voter to cast his ballot for a single party list of candidates. Voting a "split ticket," so common in the United States, was therefore impossible. The politician who hoped to be reelected had to be far more concerned about the dictates of the party secretary than he did about the feelings of the voters.[27]

Because the voter was not allowed to choose individual candidates from different parties, it became customary, even before the war, to vote for the same party, election after election, regardless of the issues. By 1911 Austria was already divided into three almost equal political "camps" or *Lager*, which have endured down to the present day: the pan-Germans, the conservative Catholics, and the Marxian Socialists. Proportional representation and the voting habits of most Austrians therefore prevented any "landslide" victories and any large government majorities.

The system of proportional representation and closed lists gave the political parties so much power that many frustrated voters, unable either to choose or oust individual politicians, began calling Austria a *Parteienstaat* (state of parties). The only way to change this system was to reform the constitution. But only the political parties had the power to do this, and they were the very groups that profited from the status quo. In this impasse it appeared to many opponents of the system that the only solution was a dictatorship.

Mortal Enemies: The Political
Parties of Austria

The hatred and contempt the Nazis felt for their opponents was by no means unique in the politics of interwar Austria. Despite a similar historical development, all three of the political *Lager* of Austria regarded each other as mortal enemies. The Christian Socials and Social Democrats managed to form a coalition government in the first two years of the Republic and cooperated during the crises presented by the Paris Peace Conference and the early postwar reconstruction. But unlike the coalition governments of the other Successor States, which faced large and hostile national minorities, there was no common enemy inside or outside Austria to hold the coalition together after October 1920.

Austrian politics was infused with a religious fervor. The Christian Socials and their Roman Catholic Weltanschauung and the Social Democrats clung tenaciously to their Marxist ideology. The CSP staunchly defended the rights of the Catholic church; the SDP was equally determined to advance the cause of anticlericalism. The Catholics regarded the "Marxists" as "revolutionaries," and the Marxists saw the Catholics as "reactionaries." The Catholic church tended to equate democracy with socialism and bolshevism, whereas the Socialists blamed all the country's problems on clericalism (and capitalism).[28]

Several factors contributed to this deep fissure in the Austrian body politic. For one thing, the Social Democrats had been virtually excluded from power before 1918. Their revolutionary ideology together with bourgeois prejudices had given rise to electoral laws that were deliberately weighted against the proletariat. Universal and equal manhood suffrage for the Imperial Parliament was not introduced until 1907; discriminatory franchise laws for some local electoral districts remained on the books until the very end of the Empire. Then, from a position of near political impotence the Socialists suddenly found themselves in an unaccustomed position of power at both the federal and local level in 1918. Thereafter the Socialists steadily increased their representation in Parliament until 1930 when they became the largest party in the country. On a per capita basis the SDP was also the largest Socialist party in the world outside the Soviet Union.[29]

The bourgeoisie, already stunned by the passing of the monarchy, was horrified enough that the dreaded Socialists were now in positions of authority. But what alarmed them still more was the SDP's continued radical rhetoric. Marxist parties in other European countries had been split over their attitude toward the Bolshevik Revolution in Russia; radicals had joined new Communist parties while the more moderate Socialists remained in Social Democratic parties. In Austria, however, such a split, for all practical purposes, never occurred. Most of the radicals stayed in the SDP, but only at a price. The left-wing radicals were appeased with a large dose of hard-line Marxist slogans about class warfare and the dictatorship of the proletariat. Indeed, the party now saw itself as a kind of bridge between Soviet communism and Western European socialism.[30]

The SDP's split personality—ideological radicalism and moderation in practical affairs—was most apparent at a party congress held in Linz in 1926. The party's left wing, headed by Otto Bauer and Friedrich Adler, the son of the party's founder, wanted to retain the party's traditional radical rhetoric; right-wing moderates, led by Karl Renner, saw slogans like "dictatorship of the proletariat" as obsolete and dangerous. The result was a tortured ideological compromise. The Linz program announced that the SDP strove to control the democratic Republic in order to place it at the service of the working class. But Bauer, the principal draftsman of the compromise, was convinced that the Austrian conservatives would resist a Socialist election victory with force. Then, and only then, would the Socialists be justified in defending their hard-earned victory with force. Violence was thus inevitable, but only for defensive purposes. The hypothetical situation envisioned by Bauer's compromise was highly unlikely. Yet the Linz program was ambiguous at best and dangerous at worst, as many Socialist leaders themselves realized. Its wording could easily be misconstrued or deliberately misinterpreted. To the very end of the Republic the Socialists could never quite decide between their ideological extremism and their pragmatic moderation. Not surprisingly, they succeeded neither in conciliating their rivals nor in eliminating them through revolution.

The continuing dogmatism and radical rhetoric of the Socialists did manage to pacify the party's left wing and to prevent the growth of a large Communist party. But the ideological extremism also alienated the bourgeoisie and peasantry. A more flexible policy, like that followed by the Scandinavian Socialists, might very well have broadened the social base of the SDP among groups such as intellectuals and the bourgeoisie, which were sympathetic towards the party in the early postwar years.[31] The breakup of opposition party meetings and rallies was also a perilous precedent that the Nazis were later only too willing to imitate. The elaborate, tight, and almost totalitarian organization of the party likewise found an admirer and follower in none other than Adolf Hitler.[32] And because the Socialists were such strident advocates of democracy and republicanism, the anti-Socialists became antidemocratic and antirepublican.

The radical rhetoric of the Socialists frightened the Austrian bourgeoisie and peasantry into believing that a proletarian revolution was imminent. In reality there was never a serious possibility of a violent revolution, except possibly by the tiny Austrian Communist party in 1919. Yet the bourgeois fears were sincere, even if unfounded, and helped lead to a conservative and even fascist reaction. Similar developments took place in other European countries between the world wars, above all in Italy and Germany.[33]

The refusal of the Socialists to enter any national government after 1920, together with their inability to win an absolute majority of the votes, meant that the Christian Socials became, by default, the ruling party for most of the First Republic. It also meant that the Socialists lost their influence in the army, police, and civil bureaucracy, something which cost them dearly in future years.[34]

The CSP likewise never succeeded in winning an absolute majority of the ballots. Consequently, it was forced to form unstable coalition governments with smaller bourgeois parties like the Greater German People's party (Grossdeutsche Volkspartei or GVP) and the Agricultural League (Landbund). Every new government was therefore a compromise, which made an energetic policy nearly impossible. Moreover, unlike the SDP, the Christian Socials were not socially homogeneous, consisting instead of genuine democrats, monarchists, capitalists, small shop owners, pan-Germans, and, above all, peasants. Only with great difficulty could these groups be held together; indeed, some of them broke away to join the Nazis in 1932 and thereafter.

The prospects for success of the new Austrian democracy were, all things considered, tenuous at best. It was born in an atmosphere of military defeat, political catastrophe, and patriotic humiliation. Conservatives associated it with socialism. The majority of its citizens doubted the permanence and viability of the state. On the fundamental questions of social welfare, church-state relations, and the Anschluss the rival political parties could reach no consensus. Extremists saw their rivals as heretics to be eliminated by one means or another. To top it all, the Great Depression struck Austria in 1930 with an especial ferocity. Thus, by the early 1930s many Austrians were prepared to believe that democracy was corrupt, inefficient, and doomed to failure. Only a fascist or semifascist system, an Anschluss with Germany, or both, could save their homeland. Eager to offer itself as the country's savior was the Austrian Nazi party.

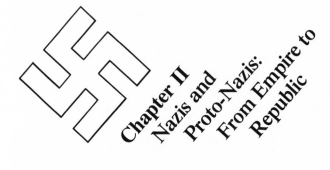

Austrian National Socialism, like the Anschluss movement, had roots that were well established before the First World War. Although the origins of any ideology are notoriously difficult to trace, it would be reasonably safe to say that there were three major ingredients of Austrian Nazism: political anti-Semitism, pan-Germanism, and the clash between the rising national aspirations of the long-submerged Czechs of Moravia, especially Bohemia, and the desire of the German-speaking inhabitants of those crownlands to preserve their superior economic and political position. A similar, though somewhat less intense, conflict occurred in Styria and Carinthia between the German- and Slovene-speaking inhabitants of those crownlands.

Austrian Anti-Semitism

Although religious anti-Judaism in Austria dates back to the Middle Ages, modern racial anti-Semitism has its Austrian origins in the emancipation of the Jews, completed in 1867,[1] and the Industrial Revolution, which followed. These phenomena were accompanied by a rapid migration of Jews from the monarchy's eastern provinces and the Russian Empire to Vienna. Whereas the capital city counted only 6,217 Jews out of a total population of 476,220 in 1857, by 1910 the comparative figures were 175,294 and 2,031,420.[2] Thirteen years later, following a mass immigration of war refugees, the city's Jewish population reached 201,510 or 10.8 percent of the total population of 1,865,780. The Austrian capital now had the third largest Jewish population of any city in Europe.[3] Outside Vienna, however, the Jewish population was minuscule, amounting to well under 20,000 after the war. Thus, Austria's Jewish population in the 1920s was only 3 percent of the country's total.[4] But this did not prevent a virulent brand of anti-Semitism from existing in the provinces.

Emancipation and migration to the big cities of the Empire were accompanied by a remarkably rapid increase in Jewish involvement in higher education. By 1914, 27.5 percent of the students at the University of Vienna were of Jewish extraction, more than three times their proportion of the city's population. Almost 35 percent of the students at the city's elite secondary schools, the *Gymnasia*, were also Jewish in 1913. On the other hand, the fact that Jewish enrollment was low, only 2.95 percent, at Vienna's School of Agriculture (Hochschule für Bodenkultur) in 1910, was seen by anti-Semites as proof that Jews were averse to dirt and manual labor.[5]

Austrian Jews used their newly acquired advanced education to enter the so-called free professions in large numbers. Whereas there were only 33 Jewish lawyers in Vienna in 1869, there were 394 of them in 1893 out of a total of 683. In the latter year, 48 percent of the medical students in Vienna were Jewish.[6] A large minority of the city's university instructors were also Jewish. An English author estimated in 1913 that no fewer than 75 percent of the Viennese journalists were Jewish.[7] The editors of Socialist newspapers were nearly all Jewish. Hence, there was some truth in the Nazis' description of the Viennese press as being "Jewish." Yet the charge overlooked the fact that Jewish journalists, like other Jews, were hardly monolithic in their political views. Some even wrote for newspapers that were notoriously anti-Semitic.[8] Austrian anti-Semites also ignored the fact that Jews made up hardly more than one-fourth of 1 percent of postwar Austria's civil service.

The coming of the Industrial Revolution to Austria was to a large extent a Jewish enterprise. Most of the country's bankers and many of its industrialists (especially in textiles, paper milling, and coal mining) were Jewish.[9] To a skilled artisan, the big industrialist with mass production seemed like a threat to his very existence. The same feeling prevailed among lower-middle-class merchants toward wealthy department-store owners. Even the poor Jewish peddler, though scarcely a product of the Industrial Revolution, was viewed by gentile businessmen as an unfair competitor. Certain trades, like furniture retailing and advertising, were 85 to 90 percent in Jewish hands by the eve of the World War.[10] To all who suffered from the inroads of capitalism it was tempting to believe that capitalism was nothing more than a Jewish invention.

The cultural and economic prominence of Austro-Hungarian Jews made anti-Semitism even more virulent in the Dual Monarchy than in Germany. And nowhere was the strength of anti-Semitism more apparent than in the Austrian universities. Indeed, it was the Austrian universities that helped to make anti-Semitism respectable throughout the country.[11]

卐

Georg von Schönerer and Austrian Pan-Germanism

Students at the universities of Vienna and Graz were among the first Austrians to adopt both racial anti-Semitism and pan-Germanism as the bases for a modern rightist movement fanatically opposed to liberalism and laissez faire capitalism. After 1859 nationalistic social fraternities called *Burschenschaften* began to spread from Germany into Austria to form the earliest focal points of pan-German activity. Pan-Germanism no doubt seemed relevant to the German-speaking students at these institutions, because their schools registered thousands of Slavic- and Italian-speaking students from the monarchy's crownlands. So zealous were these young hotheads that when they could not convert fellow students to their ideal of an all-German Reich dominated by Prussia, they used less peaceful means to try to destroy all other student organizations. Their trademark was the saber scar. "Vienna and Graz were the earliest and always remained the chief centers of pan-Germanism."[12]

At the heart of the students' political ideology was the assumption that German national unity was of supreme importance in every political question. After Austria's defeat by Prussia in 1866, and Prussia's victory over France in 1870, it became clear that German unity could best be achieved by Bismarck's new Reich. What now stood in the way of this goal was the existence of Imperial Austria. All political activity therefore was directed toward Austria's destruction. The pan-German students developed a veritable cult of Prussia, which led to speeches and pamphlets in the 1870s glorifying service to the German state. They worshiped force, had contempt for humanitarian law and justice, and criticized parliamentary government and capitalism as selfish, "individualistic," and antinational. In keeping with their idolization of all things "German," the pan-German students also sought to purify university life by eliminating all "foreign influence," which in practice often meant the expulsion of religious and ethnic Jews, as well as Slavs, from their nationalistic societies.

About 1876, contact was made between the pan-German fraternities of Vienna and Georg Ritter von Schönerer (1842–1921), at that time a left-wing Liberal deputy in the Austrian Parliament. Schönerer, who in many respects might be called the "father," or at least the "grandfather," of National Socialism, was already well-known in Austria for his bellicose German nationalism and soon made a powerful impact on the pan-German students. He taught them the importance of the social question for the political struggle and revealed how they could persuade the "masses" to defend German culture.[13]

The spiritual leader of the German national movement in Austria since the time of his election to the Lower House of Parliament in 1873, Schönerer was an extreme example of the reaction by German-speaking Austrians to the even-handed treatment Prime Minister Eduard Taaffe tried to mete out to the Slavs of the Austrian Empire during his ministry between 1879 and 1893. Taaffe's extension of political representation and language rights to the Austro-Slavs was interpreted by German-Austrian nationalists as a menace to their superior economic and political position or even to their national existence. Schönerer himself reacted by founding the nationalistic German People's party (Deutsche Volkspartei) in 1881. Elsewhere in Austria, especially along the ethnic borders, various national clubs and school leagues were founded by German-Austrians during the 1880s.

In 1882 Schönerer helped to draft the famous "Linz Program." The two most important points in this declaration were a demand for an extension of the franchise and the protection of the Germans of Austria. The latter would be accomplished by detaching the Slavic parts of the Empire (Bucovina, Galicia, and Dalmatia) from the predominantly German-speaking areas (the Alpine crownlands, Bohemia, Moravia, and Austrian Silesia). Thus the German-speaking Austrians would be raised from a 35 percent minority to an absolute majority in the greatly reduced Austrian Empire. German would become the official state language while the Czechs, Slovenes, and Italians would presumably become declining minorities. Although the Linz Program included a demand for greater civil liberties, this could not disguise the basically imperialist nature of the declaration.[14]

Anti-Semitism was not originally part of the Linz Program, as demonstrated by the fact that Schönerer's chief collaborators on the document, the historian Heinrich Friedjung and the Socialist leader Viktor Adler, were both ethnic Jews. Schönerer was simply against a "preponderance" of Jewish political influence in 1882. Three years later, however, he added a twelfth point to the Linz declaration, stating that "the removal of Jewish influence from all sections of public life is indispensable for carrying out the reforms aimed at."[15] Like Hitler after him, Schönerer was convinced that Jewish intellectuals were responsible for Marxism and internationalism, both of which were harmful to German interests.

Schönerer's racial anti-Semitism was just one of many ways in which he anticipated the ideology and tactics of postwar National Socialism. For Schönerer, who was the most effective prewar propagandist of anti-Semitism, blood was the basis of all civil rights. In 1883 he demanded the dismissal of all Jewish teachers. After another four years he was calling for legislation restricting Jewish immigration. Those Jews already in the country he wanted

GEORG VON SCHÖNERER. *The spiritual godfather of National Socialism. Karl Wache, ed.* Deutscher Geist in Österreich.

confined once again to ghettos. But in the same year (1887) Schönerer's effectiveness as an anti-Semitic rabble-rouser was sharply reduced when a Viennese newspaper published documentary proof that his wife had a Jewish ancestor.[16]

The essence of Schönerer's brand of pan-Germanism was its extremism. He demanded unconditional victory for himself and his followers, and unconditional surrender for his many enemies. Negotiation and compromise were no better than thinly disguised forms of surrender.[17] Thirty years later, the highest Nazi virtue was to be *kompromislos*.

Schönerer's most recent biographer, Andrew G. Whiteside, has also pointed out a number of contradictions in the pan-German leader. He and his followers "combined racial abuse and demands for censorship and Aryanization with courageous defense of the civil liberties of workers, demands for far reaching advances in political and economic democracy, and denunciations of police censorship and press confiscations."[18] Typical of Nazis a generation later, Schönerer deliberately provoked the state authorities and then complained about persecution. War, he felt, was a basic fact of political life and violence was a necessity. The Austrian pan-Germans, in fact, became one of the first movements in Europe to break with existing laws and normal social behavior and to resort to direct action. Force and even terrorism became a way both to attract attention and to intimidate enemies.[19]

In smaller things, too, Schönerer resembled the Nazis of the next generation, Adolf Hitler in particular. He used the title Führer, although its exact meaning was unclear. (His leadership, unlike Hitler's, rested on a mere voluntary recognition of his special position in the pan-German movement.) Like Hitler, much of his influence derived from his ruthlessness and his superior propaganda techniques. And again like Hitler, he considered himself a messiah, in his case one with a mission to save the German-Austrian people from denationalization.[20]

Even Schönerer's supporters anticipated the groups that would follow the Nazi banner after the war. Most came from the middle and lower-middle classes. These were the same classes that were the first to be influenced by nationalism in the first half of the nineteenth century. They were also the same groups that felt threatened by industrialization and Jewish competition: middle and small businessmen, and small-town intelligentsia like lawyers, doctors, teachers, and accountants. Above all, university students followed both Schönerer and Hitler because they saw their hopes of entering the liberal professions and business being endangered by the well-established, hardworking, and ambitious Jews. Young people, therefore, were the most active and ardent devotees of both Nazism and proto-Nazism.[21]

Failures of the German Messiah

The same groups that were later cool toward the Nazis were also indifferent to Schönerer: aristocrats, big industrialists, and industrial workers. An important exception in the last group were those workers living in the ethnic borderlands who did, for a time, support Schönerer and later Hitler. The comparison breaks down only with regard to peasants, who eventually flocked to Hitler, but not to Schönerer. This particular comparison is rather meaningless, however, because most Austrian peasants did not even have the right to vote until Schönerer's career was already in eclipse.

Schönerer's inability to capture either of the two largest social groups in the Austrian Empire, the peasants and the factory workers, condemned his movement to the status of a tiny minority. Even at the height of the agitation over the Badeni language laws at the turn of the century, a campaign which was led by Schönerer, his Pan-German party[22] was able to win only forty thousand votes in the parliamentary elections of January 1901. The really dedicated pan-German extremists probably made up less than 1 percent of just the adult German-speaking population. Even if we include those people who admired Schönerer but did not belong to his party, the total still does not exceed 3 or 4 percent of the German-Austrians.[23]

So despite a similarity in the social composition of prewar pan-Germanism and postwar Nazism, the former was never anything like a mass movement. It may be that Schönerer did not even want to lead a large party. He was so doctrinaire that he claimed a large constitutional party would only water down his ideas.[24]

Many of Schönerer's policies also drastically reduced the size of his potential following. After 1882 he openly called for the destruction of the Habsburg Monarchy and demanded union of all German-speaking people under Hohenzollern rule. Only then, he argued, would the German-Austrians be completely safe from Slavicization. But his irredentism attracted little support beyond university students. And even they usually became *Kaisertreu* soon after graduation.[25] When he ended a speech to the Austrian Reichsrat (Lower House of Parliament) in 1902 with the cry "Hoch und Heil den Hohenzollern," he evoked nothing but disgust.[26]

Part and parcel with his irredentism was Schönerer's *Los von Rom* (Away from Rome) movement. Not only Adolf Hitler, but also most of Schönerer's contemporaries, as well as historians, saw this policy as Schönerer's worst, and most avoidable mistake. The campaign was designed to prepare the way for an Austro-German Anschluss by first converting the German-Austrian Catholics to Protestantism. Schönerer saw such a conversion as an essential proof of uncorrupted German patriotism. Failure to convert entailed expulsion from the Pan-German party. None of this is meant to imply, however, that Schönerer was a devout Protestant; far from it.

Only about sixty thousand people actually converted to Protestantism. Potential members of the party, especially peasants, were alienated by Schönerer's agnosticism, paganism, and anticlericalism, as well as by his rejection of the Habsburgs. His bullheadedness on the Protestant question only facilitated the rising popularity of the Christian Social party among peasants and also among craftsmen and shopkeepers.[27]

Adolf Hitler also blamed Schönerer's alleged "unclear conception of the significance of the social problem" for his ultimate failure. Actually, Schönerer did not lack an understanding of social problems; and he certainly did not eschew mass agitation. He spoke out on behalf of workers as soon as he entered the Imperial Parliament in 1873. Later he proposed legislation for a minimum wage, limited work days, mandatory rest on Sundays, prohibition of child labor, and restriction of labor for women, and a state-supported old-age insurance program. It is true that he had no thoroughly revolutionary solution to social problems. But neither did Hitler.

Still another reason for the failure of prewar Austrian pan-Germanism was the inability to unite into a single party behind a common leader. The pan-Germans always remained divided into a bewildering number of parties, clubs, and associations whose names were continually changing. Chronic factionalism was the basic characteristic of pan-Germans until they were united by the Austrian Nazis after 1933. But even then they continued to quarrel.

There is no doubt that Schönerer was by far the most prominent of the prewar pan-German leaders. Without him "pan-Germanism would have remained an amorphous 'tendency' among various politically naive students, the völkisch middle class, and certain working class groups."[28] But Schönerer's insistence on blind obedience from all his followers needlessly deprived him of potentially able lieutenants. This attitude caused his most talented follower, Karl Hermann Wolf, as well as Wolf's German Radicals (Deutschradikalen) to secede from the Pan-German party in 1902.

The split with Wolf, along with a number of other minor party feuds, cost Schönerer dearly. In the parliamentary election of 1907 only three Pan-Germans were elected compared to twenty-one in 1901. The party as a whole received less than one-half of 1 percent of the total cast. Schönerer himself won only 909 votes in his district of Eger in western Bohemia, barely one-fifth that of his Socialist opponent.[29]

The break with Wolf, and Schönerer's parliamentary defeat, ended his career for all practical purposes; he did linger on until his death in 1921 as the acknowledged "grand old man" of pan-German nationalism, but lacked any political power. Even Adolf Hitler willingly conceded his philosophical indebtedness to Schönerer while criticizing him for failing to win over the masses.

✠

The Birth of the German Workers' Party

The dissolution of Schönerer's Pan-German party, his unwillingness to favor the partition of Bohemia along ethnic lines, and his conviction that the social and national questions were essentially one, all paved the way for the founding of a new German nationalist party in 1903–4, the German Workers' party (Deutsche Arbeiterpartei or DAP). The party was by no means a novelty, as numerous organizations catering to nationalistic German-Austrian workers had existed since at least the 1880s, especially in Bohemia. A fierce political and economic rivalry existed in that crownland between Czechs and Germans, which was intensified by the rapid industrialization of the 1880s and 1890s. Czechs, who were accustomed to a lower standard of living, were often willing to move into historically German-speaking areas to work for less pay. The German workers, displaced by relatively unskilled Czechs, quickly developed a burning hatred of their rivals. The Czech minority in German towns grew and sometimes even became a majority, as in Prague and Pilsen (Pizen). When this trend developed, German workers feared not only the loss of their livelihood, but the loss of their nationality as well.

Within Schönerer's pan-German movement a special group had been formed in the 1880s to represent workers' interests. The many nationalistic workers' groups in Bohemia organized themselves into a German National Workers' League (Deutschnationalen Arbeiterbund) in 1893. The nationalistic fever aroused by the Badeni decrees brought various pan-German parties together in a parliamentary club called the Pan-German Union (Alldeutsche Vereinigung). But the Schönerer-Wolf rift broke the alliance into quarreling factions after just one year. Nineteen hundred and two thus anticipated 1923, the year of Hitler's Beer Hall Putsch, as a time of disaster. In each case the movement had to begin again virtually from scratch.

The Pan-German party was the last prewar attempt to unite workers and the bourgeoisie into a single party. The breakup of Schönerer's party paved the way for the founding of a number of German national class parties for workers, peasants, and the bourgeoisie; they could agree only on maintaining traditional German predominance and in fighting all forms of Marxism.[30]

The German Workers' party was just one of these sectarian parties; but it also happened to be the direct forerunner of the National Socialist German Workers' party of Austria (NSDAP). The party was first organized in the northern Bohemian city of Aussig (Usti nad Labein) on 15 November 1903. On 17 January 1904, the first issue of the party's newspaper, *Deutsche Arbeiter-Zeitung*, appeared.

On 15 August 1904 the first big conference of the DAP met in Trautenau (Trutnou) to approve a program drafted the previous May by Alois Ciller, a founder of the party. The Trautenauer Program declared that the party sought to rescue the German-Austrian worker from his "economic, political, and cultural oppression." The worker, it went on to say, could realize his full potential only within the natural boundaries of his nationality. It rejected international organizations (meaning the Social Democratic party) and affirmed that it was no narrow class party. The program also repeated the demands found in the Linz Program of 1882 for the introduction of an equal and direct franchise and for complete freedom of speech and the press.[31]

Although the DAP, like the SDP, from whose ranks many of its members had come, was composed mostly of workers, it differed from the Social Democrats in many important respects. Unlike the SDP, the leaders as well as the party rank and file were workers, although the term *Arbeiter* was broadened by the DAP to include white-collar employees. Like the Social Democrats, but in contrast to Schönerer's pan-Germans, the DAP supported the Habsburg Monarchy right down to the last stages of World War I. On the other hand it was a proponent of the German alliance and during the war wanted to make German the official state language. The party also denounced at Trautenau the Marxist idea of the international solidarity of the working class, although it did not reject the concept of class itself. The party's announced goal was radical social and economic reform; yet it was deliberately vague about the usefulness of private property, popular sovereignty, civil liberties, and equal economic opportunity. In later years the party spoke of the need for socialism and denounced the evils of capitalism, but it never demanded the nationalization of all private property. From the start, in fact, it was far less concerned about theory than was the SDP.[32] The party's only claim to ideological originality was its idea of creating a *Volksgemeinschaft* or "people's community" of "honest" German workers whether industrial, clerical, or professional.[33]

A new party program, drawn up in the Moravian city of Iglau (Jihlava) in

1913, added little to the Trautenauer declaration. It did talk about not just the maintenance but also the increase in the territory inhabited by Germans, thus anticipating the Nazi theorist Alfred Rosenberg and his idea of *Dem Volk den Raum* (*land to the people*). The word *movement* was also used in a party document for the first time. The party's motto was declared to be "Work in German districts for German workers only!" The Iglau program concluded by saying that the party would "combat all medieval, clerical, and capitalistic privileges as well as all alien (*fremdvölkisch*) influences, 'especially the ever-increasing Jewish spirit in public life.'"[34] Thus anti-Semitism made its official appearance in the party's program, although it was well down the list of priorities as compared to those of the bourgeois German nationalist parties.

In its irrationalism, unscrupulous opportunism, nationalistic arrogance, and racism the party was clearly the heir of Schönerer. Its claim to racial and cultural superiority over Czechs and Jews was not moderated by any Christian principles of responsibility and compassion. On the other hand, its call for an egalitarian people's community did contain a note of idealism that was intended to appeal to the masses.

The German Workers' Party: Social Composition and Growth

From its founding in 1903 until its partition just after the close of the World War, the DAP drew the bulk of its following from northern Bohemia, where the Czech-German rivalry was the most pronounced. Of the first party leaders who met in Trautenau, nine came from what would later be called the Sudetenland, the German-speaking portions of Bohemia, Moravia, and Austrian Silesia. Of the others, two came from Klagenfurt, two from Linz, and one from Graz. By 1909 the party had organized fifteen *Ortsgruppen* (local groups) in Styria, four in Carinthia, one in the predominantly Slovene crownland of Carniola, and two in Trieste and Küstenland, which had mixed Italian and Slovene populations and only small German minorities. Between 1909 and 1918 the only new *Ortsgruppen* were in Upper Austria, Salzburg, and the German South Tyrol.[35]

What is interesting about this distribution is that it was confined almost exclusively to the ethnic borderlands where the German-Austrians clashed with Slavs and Italians, who aggressively sought equal political, cultural, and economic rights. The German Workers' party thus resembled other protofascist and fascist parties throughout Europe that arose both before and after the World War where nationalities came into conflict along ethnic borders.[36]

Just as most prewar members and leaders of the DAP were workers (often railroad employees and skilled craftsmen), so too were nationalist trade unions the backbone of the party. Moreover, both the union and party leadership were democratically elected by the membership. According to Whiteside, there is no evidence that either the party or its trade union was dominated by employers, the rich, or aristocrats.[37]

At first the growth of the new party was slow, in part perhaps because its members, and also those of the nationalist trade union, ran the risk of being beaten up by Marxists. In the parliamentary elections held in 1907 it mustered fewer than four thousand votes. But its fortunes began to improve in 1908 when Dr. Walter Riehl (1881–1955), a lawyer and government attorney from the northern Bohemian town of Reichenberg (Liberec), joined the party. Riehl's grandfather had been a radical during the revolutions of 1848. Like so many other members of the early DAP, the young Riehl had begun his political career as a Social Democrat. He became disenchanted as early as 1903, however, with the party's revolutionary theory. He himself preferred an evolutionary, democratic development, a conviction that would cause him to break with Adolf Hitler twenty years later. In most other respects, even in his prewar anticlericalism, Riehl still followed the Socialists' line, although he renounced their internationalism.[38]

Riehl's nationalist agitation cost him his civil-service job in 1908, but did not stop him from preaching, at mass meetings around Reichenberg, the necessity for workers and the bourgeoisie to unite in a single party to protect German interests. He tried to broaden the party's base still further by insisting on the inclusion of people with Czech names just as long as they spoke German and considered themselves Germans. (Many Czech nationalist leaders had German names, as is still the case.)

With the help of Riehl's emotional oratory, the DAP managed to gain twenty-six thousand votes and three parliamentary delegates in the elections of 1911, seven times the vote the party had received just four years earlier. Meanwhile, Schönerer's Pan-German party managed only seventeen thousand votes and soon disappeared from the political scene.[39]

It was Walter Riehl, together with Rudolf Jung, a railway worker, who teamed up to draft the DAP's new program at Iglau in 1913. The two men had complementary personalities. Whereas Riehl was gregarious, emotional, and untheoretical, Jung tended to be reserved and more philosophical. Jung hoped to become the party's Karl Marx by writing a profound analysis of society. Indeed, he did produce a theoretical study in 1918, entitled *Der national Sozial-ismus: Seine Grundlagen, seine Werdegang, seine Ziele* (*National Socialism: Its Foundations, Its Development, Its Goals*). The book anticipated the German Nazis' Twenty-five Point program by two years and Hitler's *Mein Kampf* by seven. Jung's political activity, like Riehl's, also proved costly, as he lost his job in 1910; thereafter he devoted himself full-time to party activities.

When the World War broke out in 1914 the DAP came to the defense of Austria-Hungary as the best way to preserve the interests of all Germans, including the German Reich. During the war Jung wrote an article denouncing "Western" democracy, which he claimed favored men of money and did not produce the most capable leaders. Everyone should place the good of the group above himself; therefore, the party's slogan became *Gemeinnutz geht vor Eigennutz* (the common good goes before self-interest). He called for the nationalization of monopolies, department stores, and large landed estates that were not the product of "honest work," a disguised form of anti-Semitism. He was also a proponent of an annexationist program in the East based on the need for Lebensraum.[40]

In response to Czech demands for independence, the Bohemian members of the DAP, at a meeting of the provincial parliament in April 1918, called for a separate province of "German-Bohemia." Then in May the party rejected plans to save the Habsburg Monarchy or to make German-Austria part of a Danube federation. Instead, the party reverted to Schönerer's old battle cry that the German-Austrians be united with their brethren in the Reich to create a single German state free of Jews.[41]

A large part of the membership of the German Workers' party, including Walter Riehl, served on the many Austro-Hungarian fronts during the war. By default, party leadership fell to Jung, Ferdinand Burschofsky, a printer and one of the founders of the party, and Walter Gattermayer, an aggressive trade-union leader who had joined the DAP in 1909. It was Gattermayer who suggested in April 1918 that the party's name be enlarged, for propaganda purposes, to German National Socialist Workers' party (Deutsche National-sozialistische Arbeiterpartei or DNSAP). The proposal was accepted by a party congress meeting in Vienna in August. The term "National Socialist" itself was not new. A party by that name had been founded by Czechs in 1897 after the Austrian Social Democratic party began breaking into national groups. Members of the DAP had informally used the name since about 1910 and it was proposed at a party meeting in Vienna in 1913. The Sudeten Nazis continued to use the title DNSAP until they dissolved their party in 1933.

The German Nazi party was founded in January 1919, only a few months after the name change in Austria. A controversy exists over the extent to which the Austrian Nazis may have influenced the birth and development of the German Nazis. No direct evidence has been discovered that would link Hitler with the prewar Austrian Nazis.[42] Indeed, Hitler himself, while readily acknowledging his intellectual indebtedness to Georg von Schönerer in *Mein Kampf*, made absolutely no mention of Walter Riehl, Rudolf Jung, or any of the other early leaders of the Austrian DAP. Andrew G. Whiteside has stated flatly that "the German Nazis were [not] the direct descendants of the prewar Austrian National Socialists."[43] Despite remarkable parallels between the two movements, the German Nazis, according to Whiteside, had independent origins of their own, uninfluenced by Austria.

On the other hand, as the American historian Max H. Kele has pointed out, "We know that the young Hitler was an avid newspaper reader and a student of *völkish* politics. During these very years, the DAP had its headquarters in the same Viennese district where Hitler lived. He would have had to be both deaf and blind to have escaped the pamphlets, newspapers, and rallies of the Austrian Nazis."[44]

In any event, there were certainly striking similarities between the prewar Austrian Nazis and the postwar German Nazis that may be more than simply coincidental. Both were antiliberal, anticapitalist, anti-Marxist, and of course, both were anti-Semitic, though the Austrians were much less so before the war than the Germans were after it. Even the terminology and the militancy of the two parties were much the same.[45] As Hitler himself confessed in a speech in Salzburg in August 1920, "I am ashamed to say that not until today, after so many years, the *same* movement which began in German-Austria in 1904 has just begun to gain a footing in Germany."[46]

New Beginnings: Walter Riehl
and the DNSAP, 1918–1923

When the Austro-Hungarian Monarchy collapsed in the fall of 1918, the German Workers' party, like the other parties of Austria, demanded the inclusion of both the Sudeten and Alpine Germans in the new German Republic. When the Anschluss was prohibited by the Allies, it proved to be particularly disastrous for the DNSAP. The creation of an independent Austrian Republic and the Allies' recognition of the historic unity of the "Bohemian crownlands" (Bohemia, Moravia, and Austrian Silesia) within Czechoslovakia split the DNSAP in two, with by far the larger part being isolated in the new Czech-dominated state.

Dr. Riehl, who had been elected chairman of the DNSAP in May, moved his residence to Vienna and continued as leader of the Austrian Nazis until 1923. Although he and Hitler differed, and in 1923 split over tactics, the ideologies of the two men were similar, though certainly not identical. Both advocated a strong central government (though Riehl wanted only a temporary dictatorship), and both regarded parliaments as obstacles to vigorous decision making. Proportional representation made personal responsibility impossible. Both men favored an Anschluss, and violently opposed Austria's joining a Danubian federation. Riehl also shared Hitler's anti-Semitism and, like Hitler, blamed the Jews for almost all his country's problems, both foreign and domestic. His goal was to reduce the Jews' influence to their proportion of Austria's total population. But this objective did not prevent Riehl from mixing with Jews socially, something Hitler would never have dreamed of doing in his adult years.[47]

Despite the many similarities, there were profound differences between the two men that reflected Hitler's radical brand of Nazism and the relative moderation of at least some of the Austrian National Socialists. Riehl was in many respects a typical Austrian: jovial, *gemütlich*, and helpful; he was perhaps a throwback to the popular Viennese mayor Karl Lueger. He criticized his opponents with wit and satire rather than sarcasm. On the other hand, to many Austrians, Hitler was a stereotyped, hard-nosed Prussian (despite his Austrian birth), unwilling to make concessions either in his policies or in his speeches. Riehl and his followers, moreover, unlike Hitler, took the socialism in National Socialism seriously. As a former Social Democrat he had broken with the party only because of its international and revolutionary doctrines. Riehl was also eight years older than Hitler. Therefore, the latter's uncompromising and revolutionary tactics appealed more to the younger Austrian Nazis.[48]

Nowhere were the differences between Riehl and Hitler, and between "moderate" and radical Nazis in general, sharper than over the question of the internal organization of the Nazi party. Part of the Austrian DNSAP, like its brother party in the Sudetenland, remained comparatively democratic in its structure to its very end in 1934, despite its vehement criticism of Austrian parliamentarianism. All local organizations elected a district leadership; the local and district units were subordinate to a national Staatsparteileitung (State Party Leadership) consisting of twelve members elected by the entire membership. Riehl was elected chairman of the party at these annual meetings. The Parteitag even voted on future party policies. At the 1920 gathering, for example, two-thirds of the membership voted for the resolution that "every hope for a rebirth of Austria depends on the Anschluss."[49] At the same meeting, which was held in Salzburg, there was a debate about whether the word *Arbeiter* should be retained in the party's title. Those like Walter Gattermayer and Rudolf Jung wanted to keep the DNSAP a class party of laborers; they did not even wish to recruit businessmen and peasants.[50] Although the German Workers' party had similar democratic rules when Hitler joined it in 1919, he put an end to that system soon after he took over control of the party in July 1921. By 1923 there were no more meaningful discussions at party meetings of the German NSDAP.

The debate at the Salzburg convention in 1920 was characteristic of the ideological tug of war that took place within the DNSAP in the early postwar years. Gattermayer and Jung led the party's left wing and tried to push the DNSAP in a socialistic direction. However, a demand by a delegate to the party congress in Vienna in December 1919, that the Marxist idea of class struggle be incorporated into the party's program, was rejected. Walter Riehl, the lawyer, followed a middle-of-the-road philosophy on social questions and argued that the party should represent the interests of the entire German people while recognizing the workers as the principal fighters for the National Socialist idea.[51]

But Rudolf Jung, who maintained a close contact with Austria even after he returned to Czechoslovakia in 1919 to lead the Sudeten Nazis, did not easily give up the ideological fight. In an article printed in the *DAP* in June 1921 Jung asserted that bigger industries, which represented private monopolies, ought to be socialized. Such monopolies included land, coal, water, transportation, insurance, and advertising. Workers, Jung wrote, should take part in profit sharing in both private and public businesses and should be represented equally on business-advisory councils.[52] Hitler later denounced such ideas as "Bolshevistic."

At a party meeting held in Linz in the same year, Jung attempted to strike out that section of the Nazi program which repudiated the concept of class struggle. He again called for a declaration that the National Socialists were a "class party of productive work." Once more, however, Riehl refused to accept this proposal.[53]

The party's anti-Semitism was more extreme after the World War than it had been before 1914. A headline in the *DAP* in October 1920 put *Judenherrschaft* (Jewish domination) at the top of a list of those things the Nazis opposed. Further down the catalogue were laziness, luxury, and gluttony.[54]

Walter Riehl also continued to stress the need for a temporary dictatorship. A strong leader, who did not have to worry about criticism or popularity, was needed to lead Austria out of its present malaise. But the masses should not be denied their rights indefinitely.[55]

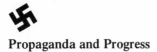

Propaganda and Progress

These ideological tenets formed the basis of much of the Nazis' propaganda in the early years of the Austrian Republic. Current events, of course, were another source of propaganda material. The Treaty of Saint-Germain was denounced, quite understandably, because it left even more Germans under alien rule than did the Treaty of Versailles. German Austria was an impossible creation consisting of a huge world city and a few Alpine valleys. Its existence would lead to a catastrophe in the long run. Mustafa Kemal of Turkey was viewed as a nationalist hero whose exploits in throwing out foreign invaders and tearing up the Treaty of Sevres ought to be emulated in Austria and Germany. All that was needed was a strong national will. Such determination had been displayed in the Soviet Union and Italy, both of which had defied the West.

Newspaper articles were by no means the only method of Nazi propaganda in the early years of the new Republic. The Nazis held their first large rally in Vienna in February 1922. Special groups were organized to put up posters advertising the demonstration; another group, the Ordnertruppen (the predecessor of the SA) was used to protect the meeting. The rally was climaxed with a speech by Hitler. Communists (or alleged Communists) tried to storm the rostrum while Hitler was speaking, but were stopped by the Ordnertruppen.[56] Such clashes between Marxists and Nazis soon became commonplace in both Austria and Germany and were always given ample headlines in the Nazi press, especially when some of the Nazi participants were killed or wounded.

Austria's dire circumstances in the early postwar years should have aided an extremist and militant party like the Nazis. Nevertheless, the growth of the DNSAP was disappointing, though on a per capita basis it was far better than that of the German Nazis. Much of the problem can be attributed to the existence of various other extremist groups: paramilitary formations like the Heimwehr (Home Guard), Frontkämpfervereinigung (Front Fighters' Association), and numerous other movements and secret organizations.[57] The Nazis' anti-Semitism and demand for an Anschluss were far from unique even among the more moderate Austrian parties.

In the first postwar elections held in February 1919 the Nazis could muster only 0.78 percent of the almost 3 million votes cast.[58] Most of the Nazis' 27,690 votes came in urban areas. In October the Nazi vote increased to just under 34,000 with the biggest increases coming in Vienna and Lower Austria. But the party still had no parliamentary mandates.[59] And the "victory" merely caused a rift to grow between the party's relatively moderate leaders and some of its more radical rank-and-file members who demanded an accelerated propaganda drive.[60]

The party's growth in 1922 and 1923 was a little more encouraging. The number of registered members tripled between August 1922 and August 1923 when it stood at 34,000. During the same period the number of Ortsgruppen doubled to 118. In municipal elections held in Linz in March 1923 the Nazis won a surprising 7.85 percent of the vote and four seats on the city council.[61] The circulation of the *Deutsche Arbeiter-Presse* rose from 4,000 to 22,000 in 1922 and 1923. The paramilitary Ordnertruppen, founded in 1922, had 9,800 members a year later.[62]

While this modest progress was being made, the Austrian Nazis succeeded in establishing contact with kindred groups in other countries. Ties with the parent Sudeten Nazis had never been broken. As early as December 1919 the Sudetens attended a joint meeting in Vienna along with some Nazis from Polish Silesia. The relative strength of the Sudeten Nazis was revealed in the fact that they were accorded four voting representatives at the conference compared to just two for Austria, and one for the German-Poles. The meeting set up the Interstate National Socialist Bureau of the German Language Territory, with Walter Riehl as its chairman.

In September 1919 Riehl sent copies of the Austrian Nazi program to the chairman of the German Workers' party, Anton Drexler. Riehl also tried to persuade Drexler to change the name of his party to coincide with that of the Austrian Nazis. In 1920 the German Nazis did change their title to one nearly identical to that used by the Austrians (except the word *German* came in the middle of the name instead of at the beginning, thus NSDAP instead of DNSAP). We do not know whether the Austrians were responsible for this change. But Drexler was prepared to collaborate with the Austrians because he shared their desire to strengthen the working-class element of the parties.[63]

Riehl was especially anxious to coordinate the program and insignia of the Austrian and German Nazis. In February 1920 he designed a flag using a swastika on a white field; the flag was first flown in public on 1 May. In the meantime Hitler had been designing his own swastika flag (apparently independently) in Munich.

It was Walter Riehl, once again, who was responsible for organizing a second conference of the federated Nazi party. This meeting took place in Salzburg and was, as far as we know, the first to be attended by Adolf Hitler and Anton Drexler. Already at this point the Munich Nazis who now joined the Interstate Bureau began to influence the Austrians.[64] However, the relationship was still far from one-sided. Riehl made a reciprocal arrangement for speakers between Germany and Austria. As a result, Hitler spoke in Innsbruck, Salzburg, Hallein, Saint-Pölten, and Vienna in 1920 and again in Vienna in December 1921 and June 1922.[65] Meanwhile Riehl, Jung, Gattermayer, and other Austrian and Sudeten Nazis spoke in Nuremberg, Munich, Rosenheim, Bayreuth, and Augsburg, always stressing the prolabor aspects of National Socialism. Riehl also wrote a number of articles in the German Nazis' official newspaper, the *Völkischer Beobachter*, and Hitler published an article in the *Deutsche Arbeiter-Presse* in February 1923. Riehl and Hitler also exchanged letters between 1920 and 1923 in which both men used the informal "Du" in their salutations.[66]

These developments meant that by the summer of 1923 the Austrian Nazis had some reason for optimism. Their party was still very small, but was grow-

Die nationalsozialistischen Führer auf der zwischenstaatlichen Tagung in Salzburg, August 1920.

NAZI REPRESENTATIVES *at an interstate meeting in Salzburg, August 1920. In the first row from left to right are Rudolf Jung, Engineer Brunner (Sudetenland), Dr. Walter Riehl, Anton Drexler, and Hans Knirsch (Sudetenland). The first person in the second row (on the far left) is Walter Gattermayer (DÖW).*

ing at a respectable rate. Ties with the Sudeten Nazis were close; and new and apparently warm relations with the German Nazis had been established. In Dr. Walter Riehl they had an admired and popular leader, not only of their own party, but of the international Nazi federation as well. As late as August 1923 few Austrian Nazis could have foreseen the disasters that lay just ahead.

Chapter III
The Nazi Civil War, 1923–1930

The year 1923 was critical for both the German and Austrian Nazi parties. For the Germans the year was climaxed by the disastrous Beer Hall Putsch in November. The uprising failed miserably; Hitler was arrested and imprisoned, and the German NSDAP had to start virtually anew fifteen months later. For the Austrian Nazis, 1923 marked the beginning of an endless series of leadership disputes and factional strife. The quarrels amounted to a veritable civil war.

The year also witnessed the efforts by older and more moderate Austrian Nazis to preserve their party's autonomy against Hitler's drive for dictatorial power, not only over the Nazis of Germany, but those of Austria and the Sudetenland as well. The attack on Austrian Nazi independence in 1923 and again in 1926 proved only a prelude to the whole national dilemma in 1938.

The Resignation of Walter Riehl

In the early postwar years the Austrian Nazis, who assumed that the German Nazi party, though younger, had the same goals as themselves, took pleasure in the Germans' success. Only years later would the more moderate Austrian Nazis deny that the two groups had anything more in common than their name.[1]

Although Riehl and his compatriots were proud of their association with the German Nazis, the feeling was by no means mutual. The Germans contributed nothing to the operation of the Interstate Bureau in Vienna, and Hitler did not even bother to answer many of Riehl's letters.[2] By the middle of 1922 the German Nazis had grown far larger than their Austrian and Sudeten cousins; and Hitler no longer had any need for his poor relations.

Hitler's attitude toward the Austrians became arrogant at the fifth and, as it turned out, last interstate National Socialist convention held in Salzburg in August 1923. By that time, as Riehl himself admitted, "The name of the powerful speaker and leader Adolf Hitler [had] grown far beyond the importance of other party leaders."[3] Having already established his dictatorial control over the German Nazis, Hitler was in no mood to see his policies contradicted by the smaller Austrian and Sudeten parties.

The main issue at the Salzburg gathering revolved around the party's policy toward future elections. The bourgeois Greater German People's party (GVP) had offered to form a coalition with the Austrian Nazis, an offer that Dr. Riehl was eager to accept. Riehl, who was reelected chairman of the Austrian party at the start of the convention, saw a coalition as the only hope of the Austrian Nazis' winning representation in the federal Parliament. With a voice in that assembly, the party would have a new and far more effective forum for its propaganda.[4] Hitler, who would himself adopt a similar philosophy in later years, rejected it in 1923 in favor of armed revolution. But Riehl believed that without a Nazi-GVP partnership, every anti-Marxist would have to vote for the Christian Social party of the Catholic prelate, Ignaz Seipel. On the other hand, a right-wing coalition could induce the Seipel government to protect the forthcoming Munich Putsch.[5]

Dr. Riehl was outvoted by the delegates at the conference and also by the Leaders' Council chaired by Hitler. Rudolf Jung, the representative of the Sudeten DNSAP, favored Riehl's proposal before the meeting, but only briefly. More solid support came from the leader of the Austro-Nazi Trade Union, Walter Gattermayer (who, however, was not on the Leaders' Council). Karl Schulz, on the other hand, even though he was Riehl's deputy (and the Gauleiter of Vienna), voted against the proposed coalition. He did so not as a matter of principle, however, but because he felt the party was too poor to campaign. Its meager resources could be more usefully spent on the paramilitary Ordnertruppen[6] and the party's press.[7] Riehl thus found himself in an embarrassing seven-to-one minority.[8]

Although Karl Schulz, who now replaced Walter Riehl as chairman of the Austrian Nazi Party, lined up with Hitler at the Salzburg convention, he would one day discover what Riehl had already learned, and what the future Austrian chancellor, Kurt von Schuschnigg, would discover years later: that Hitler was opposed not to this or that Austrian policy, but to the very principle of independence for his former homeland.

Perhaps overreacting, or more likely hoping to reverse the vote, as Hitler had done in similar circumstances in 1921, Riehl resigned his chairmanship of both the Austrian NSDAP and the Interstate Bureau (where he was succeeded by Rudolf Jung) for reasons of "health."[9] The motives for Riehl's actions became clearer during the fall of 1923. In a letter to a journalist in Salzburg, a copy of which was sent to Hitler, Riehl claimed that the executive committee that voted against him had been composed of "the most radical of the radicals." The new Austrian Nazi leaders were "young fanatics." He had resigned his offices because he did not want his name associated with the coming (Munich) Putsch, which he felt could only end in disaster. It was impossible to see how the Bavarian Nazis could profit from the weakening of the anti-Marxist forces in Austria.[10]

After his resignations Riehl received some very welcome support from Rudolf Jung. In an open letter to the Austrian leadership, which was distributed by Riehl, Jung harshly criticized an article appearing in the 25 August issue of the *Deutsche Arbeiter-Presse*. The article, written by Josef Müller, one of the editors of the *DAP*, was entitled "Kampf, nicht Wahl." Jung claimed the article could only be interpreted as a call for a Putsch. He warned that any "intoxicated enthusiasm [*Begeisterungsrausch*] could only lead to the destruction of the party. . . . Our time has not yet come."[11]

From Disaster to Resurgence: Hitler's Drive for Power, 1925–1926

Soon after Riehl's resignation the Austrian Nazi party was shaken by repercussions from the Beer Hall Putsch in Munich. Although many Austrians took part in the uprising, the party as a whole was not involved. Only three days after the fiasco, however, Karl Schulz organized a rally in Vienna to proclaim the Austrian party's unswerving loyalty to Hitler.[12] For months during the winter of 1923–24, the Austrian Nazis, who were anything but affluent themselves, also smuggled money as well as their party newspapers into Germany to aid the now outlawed German NSDAP. Numerous German exiles, including Hermann Göring, were given refuge by the Austrian party.[13] If the Austrians expected Hitler's gratitude for this assistance, however, they were soon to be disappointed.[14]

Nineteen twenty-four and the first part of 1925 witnessed a modest renaissance in the party's fortunes. In district elections held in Styria in May of 1924 the Nazis won an impressive (for them) twelve thousand votes and sixty municipal representatives.[15] The outcome was one of the first indications that Styria was to be a fascist stronghold. Otherwise, there was little the Nazis could honestly cheer about in 1924. When they attempted to hold a "German Day" in Salzburg in August, the Austrian government refused permission. The presence of eighteen thousand German gymnasts and members of paramilitary formations, it feared, would provoke unfavorable foreign reaction.[16] For similar reasons Vienna rejected an attempt by the Bavarian government to deport Hitler to his native country after his release from prison in December.[17]

The year 1925 was for a time somewhat more encouraging, because the Austrian Nazis were able to attract attention through their stormy protests and organized riots during an international Zionist congress held in Vienna in midsummer. One of the protest rallies drew an estimated ten thousand participants, of whom the Nazis were the largest single element. The impact of the Nazis' demonstrations, however, was undoubtedly blunted by the inclusion of countless other anti-Semitic groups and even by the bourgeois parties. Moreover, the Nazis could not prevent the congress from taking place, a number of their members were arrested by the police, and they found themselves financially exhausted by their propaganda expenditures. The whole episode cost Karl Schulz the respect of many of the younger Nazis.[18]

But the continued independence and relative unity of the Austrian Nazi party between 1923 and 1925 was due mainly to "fortuitous" events in Germany. The Beer Hall Putsch, and especially Hitler's subsequent imprisonment in the Landsberg fortress, interrupted—but only temporarily—Hitler's drive for mastery over the entire Nazi party, including the Austrian branch. As early as the congress of the German NSDAP in 1922 Hitler had insisted that power be concentrated at the party's headquarters in Munich. Only in this fashion, he maintained, could the kinds of splits that plagued other *völkisch* movements be avoided.[19] In writing *Mein Kampf* in 1924, Hitler made it clear that the type of federation which Walter Riehl had established among the Austrian, German, Sudeten, and Polish Nazi parties in 1919–20 was absolutely anathema to him. "By the formation of a working federation weak organizations are never transformed into strong ones, but a strong organization can and will not seldom be weakened. . . . Coalition successes bear by the very nature of their origin the germ of future crumbling, in fact of the loss of what had already been achieved."[20]

The model that Hitler thought Karl Schulz should emulate had been provided by Julius Streicher, the former leader of the German Socialist party of Nuremberg, who, in Hitler's words, "as soon as he recognized the greater and superior growth of the NSDAP clearly and beyond all doubt . . . ceased his activity for the DSP [German Socialist party]."[21]

While in prison Hitler made no attempt to take sides in party disputes so as to prevent the emergence of a successor. Thus, while the NSDAP was outlawed and disintegrating in Germany, the still legal Austrian party continued to function and even to grow. Its halcyon days were numbered, however.

Once released from prison in December 1924, Hitler immediately set to work rebuilding the party and reestablishing his own personal ascendancy. On 26 February 1925, the *Völkischer Beobachter* in Munich resumed publication; its first issue announced the "Basic Guidelines for the Reorganization of the NSDAP." The SA was subjected to strict political control and forbidden to admit into its ranks "armed groups and organizations."[22] Fifteen months later Hitler again laid down the law by drawing a sharp distinction between the NSDAP and all other völkisch groups.[23] The second volume of *Mein Kampf*, also written in 1926, claimed that the Führer was "the exclusive leader of the movement."[24]

The Social Transformation of the Austrian Nazi Party

Meanwhile, conditions within the Austrian party were undergoing dramatic changes, changes that would soon create a new crisis. The prewar Deutsche Arbeiterpartei had drawn its support primarily from trade unions, industrial workers, and the petty bourgeoisie; among these groups the bulk of the members came from northern Bohemia.[25] The first postwar elections revealed that the party was moderately strong only in the industrial regions of Vienna and Upper Styria (where there was an old tradition of radicalism), and also in Salzburg, where there was a well-established organization.[26] Not until the next decade would the party gain appreciable support from the countryside. In class terms it stood midway between the Social Democrats and the bourgeois parties. The older leaders such as Rudolf Jung, Walter Gattermayer, and Karl Schulz, all of whom were railroad workers, naturally looked to the same social groups for support after the war. Their social background likewise led them to take the socialism in National Socialism seriously.

The loss of the northern Bohemian heartland inexorably changed the social composition and therefore the very nature of the Austrian Nazi party. Trade-union influence continued to be significant in the party until 1926 (and for some Nazis even later). Many party members also belonged to a national trade union, which claimed some forty-five thousand members in 1923.[27] Trade-union influence, however, began declining after about 1922. There was now a great influx of university and high-school-aged students, hurt by the devastating inflation of the postwar years. They were frequently persuaded to join the NSDAP by their own teachers or by the German Athletes' Association (Deutscher Turnerbund). Twenty-two percent of the members of the party's paramilitary formation (whose name was changed to the Vaterländische Schutzbund in 1923) consisted of such students by 1924–25. After 1923 there was a definite decline in the relative strength of manual workers in the party and a corresponding increase in the size and importance of the lower middle class.[28]

The explosion that finally tore the Austrian party to pieces in 1925–26 basically involved a clash between trade unionists, led by men who had been born in the early 1880s, and younger members, born about fifteen years later, who lived mostly in medium-sized provincial capitals like Graz, Linz, Salzburg, and Klagenfurt. The latter faction threw its weight behind Adolf Hitler. The older men had established their careers during the relatively peaceful years of the late Empire; the young militants had grown to maturity during the World War. The younger veterans were likely to be members of the Vaterländische Schutzbund in and around Vienna.[29] The same division between older trade unionists and young firebrands existed in the German NSDAP until Hitler seized dictatorial control in 1921.

The younger members of the Austrian Nazi party had little knowledge of and even less interest in the prewar struggles of the German Workers' party. They were impatient with the party's painfully slow progress and blamed it on the party's democratic structure, which, they claimed, maximized debate and minimized action. The old leaders later recognized that the party's democratic organization, which permitted "even the lowliest Parteigenosse" to voice his opinion, had made it possible for the *Hitlergeist* to spread and disrupt the party.[30] The young hotheads admired Hitler's dictatorial leadership, radical rhetoric, and frequent, noisy mass rallies. From 1920 to 1922 they had had numerous opportunities to hear him as well as other German radicals speak in Austria.[31] They were also enthusiastic about Hitler's willingness to use force in 1923.[32] They tried, but with only limited success, to persuade the Austrian leaders to imitate Hitler's methods in their own country. But they were told that conditions were different, particularly in Vienna (with its huge Socialist and Jewish population) from those in Munich and therefore required different tactics.[33] The leadership, sensitive to the charge of undue "moderation," retorted,

> No one could say that our party has not been radical enough. . . . But the ideal of a German workers' movement does not consist of collecting

a few hundred or a few thousand desperadoes and creating an uproar like farmhands, but of saturating the mass of the German workers with the national and social ideals of our program. . . . We, too, honor the leadership principle, but that does not prevent the leader from speaking with his membership, accepting advice, and from time to time submitting an account of his activities. But the leader in Germany claims the rights of a lord toward his subjects. . . . There are no elections of the leader or subleaders, only someone who appoints himself and who is as infallible as the pope.[34]

Growing Opposition, 1925–1926

Opposition to the old Nazi leadership had been building long before a split finally occurred in 1925–26. As early as October 1920, Josef Müller persuaded the party leadership to allow him to establish a Meeting and Propaganda Committee. This group, impatient with Riehl's infrequent rallies, organized countless rallies of its own in 1921 against the Treaty of Lana negotiated between Austria and Czechoslovakia.[35] The treaty was primarily designed to reopen commerce between the countries, trade that was desperately needed by Austria. However, the treaty also stipulated a more or less "voluntary" Austrian renunciation of the Sudeten Germans in Czechoslovakia.

Walter Riehl's resignation in August 1923 was essentially a victory for the young Hitler advocates, although a major party split was avoided. But in 1925 the party was again rent by differing attitudes toward the international Zionist congress, the older party leaders not wanting to take to the streets. Another quarrel erupted in October between the editor of the *DAP* and the paper's administrative officials, who wanted higher salaries. The party's general secretary, Ernst Graber, and some leaders of the Vaterländische Schutzbund, supported the demands, while the other leaders opposed them on financial grounds.[36]

The Schulz partisans thought the party's internal problems were caused in large measure by Graber, whose alleged *Schlamperei* resulted in letters to Schulz from *Parteigenossen* in the provinces going unanswered. Subsequent indignation, they believed, had been unfairly directed at Schulz. Matters started coming to a head toward the end of October, when several local leaders (*Ortsgruppenleiter*) in Vienna got together with Müller and decided to eliminate all harmful problems "in the shortest possible time, and to arrange for an Anschluss with the Adolf Hitler movement in the Reich."

On 1 November a tumultuous meeting took place involving the Vaterländische Schutzbund of Vienna and the party leadership. After an angry debate, a majority of those present (who were not necessarily representative of all party members in Vienna or the rest of Austria) agreed with the aims of Müller and his colleagues.[37]

Nevertheless, a final split was avoided and the party's unity was patched up during an extraordinary Parteitag held in Linz in February of 1926. All attempts to sow discord were blamed on "Jewish Bolshevik newspapers." Schulz was reelected chairman, and the conference tried to distract attention from the party's internal squabbles by denouncing Italy's brutal treatment of the South Tyrol. Protest demonstrations and boycotts were ordered.[38]

All this show of unity and resolution, however, proved to be only so much bravado. In May the *Ortsgruppen* of the middle-class Vienna districts of Josefstadt, Hernals, and Währing were dissolved when they refused to recognize the federal leadership. Several conspirators were expelled from the party at the same time because of their "detrimental activities."[39]

Among the ringleaders were Ernst Graber and Richard Suchenwirth. Originally from the partly Slavic province of Carinthia, Suchenwirth (who had Germanized his name from the Slavic "Suchanek") was now a Viennese middle-school teacher and a polished speaker with consistently radical ideas. As early as 28 January 1926, he had denounced Schulz as a "Dummkopf" and other members as "people who had been thrown out of other parties."[40] Another conspirator was Josef Leopold, the head of the Lower Austrian SA, who in later years (1935–38) gained notoriety as the Führer of the entire (by then) illegal Austrian Nazi party.

Suchenwirth and his conspirators, along with two hundred of their followers, responded to their expulsion from the party by founding the NSDAP (Hitlerverein) on 4 May, and subordinating themselves directly to Hitler. The group's statutes were identical with those of the Munich party, and its program consisted of Hitler's "Twenty-five Theses." Soon other *Gaue* were founded in Styria, Lower Austria, Carinthia, and still later in the other federal states.

Another man who was instrumental in engineering the split and guiding the Vaterländische Schutzbund into the Hitler movement was Hermann Reschny. The twenty-eight-year-old Reschny was rewarded for his service when Hitler confirmed him as leader of the Austrian Sturmabteilung (as the paramilitary formation was now called) in June 1926. Reschny then extracted two promises from Hitler (both later utterly ignored): (1) that an Anschluss between Germany and Austria could take place only after a free, secret, and uninfluenced vote; and (2) that after such a union the Austrian state, party, and industry could not be staffed by Reich Germans.[41]

Hitler and the Party Schism

Efforts by Karl Schulz to head off a confrontation and work out some sort of modus vivendi with Hitler gained him nothing but insults. A meeting between the two Nazi leaders in Munich in the summer of 1925 was strikingly similar to Hitler's famous showdown with Chancellor Schuschnigg at Berchtesgaden in 1938. Schulz wrote several years later that Hitler

> allowed no exchange of ideas, but instead did all the talking. Even the slightest objection [*Einwurf*] was answered by him with a speech. I always had the feeling that Hitler was speaking not to me, but a large assembly. His voice cracked, his face became rigid, spittle flowed from his lips, and he spoke in such an ecstasy that he hit his chest and forehead with his hand so hard it smacked. After a two-hour interview I still had not a single opportunity to find out in concrete terms what Hitler expected of the Austrian movement and what he did not like.

When two other Austrian moderates met Hitler about this same time (1925), they received a similar treatment. He spoke in the rudest terms not only about the Austrian movement but also about Austria in general (again reminiscent of Schuschnigg's Berchtesgaden interview). He was particularly displeased with the Austrian Nazi policy toward Italy and the South Tyrol question.[42]

The South Tyrol issue was, in fact, almost certainly one of the major reasons for the split in the Austrian Nazi party. Contrary to popular belief, Hitler had not always favored the renunciation of the South Tyrol. In 1920 he had demanded both the Anschluss of Austria to Germany and the reunification of North and South Tyrol. In a speech at the Munich Hofbräuhaus in April 1922, he denounced the Italian administration in the South Tyrol. But his mind began to change in the fall of 1922 with Benito Mussolini's rise to power. One of the major reasons for Hitler's change of heart may have been a bribe by Mussolini. According to Konstantin von Neurath, the German ambassador to Italy from 1921 to 1930, and later the German foreign minister, the Duce gave Hitler money for his Putsch in exchange for Hitler's abandoning claims to the South Tyrol.[43]

Hitler alone was responsible for the new Nazi policy. In favoring the Italian alliance at the expense of the South Tyrol he broke with every other nationalist in both Germany and Austria. Here was an example of how Hitler was capable of formulating a policy on the basis of ice-cold logic, free from any sentiment or national prejudice.

As early as November 1922 Hitler referred to the South Tyroleans as "well treated" and said that "we must openly and honestly declare to Italy that for us the South Tyrol question does not exist." He blamed the loss of the region not on Italy, but on those responsible for Germany's defeat. Disbelieving Austrian Nazi newspapers called this "alleged renunciation" a "Jewish lie."[44]

Hitler made his policy toward the lost province even clearer in *Mein Kampf* (for anyone who took the trouble to read it) where he wrote: "I do not hesitate to declare that, now that the dice have fallen, I regard a reconquest of the South Tyrol by war as impossible. . . . If this blood were someday staked, it would be a crime to stake it for two hundred thousand Germans while next door more than seven millions languished under foreign domination."[45] Hitler's South Tyrol policy served to separate the fanatical Hitler loyalists from the more moderate Austrian Nazis. If an Austrian could swallow this policy, he could accept anything Hitler might demand.

By 1926 the membership of the German NSDAP was back to approximately the same level as before the Munich Putsch (about fifty-five thousand). The party's renewed strength was celebrated at a congress in Weimar in early July when several völkisch groups, awed by the display of unity and power, merged their organizations with the Nazis. The Parteitag ended with a resolution refusing to take a position on splits in the völkisch movement. It welcomed "all German *Volksgenossen* who recognized the statutes [Twenty-five Points of the Munich Nazis] and who announced their intention to fight for a national socialist state under the leadership of Adolf Hitler." The resolution furthermore gave Hitler the "right and duty to organize his followers in the whole party in the manner he felt to be most suitable." The resolution ended by calling on the Austrian Nazis to fulfill the above program and to annex themselves to the organization, which was valid for the entire German-language area. Such a step would "help to create a movement united in program and leadership."[46] Obviously it would also mean the death of the Schulz group and the end of Austrian Nazi autonomy. It was therefore rejected by the Austrians.

The matter did not end there, however. Schulz made one last attempt to avoid a schism when he met with Hitler in Passau (on the German side of the Inn River) on 12 August. Schulz argued that conditions in Austria and Czechoslovakia required different tactics from those used in the Reich. In Germany there were a dozen political parties including three Marxist ones (*sic*, two after 1922); in Austria there were only two major parties, one of them the powerful and united Social Democratic party. In dealing with these problems the great and guiding Nazi principles were supposed to be established in common as Hitler himself had agreed in 1920.[47]

As usual, however, Hitler permitted no real discussion. He accused the Austrians of not helping the Reich party after the Beer Hall Putsch; he refused to call another international Nazi congress, and he claimed for himself the right to break earlier agreements because he now had the power to do so. He would, he said in a revealing statement, do the same thing with the French. Schulz replied that the Austrian party had entirely different policies toward the South Tyrol, the use of the fascist salute (which was borrowed from Italy and was now fashionable with the German Nazis), and the trade-union workers whom he wished to educate in national and socialist ideas. Hitler brushed these objections aside, saying there was not enough time for education. He demanded "unconditional loyalty" from the "Schulz party." Austria, he said contemptuously, was nothing more than a German Gau to which he would send a Reichskommissar and later name a leader.[48] Here again was an ominous preview of what was in store for Austria as a whole in 1938.

When Schulz returned to Vienna he reported to an assembly of Viennese and Lower Austrian subleaders [*Vertrauensmänner*] that he had come to the shocking conclusion in Passau that although the German NSDAP was well organized militarily, it was indistinguishable from such paramilitary (and conservative) formations as the Austrian Front Fighters and the German Stahlhelm. The assembly backed Schulz in his refusal to dissolve the Austrian NSDAP, a move that was also fully supported by the Sudeten Nazi party.[49]

From his own standpoint, Hitler's policy at Weimar and Passau was both correct and consistent. To have permitted autonomy for the Austrian and Sudeten parties would have contradicted and undermined all those moves toward the centralization of authority in his own hands that he had made since virtually the day he had joined the party. Autonomy for some would have been followed by demands for the equal treatment of other groups, especially those in northern Germany. In fact, the existence of autonomous leaders in Austria and Czechoslovakia would likely have undermined the whole structure of the party. Far more than in Marxist parties, charismatic leadership, not ideology, provided the real cement holding the party together. Hitler later censured the Schulz group for "having too much Marxism in itself."[50] But this reference to ideology served only as a pretext for the break. "Ideological heterogeneity was a characteristic of the Nazi movement from its inception; it was no concern of Hitler. There was no orthodoxy in Nazi ideology; the only orthodoxy was the totalitarian principle of absolute obedience to an absolute leader. . . . By definition, the leader and the idea were the same in Nazism."[51] Therefore, by challenging the legitimizing idea of the movement, Schulz was in effect placing himself outside the party.

At virtually the same time that Schulz was confronting Hitler, the Führer (as Hitler was now being called by his supporters) was meeting secretly with several of his Austrian loyalists, including Richard Suchenwirth and Alfred Proksch, the Gauleiter of Upper Austria. All of them pledged their unconditional fealty to the German leader. Schulz's response was to have them expelled from their offices. But this was a futile gesture that could not prevent Hitler's official recognition a few days later (28 August 1926) in Munich of the so-called NSDAP (Hitler Bewegung).[52]

Civil War or Reunification?

Although there were two attempts to reunite the Austrian Nazis (one in 1927 and the second in 1929), they remained divided until the dissolution of the Schulz group in 1935. In the interval, however, they fought like mortal enemies until the Hitler Bewegung (HB) gained the upper hand following Hitler's startling electoral success in Germany in September 1930. Although each side claimed to be by far the stronger, it is more likely that they were about equally weak. In the national elections of April 1927, for example, the Hitler Movement, which campaigned independently, garnered only a pathetic 27,000 votes and won no parliamentary mandates.[53] The Schulz group joined the anti-Marxist "Unity List" of Chancellor Seipel, so its votes were not counted separately; but it is unlikely that it did any better than the Hitlerians. A year and a half later (November 1928) the Schulz people had only 6,274 dues-paying members organized into 50 *Ortsgruppen*, whereas the Hitler Movement had 4,466 members in 130 local groups.[54] Membership in the HB in the three western states of Vorarlberg, Tyrol, and Salzburg was so small that between 1928 and 1932 they were combined into a single "Westgau."[55]

The Hitlerian Nazis used "physical assault, property damage, and character defamation" against the Schulz followers. The Gauleiter of Styria, Heinrich K. Schmidt, accused Schulz and Gattermayer of having connections with Hitler's left-wing Nazi rivals in the Reich, men such as Anton Drexler, Count Ernst zu Reventlow, and Albrecht von Graefe.[56] This group had recently declared that Hitler ought not be permitted to regain his former position of power after his release from prison. The Schulz Nazis, on the other hand, labeled the HB a "fascist organization,"[57] a damning comparison with the hated Italians. To emphasize their separate identity, the Schulz Nazis exchanged their brown shirts for grey ones in 1927.

With the approach of parliamentary elections in April 1927 the feud temporarily cooled. Hitler invited Schulz to Munich on 11–12 March to discuss the possibility of reunifying the two factions. Unable to reach any agreement on reunion, however, a *Burgfriede* (truce) was concluded just in time for the elections. When resumed several months later the negotiations failed, apparently because the Austrians still insisted on retaining their own organization and policies so far as purely Austrian affairs were concerned. Local HB leaders also feared losing their positions after a merger. As usual, Hitler's own conditions were simple: "either subordination or a fight in which the stronger would decide. He hoped to be the stronger."[58]

Although 1928 witnessed some actual violence between the Nazi followers of Schulz and those of Hitler,[59] reunification efforts resumed in 1929. On 5 October 1929 the *Deutsche Arbeiter-Presse* suddenly announced that the two Nazi factions had been reunited on 30 September. As their common platform they demanded an Austro-German Anschluss, a fight against the Jewish domination of the country's economy, culture, and public life, a fundamental constitutional reform changing voting rights, and an important role for nationalist trade unions.[60] Significantly, nothing was said about party structure or the future status of the South Tyrol.

The *DAP*'s rejoicing was premature. The *Gauleiter* of the Hitler Bewegung vehemently denounced the merger in a meeting held in Vienna on 5 January 1930. In letters to Gregor Strasser at the Munich Reichsleitung and to the new Landesleitung in Linz, they objected to the selection of Leo Haubenberger, a railway official and Schulz's deputy, as the Landesleiter of the united party. The letter writers claimed that the Schulz group was now insignificant and would soon die out.[61] What really upset the Gau leaders, of course, was the horrifying prospect of losing their jobs to Schulz men.

Like Georg von Schönerer, the Hitler Nazis regarded conflicts as irreconcilable and negotiations as little better than surrender. Thus Alfred Proksch later indignantly denied the accusation made by one of his party enemies, that he had led the negotiations for reunification. It was a matter of pride that he was influential in persuading Hitler to end the talks.[62]

Hitler played a surprisingly minor role in these negotiations. When Hans Krebs, the HB Landesleiter, and Alfred Proksch spoke with the Führer in Munich, Hitler merely stated that he did not believe in the possibility of a reunification. Without firm leadership on the side of the Hitler Bewegung, however, a reconciliation between the two Austrian factions proved impossible. Negotiations broke down on 2 March 1930, with each side blaming the other for the failure. It is impossible to say for certain which side was more responsible for the fiasco; but the attempts of Hans Krebs, to organize an opposition to Schulz within Schulz's own membership, did not go unnoticed and did little to improve mutual trust and good will.[63] The unification efforts were not a total failure, however, as Walter Riehl and his tiny Deutschsozialer Verein (which he founded in 1924 after resigning from the party) rejoined the Hitler movement in September 1930.[64]

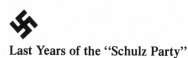

Last Years of the "Schulz Party"

The "Schulz party," as it was contemptuously called by its Hitlerian opponents, lingered on for more than five years after the failure of the last reunification efforts in 1930. Although they did not then have the facts to prove it, the *Gauleiter*'s prophecy that the Schulz faction would die a natural death was basically correct. Karl Schulz simply did not have the ability to build a mass party. But more importantly, Adolf Hitler's local electoral victories in Germany in 1929 and his much more impressive national victory in September 1930, when the Reich Nazis won over 6.4 million votes and became the Reichstag's second largest party, gave the Austrian NSDAP (HB) a badly needed boost. Although still hampered by the popularity of other right-wing groups, the Hitler Nazis nevertheless gained 111,000 votes in the November 1930 parliamentary elections, thus quadrupling their vote of 1927.[65] Thereafter the Schulz Nazis became a politically insignificant splinter group, although they still refused to disband.

Nonetheless, the Schulz faction in its final years has a certain interest for historians of fascism if only because of its impotence. Although it possessed much of the ideology of Nazism and fascism in general, it lacked the ruthless fanaticism, imperialistic program, hierarchical structure, and especially the charismatic leadership of successful fascist movements. The Schulz Nazis preferred ideological purity to political success. Typical of its attitude was an editorial of 1931 in the *DAP*, which stated that "to fight for the purity of an idea is certainly a more difficult task than to grow in a movement in which national socialist ideas are watered down and interspersed with the most different borrowings."[66]

In general, the last years of the Schulz group were devoted to dissociating itself from embarrassingly similar movements. Mussolini's Italy was condemned for being antiworker, for censoring the press, for dissolving political parties, and for establishing a permanent, rather than simply a temporary, dictatorship. Likewise, the Fascist state was criticized for not recognizing racial distinctions; it was no better than bolshevism with reversed value signs (*Vorzeichen*).[67]

The *DAP*'s greatest ire, however, was reserved for the Hitlerian Nazis. Their election tactics in September 1930 were comparable to those of the Communist party. The Nazis and Communists were trying to outbid each other in their radicalism. Both parties hoped to build a new Germany on the ruins of the old one. The German Nazis, in fact, were not really true national socialists at all, but reactionary fascists using national Bolshevik methods.[68] In 1931 the swastika, which had been part of the *DAP*'s masthead since 1922, quietly disappeared. And when Chancellor Engelbert Dollfuss dissolved the Hitler Bewegung in June 1933 following a wave of Nazi terror, the *DAP* applauded, hoping in vain to pick up some new members.[69]

The *Deutsche Arbeiter-Presse* did not even object to the dissolution of all Austrian political parties in 1934, including the DAP, because it had always regarded the movement "as an association of like-minded people and especially after the appearance of Hitlerism in Austria . . . as the founders and protectors of true national socialism."[70] The newspaper itself disappeared without a whimper in July 1935 after twenty-seven years of publication.

That the Schulz group survived as long as it did was in part a tribute to the strength of Austrian patriotism. When the north German left-wing Nazi Otto Strasser (brother of Gregor) broke away (or was expelled) from the Nazi party in 1930, he carried almost no one with him. But Schulz, who believed in many of the same ideas as Strasser, could count on Austrian separatism to maintain his political independence for nine years. However strong the yearning was for an Anschluss with Germany, Austrian Nazis, and not just the followers of Schulz, were still primarily Austrians. In effect, Hitler forced Schulz and his followers to choose between Hitler's brand of Nazism and their Austrian loyalties. They chose Austria. Ironically, even the Hitlerian Nazis would one day be faced with that same painful choice.

To some extent the survival was also a matter of institutional loyalty. Walter Gattermayer expressed this sentiment very well several years later when attempting to explain why he had not joined the Hitler movement until 1932. "It is difficult," he wrote, "to give up an enterprise which one has helped to create."[71]

The decade of the 1920s, which had begun so promisingly for the Austrian Nazis, thus ended on a decidedly sour note. The progress achieved between 1920 and 1925 could not be sustained into the more prosperous second half of the decade. The split in 1925–26 proved to be permanent and had a debilitating effect on the party's success for the next five years. After the resignation of Walter Riehl in 1923, the party never again found an entirely satisfactory leader. Karl Schulz was acceptable to the older and more conservative members, but not to the young radicals, who turned to Adolf Hitler. But Hitler, even though providing his followers with ideological guidance, was prohibited from entering Austrian territory and in any case was too preoccupied with German affairs to provide the Austrian Nazis with practical day-to-day leadership. Therefore, the late twenties proved to be a time of frustration and stagnation for both wings of the Austrian Nazi party.

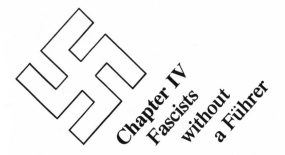

The German-speaking people have an old proverb, *Man braucht Feinde* (one needs enemies). The Nazis of both Germany and Austria were fervent believers and practitioners of this philosophy. Even before the rivalry between the Schulz and Hitlerian Nazis ended for all practical purposes in 1929–30, new foes appeared on the horizon. One of these was the paramilitary Austrian Heimwehr; the other, amazingly enough, consisted of the party's[1] own leaders.

Germany and the Leadership Principle

It was one of the major ironies of the Hitlerian Nazis (and also of the fascists in the Heimwehr movement) that however much they prattled about the glories of the Führerprinzip, when it came to following a leader unconditionally, they often acted more like anarchists than disciplined followers of the German Messiah.

Of course, Hitler remained the supreme leader, a remote "umpire" who was able to prevent the outbreak of the kinds of ideological disputes that plagued the Heimwehr. But the Führer's strategy was to concentrate on gaining power in Germany first, before shifting his money and attention to the struggle in Austria.[2] Being forbidden by the Austrian government from entering the country no doubt made it difficult for Hitler to intervene in day-to-day party quarrels there.[3] But a more fundamental problem was Hitler's unwillingness to bother with the mundane aspects of running a party (or, later on, a government). Hitler's only real interests were art and war. Thus he contented himself with laying down only a few broad outlines of policies for the party and seldom even issued written orders. His underlings were left to carry out his programs as best they could interpret them, with whatever means they chose. Hitler intervened in everyday party affairs in both Austria and Germany only if they seriously threatened to disrupt the party or to interfere with his overall international objectives. Gregor Strasser, as head of the party directorship (Reichsleitung) in Munich between 1928 and 1930, also made administrative decisions concerning Austria, but was often too busy to handle the incessant feuds.[4]

Most historians have firmly believed that after 1926 the Austrian Nazi party was "a mere appendage of Hitler's movement [which] must be ruled out as representative of Austrian fascism."[5] Although the Austrian *Landesleiter* were appointed (if at all) in Munich, local Nazi functionaries felt little control from Germany. For the Austrian Nazis, the problem was a lack of Reich German interference rather than too much, especially between 1926 and 1931. (In later years, however, they frequently made the opposite complaint.) So jealous were the Austrian *Gauleiter* of each other that they never could agree to give unconditional allegiance to one of their colleagues as Landesleiter of the whole Austrian party.[6] Their mistrust and envy were to remain chronic problems for the party, not only in the late twenties, but also even up to the Anschluss in 1938.

Munich's laissez faire policy was more than simply the product of Hitler's natural inclinations toward laziness and indecisiveness. If the Austrian party were kept in a *führerlos* condition, there would be little likelihood of Hitler's authority being challenged again by a powerful native leader the way it had been between 1923 and 1926 by Riehl and Schulz. Such a policy of "benign neglect" had been successfully employed by Hitler in Germany to prevent the emergence of a successor while he was imprisoned in 1924.

The Führerlos Party

At any rate, there simply was no *strong* centralized Nazi leadership for Austria between 1926 and 1931, and sometimes no centralized leadership at all. Following the schism in 1926, Hitler appointed a fifty-five-year-old retired colonel from Styria, with the very un-Nordic name of Friedrich Jankovic, to be his first Landesleiter of Austria. Although a member of the party since 1921 and a hard worker, Jankovic had at best only limited success in bringing order to the movement, despite his claims. According to one of his successors, Alfred Proksch, the party's pathetic showing in the 1927 parliamentary elections (when it tallied only twenty-seven thousand votes) was a result of no one knowing what to do.[7] Even though the mediocre accomplishments of Jankovic may have had something to do with his premature demise as federal leader, intraparty intrigue was the immediate cause.

Instead of replacing Jankovic with a new state leader, the Führer placed the six Austrian *Gaue* directly under the Reichsleitung in Munich and named Gregor Strasser as his plenipotentiary to reorganize the Austrian party. The Gauleiter of Styria, Heinrich Schmidt, was given the thankless job of enrolling new members throughout the country but few other responsibilities. Schmidt's highest qualification was possibly that he had avoided making enemies through the simple tactic of expressing no opinions![8]

Schmidt, in turn, was relieved of his job in October 1928 when Hitler appointed a full-fledged Landesleiter, Hans Krebs. But the new leader was never very popular with the *Gauleiter* because of his willingness to compromise with the Schulz group.[9] Although Krebs was the founder of the *Deutsche Arbeiter-Presse* and had led the party from Vienna in the six years preceding the World War, he had moved to Aussig in northern Bohemia at the war's end. His absentee leadership did nothing to enhance his prestige in Austria.[10] Worst of all, Krebs, as he himself admitted, simply did not have enough time for Austrian politics.[11] As leader of the Sudeten Nazi party and a member of the Czechoslovak Parliament, he could never regard the Austrian party as more than a minor event. He did move the offices of the Landesleitung from Vienna to the more centrally located and less "Marxist" city of Linz, and under his authority the party made some modest progress. But Krebs's administration lasted only until March 1930, causing one leading Nazi to remark that "no other party in Austria has had so large a turnover of leaders as ours."[12]

Because the Austrian *Gauleiter* could not agree on a new federal leader, Strasser ordered them to form a leadership council among themselves and appointed Alfred Proksch, the Gauleiter of Upper Austria, to be a mere administrative (*geschäftsführenden*) Landesleiter. But this post carried with it (at least technically) no authority in political questions. The arrangement lasted until the middle of 1931, and does not appear to have pacified any of the provincial Austrian leaders. Proksch, who held various offices, including those of press leader, organization leader, publications leader, city councilman, and trade-union functionary,[13] had just enough power to arouse the envy of other *Gauleiter*, but not enough to stamp out opposition.

Proksch was born in Morischau, Silesia, in 1891 of Sudeten German ancestry. One of his enemies in Linz accused him of being a German-Slavic "mixbreed." However, Proksch boasted that he had no Slavic ancestors and could speak no Slavic languages. Like so many other Austrian Nazi leaders, he was a railway employee and joined the Deutsche Arbeiterpartei in 1912. After serving in the World War, he was forced to flee from his home in the newly created state of Czechoslovakia, owing to his political activities. Following the example of twenty-two thousand other Sudeten Germans, he emigrated to Linz and founded the first Nazi Ortsgruppe there in 1919. In 1926 he was one of the ringleaders in the establishment of the Hitler Bewegung.[14]

First as an agent of Hans Krebs in 1929 and then as the administrative Landesleiter, Proksch made many enemies through his willingness to form electoral coalitions with non-Nazi parties (the same policy that cost Walter Riehl his job in 1923).[15] In 1930 he tried unsuccessfully to form a coalition with the Heimwehr. By the middle of the same year Proksch had acquired the reputation, deserved or not, for operating behind people's backs and playing off his rivals against each other.[16] But with Gregor Strasser apparently still too busy to intervene, the Austrian party continued to drift in its leaderless condition until the middle of 1931.

The Party Hierarchy

Fortunately for the Austrian Nazis, local success did not entirely depend on a strong central leadership. As in Germany there was an elaborate party hierarchy, which gave local leaders, especially *Gauleiter*, considerable powers.

At the bottom of the leadership structure were the *Ortsgruppenleiter* or local group leaders, who were responsible for judging the qualifications of prospective party members and for collecting dues. They were supposed to hold regular membership meetings and to distribute orders that came to them from higher up. They were also expected to carry out minor propaganda activities, such as passing out leaflets and posting displays. Elections brought new responsibilities, including assessing the strength of opponents.[17]

The *Ortsgruppenleiter* were subordinate to the *Kreisleiter* (district leaders) who, until 1938, were relatively weak. Most of the local organizations of the many Nazi subsidiaries, such as the teachers' and doctors' leagues, were also under their control. This power did not apply, however, to the Hitler Jugend, the SA, or the SS.[18]

The *Ortsgruppenleiter* were appointed by a Gauleiter upon the suggestion or recommendation of the *Kreisleiter*. District leaders were appointed by Hitler himself, or the party cabinet, upon the recommendation of the Gauleiter. In sharp contrast to the "Schulz party," no Nazi leaders were elected by the men they commanded.[19]

A key role in the party hierarchy was played by the *Gauleiter*. Hitler himself had made that role clear in *Mein Kampf*, especially in the second volume, where he stated that the *Gauleiter* were to be appointed directly by the Führer and were responsible to him alone, not to the members of their own Gau. In the words of one Nazi handbook, "The Gauleiter lays down for the area of his Gau the tactics of political activity, the line to be taken, the holding of meetings in the individual Kreise districts and branches and the construction of the organization."[20]

Given the intensity of some of the rivalries within the lower echelons of the party, Hitler was most reluctant to allow the overthrow of a Gauleiter, because that would create disorder and undermine discipline. He would tolerate corruption and even incompetence, but never disloyalty or the kind of anarchy that threatened to create a public scandal.[21] Those who rebelled against their Gauleiter found little sympathy among the party's hierarchy,[22] at least as long as the Gauleiter still enjoyed the Führer's confidence. In a system that deliberately encouraged cutthroat competition, utter loyalty to Hitler was one's only security.

Although as late as 1928 the position of Gauleiter was still not fully clarified, Hitler had at least transformed the Gaue from neighborhood clubs into propaganda-distribution centers. Because propaganda was so crucial to the party's progress, this function alone gave the Gau leaders substantial power. An ambitious man, especially if he were a good public speaker and a tolerable writer, could make a real difference to the success of the party in his region.

In theory, the six *Gauleiter* of Austria (seven after 1932) were subordinate to the Austrian Landesleitung, which in turn was subordinate to the Reichsleitung in Munich. But because there was sometimes no regular Landesleiter at all in Austria, and never a strong one before 1931, "every Gauleiter [acted] like a princeling of the prewar Reich."[23]

Two of the Austrian *Gauleiter* were particularly effective in the otherwise dismal years between 1928 and the end of 1930: Walter Oberhaidacher of Styria and Alfred E. Frauenfeld of Vienna. It was probably no mere coincidence that Oberhaidacher, like so many Austrian pan-Germans inside and outside the Nazi party, was born (1896) in what later became an Austrian *terra irredenta*, the South Tyrol. Before the war Oberhaidacher attended the Technical Institute (*Hochschule*) for Mechanical Engineering in Graz. During the war he fought on the Italian front where he won several decorations. He joined the Nazi party in 1924 and was one of the charter members of the Hitler Movement in 1926. In May 1928 he was made deputy Gauleiter and propaganda leader and was promoted to Gauleiter in November of the same year. Although privately anxious to attain that coveted post, he had been careful to avoid appearing overeager.

Oberhaidacher enjoyed a number of political advantages. His Nazi superiors in Austria credited him with good political judgment and speaking and debating skills. Perhaps only his relative youth stood in the way of his becoming the Austrian Landesleiter. Oberhaidacher's vocation as superintendent of his father-in-law's featherbed factory gave him an independence and financial freedom unusual in a fascist leader. Although he later had his detractors, there can be little question that the Styrian Gau could not have attained its status in 1930 as having the largest per capita Nazi membership and soundest finances in Austria had it not been for Walter Oberhaidacher.[24]

Even more important to the eventual success of the Austrian Nazi party was Hitler's confirmation of Alfred Frauenfeld as provisional Gauleiter of Vienna on 27 January 1930. Coming from a family of artists and architects, Frauenfeld was somewhat unusual in having been born (1898) in the same city where he later pursued his career as a Nazi. He resembled Oberhaidacher and a good many other Nazi leaders in having attended a technical institute[25] rather than acquiring a humanistic education. On the other hand, he departed once again from the Nazi stereotype in being a onetime actor, an experience that no doubt proved useful when he became a Gauleiter. He served on the Italian front as a lieutenant in the Austro-Hungarian air force during the Great War and was a stone mason from the war's end until 1922. Like so many German nationalists, Frauenfeld had not started his political life as a Nazi. He entered politics as a Christian Social, but soon joined the Front Fighters' Association in 1920. Although he attended a Nazi meeting as early as 1924, it was a passionate speech by Hitler in Nuremberg together with Austria's slow economic progress which ultimately induced him to become a party member on 3 August 1929, an act that persuaded many Front Fighters to follow suit.[26]

Before Frauenfeld's conversion, the Vienna Gau had been so undisciplined and chaotic that Hitler had been forced to step in and temporarily dissolve it in April 1927.[27] When Frauenfeld assumed his duties in 1930, the Gau could claim only six hundred members. The failure of the Bodenkreditanstalt in 1931 cost him the job as bank clerk that he had held since 1923, but freed him to devote all his energies to his many political activities. Besides being a Gauleiter, he was a member of the provincial parliament of Vienna and the leader of the Nazi faction in the city council (*Gemeinderat*). His previous

ALFRED FRAUENFELD. *Gauleiter of Vienna, 1930–1933. Karl Wache,*
ed. Deutscher Geist in Österreich.

experience as a short-story writer was undoubtedly helpful to him when he founded a number of Nazi publications, including the Gau's official newspaper, *Der Kampfruf*.[28]

Frauenfeld now succeeded where Walter Riehl and Georg von Schönerer had failed, namely in building a mass movement. To accomplish this task he replaced about one-third of the *Ortsgruppenleiter*, appointed a new treasurer, and established a number of new committees. Even more important was his founding of the Austrian SS. The new Gauleiter was extremely prolific. In the first half of 1930 alone he gave over one hundred speeches, most of them to large audiences. To the city's unemployed (who comprised one-half and sometimes as many as two-thirds of the country's jobless) he promised that trade and prosperity would return to the metropolis as soon as the Anschluss with Germany was consummated.[29]

Frauenfeld's work was facilitated by his connections with major German Nazi leaders, which enabled him to bring "big name" Nazi speakers to Vienna. His younger brother, Eduard, believed that the real turning point for the party in Vienna came in March 1930 when Josef Goebbels and Hermann Göring spoke to a crowd of three thousand people in the Konzerthaus.[30] Göring spoke at another rally in Vienna's huge Heldenplatz in October 1932, along with Robert Ley, Julius Streicher, and Hans Frank, all leading German Nazis.[31] By such means the elder Frauenfeld was able to create the most intensive organization in the country and expand the Gau's membership to forty thousand in just three years.[32]

Leadership Quarrels

Frauenfeld paid a price for this spectacular success. Only a few weeks after he had assumed his office he had to oust one Ortsgruppenleiter, Ernst Sopper, for insubordination over a controversy involving the Hitler Jugend (HJ) and the Nazi League of Students.

Frauenfeld's trouble with the Vienna Hitler Youth was by no means unusual. The Austrian HJ, the Sturmabteilung (SA), and later also the SS, all attempted to follow policies independent of the party's political leadership and managed to do so with considerable success, especially when there was no strong central leadership.[33] One party member complained to Hitler in February 1931 that "the battle inside the party absorbs its greatest strength and directly hampers its external struggle. The political leadership fights the SA for not achieving enough. The SA is against the women's and girls' groups and vice versa, and these in turn are against the Hitler Youth; the SA is dissatisfied with the political leadership for not organizing enough events."[34] A decree by Hitler making SA members part of the Political Organization, the main body of the party, was largely ignored in Austria.[35]

The struggle in Vienna reached a climax when Sopper reacted to his dismissal by sending a circular letter to the rank-and-file party members of Vienna denouncing his dismissal, pointing out that Frauenfeld had only recently joined the party, and claiming that Frauenfeld was not even the legitimate Gauleiter of Vienna. Sopper's appeal to the Reichsleitung found little sympathy, however, as Strasser reaffirmed Frauenfeld's authority and acidly remarked that acts such as Sopper's were responsible for the party's lack of progress in Austria.[36]

Sopper's challenge to Frauenfeld's leadership was not unique. But more serious were Frauenfeld's confrontations with Alfred Proksch. The Gauleiter's phenomenal progress evidently caused Proksch to see Frauenfeld as a possible obstacle to his becoming the full-fledged Landesleiter of Austria. Frauenfeld's repeated requests to Strasser that a new Landesleitung be established in Vienna could have been fulfilled only at Proksch's expense. In April 1931 Proksch wrote a letter to the party court or USCHLA (Untersuchungs- und Schlichtungsausschuss) in Linz complaining that Frauenfeld had founded *Der Kampfruf* in order to compete with Proksch's paper, *Die Volksstimme*. Proksch also called Frauenfeld a "Jewish shyster" (*Geschäftspraktiker*), and claimed that the Vienna Gauleiter had ridiculed him before the Reichsleitung.[37]

Frauenfeld counterattacked by denying Proksch's charges about his alleged Jewish ancestry. Proksch had also claimed that Frauenfeld had written for a pornographic magazine and had dedicated a book to a Jewish bank president. These accusations, Frauenfeld maintained, had all originated with Marxists and Czechs. The controversy was temporarily stilled when Frauenfeld was acquitted by the party court. But only a few months later Proksch tried to oust Frauenfeld from his post as Gauleiter; however, Frauenfeld was again reinstated by the Reichsleitung.[38]

Although Proksch finally realized his ambition of becoming a regular Landesleiter, he did so only against the wishes of the Austrian Gau leaders. His appointment in July 1931 did nothing to improve his popularity or probably even his authority. Hardly any Austrian Nazis recognized him as their real leader. He was accused (with how much justice it is impossible to say) of wanting to rid himself of anyone who was intellectually superior, of making the *Gauleiter* financially dependent on the Landesleitung, and of using the USCHLA like the Russian Cheka (the police court, which carried out a policy of deliberate terror).[39]

Obstacles to Progress

The absence of a centralized leadership and the resultant intra-party feuding clearly slowed Nazi progress in Austria between 1928 and 1931. They were far from being the only problems, however. No doubt the most serious difficulty was the competition provided by kindred groups, especially the Austrian Heimwehr, which was reaching the peak of its popularity in these same years. The improvement of the Austrian economy, which briefly approached its prewar level of prosperity in 1928 and 1929, also blunted considerably the impact of radical propaganda coming from parties like the NSDAP.

If these conditions were beyond the Nazis' control, there were many others that were very much self-inflicted. A favorite charge made by their opponents was that the movement was "imported." Indeed, many points in the party's program, such as the struggle against reparations, were simply irrelevant in Austria; the Allies had long since abandoned hope of collecting payments from the impoverished new Republic. Anti-Nazis could also point to the large number of Nazi speakers who came from the Reich. It was also a fact that the most aggressive Nazis in the Austrian universities were German citizens. Their number had risen dramatically from 210 in 1912 to 2,500 in 1930. In later years even many of the "Austrian" Nazi leaders were actually either Reich Germans or from the Sudetenland.[40]

Compounding the problems of the Austrian Nazis was the fact that Hitler and other leading Nazis in Germany, apparently indifferent to the fate of the HB, made many speeches in 1927 and 1928 denouncing the folly of opposing Mussolini's Italianization of the South Tyrol.[41]

The Austrian National Socialists, like their comrades in Germany, were also constantly grappling with financial headaches throughout the 1920s. Potential financiers could hardly be impressed by the Beer Hall Putsch, by the Austrian party's split in 1925–26, or by the incessant bickering among party leaders. And in a country like Austria, where so many capitalists were Jewish, the party's anticapitalist program (especially before the 1926 schism) and anti-Semitism had serious financial consequences.[42]

Lacking significant benefactors before the 1930s, the party depended on admission fees charged for public rallies, profits from party newspapers (if any), and especially membership dues. Intraparty feuds, however, sometimes resulted in local groups' not even paying these dues, as occurred in Austria in 1925–26. As a consequence, by September 1926 the Landesleitung had monthly expenses of 2,500 Schillings ($280), but an income of only 800 Schillings ($90). Rent for its office alone was 250 Schillings ($28).[43] Although some aid from the German party may have reached the Austrians as early as 1920, an urgent plea for money in the fall of 1926 was turned down by the almost equally impoverished Reichsleitung in Munich. Not until at least 1928 did any significant financial assistance from Germany reach the Austrians.[44] On the contrary, the Organisationsabteilung of the party in Munich wanted SA dues sent to Germany following the dissolution of the Austrian Landesleitung in 1927. So for years the party had to stagger along as best it could.

In later years the financial woes of the twenties became almost legendary. For example, in early 1926 the *Deutsche Arbeiter-Presse* did not have enough money to pay its phone bills. The purchase of a single typewriter was a major expense, and the electricity bill was a perennial nightmare for the treasurer. In 1926 the party was so poverty-stricken that the cost of posters and leaflets advertising a meeting exhausted the treasury to the point that another rally could not be held for eight to fourteen days while the party's coffers were replenished.[45] As late as September 1928 a *Deutscher Tag* for all members of the Austrian SA had to be cancelled, because fewer than three hundred of the two thousand members had agreed to attend the event. To avoid embarrassing publicity, the pan-German governor of Styria, Anton Rintelen, was asked to "forbid" the gathering![46]

By the Nazis' own admission, the party was regarded as "a ridiculous little group" in 1928 insofar as anyone noticed it at all.[47] The situation did not improve markedly in 1929. And as late as March 1930, an Austrian Nazi *Parteitag* resolution pointed out the need for electing parliamentary deputies "so they could be paid by the state to carry on agitation [and could] then devote themselves entirely to the party." The resolution pointed out that only 20 percent of the campaign costs for the November 1930 elections were being paid by Munich.[48]

Equally worrisome was the sorry state of Nazi journalism, which was characteristic of the party not only in Austria but in Germany as well. Hitler firmly believed that the spoken word was superior to the written one and proved his point in the writing of *Mein Kampf*. But a newspaper was important for the party's prestige; it was a sign that the movement was flourishing. And a newspaper was preferable to leaflets and posters as a means of announcing meetings and other party activities, giving party orders, and presenting the party's ideology. However, not until the 1930s did the newspaper press assume its status as the Austrian Nazis' most important propaganda weapon.[49]

Nazi newspapers confined themselves almost exclusively to party affairs, except occasionally to denounce the government or other enemies of the party. They suffered from too strong a control by the party's central office, despite the party's generally weak leadership. To read one is therefore much like reading them all. In fact, provincial Austrian Nazi papers often simply reprinted articles of the party's two leading journals, *Die Volksstimme* in Linz and the *Österreichischer Beobachter* in Vienna.

Because the press for a long time had so little status within the movement, there were few journalists with any ability, let alone real talent. In Austria most of them were simply *Gauleiter* who "moonlighted" as journalists. The party's emphasis was on winning the support of the masses, and it was assumed that few converts could be won by reading a newspaper.[50]

The *Deutsche Arbeiter-Presse* was a partial exception to the generally mediocre journalism. Mainly owing to the early editorship of Dr. Walter Riehl, the paper's circulation was built up to a respectable twenty-four thousand copies in 1924. In later years, even members of the rival Hitler Bewegung admitted (or charged) that the *DAP* was superior to their leading paper, *Die Volksstimme*, edited by Alfred Proksch.

After the founding of the Hitler Movement in 1926, the *Österreichischer Beobachter* was first published on 20 May of that year. A few months later, the *Linzer Volksstimme* dropped its first name and began covering news for all the Alpine provinces, including Upper Austria, Carinthia, Styria, Salzburg, Tyrol, and Vorarlberg. After the party began its rapid growth in 1930, nearly every federal state had its own Nazi organ, and members were under orders to find new subscribers and if possible new advertisers. The party's appeal to so many different social groups, however, made it difficult for a Nazi paper to satisfy the literary tastes of, for example, both academicians and peasants.[51]

Changing Fortunes: The Great Depression and the Parliamentary Elections of 1930

Not surprisingly, the economic fortunes of the Nazi party did not improve until the Austrian economy began plummeting. Austria's postwar economy, of course, had never been robust. If 1928 and 1929 were "good years," they were so only in relative terms. In 1929, 12.3 percent of the country's workers were unemployed compared to 10.4 percent in Great Britain, 9.3 percent in Germany, and 2.2 percent in neighboring Czechoslovakia.[52] Industrial production in Austria was only 95 percent of the 1913 level for the same area and just 80 percent of capacity.[53] Nevertheless, if we use the figure 100 to represent Austria's unemployment rate in 1929, then already by the next year the rate was down to 95.1 and reached 70.6 in 1933. The following table shows how poorly Austria compared to other industrial countries in Europe during the Depression. These figures clearly reveal that except for the first three years of the slump, when Austria and Germany were about equally affected, no other country in Europe (or probably in the world) was so devastated by the economic crisis as Austria.

Employment Rates in Europe, 1929–1937
(as percentages of 1929 employment rate)

Year	Austria	Czechoslovakia	Germany	Great Britain
1929	100	100	100	100
1930	95.1	97.6	93.3	95.8
1931	86.6	92.3	81.5	92.2
1932	76.4	82.6	71.7	91.4
1933	70.6	76.4	74.0	94.7
1934	69.8	75.0	85.5	99.2
1935	66.8	76.6	90.6	101.5
1936	64.6	82.4	97.2	106.7
1937	67.4	90.0	104.3	112.3

SOURCE: Friedrich Hertz, *The Economic Problems of The Danubian States*, p. 147.

The Nazis profited very little from *industrial* unemployment, as the proletariat generally remained faithful to its Marxist parties,[54] at least until 1938. On the other hand, there is abundant evidence to prove that the unemployed Austrian intelligentsia were solid supporters of the Nazi party from an early date and for primarily economic, not ideological, reasons.[55]

The relationship between the unemployment rate and the Nazis' popularity was not so immediate or direct as it was in Germany. If they were able to pick up 111,000 votes in the parliamentary elections of 9 November 1930, that can only be regarded as pathetic compared to the 6,409,600 votes captured by the Reich Nazis two months earlier. Moreover, it is probable that the Austrian Nazi vote would have been even lower had it not been for the "coattail effect" created by the Nazi victory in Germany.[56] In Styria, where Nazi membership had increased by a comparatively modest 11.5 percent, 30 percent, and 31 percent in the first three quarters of 1930, the growth rate suddenly shot up to 67 percent in the last quarter of the year.[57]

The Nazis' relatively poor showing in the Austrian elections resulted in large measure because of the continued absence of a strong central leadership.

But the pan-German vote was also divided by the failure of the Nazis to conclude an electoral coalition with the Heimwehr. The failure, however, did not result from a lack of interest on either side. The pan-German, anticlerical wing of the Austrian Heimwehr, which was strongest in Styria, Carinthia, and Salzburg, was very much in favor of such an alliance. The clerical wing of the Heimwehr, on the other hand, which drew its support mainly from the eastern provinces of Lower Austria, Burgenland, and Vienna, wanted nothing to do with the anticlerical Nazis, and, in fact, objected to any kind of Heimwehr campaign, as it would inevitably draw votes away from the pro-Catholic Christian Social party.[58]

On the Nazi side, Gregor Strasser met with the Heimwehr chief of staff, Hanns Rauter, to discuss an electoral coalition in early October 1930. The more serious discussions were conducted between Strasser and the recently (and controversially) elected Heimwehr leader Prince Ernst Rüdiger Starhemberg. During their three meetings (one of which included Adolf Hitler) no fundamental obstacles to an election alliance arose, except the problem of how to divide the presumed spoils of victory: the parliamentary mandates. The Nazis, still euphoric over their sensational victory in Germany the previous month, confidently expected a repetition in Austria. Consequently, they asked for an equal share of the mandates. After some quibbling, Starhemberg agreed, but only on the condition that he be made the head of the joint parliamentary delegation.[59]

Strasser saw the election as an opportunity for long-term cooperation between the NSDAP and the Heimwehr and was willing to pay a high price for it. He therefore offered to place the Nazis' paramilitary and sporting organizations in Austria under Starhemberg's command. The Prince turned down the tempting offer, however, because Strasser indignantly refused Starhemberg's demand for leadership over the joint parliamentary delegation. The promising negotiations thus ended in failure.[60]

The two fascist groups therefore campaigned independently. Typical of Nazi propaganda in general, the Austrian NSDAP tried to please everyone. The universally detested Treaty of Saint-Germain was blamed for the Great Depression. The hard-pressed middle class was told that its predicament was due not only to the inflation of 1921–22, but also to the restoration of the currency by Seipel at an artificially high rate, as well as by money speculation that had allegedly caused the collapse of several banks. To the peasants, struggling against the competition of more efficient Czech and Hungarian farms, the Nazis promised high agricultural tariffs. For the unemployed or underemployed industrial worker, the Nazis demanded the expulsion of tens of thousands of foreign workers and Jews. But the Nazis spread their propaganda effort too indiscriminately across the length and breadth of the country for these messages to have much effect.[61]

The Nazis' anemic showing at the polls was difficult even for their own superoptimistic press to disguise. Although the count was four times the 27,000 votes registered in 1927, the total of 111,000 was less than half the 228,000 amassed by the Heimwehr.[62] And while the Heimwehr was garnering eight parliamentary mandates, the Nazis won none. Alfred Proksch's mouthpiece, *Die Volksstimme*, denounced Austria's complicated voting system, which had prevented the Nazis from winning any representation. Yet the paper also admitted that the party had been hurt by the charge that it was antireligious.[63]

In a report sent to the Munich Reichsleitung, Walter Riehl, who had just rejoined the party in September 1930, made a more detached analysis of the disappointing showing. He agreed that the Nazis, and also the Heimwehr, had lost votes because many people believed they would be throwing away their votes if either party failed to win the indispensable *Grundmandat* (basic mandate, which required an absolute majority vote). The Social Democrats had retained their popularity because of their great building program in Vienna. The Anschluss program, which was still advocated by both the SDP and the CSP, had also stolen much of the Nazis' thunder, as had the Heimwehr's antiparliamentarianism. Finally, the Nazis needed to put forward prominent men with distinguished names, even if they were not party members, rather than professional politicians who were unknown to the general public.[64] Riehl might have also mentioned that the Austrian Nazis received almost no assistance in the campaign from Germany. Except for one speech by Strasser in the small Carinthian town of Völkermarkt, no major German speakers came to Austria for the election. Two German diplomats in Austria thought this might have been the result of an understanding between Hitler and Starhemberg.[65]

The Party at the End of 1930

The German envoy to Austria, Count Hugo Lerchenfeld, summarized the Austrian political scene in a year's-end report to his home office. He noted that he had dealt with the Austrian Nazis only incidentally in his previous reports, because they had had no special significance as long as the Heimwehr was united. The Heimwehr, with its antiparliamentarianism, had been a kind of Nazi substitute. National Socialism had failed in Austria because the necessary preconditions were lacking. The Nazis in Germany had

POSTER OF A NAZI WORKER *slaying a Socialist dragon with the head of a Jew. DÖW.*

done so well because of the reparations issue and the government's policy of fulfillment (that is, complying with the terms of the Treaty of Versailles). These arguments made no impression in Austria. The Nazis had also succeeded in those parts of Germany which had been occupied by the Allies. But no such territories existed in Austria. The economic status of the Austrian peasants was also better and more stable than that of their counterparts in northern and eastern Germany. Moreover, the Weltanschauung of the Christian Social party was to some extent immune to the teachings of Nazism. But above all, the Austrian Nazis had failed to achieve a breakthrough because they lacked a strong and popular (*volkstümlich*) leader.[66]

The year 1930 thus ended with mixed results for the Austrian party. On the one hand, it was undeniably growing, attracting four times its vote of three years earlier. The feud with the Schulz faction no longer drained the party's energies, because the November 1930 elections had left the Schulz group far behind the Hitler Bewegung. The party's stupendous success in Germany was, of course, also a source of pride and optimism. On the other hand, the party still had no representatives in Parliament, was overshadowed by the Heimwehr, and, worst of all, was without any centralized leadership. If the party hoped to become a major force in Austrian politics, it would have to have a strong leader and destroy, or at least disrupt, the Heimwehr movement.

The two perennial problems that had been plaguing the Hitlerian Nazis since their founding in 1926 were at least ameliorated, between
1931 and 1933: the lack of an effective centralized leadership and the competition of other völkisch groups, especially the Austrian Heimwehr.

Theo Habicht as "State Inspector"

The man who brought about these changes was a German
citizen named Theo Habicht. Born in Wiesbaden in 1898 (coincidentally the
same year as both Frauenfeld and Reschny), Habicht had been a member
of that town's city council, an Ortsgruppenleiter, and a Kreisleiter before
becoming the de facto leader of the Austrian Nazi party on 11 July 1931. In
September of the same year he became a member of the German Reichstag.
According to his enemy Prince Starhemberg, he was also a "former window
dresser and an ex-Communist agitator."[1]

Habicht (which appropriately enough means "hawk" in German), was
anything but a prototype of the Nazis' Nordic hero. According to Starhemberg
(whose views are largely verified by photographs), the Nazi leader "was a
small, embryonic character who was slender and insignificant, with a disproportionately large head and who wore large horned-rim glasses. . . . He
actually incorporated that which in Nazi theory was regarded as an inferior
race to be fought."[2] His physical appearance proved to be no insurmountable
handicap, however, perhaps because all but one of the Austrian *Gauleiter*, not
to mention the top German Nazi leaders, were equally un-Nordic.

More damaging was Habicht's limited acquaintance with Austria. According to another rival, the former German chancellor and later special

envoy to Austria, Franz von Papen, Habicht was unencumbered by any historical knowledge of Austria or insight into its complex political problems. In short, he was a "revolutionary Impressario."[3] Habicht's impulsiveness and either ignorance of, or indifference to, diplomatic dangers did lead to near disaster in July 1934. These characteristics may have also aroused a certain amount of resentment from his Austrian subordinates.[4] Nonetheless, in his three years of leadership between 1931 and 1934 Habicht succeeded in galvanizing the Austrian Nazi party into a large and effective weapon, possibly because he was courageous, energetic, influential, and an excellent speaker.

Habicht's official position in 1931 was merely that of *Landesgeschäftsführer* (state business leader). As such he stood above the *Gauleiter*, but was technically subordinate to Alfred Proksch, who now realized his longtime dream of becoming the full-fledged Landesleiter of Austria. This position reaffirmed his financial control over the *Gaue*. Evidently in response to the antagonism felt toward Proksch by many of the *Gauleiter*, the new federal leader was placed under the "supervision" of Habicht. From the outset, however, Habicht, with full authority to consolidate and expand the movement and its auxiliary organizations into a united force, took over as the real leader of the Austrian party, including the signing of membership cards. Nevertheless, there remained a dualism at the top of the Austrian party that typified Hitler's reluctance to create the rational kind of party organization desired by Gregor Strasser. Only Hitler could hold the fragmented offices and interests together with his charismatic leadership.

In 1932 Habicht's official status was elevated to that of *Landesinspekteur* (state inspector). This post made him one of ten inspectors assigned to the party in Germany and Austria. Although entirely dependent on Hitler, of course, his powers included the right to supersede the authority of individual *Gauleiter* if need be.[5]

Although far from universally liked, Habicht gave the Austrian Nazis the strong leadership and direction they had so desperately needed. He did not hesitate to use his new office to suppress long-simmering party feuds. For example, in the Westgau of the Tyrol, Salzburg, and Vorarlberg, which had long been torn apart by "mutual accusations, suspicion, and unproven assertions," he managed to restore order by expelling the former Gauleiter, Heinrich Suske, and by threatening to expel anyone who "made war on his own or who broke party rules."[6]

The new unity and leadership was purchased at the price of local autonomy. No longer could the Austrian *Gaue* communicate directly with the Nazi headquarters or Reichsleitung in Munich. Instead, all business had to be referred to the Landesleitung in Linz, which meant in practice Habicht. The Landes-

THEO HABICHT. *The leader of the Austrian Nazi party, 1931–1934.* Gerd
Rühle, Das Grossdeutsche Reich.

leitung was subordinate to the Reichsleitung and carried out its directives. The Austrian *Gauleiter*, who were now appointed by the Landesleiter and confirmed by the Reichsleitung, carried out the policies of the Landesleitung.[7]

Aside from appointing Habicht, Hitler, like Gregor Strasser, continued to show surprisingly little interest in Austria. The Führer was simply too preoccupied with the task of attaining power in Germany and of maintaining party unity and his own leadership to devote much attention to Austrian affairs. Thus a political vacuum was created that served to increase the effective authority of middle-range functionaries like Habicht. Hitler told a prominent Heimwehr leader in early 1931 that once he was Reich chancellor he would send his best speakers and a good deal of money to Austria.[8] But that day was still far off.

In a party manual (*Dienstbuch*) published in March 1932 Habicht revealed the party's goals to be the overthrow of the Austrian government and the union of Austria and Germany. "Whoever controls Austria, controls Central Europe," he maintained. "Victory is not a question of numbers, but of determination."[9] His more immediate tasks, however, were the enlargement of the party and concomitantly the "capture" of other right-wing forces, especially the Heimwehr.

Thanks to the worsening Depression and the disillusionment within the Heimwehr over that group's poor showing in the 1930 elections, Habicht made substantial progress on both fronts during 1931. In local elections held in Upper Austria in April 1931 the Nazi vote rose to 15,770, an increase of 36 percent since the previous November, while the Heimwehr's vote dropped precipitously from 40,000 to under 19,000. In Carinthia, always a pan-German stronghold, Nazi membership increased by 150 percent between November 1930 and August 1931,[10] while in Klagenfurt, the provincial capital, the party became the city's second largest. In neighboring (and equally pan-German) Styria, the party's membership tripled during 1931 when some 4,000 public meetings were held.[11] Aiding the struggle in both states was the establishment of the two Nazi newspapers, *Der Vormarsch* in Klagenfurt and *Der Kampf* in Graz.

For the country as a whole the police estimated that there were about fifteen thousand members in September 1931. One-third of these men belonged to the SA and another three thousand were members of the Hitler Youth.[12] Although in absolute numbers the party was still one of the smallest in the country, it now had the precious "momentum" that all political parties need for real success.

Fascist Competitors: The Austrian Heimwehr

While the Austrian NSDAP was thus making impressive if not spectacular progress, the Heimwehr was in danger of falling apart. Because the Heimwehr was the Nazis' biggest rival, especially between 1930 and 1933, it is important to review here briefly its early development.

The Heimwehr was actually much younger than the Austrian Nazi party, being purely a postwar phenomenon. Like the Austrian Nazis and many other fascist movements, it originated in an area having extreme ethnic conflicts.[13] The Heimwehr's early strength had been in Carinthia and Styria, where it fought Yugoslav territorial ambitions in 1919. Almost from the beginning, however, and increasingly as the external danger waned, the Heimwehr and other right-wing paramilitary formations in Austria concentrated their energies against the internal "Marxist threat."

The modest size of the country's army, which Saint-Germain limited to only thirty thousand men (but which was really far smaller than that) and its early control by the Socialist war minister, Julius Deutsch, also induced many veterans to continue their military pursuits outside the regular army. They were joined by peasants, lower-middle-class shopkeepers, teachers, and other professional people, in addition to certain aristocrats who were still angry over being declassed by the Republic.[14]

The Socialist participation in the Austrian government ended in October 1920, and the Austrian economy began to improve after the reestablishment of the currency in 1922. Thereafter a certain stability returned to Austrian politics. No longer having major unifying issues or an effective leader, in early 1923 the Heimwehr broke into a clerical faction and a radical pan-German wing concentrated in Styria, Vienna, and Lower Austria.[15]

While the two wings barely survived the calm and relatively prosperous years between 1923 and 1926, another anti-Marxist paramilitary formation, the Front Fighters' Association with some fifty thousand members, was flourishing in eastern Austria.[16] It was the Heimwehr, however, that profited most from the apparent revival of the Marxist "threat" in 1926–27.

As we have seen, the Austrian middle class was alarmed by the Socialists' Linz Program of 1926 when the party announced the possibility (under certain highly unlikely circumstances) of a "proletarian dictatorship" to defend democracy.[17] Alarm changed to panic the next year after an uprising in July in Vienna when workers rioted and burned down the Palace of Justice following the acquittal of a group of Front Fighters accused of murder. The nationwide general strike, called by the Social Democrats in the aftermath of the riot, was quickly squelched by the mobilization of several provincial Heimwehr units, above all, the one in Styria. The Heimwehr could now claim to have saved Austria from "bolshevism," all the more so because the Nazi party was too divided to exploit the situation.[18] The grateful bourgeoisie soon rushed to join the ranks of the Heimwehr.

The Heimwehr's unity was restored in October 1927 when Richard Steidle and another lawyer, the Styrian Walter Pfrimer, began serving as co-leaders. The movement grew rapidly during the next two years, thereby contributing to the Nazis' lackluster growth rate. However, the swift progress of the Heimwehr served to mask serious internal problems. Neither Steidle nor Pfrimer were particularly effective leaders. Steidle, the leader of the more moderate, clerical wing of the Heimwehr, was popular with his own Tyrolean followers and was a talented speaker. But he had a reputation for extreme laziness and indifference. Pfrimer, who led the radical, pan-German wing of the movement, a movement that glorified youth and military virtues, was overweight, balding, nearly deaf, and a poor public speaker.[19]

The dual leadership, although giving equal recognition to both wings of the Heimwehr, probably created more problems than it solved. Before long the two leaders were so jealous of each other that they did not even communicate. Their main handicap however, was that real power in the Heimwehr rested with the provincial, not the federal, leaders. Ironically, members of the Heimwehr, which like the Nazis placed so much emphasis on the leadership principle, could not even unite their own movement behind a single leader, let alone the whole of Austria.

As the fear of Marxism again began to dissipate in the late twenties, the Heimwehr movement seemed to require a more "positive" program than mere anti-Marxism to maintain its raison d'être. At least as early as 1926 Heimwehr leaders began to formulate fascist and corporative objectives.[20] In June 1929 the German consul in Klagenfurt noted that the Heimwehr believed that "all the social, economic, and political ills of Austria could be cured through a dictatorship."[21] But not until May 1930 did the Heimwehr make an almost official avowal of typically fascist principles in the notorious "Korneuburg Oath." Denouncing "Western" democracy, liberal capitalism, and political parties, the declaration demanded the establishment of economic corporations, a "new German national outlook," and the creation of a Heimwehr dictatorship.[22]

The Oath marked both the peak of the Heimwehr's power and the beginning of its decline; it was far too radical for the clerical wing of the movement. The Oath, the controversial election of Prince Starhemberg as federal leader in

September 1930, and Starhemberg's decision to enter the November 1930 election all reopened the old schism between the clerical and pan-German wings. The parliamentary election was particularly disastrous, because the Heimwehr's showing (partly attributable to its late entry into the campaign and its inexperience in electoral politics) fell far short of its members' unrealistic expectations. The Heimwehr was further hurt in January 1931 when Alfred Proksch ordered all Nazis holding dual membership in the Heimwehr to withdraw from one organization or the other.[23]

Walter Pfrimer, who briefly replaced the discredited Starhemberg as Bundesführer in May 1931, saw a "March on Vienna" (à la Mussolini and Pilsudski) as the only way to revive the Heimwehr's flagging fortunes and to gain dictatorial power. His Putsch in September turned out to be a fiasco, however (in many respects resembling Hitler's Beer Hall Putsch), because the other provincial Heimwehr leaders refused to join the escapade. Unable to achieve power through the ballot box or violence, many frustrated members of the Heimwehr, like those of the paramilitary Combat Leagues in Germany after 1928, became receptive to the call of Nazism.[24]

Capturing the Pan-German "Right": Phase One

Thus Theo Habicht's appointment, just two months before the Pfrimer Putsch, came at an opportune time for the Nazis. Habicht was eager to exploit Heimwehr disillusionment by winning over, if possible, the entire movement to the Nazi side, or failing that, to capture at least the Heimwehr's pan-German wing. If either goal could be attained, it was likely that other pan-German and anti-Marxist groups, such as the Front Fighters' Association, the Greater German People's party, the Agricultural League, and even part of the ruling Christian Social party, would follow the Heimwehr's lead.

Back in 1926 Hitler himself had tried to subordinate the many German paramilitary formations to his political leadership, although momentarily without success. Hitler's efforts were productive, however, as far as the Styrian section of the Heimwehr (which preferred to call itself the "Heimatschutz") was concerned. Discussions between Styrian representatives and Hitler took place in Passau and Freilassing (both just across the Austro-German border in Bavaria) in 1926 and 1927. The diplomatic vulnerability of Germany and Austria, however, militated against a formal alliance between the two organizations, at least for the time being. Hitler instead preferred to use the Styrian Heimatschutz as a kind of Nazi agent, spreading National Socialist ideas throughout Austria at a time when the Austrian Nazi party was still extremely weak.[25]

Alfred Proksch had tried to reach some sort of understanding with the Heimwehr in early 1930 but was blocked by the Austrian SA and Hitler Youth. We have also observed the breakdown of negotiations between Gregor Strasser and Prince Starhemberg for an electoral coalition in the fall of 1930.

The key to absorbing the whole pan-German Right in Austria rested in the fate of the Styrian Heimatschutz. It was by far the largest and best organized of all the Austrian *Heimwehren* and comprised perhaps one-third of the Heimwehr's total membership. It also happened to be the most radically pan-German, anti-Semitic, and especially after the Pfrimer Putsch, the most restless segment of the Heimwehr. In its broad social composition, which included students, industrial workers, and civil servants, it more nearly resembled the Nazis than did any other provincial unit of the Heimwehr.[26]

Habicht wasted no time in establishing contact with Walter Pfrimer (who was still both the federal leader of the Heimwehr and the head of the Styrian Heimatschutz) in July 1931. Their exploratory talks soon led to a Burgfriede or civil truce. In plain language, this agreement amounted to a promise to refrain from the exchange of insults between members of the two organizations. Further negotiations were interrupted by the Pfrimer Putsch before anything more substantial could be accomplished.[27] The aftermath of the Pfrimer Putsch had left the Styrians completely isolated, even from other sections of the Heimwehr. An alliance with Nazis would prove that it was still politically alive and vigorous.

After only two days of discussions the first *Kampfgemeinschaft* (fighting alliance) between the Austrian Nazis and the Styrian Heimatschutz was concluded in Klagenfurt and ratified at a public meeting in Graz on 31 October. The terms of the agreement were vague: both organizations agreed to work together for an Anschluss and to oppose any action that would hinder the attainment of this goal, in particular a Habsburg restoration. Secondly, both groups promised to fight bolshevism, Marxism, parliamentary democracy, and capitalism.[28]

At first glance, this Kampfgemeinschaft would appear to fly in the face of Hitler's tactics of opposing federations, which he outlined in *Mein Kampf*. But Hitler had left himself a loophole: "It can occur that from purely tactical considerations the top leadership of a movement which looks to the future nevertheless enters into an agreement with such associations for a short time as regards the treatment of definite questions and perhaps undertakes steps in common. But this must never lead to the perpetuation of such a state of affairs unless the movement itself wants to renounce its redeeming mission."[29]

Following the Klagenfurt Kampfgemeinschaft, Nazi speakers were ordered to draw a sharp distinction between the pro-Anschluss Styrian, Carinthian, Salzburg, and Lower Austrian *Waldviertel* (forest district) units of the Heimwehr, and all other Heimwehr groups that either directly or indirectly opposed the Anschluss; the latter were to be designated as "separatists, Francophiles, and traitors." To bind the Styrian Heimatschutz still closer to the Nazis, Heimatschutz members would be privately permitted to hold dual membership in the NSDAP, provided they recognized the Nazi political leadership.[30]

In an effort to split the Styrian Heimatschutz from the rest of the Heimwehr, the Nazi press leveled the improbable charge that a Heimwehr dictatorship would lead to a Habsburg restoration and claimed (this time with considerable justification) that the Heimwehr was unclear on the Anschluss question. The Heimwehr was supposedly France's loyal "foreign legion" and the "storm troopers" of the Habsburgs.[31]

As it turned out, the attack on Starhemberg misfired. Torn between its revolutionary, pro-Anschluss, antigovernment ideology, which drew it to the Nazis, and its traditional ties with the rest of the Austrian Heimwehr, the Styrian Heimatschutz decided to choose the latter, at least for the moment. When Nazi attacks on the Bundesführer increased, the Heimatschutz demanded that they cease. The Nazis refused, and consequently the Kampfgemeinschaft was dissolved on 30 December 1931.[32]

Once this "fighting alliance" was terminated, the Nazi-Heimatschutz friendship was quickly transformed into a bitter rivalry into which the whole Heimwehr was drawn. Although ideological differences continued to be slight (especially between the Styrian Heimatschutz and the Nazis), the two movements came to regard each other as mortal enemies.[33]

The Heimwehr lashed out against the Nazis by ridiculing the fact that many Austrian Nazi leaders had Germanized Slavic names. A favorite charge was that the Nazis (unlike the Heimwehr) had played no role in suppressing the Viennese workers' uprising in 1927. There were also personal attacks. The Heimwehr's official newspaper, the *Österreichische Heimatschutz-Zeitung*, accused Frauenfeld of being a one-time Legitimist (in 1923), and Starhemberg described Proksch as being a "little, unpatriotic demagogue." Perhaps the most vicious Heimwehr accusation against the Nazis was that the latter resorted to using "American propaganda."[34] In Styria, the Heimatschutz accused the Nazis of attacking them "in a Jewish way" and denouncing their members to the police, a charge the Nazis only half denied by saying they had done so "only when circumstances demanded it."[35]

Of all the Heimwehr's criticisms aimed at the Nazis, probably the most interesting was the oft-repeated assertion that the Austrian Nazis were somehow completely different from their counterparts in Germany. Starhemberg himself wrote in an open letter to Alfred Proksch that "the German NSDAP is a genuine national renewal and freedom movement. It is impossible to believe that a national fighter like Hitler could approve of an [Austrian Nazi] policy which means nothing else but the support of Austro-Bolshevism."[36]

In reality the policies and ideology of the German and Austrian Nazis were in most respects very similar, because the Austrian NSDAP was part of the larger Gesamtpartei. The contrast lay only in different local circumstances that required altered tactics and the desire for autonomy by Austrian leaders. Yet misconceptions over the true nature of German National Socialism continued, not only in Heimwehr quarters, but also among the general Austrian population, and played a significant role in the willingness of so many Austrians to welcome or at least to tolerate the Anschluss in 1938.

The Nazi Breakthrough

The spring of 1932 proved to be one of the major turning points in Nazi-Heimwehr relations and in the whole history of the First Austrian Republic. Within a span of just ten weeks the Nazis had made their first real breakthrough in the local elections of 24 April, a new government was organized by the former minister of agriculture, Engelbert Dollfuss, and the Austrian pan-Germans were outraged by conditions attached to the League of Nations' "Lausanne" loan, which was ratified by the Austrian Parliament on 30 June.

The local elections took place at a time when 600,000 Austrians were both unemployed and under the influence of another impressive Nazi victory in Germany. In the contest for the presidency, which occurred just two weeks before the Austrian elections, Hitler had amassed 13.4 million votes, or double the Nazis' effort in September 1930. Although Nazi successes in Austria were more modest, they can still be fairly described as a genuine breakthrough.

In the three federal states holding elections for their *Landtage* (state parliaments), Vienna, Lower Austria, and Salzburg, the Nazis' vote was 336,000, as compared to just 66,000 for the same three states in 1930. The Nazis gained another 42,000 ballots in municipal elections held at the same time in Styria and Carinthia, thus raising their total to 378,000 or over 16 percent of the 3,149,000 votes cast.[37] In Vienna alone their vote jumped from 27,540 in 1930 to over 201,000 a year and a half later.[38] Alfred Proksch was probably not far wrong in claiming that new national elections would give the

Nazis 500,000 votes and thirty-three parliamentary mandates among the 165 members of Parliament.

Several historians have pointed out that the Austrian Nazi vote in 1932 was less significant than raw statistics might seem to indicate. For one thing, Nazi gains were made mostly at the expense of other pan-German groups, like the Heimwehr, the GVP, and the Landbund, the last two of which were virtually wiped out. Of the Nazis' 174,000 net gain in Vienna, for example, 115,000 votes came at the expense of the Greater Germans. In Lower Austria the Nazi vote increased by 76,400, with over 61,000 coming from the Landbund. The Nazis of Salzburg added 20,000 ballots to their 1930 total, with 13,600 of these coming from the GVP and another 2,000 from the Heimwehr.[39]

On the other hand, the Nazis' success was by no means confined exclusively to the pan-German *Lager*. In Vienna, 49,000 votes or 24 percent of their total came from the ranks of the Christian Socials and another 17,000 (8.5 percent) switched over from the Social Democrats.[40] In Salzburg, the Socialists' vote dropped by 7,000 ballots or about 26 percent.[41] The losses of the CSP in Vienna and Lower Austria would have been even higher if the Heimwehr had not declined to stand for election.

In a curiously delayed fashion the Nazi vote in Austria nearly duplicated that in Germany. In the Reichstag elections of May 1928 the German Nazis collected a mere 2.6 percent of the vote compared to 3 percent in Austria two years later. In the September elections of 1930 the German Nazis captured 18.3 percent of the vote[42] compared to 16.4 percent for their Austrian brethren in 1932.[43] Nonetheless, it would be a mistake to assume that the Austrian Nazis were capable of matching nationwide the 37.4 percent of the vote the German NSDAP won in July 1932.

Austria's party structure and voting habits were simply too different from those in Germany to make any such projection likely. In Austria almost 80 percent of the electorate habitually voted for one of the two established parties.[44] By contrast, in Germany the SDP and the Catholic Center party, together with the latter's Bavarian People's party ally, could muster a combined total of only 43.3 percent of the vote in the relatively normal election of 1928.[45] For their great victories in the 1930s the German Nazis drew heavily on the *Wahlmüde* or traditional nonvoter, who had made up 30 percent of the potential electorate during the 1920s. But in Austria, where 90 percent of the electorate usually voted, no such reservoir existed. Nonparticipation actually increased by 4 percent in Vienna in April 1932.[46]

The formation of the Dollfuss government on 20 May 1932 was itself significant in bringing about a shift in the country's political balance of power, a shift ultimately advantageous to the Nazis. The new chancellor, a thirty-nine-year-old illegitimate son of a woodcutter and peasant, would soon be regarded by the Nazis as their mortal enemy. What interests us here, however, is the effect the new government had on the non-Nazi, pan-German parties.

Since 1920 every bourgeois coalition government had included, of necessity, the Greater German People's party. But the party's smashing defeat in the elections of 1932 made it fear still further losses to the Nazis if it should join the Dollfuss ministry. This apprehension was especially strong in the spring of 1932, when the Austrian government was considering a 300-million-Schilling (or $36-million) Lausanne loan from the League of Nations. Britain and France took advantage of Austria's desperate economic plight by demanding that in exchange for the loan, Austria renounce an Anschluss with Germany for another ten years beyond the twenty years already stipulated in an earlier "Geneva" loan in 1922. Pan-Germans of all stripes were incensed by the prohibition. Among them were the Greater Germans, who now refused to join the new Dollfuss ministry.

The GVP's short-sighted policy was useless in preserving the party's integrity; its only real consequence was to undermine the already weakened Austrian democracy. Without the GVP's support Dollfuss had to look either to the Socialists or to the Heimwehr to maintain his fragile majority. But the Socialists refused to enter a coalition; Dollfuss's only other alternative was to move to the right by bringing the Heimwehr into his government.[47]

Capturing the Pan-German "Right": Phase Two

Nazi electoral successes in both Germany and Austria, as well as Starhemberg's decision to join the Dollfuss government and support the Lausanne treaty, simply accelerated the drift of the Austrian pan-Germans toward the NSDAP. The trend, which had begun in the latter part of 1930, would culminate in 1933 with Hitler's takeover in Germany.

This pro-Nazi tendency became apparent in the ideology of the Heimwehr even before parts of the organization broke away to join the Nazis. A frequent Nazi attack, which had been used earlier against the independent German Combat Leagues, was that the Heimwehr lacked a clear, positive program. Whereas they (the Nazis) "had a great overriding idea [racism] which incorporated all aspects of political, economic, and cultural life,"[48] the Heimwehr was "soft" on Jews and indecisive on the Anschluss question. These accusations were essentially true, though no one should assume that the Heimwehr was philo-Semitic or anti-Anschluss. Fascists in all countries were notorious for their ideological "flexibility."[49]

Although the Heimwehr had its rabid anti-Semites, especially in Styria, the movement as a whole was only mildly anti-Jewish. It was closer to the relatively easygoing, nonracial anti-Judaism of the early twentieth-century Viennese mayor Karl Lueger, who was famous for his assertion that he determined for himself who was a Jew. But to any truly bigoted anti-Semite this philosophy was pure heresy; no such "compromises" were found in the Nazi ideology.

On the Anschluss issue the Heimwehr was equally fuzzy. Although its pan-German members adamantly supported this goal, its clerical wing, which included aristocrats and peasants, was at best lukewarm, at worst hostile. To minimize internal quarreling over the question and to avoid offending the Heimwehr's financial benefactor, Mussolini, the Anschluss issue was simply shelved. The Heimwehr's Korneuburg Oath of May 1930 did not even mention Anschluss. A compromise "Nine Point" program drawn up by the Styrian Heimatschutz on 30 November 1932 Delphically proclaimed that the "Heimatschutz undertakes to develop German-Austria into a German state, both internally and externally, which will *one day* be regarded by the great German fatherland as a valuable German branch *worthy* of being annexed."[50] By February 1932 this program had been accepted by the rest of the Heimwehr.

While the Heimwehr was performing intellectual gymnastics in an attempt to pacify its two disparate wings, the Austrian Nazi party was growing at an ever accelerating rate. Whereas it had had only 4,400 members in June 1928, it could boast over 43,000 in January 1933. This spurt was but a prelude to the dramatic progress it achieved following Hitler's appointment as German chancellor on 30 January 1933. In the next four and a half months another 25,000 Austrians rushed to join the NSDAP.[51]

With the anticlerical and anti-Socialist Nazis now controlling the German government, Austria's two largest parties, the Christian Socials and the Social Democrats, dropped their longstanding demand for an Austro-German Anschluss. Because the Greater German People's party and the Agricultural League had already been decimated by the Nazis, this left the NSDAP as the only major Austrian party still demanding the Anschluss. Anyone regarding the union of the two German-speaking countries as Austria's most important objective had little choice but to join the Nazis.

As early as the summer of 1932 the so-called German Legion of Honor, a veterans' organization whose members were in the federal army, police, gendarmerie, and judicial system, asked Gauleiter Frauenfeld to join the

NSDAP. Another group that originated as a veterans' organization, the Front Fighters' Association, was also rapidly losing its membership to the Nazis during the same summer.

Following Hitler's takeover of power the Styrian Heimatschutz, not surprisingly, was the first important pan-German unit to "recognize the signs of the times."[52] On 9 March 1933 the Heimatschutz joined with the Nazis to form the "Pan-German Front." In quick succession other pan-German Austrian groups now rushed to jump on the Nazi bandwagon. On 18 April the Front was enlarged by the paramilitary Bund Oberland of Tyrol and a few days thereafter by the "German Employees Union" along with thirty *Ortsgruppen* of the Upper Austrian Heimwehr. The immediate objective of this coalition was the creation of a "strong government of national concentration."[53]

To solidify their new partnership, the Styrian Heimatschutz concluded a second Kampfgemeinschaft with the Austrian Nazis in the Upper Styrian town of Liezen on 22 April. As late as January 1933, Walter Pfrimer's successor as leader of the Heimatschutz, Konstantin Kammerhofer, had declared that any Heimatschutz member who joined the Nazis was a "traitor." Four months later, his newspaper, *Der Panther*, was calling every Austrian who opposed the Liezen Agreement "not only a traitor to the eternal idea of German unity . . . but an idiot."[54]

The Liezen pact decisively shifted the balance of power within the various pan-German groups in favor of the Nazis. The isolated GVP (and later the Landbund) thereafter felt compelled to line up with the Nazis themselves.[55] The GVP had been declining disastrously ever since "peaking" in the national elections of 1930 when, together with its Landbund ally, it had collected 472,000 votes.[56] The rise of other, far more radical, pan-German groups proved to be its undoing. The Heimwehr's Korneuburg Oath, for example, contained many ideas long advocated by the GVP. Like the Heimwehr, the GVP was a loose coalition of heterogeneous social groups and several older national organizations. Its composition prevented the party from taking a strong stand on anything positive except the Anschluss. By the same token the GVP was never a party of members whose dues could support it, but simply a party of voters which, from the beginning, required outside financial support, above all from Germany. It was also the only significant party in Austria without its own press.

An intensive love-hate relationship developed between the GVP and the NSDAP (starting with the parliamentary elections of 1930), just as occurred between the Nazis and the Heimwehr. The Nazis and GVP were in obvious agreement over the Anschluss question, and the GVP tolerated Nazi attacks on parliamentarianism. But the GVP differed sharply with the Nazis concerning the Führerprinzip, the South Tyrol question, and the Nazis' utopian economic thought. The GVP (Greater Germans) tried to form an electoral coalition with the Nazis before the April 1932 election, but Habicht, probably wisely, turned the offer down. Younger members of the GVP wanted to subordinate the party to the NSDAP, but in a split resembling the Nazi schism of 1925–26, older members rejected this idea.[57]

From late 1930 to early 1933 the Nazis regarded the GVP as one of their chief recruiting grounds. They frequently disrupted the latter's meetings. The Greater Germans reacted by attacking the "Hitler papacy" (their own hierarchy was never very disciplined) and the Nazis' sell-out of the South Tyrol.[58] But it was all to no avail. The GVP's losses to the NSDAP in the local elections of 1932 were catastrophic. In Vienna alone the 124,000 votes they received in 1930 shriveled away to a paltry 9,000 two years later.[59] Hopes for a renaissance such as that experienced in November 1932 by the GVP's brother party in Germany, the German National People's party (DNVP), proved illusory.

In order to salvage something from the wreckage, the GVP, after long negotiations, joined the Pan-German Front on 15 May 1933. Like the Styrian Heimatschutz, the Greater Germans preserved their organizational independence. But the Nazis were by far the biggest gainers. The GVP promised to push for new elections and the victory of the national movement. Until that day arrived, however, the Nazis gained a new respectability in their association with the GVP and its relatively distinguished membership. More specifically, the Nazis could utilize the still considerable number of GVP deputies in Parliament and in those cities and states where there had not been recent elections.[60] These men were especially useful as intermediaries between the Nazis and the government after June 1933 when both the Nazis and the Styrian Heimatschutz were outlawed. The Nazis' new respectability also made it easier for still more middle-class professional people to switch their allegiance to the Nazis. When the Nazis increasingly resorted to the use of terror in the late spring and summer of 1933, some members and former members of the GVP began to dissociate themselves from the NSDAP. But they were driven right back into the Nazi camp when Dollfuss outlawed the remaining political parties and their public officeholders in 1934.[61]

The Pan-German Front was joined in May 1934 by the Landbund, or what was left of it. A purely political and democratic party made up of peasants, mostly in Styria and Carinthia, its pan-Germanism and anti-Marxism made it vulnerable to the Nazi siren song. Rumor had it that the functionaries of the Agricultural League received 340,000 Schillings (or $38,200) in exchange for making common cause with the Nazis.[62] The Landbund was finally dissolved by the government in August 1934 because of its close association with the NSDAP.[63]

The Pan-German Front proved highly useful to the Nazis. Not only were the GVP and Landbund public officeholders able to remain active until 1934, long after the NSDAP and the Styrian Heimatschutz had been outlawed, but the weapons and military experience of the Heimatschutz were also crucial to the Nazi attempt to overthrow the Dollfuss government in July 1934.

The two years between the spring of 1931 and the spring of 1933 thus marked a decisive turning point in the history of the Austrian Nazi party. The leadership problem, which had severely hampered its growth during the preceding five or six years, had been resolved by the appointment of Theo Habicht. The electoral victories of the Nazis in Germany had provided an inspiring example, which their Austrian comrades were eager and to a considerable degree able to emulate. The worsening of the Great Depression again made an Anschluss with Germany seem an attractive alternative to Austria's alleged economic nonviability.

But at the very time the Anschluss was reviving as a major issue, Austria's two largest parties became alarmed by the treatment of their brother parties in Germany and eliminated the Anschluss plank from their platforms. The Austrian NSDAP was therefore left as one of the country's few parties still unequivocally in favor of the Anschluss and the only one that had a realistic chance of implementing it in the near future. Consequently, Austria's pan-Germans, who had previously been scattered throughout all of the country's political parties, now gravitated to the Nazis. So with virtually all the pan-German Right either in the ranks of the Austrian NSDAP or closely allied to it by the spring of 1933, the Nazis were justifiably confident about their prospects for seizing power.

Nazi Optimism in the Spring of 1933

With Adolf Hitler and the Nazis securely in power in Germany and with the pan-German Right in Austria largely "captured," Austrian Nazis in the spring of 1933 had every reason to believe that it was just a matter of time—and a short time at that—until they too would be at the gates of power. To be sure, caution had to be taken not to provoke an intervention by the anti-Anschluss powers (Italy, France, and Britain) at a time when the Third Reich was still militarily weak. But the "inspiring example set by the course of events in the Reich,"[1] along with the almost scientifically organized propaganda, would inevitably produce the same results in Austria as they had in Germany.

Hitler himself must have shared this optimism in early 1933. Two prominent historians of Nazi Germany, the American Gerhard Weinberg and the German Jens Petersen, both believe that Hitler, as chancellor, at first viewed Austria not as a foreign, but as a domestic problem to be solved in the same way he had achieved power in Germany: through agitation, elections, and coalition governments.[2]

The Nazis' dream was soon to be shattered by the Austrian chancellor, Engelbert Dollfuss, and his successor, Kurt von Schuschnigg, as well as by the constitutionally weak, but nevertheless determined, anti-Nazi president, Wilhelm Miklas. Although there are many parallels between the histories of interwar Germany and Austria, there was no Heinrich Brüning in the Alpine republic to dissolve Parliament prematurely and call for parliamentary elections in the middle of the Great Depression. There was no Paul von Hindenburg to appoint a Nazi chancellor in 1933. And there was no Reichstag fire to create mass hysteria at a time when the Austrian Nazis were strong. So instead of residing comfortably in the federal chancellery, the Austrian Nazis were more likely to be found in detention camps between 1933 and 1938, if indeed they had not been expelled from the country.

Nazi optimism also appeared to be well justified owing to the local elections at the end of 1932 and during the first four months of 1933 when the Nazis gained anywhere from 16 to nearly 42 percent of the vote.[3] Nazi strength was greatest in Carinthia and Styria where they drew 20 and 16 percent of the votes for the provinces as a whole. However, in individual towns the Nazis sometimes attracted as much as 40 percent of the vote, as for example in the Lower Austrian town of Zwettl and in Innsbruck in March and April 1933. On the other hand, the Nazis were weakest in Upper and Lower Austria and in the Burgenland.

Although no one will ever know the exact extent of Nazi popularity after April 1933, because no more elections were held, an estimate of 20 to 25 percent would probably be reasonable. Perhaps another 10 percent supported the idea of an Anschluss with Nazi Germany without accepting other aspects of the Nazi ideology.[4] Even though the Nazis continued to gain new members after the spring of 1933, it is likely that their appeal among the general population was actually reduced by their willingness to resort to terror and assassination.[5]

Legal Propaganda

To a substantial degree Nazi popularity in Austria, as in Germany, was the product of propaganda, both legal and illegal. Hitler discovered that one way to combat radical Marxist propaganda was by a still more radical propaganda from the far Right. The rational and peaceful atmosphere of bourgeois party meetings, as Hitler noted in *Mein Kampf*, would never appease the fears and hopes of the previously nonpolitical lower-middle class.[6] The Nazis offered instead all kinds of exciting entertainment. Their torchlight processions, huge rallies illuminated by bonfires and searchlights, and enormous funerals for "martyred" heroes were all comparatively well known and, particularly in rural areas, provided a welcome alternative to the usual fare of motion pictures and an occasional play.

Not so well known, however, was the Nazis' attempt to bring high or at least middle-brow culture to the masses. This tactic involved so-called German Evenings, which might consist of military marches, readings from Goethe, German Lieder, Nazi party songs, violin music, and humorous impersonations.[7] Similarly, there were also concerts, plays, films, and slide showings, all designed to prove that the Nazis were interested in *Kultur* and, more subtly, to demonstrate the similarity of the fine arts in Austria and Germany. These affairs also strengthened the Nazi claim that their movement was classless and nonpartisan. In so doing they hoped to attract the attention of those people who ordinarily were not interested in party politics. The German Evenings, as well as various festivals and memorials, also helped to verify the Nazis' contention that they did not simply want to gain power, like every other party, but also wanted to create a new style of life.[8]

Part of the Nazis' success was a matter of timing. The beginning of their meteoric rise virtually coincided with the rapid improvement of mass communications after 1929. The newspaper press was, of course, available to the Nazis almost from the beginning. But the introduction of sound films, the radio, airplanes, and perhaps most of all, loudspeakers, made it possible for Nazi propaganda to reach a far larger audience than ever before at the very time it was most advantageous.

The Nazis' timing was also fortunate with regard to the Great Depression. When the crash came in 1929, the NSDAP was the only significant party in either Germany or Austria that had never belonged to a national (or even state) government; thus it could not be blamed for the Depression or any of the other disasters of the Republican period. Even after the great victory of April 1932 Walter Riehl advised Alfred Proksch to avoid any parliamentary involvement while the party was still weak. When the Nazis finally attained power in Germany in 1933 and Austria in 1938, the economic recovery had just begun in both countries and the Nazis naturally claimed full credit for it.

The Nazis left little to chance in their propaganda drive. Each Gau had its own Propagandaleiter, who had a wide variety of responsibilities. The Nazis believed that unity of propaganda leadership and careful planning would guarantee success. Propaganda in a brand new district was supposed to begin suddenly with posters, leaflets, newspapers, and marchers all asking: "Who is Hitler?" "What does Hitler want?" To give an impression of strength, the propaganda campaign in a new region was to begin with several meetings being held in different places on the same day, or within a short span of time. Because first impressions were often the longest lasting, only experienced speakers familiar with local conditions were to be used in a district's first Nazi meeting. A "big city" speaker was considered unsuitable for a rural area and vice versa.[9]

Propaganda leaders were supposed to follow the activities of Nazi opponents with great care. Quarrels and conflicts within a rival party were to be quickly publicized, and all contradictions between theory and practices, between promises and fulfillment, were to be pointed out. Comparisons favor-

REVIEWING STAND *for a Nazi Gauparteitag parade, September 1932. Standing on the top row (from left to right) are SA leader Ernst Röhm and Hermann Göring. Standing in front of Röhm and to the viewer's left is Theo Habicht. Next to him with the bouquet and bandaged forehead (which resulted from a brawl with Socialist Landtag deputies) is Alfred Frauenfeld. Austrian National Library Picture Archive.*

able to the Nazis were also supposed to be made by the Propagandaleiter whenever possible.[10]

Because the Nazis far outstripped all their rivals in the number of public meetings they held, there was always an enormous demand for new party speakers. Here again, it was the duty of propaganda leaders to set up special speakers' courses, lasting for four months, to train new speakers in both Nazi theory and in the practical aspects of public address. The trainee had to make thirty trial speeches culminating in one made in the presence of the local Gauleiter.[11]

Special leaders (called *Versammlungsleiter*) were in charge of the smooth operation of public meetings. Such meetings were to be well publicized several days in advance, first in the local press and then on wall posters. About a day before the meeting Hitler Youth distributed leaflets and pamphlets and a notice would again appear in local newspapers. Finally, on the day of the meeting itself "town criers" (*Sprechchöre*) consisting of the SA, SS, and HJ, would march through the streets announcing the meeting. Care was also taken to remove posters after every meeting so new ones would be readily noticed.[12]

To provide a sharp contrast with traditional Austrian *Schlamperei*, Nazi leaders were instructed to begin meetings punctually regardless of the number of people present. Introductions were to be kept short, and people at the head table were under orders to maintain strict silence and not to smoke during a speech or report. Hecklers and other disturbers of the peace who ignored warnings were to be thrown out by the SA, and those who insulted the Führer or the movement were to be dealt with severely.[13]

Because factual statements generally make the best propaganda, Nazi speakers were ordered to stick to the truth. Non-Nazi speakers were excluded from the meetings unless their views were indistinguishable from those of National Socialism. If the leader of the meeting were absolutely convinced that the Nazis were in a majority of those present, the assembly would close with a "Heil Hitler," the singing of the German national anthem, and the *Horst Wessel Song*.[14] In short, the audience was to be left with an impression of efficiency, seriousness, and credibility.

Such civilized behavior, however, was confined only to the Nazis' own meetings. One of the Nazis' favorite pastimes was breaking up opposition party meetings by howling, screaming, prolonged applause, coughing, and various other assortments of noisemaking, employed to embarrass, confuse, and drown out the speakers.[15] Similar techniques were used against pacifistic and pornographic movies, such as *All Quiet on the Western Front* and *Secrets from the Portfolio of a Sexologist*. In the latter case, however, the Nazis' righteous indignation was somewhat slow in rising to the surface, as a performance in Graz was nearly over before a group of young Nazis unleashed their loud speakers, stink bombs, and generally raucous noise![16]

Although the Nazis had few opportunities to use them, Theo Habicht outlined still more propaganda tactics for future electoral campaigns following the Nazis' stunning success in April 1932. The party's principal opponents were to be the pan-German parties (which, as we have already seen, were virtually destroyed during the next twelve months). The Nazis' attack was to be especially sharp in those areas where their rivals still held a *Grundmandat*. The Christian Socials were to be accused of committing treason against the (anti-Semitic) ideas of Karl Lueger. In dealing with the Social Democrats, positive Nazi programs were to be emphasized. To speed important Nazi speakers from one rally to another and to utilize an impressive technological innovation, airplanes were to be used for the first time in Austrian campaign history. All party affairs not directly related to the election were to be set aside in the last five to six weeks of a campaign. The propaganda "storm" was to increase two to four weeks before the election and to reach a peak during the last week.[17]

These techniques may help account for the Austrian Nazis' greatest local election victory ever in April 1933. The municipal elections held in Innsbruck gave the NSDAP a staggering 41.2 percent of the 36,400 votes cast[18] (thus nearly equalling the 43.9 percent won by the German Nazis in the Reichstag elections of 6 March 1933). In the meantime, the number of Nazi *Ortsgruppen* throughout Austria had nearly doubled between April 1932 and April 1933.[19]

In view of the enormity of this victory it is hardly surprising that the Dollfuss government announced on 11 May that "to prevent economic damage during the tourist season" further elections would be prohibited until after 31 October.[20] In fact, democratic elections were never again held during the First Republic. In one sense, of course, this prohibition was clearly an undemocratic and unconstitutional act. But given the Nazi view of democracy and constitutionalism in general, the chancellor's move is at least understandable. Nazis in both Austria and Germany cynically and publicly announced their intention to use parliaments to destroy democracy. As Theo Habicht put it: "Where National Socialists enter a parliament their duty is not to conform to and respect the questionable 'dignity' of the high house, to walk softly and to speak softly so that 'peace and quiet' are preserved, but instead . . . to change everything. The NSDAP is a fighting movement whose goal is to conquer power in the state. But conquerors don't walk in felt slippers but instead in boots."[21] The people of Germany had to learn the deadly seriousness of these convictions the hard way.

It is also a fact that the Nazi party demanded an unending series of victories to maintain its heterogeneous following. In Austria and Germany where good economic and diplomatic news was in short supply, the Nazi electoral victories were themselves a startling contrast to governmental failures. To allow them to continue would give the Nazis still more prestige and social respectability. Habicht observed shortly after the local elections of April 1932, "The experiences in the Reich show that once a mass movement is set into motion it gains more momentum from election to election. After our great victory there can be no doubt that the next election will bring even greater success."[22] Therefore, the Nazis were probably justified in believing that their momentum and unscrupulous tactics, together with moral and financial resources of the Third Reich, were likely to produce ultimate success. But denying the Nazis the opportunity for still more electoral victories was demoralizing. A clash between government and party became inevitable.

The Social Composition of the Austrian Nazi Party

The nature of the five-year struggle between the Austrian regime and the Nazis is intimately related to the social composition of the
Austrian NSDAP. National Socialism traditionally has been seen as a lower-
middle-class movement, particularly by Marxist historians. In reality, however, it drew support from a wider social spectrum than the democratic or
Marxist parties of either Austria or Germany.[23] Nowhere was the breadth of
this support more obvious than among Austrian youth.

Young People

It is reasonably well-known that fascist (as well as Communist) party members
were substantially younger than those of bourgeois parties and the many
Social Democratic parties of Europe. More than half of the fascist leaders of
Europe were born between 1890 and 1910. We have already noted that Theo
Habicht, Alfred Frauenfeld, and Hermann Reschny were all born in 1898,
whereas Walter Oberhaidacher had been born in 1896. Alfred Proksch was
only slightly older, having been born in 1891. By contrast, of the forty-five
Austrians who were cited in a Nazi enemies' list in 1939, only four had been
born after 1900, fourteen had been born between 1890 and 1899, seventeen
during the 1880s, nine during the 1870s, and one in 1856.[24]

The fascist leaders were all part of the "front generation" that had reached
maturity during the First World War. They had learned to associate democracy
with military defeat and parliamentarianism with frustrating ideological conflict and obstructionism. They had grown accustomed to making quick decisions in battle and had little patience with compromises. Their involvement in
the war and their inability to find employment after its conclusion had in many
cases prevented their firm attachment to any of the older parties or well-
defined social classes.[25]

Although no statistics are available concerning the age structure of the
Austrian Nazi party, nearly all contemporary observers as well as historians
have noticed the disproportionately heavy concentration of young people
between the ages of eighteen and thirty-five.[26] In early 1932 the Nazis expected most of their new members and some of their new *Ortsgruppenleiter*
to come from the youth. By 1933, their claim that two-thirds of the Austrian

youth stood in their ranks[27] may not have been far off target. The American historian R. John Rath, who was a graduate student in Austria shortly before and after the Anschluss, estimated that at least 75 percent of the active Nazis were youths, many still in their teens.[28]

Nazi activism, which stressed quick, radical, and simple solutions to complicated problems instead of hair-splitting ideological debates, had a natural appeal to young minds. The party's moral absolutes made Nazi youths feel they were being guided by the highest moral principles. In the words of one American historian, "They liked to parade their principles before the tawdry world of social prejudice, selfishness and compromise of their elders."[29] The numerous Nazi organizations also gave young people a welcome sense of comradeship. Equally attractive for them was the party's emphasis on charismatic leadership, personal commitment, and a sense of belonging.

Already in 1923 an organization called Deutsche Arbeiterjugend Österreichs (German Workers' Youth of Austria) was founded, although its membership remained small for the next two years. After the split in the Austrian Nazi party, the pro-Hitler faction founded its own Hitlerjugend in 1927. In the years of illegality between 1933 and 1938 the Hitler Youth, to which "every reputable member of the German people of pure Aryan ancestry and between the ages of eight and twenty could belong," maintained uninterrupted contact with the parent group in Germany.[30]

Just as in the Reich, young boys between eight and fifteen were eligible for the Jungvolk, which engaged in largely nonpolitical activities, such as taking trips together, camping out, and holding weekly club meetings. All of these activities were designed to develop a völkisch way of life (*Lebenserhaltung*). For girls between twelve and twenty-four there was the Bund Deutscher Mädel (BDM, or League of German Girls) which had about the same regulations as the HJ. The activities of the BDM, however, were kept strictly segregated from those of the HJ except for certain public events. For the training of future leaders, the Austrian Nazis, like their comrades in Germany, established Führer schools.

Great care was taken by party leaders to make their young followers feel they were a vital part of a movement that was reshaping history. They were given tasks like distributing propaganda for party rallies and helping in the Nazi campaign to eliminate corruption and pornography.

The unhappy interwar economic, social, and political conditions of Austria also heightened the party's attractiveness for young people. The German-speaking Austrians had for centuries provided by far the highest percentage of the old monarchy's professional class: public servants, professional soldiers, teachers, lawyers, doctors, and the like. With the war's end many of these people became superfluous to what was left of Austria. There is no question that in Austria, at least, the Nazis drew their strongest support from the unemployed, particularly the unemployed intelligentsia.[31]

Students

Employment difficulties were especially severe for university graduates, of which there were many in Austria owing to the high prewar birthrate. Of course that problem existed in nearly every European country; but it was worse in Austria, where there were 38.3 students for every ten thousand people, or nearly twice the ratio of the next highest country, France, with 20.9.[32] And no other European country faced Austria's staggering economic problems.

The situation was perhaps worst in Vienna where, as we saw in chapter two, Jews enjoyed a near monopoly in the fields of journalism, banking, and medicine. They were also disproportionately strong in the cultural and intellectual life of the Austrian capital.[33] Consequently, Jewish graduates, with their personal connections, had a considerably easier time entering the professions than did gentiles.[34] The Nazis, of course, promised to change all this by expelling Jews from the city and by opening up new economic opportunities through an Austro-German Anschluss. Students in universities and advanced technical and agricultural schools were therefore especially susceptible to National Socialist ideas. Enhancing the appeal was the Nazi Student League (Studentenbund).

As we have already seen, the affinity for right-wing extremism and pan-German nationalism of university students long preceded the First World War.[35] After the war, when the Nazi party was virtually unknown in Austria, Nazi students at the universities of Graz and Vienna were already so numerous that they succeeded in closing their schools with a series of demonstrations in the fall of 1923. By February 1931 Nazi students at the School of Agriculture in Vienna captured two-thirds of the mandates in the student senate.[36] Six months later the Nazis won an absolute majority of the votes in Graz at a congress of the Deutschen Studentenschaft (or German Student Association), which included students from Germany, Austria, and the Sudetenland. In 1933 the University of Graz became the scene of violent student demonstrations by Nazis. For four hours the university's main building was turned into a veritable fortress, with only professors and their assistants allowed entrance.

The whole university was decorated with Nazi propaganda, while clashes between students and police occurred in the inner city. Similar episodes were also common at the University of Vienna.[37]

The Intelligentsia, Middle Class, and Civil Servants

A major reason for the Nazi proclivities of young academicians can be traced to many of their schoolteachers and professors who were at best indifferent to the new Republic if not actually members of the NSDAP themselves.[38] The proportion of academicians in the Austrian Nazi party was even higher than in Germany.[39] Walter Riehl was able to report after the local elections of April 1932 that "the entire Aryan intelligentsia and a large part of the academicians . . . voted for us."[40]

In addition to teachers, the pro-Nazi intelligentsia included lawyers, veterinarians, pharmacists, architects, and engineers. Many of these people, particularly in the small towns, had supported the Heimwehr until about 1932, but thereafter they shifted their support to the National Socialists.[41]

As with every social group, the Nazis had special organizations for every profession. Teachers were encouraged to join the National Socialist German Teachers' League (Lehrerbund) to help fight "cultural bolshevism." For physicians there was the NSD Ärztebund. Lawyers could find a home in the NS Juristenbund. Industrial workers were organized in NS Betriebszellen. These organizations in turn helped to spread propaganda to non-Nazi professional people.

Other middle-class groups attracted to National Socialism in Austria included private employees, civil servants, hotel keepers, and merchants and small businessmen. Further down the social scale were chauffeurs and railroad and streetcar workers.[42] German-owned firms or those with German managers were also pro-Nazi. Merchants and artisans, with their traditional anti-Semitism, were particularly susceptible to Nazi propaganda. On the other hand, most big industrialists were staunchly anti-Nazi, sometimes because they were Jewish, but more often because they feared the economic competition an Anschluss would bring.[43]

Civil servants were also likely candidates for Nazi membership. The superabundance of civil servants both before and after the war grew still worse in the Depression years. In 1932 nearly 100,000 government workers were dismissed in order to comply with the stipulations of the Lausanne loan, even though Austria did not receive the money until 1934. Unemployed civil servants were hopeful that an Austro-German Anschluss would put them back to work. Those fortunate enough to retain their jobs often surreptitiously joined the Nazi party as a kind of insurance policy in case of a Nazi takeover, or to gain a second position in the elaborate Nazi hierarchy. These "closet" Nazis were thus in an excellent position to give away vital government secrets. In Vienna, where fewer than 5 percent of the total population were civil servants, around 19 percent of the party consisted of public employees. The risk of being dismissed from their posts during the illegal period, however, caused the number of civil servants and other public employees to decline by around 20 percent from the previous decade, if Linz can be used as a model.[44] Railroad workers acted as couriers, customs officials smuggled propaganda material and explosives, and Nazi policemen warned their comrades of impending arrest. Nazi attorneys and judges also discriminated in favor of accused party comrades. And in contrast to pre-1933 Germany, Nazis could be found in the Austrian civil service from the bottom to the very top, including the Security Directorate.[45]

The middle-class nature of Austrian Nazi support was clearly revealed in voting patterns. Already in 1930, when the party was still very small, it did best in provincial capitals and county seats. The Nazi vote in Klagenfurt, Graz, and Linz was two to four times the national average.[46]

Peasants and Miners

The Nazis were particularly eager to win over the peasants. Nazi ideology held the peasantry to be "the backbone of Austria." It was a matter of urgency that they be won over to the Nazi cause. Habicht's *Dienstbuch* emphasized in 1932 that "if we have seized the mass of the peasants we have the whole land and with it the state."[47] This was not to be an easy task, however.

Until the beginning of 1931 Austrian peasants and agricultural workers had been solid supporters of the Christian Social party and the Heimwehr. But with the deepening of the Great Depression, Nazi strength in rural areas began to increase, above all in Styria and Carinthia.[48] A Bauernschaft (Peasants' Association) was organized for the many peasants who could not afford the party's membership dues. A legal and later illegal newspaper supplement called *Bauernsturm* painted a rosy picture of agricultural conditions in Germany. It may have been such stories that encouraged many farm workers to seek employment in the Reich in the mid-1930s. When they returned to Austria, well clothed and with money in their pockets, they were full of enthusiasm for the new Germany. Finally, mine workers, especially in northern Styria, were also hard hit by the economic crisis and began to join the Nazis in ever-increasing numbers during the early 1930s.[49]

Economic considerations, though extremely important, were not the only reasons for the Nazis' growing popularity in rural districts. If Austrian peasants were traditionally Catholic, many others were traditionally anticlerical and deeply resented the Church's increasing political influence during the Dollfuss and Schuschnigg regimes. Growing Nazi strength among the peasantry was demonstrated in local elections in early 1933 and in a more alarming way during the Nazi Putsch of 1934.[50]

Protestants

An entirely different kind of pro-Nazi group was the Austrian Protestants. Numbering only 248,600 in 1933,[51] they were the remnant of a once far larger minority that had barely survived the persecutions of the Catholic Counter-Reformation. Although Protestants were officially tolerated by Joseph II in 1781, discrimination continued at the local level. Therefore, an antigovernment tradition arose among Protestants, which was first exploited politically by Georg von Schönerer in his anti-Habsburg *Los von Rom* movement.

The anticlerical Nazis, following in the footsteps of Schönerer, had a similar success identifying Protestantism with pan-Germanism, promoting conversions, and in securing the support of many longtime Protestants. Within a span of just one year, 1933–34, the number of evangelical Christians increased by 24,357, or six times the annual rate for the previous ten years.[52] In the local elections of April 1932 the only community where the Nazis gained an absolute majority was the Carinthian town of Weissbriach, which was 88 percent Protestant. Of the 13 Carinthian communities where the Nazis polled between 30 and 40 percent of the vote, 4 had Protestant majorities even though there were only 13 such towns in the province out of a total of 249.[53]

Certainly aiding the Nazi cause among Austrian Protestants was the repeated emphasis by the Dollfuss and Schuschnigg regimes on the *Catholic* (not just Christian) character of the Austrian state. Nazi propaganda was quick to claim that government measures taken against individual Protestant clergymen, who were allegedly 100 percent National Socialists, were directed against Protestants as a whole. Protestants themselves had the impression that they were all assumed to be friends of the Reich and enemies of the Austrian state.[54]

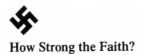

How Strong the Faith?

To what extent the various Nazi supporters really accepted the imperialistic, anti-Semitic, and anticlerical Nazi ideology will always remain a mystery. In most cases the pro-Nazi Austrians probably resembled the Germans in having an aversion to other political ideologies rather than having a clear understanding of Nazi beliefs.[55] The head of the Austrian Security Directorate, Eduard Baar-Baarenfels, wrote in a long report dated 4 April 1936, that "the rejection of Austrian state thought (*Staatsgedankens*) for fifteen years, the propagation of the Anschluss idea by representatives of all the former political parties, and not least, the great-power idea, which has survived after the destruction of the Austro-Hungarian Monarchy by members of the prewar and war generations, have contributed to the rise of the National Socialist party."[56]

According to Alfred Persche, the leader of the Austrian SA from 1936 to February 1938, of those party members who came from the working class, 90 percent were "true believers"; but among officials and peasants the figure was only 10 percent. Of the well-to-do intelligentsia only 3 percent really took the Nazi principles seriously. Altogether, these groups had in common only their nationalism. Persche's analysis is borne out by the findings of the Austrian historian Gerhard Botz. Whenever the Nazi party shrank in size, Botz contends, the Nazi wage workers grew in relative importance, whereas the significance of the self-employed party members declined.[57]

The Nonbelievers

Social Democrats

The social base of the Austrian Nazi party was clearly widespread, yet many large groups stubbornly remained immune from its magnetism even during the desperate years of the Great Depression. The most significant of these groups was the industrial workers, who continued to belong to the underground Socialist movement even after their party had been outlawed in February 1934.

The Nazis were fully aware that if they were ever to capture an absolute majority of the Austrian people it would have to be at the expense of these "irreconcilable enemies." The Nazis had reason to be optimistic about their chances of winning the Socialists over to their ranks. Both groups had no use for Austria's traditions and they rejected clericalism. Both professed to be anticapitalist and antiliberal. And the Nazis had deliberately imitated the SDP's mass organization. The illegal Nazi press took a cautiously friendly attitude toward the Austrian working class and cited the declining unemployment rate in Nazi Germany. Further proselytizing was conducted in factories by the NSDAP Betriebszellen.[58]

The Nazis' efforts did not go entirely unrewarded. For young workers and those who had lost their jobs, the Nazis' promise of better times to come was too tempting to resist. This was seen when the Nazis attracted 17,000 former Socialist voters in Vienna in April 1932 and another 7,000 in Salzburg. Between 1929 and April 1933 the Socialist vote in Innsbruck declined from 14,016 to 9,932, while the Nazis' jumped from 202 to 14,996.[59] The Socialists also lost 4,000 of 16,000 votes in Vorarlberg in 1932. Their losses, however, tended to be in areas where they were already weak. In Vienna the Socialists consistently drew around 78 percent of the vote of the industrial workers and employees, and most of the voters they lost gravitated to the Communist fold.[60] Nevertheless, of those people who joined the Nazi party in Vienna between 1926 and 1933, nearly 14 percent were manual workers (compared to 32 percent of the city's total population). The percentage of *Parteigenossen* who were workers rose significantly to 24.6 percent between 1933 and 1938, but was still well below the workers' proportion of the city's population.[61]

When the brief Socialist uprising of February 1934 was crushed with needless brutality by the Dollfuss regime (or to be more exact, by the Heimwehr), the Nazis expected at least half of the Socialist party to cross over to their ranks. Some condemned Socialist leaders did flee the country with the aid of the Nazi underground, especially those from Upper Austria, and some Social Democrats even joined the Austrian Legion, the Nazi paramilitary formation for Austrian exiles in Germany. But by June a German observer in Austria noted that Socialist conversions had lasted for "only a very short time" after the February revolt.[62] When Nazis and Socialists were forced to mix in detention camps, some Socialists did convert to Nazism (never the other way around), yet the number of such converts was insignificant.[63]

Roman Catholics

The attitude of Austrian Catholics and the Roman Catholic hierarchy in Austria toward National Socialism is difficult to assess. The Nazis themselves regarded Catholicism and also legitimism as "the chief sources of anti-German hate" in the country.[64] The Nazi cause was badly hurt in the Alpine republic by the state-church conflict in Germany. The Austrian bishops, in numerous open letters to the faithful, condemned the extreme nationalism of Nazism along with its hatred of religion and the Church. They warned that the strivings of Nazi leaders could soon result in revolution and both civil and foreign wars. The general vicar of St. Stephen's Cathedral in Vienna turned down a request in 1932 to permit the SA Gauparteitag to attend a mass at the church en bloc and the Catholic journal, *Neues Reich*, took an uncompromising stand against the Nazis.

On the other hand, not even the Church leaders were consistently anti-Nazi in their pronouncements. The priest and former chancellor Ignaz Seipel was quoted by a Berlin newspaper in February 1932 as saying that there were "two sides to National Socialism" and Cardinal Innitzer, who came from the ultranationalistic Sudetenland, accepted a proreligion statement by Hitler at its face value.[65] The Nazis loved to quote from a "Hirten" letter to the faithful written in January 1933 by the bishop of Linz, Johannes Gföllner, in which he said that Christians ought to break with the harmful influence of Jews who poisoned their souls. The Jews, Gföllner wrote, were responsible for capitalism, socialism, and communism. The Nazis were careful, however, to avoid mentioning that in the same letter the bishop said it was impossible to be both a good Catholic and a good Nazi. Nor could they have been pleased when later in the same year the entire Austrian episcopate denounced Gföllner's letter for arousing social hatred and conflict.[66]

Another Austrian bishop, Alois Hudal, published a book in 1937 entitled *Das Grundlagen des Nationalsozialismus*, in which he sought an understanding between Christianity and Nazism. He discovered a common ground for compromise in the Nazis' idea of Volksgemeinschaft, the German language as the spiritual expression (*Raum*) of the nation, the mutual desire to solve the Jewish problem and to have large and healthy families, military preparedness, and the aristocratic Führerprinzip. The racial teachings of the Nazis were approved by Hudal as long as they did not challenge the philosophy of the Roman Catholic church.[67]

Josef Eberle, editor of the Austrian Catholic journal *Schönere Zukunft*, reflected the ambiguous attitude of many Austrian Catholics toward National Socialism. He rejected Nazis as an enemy of the Church, but believed the best way of fighting them was to take over those Nazi ideas that were "correct,"[68] advice which, in fact, was followed by chancellors Dollfuss and Schuschnigg. The *Schönere Zukunft* claimed to approve the goals, but not the methods, of the Nazis in defending Germany against the Jews, but the journal supported the burning of books by German Nazis in May 1933. Other Austrian Catholic periodicals rejected the anti-Semitic policies of the German (and Austrian) Nazis, as too harsh, but said they were understandable. In many instances the papers chose to report anti-Semitic actions by Nazis without comment.[69] Finally, Austrian Catholics were both confused and shocked by the Concordat signed between the Vatican and Nazi Germany in July 1933.[70]

The Nazis tried to improve their image with the Roman Catholic hierarchy in a meeting attended by Cardinal Piffl and Theo Habicht on 17 November 1932. The cardinal objected to the use of the term "positive Christianity" by the Nazis. But Habicht, who had postponed an important conference in Berlin to attend the meeting, insisted that Hitler had made a point of declaring that the term represented merely the private opinion of Alfred Rosenberg in his book, *The Myth of the Twentieth Century*, and not the official policy of the party. Habicht also reminded the cardinal that Hitler had specifically rejected the *Los von Rom* movement in *Mein Kampf*.[71]

At about the same time that the above meeting was being held in Vienna, Alfred Frauenfeld was assuring the archbishop of Vienna that he was willing to confer with the clergyman at any time to clear up misunderstandings concerning the Nazi attitude toward Christianity. Although he currently opposed the policies of the Christian Social party, he hoped that at some future date all Christian, nationalistic, and patriotic elements would form a common front against bolshevism.[72]

Not surprisingly, then, there was no one position on Nazism held by Austrian Catholics. Even though the country was officially more than 94 percent Roman Catholic, probably no more than 40 percent were practicing Catholics in good standing and not even these people were uniform in their political beliefs. Arthur Seyss-Inquart, for example, who later was to be unfairly given so much of the blame for the Anschluss, was a practicing Catholic, as were many other Nazi and pro-Nazi leaders.[73]

Legitimists

Among the Catholic anti-Nazis probably the most ardent were the Legitimists. Aristocrats, officers of the World War, and many middle-aged civil servants were stunned by the breakup of the Habsburg Monarchy and longed for its restoration. They adamantly opposed an Anschluss with Germany, preferring instead a Danubian confederation. Although many Legitimists enrolled in the ranks of the Heimwehr, they kept their political views relatively quiet during the 1920s.[74]

The Legitimists' goal of a restoration would have provided Nazi Germany with a welcome pretext for invasion. As a matter of fact, their only contingency plan for an invasion of Austria was labeled "Case Otto" in reference to the former crown prince, Otto von Habsburg. A restoration would also have aroused the wrath of secessionist states like Czechoslovakia and Yugoslavia that, surprisingly, preferred an Anschluss to a return of the Habsburgs, which they feared would only increase the unrest of their already highly dissatisfied minorities.

It is impossible to measure the strength of legitimism though its adherents were certainly a fairly small minority. They were rejected by the Socialists as well as by the Nazis. In any event, their usefulness in the anti-Nazi cause was dubious because they were a liability in Austria's international relations. And as the English historian F. L. Carsten has pointed out, "It is virtually impossible to create an activist mass movement based on the support of the middle-aged."[75]

Feminists

Another group that was relatively impervious to Nazism prior to Hitler's coming to power was women, especially feminists.[76] There had long been a definite connection between antifeminism and anti-Semitism, and the Nazis were the heirs of this tradition. Although the Nazis devoted little thought to the role of women, especially before 1933, what they did think was ultra-conservative. Family life, they believed (or at least said they believed), had been destroyed by the Industrial Revolution when women started working outside the home. For family life to be restored, and the declining birthrate of Germany and Austria to be reversed, women would have to revert to their time-honored tasks of caring for children, attending church, and preparing meals (*Kinder, Kirche, Küche*).

A National Socialist Frauenschaft was established for Nazi women, but it was no true organization because it had no leaders of its own and did not collect dues. It was subordinate to the party's political leadership in every respect. Insofar as it was given any responsibilities at all in party affairs they were again traditional ones: doing charitable work; caring for unemployed, sick, and imprisoned party members; and rooting out "scandalous" films and plays, "shameless" fashions, and "Negro music."[77] For Nazi university coeds there was also an *Arbeitsgemeinschaft Nationsozialistischer Studentinnen* (Study Group for National Socialist Women Students).

However, not even all women who were otherwise convinced Nazis were happy with modest roles. The Nationalistic (völkisch) Women of Vienna, for example, drew up a resolution in April 1932 requesting that "women's affairs" within the party be controlled by women. If not, votes would be lost to Marxist parties, which charged that Nazis did not value the well-being of women. Theo Habicht was apparently aware of this possibility, because he ordered Nazi speakers to "deny the lie that [the party regarded] women as servants."[78]

Habicht also assured the same Viennese women's group that the absence of women from Nazi electoral lists did not imply any disrespect for women in general. On the contrary, the party wished to protect the delicate sensibilities of women by keeping them off the parliamentary battlefield where representatives acted like front soldiers. But this policy did not mean that the party did not welcome the active participation of women in other political affairs.[79]

Although women held some positions within the Austrian hierarchy during the 1920s, by the early 1930s they had been eased out, in at least one instance by Hitler himself.[80] This may have been one reason that in the Viennese municipal election of April 1932, 18.6 percent of the male population voted for the Nazis, whereas only 16.2 percent of the Viennese women followed suit. Only the Communists had a smaller female vote, whereas the Christian Socials continued to attract the highest percentage of feminine voters.[81]

In terms of membership, the party in Austria was even more overwhelmingly composed of males. In Vienna, for example, housewives (having no outside employment) made up 21.4 percent of the city's total population in 1939, but 2.5 percent of the party's membership between 1926 and 1933. That figure rose substantially to over 10 percent for the party's years of illegality, but was still less than half of all housewives in the total population. By 1938 women of all professions made up just under one-fourth of the party's membership in the Austrian capital.[82] However, membership figures alone do not tell the whole story. Whatever the Nazi women lacked in numbers they made up for in enthusiasm for the cause.[83]

As we have seen, the Austrian Nazi party was probably at the peak of its strength and popularity during the first half of 1933, when it could legitimately claim to be a mass movement. About one-third of the country's population subscribed to at least part of its program. To a very large extent this popularity resulted from the party's extremely well-organized propaganda, which utilized all the latest technological means of dissemination and was aimed at virtually every segment of Austria's population. The Nazis took care—unique in Central European history—to make their propaganda entertaining as well as prolific. The Nazis' propaganda storm produced some of their biggest electoral victories in the spring of 1933 and induced Dollfuss to cancel all further elections.

Although the Nazis' propaganda never succeeded in winning over the majority of the Austrian population, its appeal was widespread and was by no means confined, as has so often been assumed, to the lower-middle class or even to the middle class as a whole. Peasants, miners, Protestants, Catholics, civil servants, merchants, and artisans, all joined the ranks of the Austrian NSDAP in considerable numbers. Young people and the intelligentsia were particularly attracted by the Nazis' appeal, whereas industrial workers, and to some extent women, were less eager to join the Nazis' ranks. With such a mass following, in the spring of 1933 the Nazis appeared to be well prepared to challenge the government in a test of strength and will power.

Chancellor Dollfuss refused to be intimidated by either the growing popularity of the Austrian Nazis or even by the victory of the German Nazis in the Reichstag elections of 5 March 1933. Instead, he took advantage of circumstances to make sure the Nazis would not even be able to enter the Austrian Parliament, let alone dominate it. And not long thereafter he outlawed the Austrian NSDAP altogether. Thus began a violent five-year struggle between the Austrian government and the Nazis, which did not end until the Anschluss of 1938.

Rule by Decree

On the day before the German elections the Austrian Parliament had inadvertently "dissolved itself" when its president and two vice-presidents impetuously resigned over a minor voting technicality. Far from reconvening the Parliament, Dollfuss seized this incident to avoid both Socialist obstructionism and the certainty of the Nazis' entering Parliament after the next elections and using it as a stepping stone to power as they had just done in Germany.

Therefore, on 7 March, posters appeared throughout the country announcing that henceforth the government would rule without Parliament. Moreover, all public meetings and marches were forbidden (though in practice not those of the Christian Social party and the Heimwehr). Censorship of the press also began on the same day. The subsequent government by decree was based on a legal pretext, a wartime emergency economic law dating back to 1917 that had never been rescinded.

The battle lines between the Nazis (and to a lesser extent the Socialists) and the government were now more sharply drawn than ever. In early May the chancellor issued a decree prohibiting the wearing of uniforms and insignia in public, though once again progovernment groups were excluded from this ruling. But these decrees did not even faze the Nazis. The Austrians were well aware that the Prussian government had once forbidden the wearing of SA uniforms, but had succeeded only in giving a boost to Nazi propaganda. A second ban by the German government in April 1932 was only temporarily successful and was soon revoked by the Papen government. The Austrian Nazis answered the Dollfuss decree forbidding their SA brownshirts by wearing white stockings (or sometimes no shirts) and tall silk hats. On the nineteenth of May, Alfred Frauenfeld, still the Gauleiter of Vienna, was ordered by the government to make no more public speeches. Eight days later the University of Vienna, along with several other Austrian universities and other institutions of higher education, were temporarily closed because of Nazi activities. The Nazis refused to be intimidated, however, simply because they were convinced that the Dollfuss regime was too weak to enforce these measures for any length of time.[1]

The situation became far more serious for the Nazis when on 10 June the government proscribed the sale of their official newspaper, the *Völkischer Beobachter*. Then, on the following day, an attempt was made to assassinate the Tyrolean Heimwehr leader, Richard Steidle. Although the Nazis denied all responsibility for the act, and no proof of their complicity was ever found, all "Brown Houses" (Nazi headquarters) throughout the country were closed and sealed by the police. This decree was followed by another on 11 June expelling all soldiers from the Austrian army who belonged to the Nazi party or who had engaged in Nazi activities.[2]

Nazi Bombings

The Nazis retaliated during the next week (12–19 June) by carrying out a series of bombing attacks in Vienna and other tourist centers. Violence had begun escalating in 1932 when there were twenty-four armed clashes between Nazis on the one hand and Socialists and Communists on the other. Most such fights involved the Nazis' armed formations and the Socialists' paramilitary Schutzbund. These Nazi acts of violence were more or less spontaneous, however, and were not directed by a centralized leadership.[3] In theory, violence was to be used only in self-defense. Yet Nazi activities were often so deliberately provocative—for example, SA marches through solid working-class districts—that they invited attacks.[4]

All these early disturbances were but a prelude to the prolonged and well-organized terror of 1933 and the first half of 1934. During the violent June days of 1933 two businesses in Vienna were nearly destroyed, two people were killed, and nine others were wounded. Nazi propaganda disclaimed any responsibility for these "spontaneous" acts. But German diplomats in Vienna privately admitted to their Foreign Ministry that the terror had been orchestrated by the Austrian Nazi leadership, which had used fifteen- and sixteen-year-old youths to do the dirty work.[5]

The bombing incidents provoked the Austrian government into arresting known Nazis on 13 June. All those under suspicion of conducting subversive propaganda were deported. In hopes of preventing still more violence, public buildings and homes of political leaders were placed under police surveillance. Membership in the NSDAP was prohibited for all public officeholders and government pensioners. The army and police were also purged of all Nazis.[6]

Far from ending the assaults, however, the government's measures only aroused the Nazis to commit still more violent acts. Beginning in October, tear-gas attacks were made on stores, coffeehouses, and in cinemas. After the twentieth, small bombs made of cardboard filled with black gunpowder and ignited by a cigarette or a match were tossed into busy streets or even into coffeehouses frequented by Jews. Although they did little damage to property, they were sufficient to wound and occasionally even to kill people.[7] Sometimes more powerful explosives were used; these were mixed with clay to create tiny bulletlike missiles, which were used against shops and in public parks, beginning in December. By early February 1934 there were as many as forty explosions a day throughout Austria perpetrated by members of the Austrian SA and SS, the Austrian Legion (the newly organized armed formation of Nazi exiles stationed in Germany), the Hitler Jugend and, quite possibly, German citizens residing in Austria. All of these groups made use of explosives smuggled into the country from Germany.[8]

The purpose of the bombings, which were directed mainly against streets, bridges, government buildings, and railroads, was partly to weaken the Austrian economy by frightening off foreign tourists, and partly to demonstrate the inability of the Dollfuss government to control the situation.[9] The bombings can be seen in large measure as a sign of the Nazis' frustration over their own inability to bring down the hated Dollfuss regime. In the long run, these bombings not only failed to have any serious impact on the Austrian economy, but they also culminated in a near disaster for the Nazi cause. Hitler forbade the use of terror in August 1933, but took no action against Habicht to make him stop it.[10]

Outlawing the Nazi Party

The first wave of terror reached a climax on 19 June 1933, when fifty-six unarmed "Christian German Gymnasts," a police auxiliary, were attacked near Vienna by two Nazis armed with handgrenades. One man was killed and thirteen others were seriously wounded. In an emergency meeting held the same day, the Dollfuss cabinet decided to outlaw the Austrian Nazi party together with all its subordinate organizations; the Styrian Heimatschutz, firmly allied with the Nazis by this time, was also included in the prohibition.

There has been considerable debate about both the justification and the wisdom of outlawing the Nazi party. The Nazis themselves either blamed the terror on the Communists, whose party had been outlawed on 26 May, or said that the acts of violence were merely "harmless shows of strength."[11] At other times they claimed that the terror was the work of isolated fanatics operating on their own initiative. And it is true, as the Nazis charged, that the Austrian government had in a sense provoked the terror by denying the Nazis freedom of the press and the possibility of running for office. It is equally true that the terror was an embarrassment to some Nazis. Walter Riehl and Alfred Frauenfeld told Dollfuss that they opposed such acts and objected to them in intraparty debates.[12] One could also argue, as some Socialists (and Nazis) did at the time, that the government was doing nothing more than driving the Nazis underground, where they would be even more difficult to control and where they could pose as martyrs.[13]

Nevertheless, short of committing political suicide, it is difficult to see what else the Austrian government could have done under the circumstances, given not only the Nazis' goals but also their tactics in achieving them. In view of the total abolition of political parties (except the NSDAP) and civil liberties in Germany, the Nazis were in no position to complain.

Despite the many measures taken against the Nazi party in May and early June, Theo Habicht and the remainder of the party leadership were surprised by the party's proscription.[14] Habicht, as well as most of the Nazi *Gauleiter*,

CAPTURED NAZI EXPLOSIVES *and propaganda materials. DÖW.*

was no longer even in Austria when the party was dissolved. Despite Hitler's attempt to give him diplomatic immunity by making him a press attaché in the German embassy (an action the Austrian government refused to recognize), Habicht was deported on 13 June along with 1,142 other Austrians and some Germans.[15]

Undaunted, Habicht, Proksch, and most of the Austrian *Gauleiter*, together with the leaders of the Austrian SA and SS, proceeded to establish a new Landesleitung in Munich with Habicht himself as chief. On the other hand, Walter Riehl, Alfred Frauenfeld, and Captain Josef Leopold, the Lower Austrian Gauleiter, refused to obey Hitler's order to flee to Germany. Of course, Karl Schulz and his long-forgotten followers also stayed in Austria and their activities remained legal. The Gauleitung of Salzburg moved just across the border to Freilassing, Bavaria, whereas the Carinthian Gauleitung was relocated for a time in Tarvisio, in northeastern Italy, until Mussolini forced it to move to Germany.[16]

For those who fled or were expelled, the consequences were serious: their property was confiscated and they could lose their citizenship. Not only did these measures punish those who fled, but they also served as a strong deterrent to those who otherwise might have joined the movement, especially members of the propertied middle class. For the Nazis, accustomed to the gentle approach of the Weimar governments in Germany, the determination shown by the Dollfuss regime must have come as a very unpleasant shock.

The Nazis were not the only losers in this struggle, however. Nazi terror in the spring and early summer of 1933 restricted the political freedom of Dollfuss and drove him more firmly than ever into the arms of the Heimwehr as his only dependable security prop. The Austrian army alone was simply too small to handle all emergencies. And there may have been some doubts in the chancellor's mind about its loyalty, although such doubts proved to be exaggerated in July 1934.

Dismissals and Detention Camps

Starhemberg says in his memoirs that sometime during the middle of 1933 he told a discouraged Dollfuss to abandon the defensive and go over to the offensive.

"We must show the Austrian people that there is an Austrian power. They must have the feeling that there is a force which will protect them from the Nazis. And the faint-hearted, above all the state officials, officers, gendarmes, and police, must not doubt from whom they have the most to fear: us or the Nazis. . . . " I argued that we must answer the Nazi terror with an even stronger Austrian terror. Dollfuss agreed. "I know Hitler. . . . It is complete nonsense to believe that one can fight National Socialism with intellectual arguments."[17]

That there was an Austrian "terror" comparable to Hitler's in Germany may be doubted, though it was risky business indeed to be a professed Nazi in Austria, particularly from the middle of 1933 to the middle of 1936. Between late July and early August 1933 Nazi deputies in state parliaments were removed from office. Martial law was instituted in November with drumhead courts being used for political cases involving murder, arson, and explosives. Some political crimes were punishable by a 20,000-Schilling (or $2,256) fine and a two-year imprisonment.[18] By April 1934 some 50,000 Nazis had been convicted of various political and civil offenses.[19] In June 1934 the death penalty was restored for the mere possession of explosives.

The Austrian government was determined to purge itself and Austrian society of Nazi party members and sympathizers. By February 1934 Nazi or pro-Nazi civil servants, including teachers and university professors, were

ENGELBERT DOLLFUSS *(second from left)* AND PRINCE STAR-
HEMBERG *(center) at a Heimwehr rally at Schönbrunn palace in May 1933.
Emil Fey, leader of the Vienna HW, is on the far left. Austrian National
Library Picture Archive.*

sometimes dismissed or forced into early retirement without benefit of a trial;
they were replaced by loyalists.[20] All private clubs tainted with Nazi sympathies, especially sporting clubs that were traditionally pan-German and
völkisch, were outlawed by the government. Provincial governments in Upper
Austria and Salzburg also required the huge Kreditanstalt banking firm to fire
pro-Nazi officers and employees. Beginning in January 1934 hostages were
placed under "preventive arrest." Mere suspects could be imprisoned after
September. Likewise, the principle of "collective" or mass arrest of known
Nazis was used when the real perpetrators could not be apprehended.[21] August
Eigruber, the Gauleiter of Upper Austria after 1936, was arrested nineteen
times by the Dollfuss-Schuschnigg regime, sometimes as a preventive measure, sometimes to make him a hostage, and only occasionally because of
actual illegal activity. The first time he was arrested in 1933 he spent nearly
five months in the Wöllersdorf detention camp.[22]

Indeed, detention camps became important weapons of the government
against all its political opponents. Of the four camps scattered throughout the

country, the largest and most famous (or infamous) was the one at Wöllersdorf near Wiener Neustadt (just south of Vienna). After it was established in October 1933, the number of its inmates varied substantially from time to time, reaching a peak of 5,302 in October 1934, of whom 4,747 were Nazis and 555 were Socialists. But by 1 January 1935 Wöllersdorf held only 825 inmates, 654 being Nazis.[23]

Nazis, therefore, obviously outnumbered Socialists in Wöllersdorf (and elsewhere), but only because they were more active in resisting the regime. However, Socialists who participated in the civil war of February 1934 may have received harsher sentences than the Nazi Putschists of July.[24]

For the dedicated Nazi time served in a detention camp was a badge of honor, a testimony to his faith in the cause. Although treatment of prisoners differed according to who happened to be the commandant, Nazis privately referred to the camps as "nationalist convalescent homes." Individual differences between prisoners were suppressed, but there was no attempt to "reeducate" them as in Nazi Germany. The prisoners were given opportunities to participate in various sports and pursue hobbies at will. They were entertained by movies, singing, and lectures and were free to attend or not a religious service of their choice. Inmates could entertain their girlfriends, and businessmen could meet partners during emergencies. These visits also made possible the exchange of news and party orders. Better food could also be brought to prisoners from their homes.[25]

The British journalist G. E. R. Gedye, who was anything but a friend of the Austrian dictatorship, described life in the Wöllersdorf camp he visited in April 1934 as "easy if boring. . . . There were no cells, no plank beds. All the inmates, mostly young men, had photos of their best girls upon the walls. There were no restrictions on smoking and no hard labor to be done, as in the German camps. . . . Except for a few simple chores the time was their own and seemed to be devoted chiefly to football, sunbathing, or reading under the trees."[26] Disciplinary punishments might include some unpleasant work, a denial of visitation or reading privileges, deprivation of warm breakfasts, or solitary confinement for as long as a week.[27]

Another view of Wöllersdorf is provided by Eduard Frauenfeld, who was incarcerated at Wöllersdorf from 10 December 1933 to 16 December 1935. He describes the sanitary conditions at the camp as bad, and because it was located on the site of a former munitions dump, nothing would grow there (even though Gedye mentions having seen trees). Eight hundred men were crowded into a single barracks and slept in bunk beds three tiers high. In 1934 mail service to the camp was irregular, though in 1935 letters could be received every two weeks. The commandant of the camp, according to Frauenfeld, was a brutal homosexual named Stillfried.[28]

It is impossible to reconcile these two diametrically opposed impressions of Wöllersdorf. In all likelihood, Gedye was shown only the best parts of the camp and Frauenfeld remembered only the worst aspects.

German Economic Pressure

Even before the Austrian Nazi party was outlawed, Hitler realized that the German policy of nonintervention had failed. Instead of a direct annexation of Austria by Germany, the Austrian NSDAP was to carry out the *Gleichschaltung* (political coordination) of the country with only a minimum of outside guidance. But if anything, the Dollfuss regime was growing stronger, not weaker. Therefore, Hitler told a conference of ministers on 26 May, over the objections of Foreign Minister Neurath and Vice-Chancellor Papen, that he intended to launch a new two-pronged Austrian policy. A virtual economic boycott, including the cessation of German tourist traffic to Austria, was to begin immediately. The economic squeeze was to be accompanied by a massive propaganda offensive involving the dissemination of hundreds of thousands of leaflets explaining the reasons behind the German policy. Such a double-barreled approach would "lead to the collapse of the Dollfuss Government and bring new elections . . . before the end of the summer." The official explanation for the tourist boycott given to the press was the desire of the German government to avoid possible embarrassing incidents resulting from the prohibition of Nazi uniforms and insignia by the Austrian government.[29]

So after 1 June 1933 German citizens could travel to Austria only upon payment of a 1,000-Mark (or $250) visa fee. Although the Austrian government countered with its own exit fee, the main purpose of which was to hinder communications between German and Austrian Nazis, Austria, of course, was hit much harder than Germany. Thirty percent of Austria's tourist income was normally from Germany alone.[30] But in July 1933 only 8 Germans visited Austria compared to the 98,000 the year before. In all, the number of German tourists declined from nearly 750,000 in 1931–32 to 70,718 in 1933–34.[31] Although this diminution was partially compensated by an increase of tourists from other countries, the consequences were serious nevertheless, especially for the western provinces nearest Germany. In those areas most affected by the "blockade," and by other economic conditions, the Nazi party experienced a rapid growth in the summer of 1933.[32]

Eleven months later Hitler tightened the economic screws even more by "a curtailment of the imports of all those Austrian articles of export which were of particular importance to the Dollfuss Government in its domestic political struggle."[33] These items were to include lumber, fruit, and cattle. In case the Austrian government complained, the German Foreign Office was instructed to reply that "this was a spontaneous reaction of German consumers against the policy of the Austrian Government toward the NSDAP."[34]

The German economic vise only intensified an already desperate situation for Austria. As one of the European countries most dependent on foreign trade, Austria was especially devastated by the sharp decline in world trade during the Great Depression. In few if any other countries did the employment rate drop so low and remain depressed so long as in Austria. Whereas in Germany the bottom of the Depression was reached in 1933 when 71.7 percent of those employed in 1929 were still working, in Austria the nadir was not reached until 1936, when the rate was just 64.6 percent of the already high 1929 level of unemployment. In 1937 the unemployment rate in Austria was still only 67.4 percent of the 1929 norm compared to 104.3 percent in Germany.[35] In all, about 600,000 Austrians were unemployed at the beginning of 1936 or more than one-third of the country's total labor force. Meanwhile industrial production fell by 38 percent and foreign trade by 50 percent between 1929 and 1933.[36]

These statistics are not just a matter of idle curiosity. The strength of pro-Anschluss sentiment since 1918 had always been related to comparative economic conditions in Austria and Germany. To a considerable extent this phenomenon continued during the Depression years. As long as the Austrian employment rate dropped more slowly than Germany's, as it did from 1930 through 1932, the temptation to look with envy toward Austria's northern neighbor was weakened. But when the German economy began improving rapidly following Hitler's takeover in 1933, while the Austrian economy continued to sink even lower, many previously uncommitted people quite naturally drew the conclusion that only an Anschluss could reverse the trends. Probably nothing raised Germany's prestige in Austrian eyes so much as its flourishing economy. And nothing could so enhance the effect of Nazi propaganda in Austria as the very real difference in the two countries' economies.[37]

The Nazis never tired of repeating the old legend, so popular in the twenties, that little Alpine Austria was simply not *lebensfähig* (viable).

Economic salvation, they argued, could come only from Germany. Of course, they carefully avoided mentioning that Austria's miserable situation was in part caused by Germany itself.[38]

Nazis in both Austria and Germany were divided about the usefulness of German economic pressure. Those Austrian Nazis hurt by the German boycott favored reopening the boundary as a means of bringing more Nazi propaganda into the country. And even German diplomats admitted in 1934 that the economic measures were unlikely to bring about a change in the Austrian government in the near future. A diplomatic report of 2 June said that the attempted disruption of the Austrian tourist trade and other measures such as a Nazi smokers' strike had brought some "hardships" for the Austrian government, "but no decision." The Austrian budget, the report continued, was fairly well balanced, the currency was sound, and exports were actually increasing.[39]

Illegal Nazi Propaganda: Phase One

As already noted, the other half of Hitler's new policy of 26 May 1933 was a "massive propaganda offensive."[40] This new wave of propaganda was to take a variety of forms, some nearly as violent as the Nazi bombing attacks, and some more subtle and insidious. Though both forms were used simultaneously, it was the more violent and noisy type that predominated in the beginning, especially between June 1933 and February 1934.

In promoting propaganda the Nazis took advantage of a relatively new medium: the radio. Safe in Munich, Landesleiter Habicht was able to direct the world's first radio "war" against Austria. In July 1933, he began a series of eighty-four speeches carried from transmitters in Munich, Leipzig, Breslau, and Stuttgart. Habicht himself gave twenty-one of these talks, which ridiculed the Austrian government and called on Austrians to carry out new acts of terror. The other speeches were made mostly by Nazi refugees who belonged to the party's Landesleitung in Munich. Austrian protests against these broadcasts were answered with the assurance that they were merely intended for the information of the German people.[41]

Equally innovative for nominally peacetime conditions was the Nazis' use of the airplane to literally spread their propaganda over Austria. During the second half of July 1933, several German planes flew over Austrian territory and dropped leaflets urging the population to withdraw their bank deposits and to refuse to pay their taxes. Again, the German government "could do nothing" to prevent these incursions, although they were finally halted in August after the intervention of the Western powers, including Italy.[42]

More of a nuisance than a real threat, but equally difficult for the Austrian government to control, was the use of loudspeakers in German territory. One gendarme in the border town of Hallein, for example, reported how in March 1933 Bavarian Nazis set up a powerful loudspeaker within a few meters of the Austrian border and then broadcast insults against the Austrian government from early in the morning until late at night. Interspersed between the pejoratives were military marches and nationalistic songs, which could be heard for over two kilometers.[43]

Young Nazis particularly enjoyed dreaming up ingenious ways to display the forbidden swastika. Hair was sometimes cut in the form of a swastika in the middle of the scalp. Fireworks were sent into the air with parachutes holding the Nazi emblem and reclining sunbathers along the Danube sometimes joined to form the shape of the twisted cross. Cattle were branded with it and burning candles in its shape were floated down rivers. Swastikas were frequently painted on walls or even formed by forest fires. Dogs and pigs were sometimes named "Dollfuss" so that they might be cursed and kicked.

The purpose of these antics was less to win converts than it was to prove that the Nazi party was still very much alive and fully capable of defying the regime. More mature Nazis admitted that the displaying of swastikas had little or no real propaganda value and believed that dangerous pranks even weakened the strength of the party. It was safer and more effective, they believed, to place propaganda leaflets in mail boxes.[44]

Illegal Nazi Propaganda: Phase Two

By February 1934 it was becoming increasingly apparent to Hitler that neither terror nor the more extreme forms of propaganda could bring down the Dollfuss government. The German Foreign Office had reached the same conclusion as early as the summer of 1933. Concerned that Austrian Nazi activities might endanger other more important areas of German foreign policy (such as the Saar and disarmament), the state secretary in the German Foreign Ministry, Bernhard von Bülow, summoned Theo Habicht to Berlin for a conference on 31 July 1933. Habicht assured him that everything in Austria "was going according to plan." Austria's economic situation was growing steadily more intolerable and would soon bring the collapse of the regime. His radio broadcasts to Austria did not break any international law and the airplane propaganda "raids" did not have an "official" character. The terror was being carried out by individuals acting on their own initiative and Habicht was attempting to control it. Bülow was not entirely satisfied by these explanations and told Habicht that the international community would not accept the argument that the radio broadcasts did not technically violate international law.[45]

In a letter to Foreign Minister Neurath, Bülow observed that it was "understandable how Habicht could get so absorbed in his job that he could ignore Germany's other foreign-policy questions." The state secretary went on to urge Neurath, however, to see Hitler and impress upon him the dangers involved in the Austrian situation.[46] But when the foreign minister passed on Bülow's warning to Hitler two weeks later, the Reich chancellor merely became infuriated and railed against Mussolini's recent intervention in the Austrian question. He had already ordered the cessation of the airplane raids, but would not agree to end all forms of propaganda.[47]

Hitler changed his mind, however, about the wisdom of his laissez faire policy toward Austria as a result of events in February 1934. The Dollfuss government displayed surprising strength in crushing a three-day Socialist uprising in Vienna. And a radio speech by Habicht promising Dollfuss a temporary "armistice" in the Nazi-government "war" only angered international public opinion, especially in Italy. The speech was generally interpreted abroad as proof that Habicht and other German authorities were directing the Nazi terror campaign.[48]

In response to the international uproar, Hitler repeated his order of August 1933 to end the violence in Austria. In the place of terror an increased emphasis was to be given to the more subtle forms of propaganda while at the same time expanding the illegal NSDAP. A diplomat in the German Foreign Ministry summarized the new policy as follows: "The fight in Austria will continue under the old leadership but will be fundamentally changed. The use of force and direct attacks [on the Austrian government] will be avoided in the press and radio. The emphasis will be placed on the strengthening of internal Austrian propaganda and the organization and growth of the party which should lead to a situation where no government can last without Nazi cooperation."[49] Special weight in the future was to be given to the achievements of National Socialism in Germany since the Machtergreifung.[50]

The new "soft-sell" propaganda approach was actually far more difficult to combat than the older, more blatant variety, which had outraged international public opinion. Such propaganda could take an almost unlimited number of forms. Even before the German trade war was nominally ended with Austria in July 1936, all aspects of culture imported into Austria from Germany had to be carefully screened for subtle Nazi influences. Films, stage plays, and even concerts could have Nazi overtones. Austrian authors and teachers could be influenced by the censored German publishing industry.[51]

For two or three weeks after the termination of Habicht's broadcasts, the Austrian Nazis were in a state of leaderless confusion.[52] But with terror, radio broadcasts, and airplane raids all ruled out because of their negative effect on Germany's diplomatic posture, and with public speeches, demonstrations, rallies, and posters against the law, it finally became clear that the illegal Nazi press would have to assume a new importance.

The Nazi press between 1933 and 1934 consisted of two types: legal newspapers, which were often secretly subsidized from Germany and which took as pro-Nazi a stand as they dared, and an underground illegal press. The outlawing of the overtly Nazi newspapers in the early summer of 1933 forced the Nazis to think of more subtle ways of getting their message to the Austrian public. Thus, for example, they bought the inexpensive Viennese newspaper called *Depeschen* through "straw men" and for a time were able to operate the paper as an "independent daily" despite the close scrutiny of the police.[53] Two other Viennese newspapers, the *Neue Zeitung* and the *Zwölf Uhr Blatt* were secretly financed by a pro-Nazi German, Prince Philipp Josias von Coburg.

Far better known and more successful, at least for a time, was the *Wiener Neueste Nachrichten*. Having little else of a legal nature to read, Viennese Nazis subscribed to that paper almost exclusively so that its circulation rose to over 50,000 by July 1934. It too was subsidized from Germany and printed numerous anti-Semitic articles while carefully avoiding anything critical of Germany. But the censorship of this and other disguised Nazi newspapers, like the *Innsbrucker Nachrichten*, remained so tight that even German diplomats doubted whether it was worth continuing the subsidies.[54]

There were three categories of illegal press propaganda: the centralized variety was used for the whole of Austria; regional propaganda was intended for the provinces; and local publications were geared for individual towns. The central propaganda originated in Munich and consisted of leaflets, brochures, and sporadically appearing newspapers, all of which were smuggled into Austria at Passau.[55] Centralized propaganda was aided by a news service whose job it was to keep abreast of the plans, tendencies, and equipment of the government and rival groups, such as the Socialists and Communists. At the same time it was supposed to establish a common Weltanschauung and foreign policy. It was likewise responsible for distributing news to the various Austrian *Gaue*.[56]

The most important illegal Nazi newspaper, and perhaps the only one having a national circulation, was the *Österreichischer Beobachter*. Its sixty thousand copies began appearing on 28 July 1936; the Nazis fondly referred to it as the "littlest and biggest newspaper in Austria."[57] The *ÖB* succeeded in giving the impression that there was still a central party leadership in Austria itself even when the leaders were forced to remain underground.[58]

Propaganda for the individual Austrian states was printed locally but followed certain general themes. However, it concentrated on items of local importance. The publications consisted mostly of very small mimeographed newspapers distributed from bicycles or motorcycles by young people thrilled with the idea of defying authority and proving their courage. Local propaganda was confined mostly to the scattering of swastikas.[59]

It was nearly impossible for Austrian authorities to suppress the flow of propaganda, either foreign or domestic. The police did occasionally discover printing presses, but strict party discipline prevented them from all being discovered at any one time. Some propaganda was printed in northern Yugoslavia, where there was a German-speaking minority. This material was then smuggled across the border in automobiles or even in baby carriages at times when a "friendly" customs official was on duty.[60]

Goals and Themes of Nazi Propaganda

The illegal Nazi press could not be described in any literal sense as "news" papers, because the stories consisted almost entirely of opinions. Nor was it really any more effective at winning converts to National Socialism than its legal predecessor had been. Its essential goal was to maintain morale during the five years the party was outlawed. To a discouraged Parteigenosse, frustrated over his inability to topple the hated government, making and distributing propaganda had a certain therapeutic value as a means of reconfirming his own dedication to the cause.[61]

The illegal press made repeated exhortations to the faithful to believe in the party's leadership and to maintain unity. Certain anniversaries, like Hitler's birthday, 19 June (the day on which the party was outlawed), or later, the 25 July Putsch of 1934, were celebrated by special issues. On 19 June 1937, for example, the *Österreichischer Beobachter* declared that "the whole world" knew that "the Nazi freedom fighters [had] been brutally mistreated by a shameless dictatorship." The paper went on to say that the Austrian Nazis would never succumb to brute force.[62]

Although attacks on the "political" clergy were still commonplace in the Nazi press, care was taken to use this weapon only where the population was considered receptive, as in Vienna, in other large cities, and in Carinthia. In other, more religious areas (like the Tyrol), the Nazis posed as friends of the Church. Direct attacks on the Catholic religion itself were verboten in order to facilitate a reconciliation with the Church once power was achieved. Party members who forgot this rule could expect a severe reprimand.[63]

The Nazi press pointed out that National Socialism insisted merely that there is an inequality of bodies between the races whereas the Catholic Church was concerned only with the equality of souls.[64] When a woman wrote to Gauleiter Frauenfeld protesting Nazi racism, he replied by quoting Jesus' statement that he had not come to bring peace on earth but the sword. Nevertheless, the Nazi effort to win over Catholics was far from being a complete success. Many Austrians continued to believe that "all forms of Christianity [were] endangered [in Germany] by a new hedonistic paganism."[65]

These and other themes expressed in the illegal Nazi press did not differ radically from those of the legal press prior to June 1933. There were, however, a few changes in the contents of the Nazi propaganda during the five years between 1933 and 1938. After 1934 the connections between the Austrian and German Nazis were played down.[66] Peasants were assured that the Nazis respected the sanctity of their property whereas in Vienna and other industrial areas the alleged socialist character of National Socialism was stressed. Just prior to the outbreak of the Ethiopian War, Nazi propaganda against Italy ceased and Italy's differences with Britain and France were noted in the Nazi press.[67]

Illogical as it may seem for a party that had been bitterly denouncing democracy since 1919, the Nazis suddenly became staunch defenders of the *Rechtsstaat* idea (a state based on the rule of law) once they had been outlawed. The Nazi press of both Austria and Germany invariably depicted the Austrian Nazis as "freedom fighters" bravely fighting against the "system," which lacked any legal basis or popular mandate.[68]

Humor was another useful weapon in the Nazis' propaganda arsenal. Although Nazis in general were known primarily for their deadly seriousness, the Austrian Nazis shared the barbed wit of their countrymen. Dozens of jokes ridiculing the government originated in Nazi ranks and circulated throughout the general public.[69] Many of these stories were plays on words and therefore are untranslatable.

An exception was known as "The Last Triumph" and purported to be a conversation between the German and Austrian chancellors. Hitler told of all the things that were being done in Germany. Schuschnigg at first couldn't think of a good comparison. Finally he blurted out: "We hang more people in a week than you do in a whole year!"

In another story, an Austrian state minister asked a German party leader how strong the opposition was in Germany. " 'Unimportant,' was the answer. 'Just over 6 million.' Excitedly the Austrian shot back: 'It's no larger than that in our country, too.' "

Still another tale described three different types of brassieres. One, called the "Hitler bra," was used for uplifting the masses. The "Mussolini bra" was good for holding the masses together. The "Schusschnigg bra," on the other hand, was used for covering false pretenses.

Finally, to illustrate Austria's dependence on Italy, there was an anecdote of how God asked Hitler, Pierre Laval (the foreign minister of France), and Schuschnigg what their favorite wishes were. Hitler said he wanted to bring all Germans under his leadership. Laval wanted all people to become Frenchmen. Schuschnigg at first didn't know what to say. He fumbled around in his pockets for a long time and then at last said: "Mussolini gave me a piece of paper with everything on it, but I lost it."

Illegal Nazi Propaganda: How Effective?

It is far easier to describe Nazi propaganda than it is to evaluate its effectiveness. Although it is unlikely that even true believers swallowed all the material, its credibility was enhanced by two factors. First, the Austrian people distrusted the legally published periodical press because they knew it was highly censored. Consequently, there was a tendency, not uncommon in dictatorships, to disbelieve official publications even when they were completely accurate.[70] This lack of confidence in their own press somehow made the Austrian people receptive to articles and even rumors put out by the Nazis.[71] Nevertheless, Austrians were by no means totally naive about Nazi propaganda. They were well aware, for example, of the suppression of all criticism in Germany; and they knew that one could not believe everything printed in the German newspapers.[72]

Secondly, much of the Nazi propaganda contained more than a particle of truth. And as two specialists on the subject have put it: "No propagandist worth his mettle will prefer an untruth to a truth, if the truth will do the job."[73] There were plenty of achievements in Germany that Nazi propagandists could "point to with pride." Hitler's foreign policy successes in the Saar, rearmament, and the remilitarization of the Rhineland were indisputably impressive. German economic progress, particularly in the area of unemployment, was equally concrete and stood out in stark contrast to the dreary conditions in Austria.

Even if the Nazis' propaganda did not have as its sole or even primary goal the winning of new converts, there can be no doubt, as Austrian officials themselves admitted, that it helped to maintain the morale of party members while sowing distrust and pessimism among government loyalists.[74]

All in all, political power, which seemed tantalizingly close to the Austrian Nazi party in the spring of 1933, remained beyond their grasp during the succeeding year. All the proven methods, employed so successfully by the Nazis in Germany, failed to bring about the *Machtübernahme* (takeover of power) in Austria. Although encouraging progress was made by the Nazis in local elections in the spring of 1933, that road to power was blocked by Chancellor Dollfuss, who prohibited further elections and allowed Parliament to "dissolve itself." The Nazis were forbidden from wearing their uniforms, marching, giving public speeches, or printing newspapers. Finally, the party itself was outlawed on 19 June and large numbers of Nazis were sent to detention camps. These actions by the Dollfuss regime presented the Nazis with a totally new situation. Never had a government in Germany shown such determination to suppress the NSDAP.

The Nazis retaliated in every conceivable way. Backed by a virtual economic boycott of Austria by Germany they bombed public facilities and private businesses, and launched a "massive propaganda offensive" that utilized every technological device possible. But neither radio broadcasts nor legal and illegal newspapers, nor various adolescent pranks worked. By the summer of 1934 political power was becoming an ever-receding mirage. Chancellor Dollfuss had crushed a Socialist uprising and exiled or imprisoned most of the Nazi leadership. To the befuddled Nazis, only some extraordinary action could reverse this situation and realize their long-anticipated dream of power.

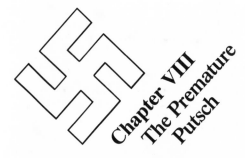

By the end of 1933 and the beginning of 1934 Theo Habicht and his Austrian Nazi followers were becoming increasingly frustrated. The buoyant optimism of the previous spring had steadily dissipated as legal propaganda, terror, economic pressure, and finally illegal propaganda all failed to intimidate Chancellor Dollfuss and the Austrian government. Their original objective of an Austro-German Anschluss had given way in the face of Germany's overall foreign-policy goals, to the more subtle policy of Gleichschaltung. But by the end of 1933 the Austrian chancellor's growing strength had forced Habicht to scale down his immediate ambitions once more to mere participation in the federal government. When even this modest ambition was not attained, Habicht, in desperation, resorted to a Putsch, only to fail once again. It would take a virtual revolution in the European balance of power in 1935–36 to improve the fortunes of the Austrian Nazi party.

The Habicht-Dollfuss Negotiations

Habicht had turned to negotiations as a means of subverting the Austrian government in the spring of 1933. The talks went nowhere, however, as Habicht was not interested in the two ministerial positions Dollfuss offered him, and the chancellor rejected the Nazi demand for new elections. Not until September would serious discussions begin anew.

Both Dollfuss and the Nazis imagined that they would be the big winners in any negotiated agreement. The Nazis, with the example of the Hitler-Papen coalition and the Gleichschaltung of Danzig in mind, were convinced that they could dominate any coalition by means of their growing and dynamic organization.[1] Dollfuss, on the other hand, believed a settlement with the

Nazis would soothe strained Austro-German relations, solidify his position vis-à-vis the restless Heimwehr, and reduce his dependence on Italy. He also expected that such an agreement would increase the army's reliability. The chancellor feared, and with good reason, that if he did not reach an understanding with the Nazis, the Heimwehr would, and at his expense.[2]

These negotiations, the first phase of which extended from September to November 1933, were initiated by Habicht from his Munich Landesleitung, although neither he nor Dollfuss actually took part in the discussions themselves. The Nazi demands, which remained fairly consistent throughout the talks, were outlined by an official in the German Foreign Ministry:

[1] Complete equality of rights for the two partners, i.e. the new Austrian cabinet to be made up of the Dollfuss group and the Habicht group, fifty percent each, with Dollfuss receiving the post of federal chancellor and Habicht that of vice-chancellor with enlarged responsibilities.
[2] . . . Lifting the ban on the party, the SA, the SS, the National Socialist press; cancellation of the expulsions. . . .
[3] Naturalization [of Habicht]. . . .
[4] The most vigorous [joint] struggle against Marxism. . . .
[5] The establishment of a friendly relationship with the Reich.[3]

Dollfuss, for his part, remained adamant that any agreement had to include the renunciation of all organizational ties between Germany and the Austrian NSDAP, the abandonment of any encouragement or toleration of propaganda directed against the Austrian government, and the end of all German interference in the internal affairs of Austria.[4] A letter by the German consul in Linz to the Foreign Ministry reported that Dollfuss was willing to lift the ban on the Nazi party, but not to allow new elections.[5]

The first phase of the Habicht-Dollfuss negotiations remained fruitless allegedly because the chancellor felt the Nazis' terms were too high. But the real reason was more likely that neither side regarded a compromise as absolutely necessary at the time. Dollfuss changed his mind, however, when Mussolini put pressure on him to eliminate the Social Democratic party. The Duce was hoping that such a move by the Austrian chancellor would offend France and Britain and thus make Dollfuss more dependent on Italy. The chancellor's response was to strengthen his hand by reopening negotiations with the Nazis.

In mid-December (1933) Dollfuss asked a confidant to arrange a meeting with Habicht through the Landesleiter's representative, Franz Schattenfroh. A meeting in Vienna was finally arranged for 8 January 1934. The Austrian ambassador to Berlin, Stefan Tauschitz, had secured Hitler's approval of the conference. Moreover, the German Foreign Office was willing to agree to Dollfuss's wish for the cessation of hostilities, the postponement of new elections, and the recognition of the sovereignty and independence of Austria.[6]

The only permission Dollfuss neglected to attain was the Heimwehr's. Not until 7 January did the chancellor finally inform Starhemberg and Emil Fey (the new vice-chancellor) of his intentions. Starhemberg, fearing the immediate end of the Heimwehr's raison d'être, called the scheduled meeting *Wahnsinn* (madness) and threatened to break with Dollfuss should he go ahead with his plans.[7] Thus Dollfuss was forced to cancel his meeting with the Nazis at the very last minute, citing recent acts of Nazi terror as his excuse.[8]

Having failed in his negotiations with Habicht, Dollfuss turned to two local and relatively moderate Nazis, Alfred Frauenfeld and Hermann Neubacher. In late May or early June 1934 the chancellor, in a possible attempt to split the Nazis, offered Frauenfeld a position in the federal cabinet. But Starhemberg once again heard of the negotiations and wanted Frauenfeld arrested. Habicht was equally unenthusiastic about the talks and repeatedly ordered the former Gauleiter to leave Austria, threatening him with reprisals if he refused. Facing danger from two sides, Frauenfeld finally moved to Germany, where he was "ungraciously received" by the Landesleiter and assigned to minor propaganda activities.

Still later negotiations in June between Dollfuss and Neubacher also proved fruitless. The chancellor once again rejected the demand that Habicht be made the chancellor or vice-chancellor.[9]

The July Putsch: Motives and Early Rumors

The failure of the negotiations left Habicht and the Austrian Nazis more baffled than ever. Adding to their sense of frustration was Hitler's new policy, which he had launched on 2 March 1934. According to his orders, all "direct attacks on the Austrian Government in the press and radio [were] to be strictly avoided."[10] Once tranquillity had returned to Austria the Germans would try to gain freedom for the Austrian Nazi movement. But this time the Austrian Nazis would not be influenced by the Reich.[11]

Habicht, to say the least, was uninspired about the new policy and pointed out to the German foreign minister, Konstantin von Neurath, that "the total ban on propaganda against the Austrian Government, as well as the instructions issued to him personally not to make any more speeches of any kind against Austria, could result in the gradual disintegration of the National Socialist movement in Austria."[12]

As early as the summer of 1933 Habicht had had a hard time controlling the activities of his Austrian followers; in October he had to threaten them with "sharp action against everyone who did not obey."[13] Beginning on 27 April, Nazi terror resumed with an assassination attempt against Emil Fey in Salzburg. Thereafter it continued almost unabated throughout May, June, and July, except for brief interludes during the Hitler-Mussolini conference in Venice in mid-June, and for a time following the Röhm Purge of 30 June. This activity still had the general objective of ruining the Austrian tourist trade and weakening the morale of the Austrian people.[14] Some of it was directed against public buildings, barracks, prisons, and other government buildings as well as against judges, police officials, and politicians. Most explosions, however, occurred near tourist areas, waterworks, and power plants.

It is impossible to say who was responsible for this complete collapse of the "evolutionary" policy initiated in March. As the leader of the Austrian party, however, it was Theo Habicht who bore the ultimate obligation to control these activities. The consequences of the party's reckless defiance of international law were the diplomatic isolation of Germany and the near destruction of the party itself.

The climax of the new wave of terror came early in the afternoon of 25 July when 154 members of the Viennese SS Standarte Eighty-nine, disguised in uniforms of the Austrian army, broke into the federal chancellery on the Ballhausplatz in Vienna and mortally wounded Engelbert Dollfuss. This act was just the beginning of the notorious July Putsch, which ended three days later after 153 Nazis had been killed in battle (or later executed) and thousands more had fled to Germany and Yugoslavia.

The story of the Putsch, which has been told and retold in almost excruciating detail, need not be repeated here. Still of interest, however, is what induced the Austrian Nazis to take this desperate gamble, why the action misfired, and what impact its failure had on the subsequent history of the illegal party.

The idea of a Putsch was an old one. The first rumors of a plot to overthrow the government reached the German Legation in Vienna on 26 July 1933, only five weeks after the party had been outlawed. This plan, to be carried out in September, was never implemented. The SA also began to work on Putsch plans during the summer, which led to conversations in October between Ernst Röhm, Hermann Reschny (the leader of the Austrian SA), Habicht, and

Proksch. At a meeting in Passau the conspirators agreed that the Putsch should take place on 9 November (the tenth anniversary of the Beer Hall Putsch). It was supposed to begin in the Nazi stronghold of Carinthia and lead to a nationwide strike. A lack of weapons in Carinthia, however, prevented the execution of this plan.[15]

The rumors subsided during the fall and winter months of late 1933 and early 1934 while the Habicht-Dollfuss negotiations were in progress. But with their complete collapse in January rumors again began to circulate.

One of these tales, which reached the ears of German diplomats in Vienna, was reported on 31 January 1934. It is particularly interesting because it helps explain the failure of the actual Putsch six months later. The German military attaché, Lieutenant General Wolfgang Muff, wrote to Berlin that "the Austrian SA leaders [had] received from their *Obergruppenführer*, Hermann Reschny, the definite order from Munich to make preparations for action on March 15. . . . This order [was] to be kept strictly secret from the political leadership of the party both in Munich and in Austria, so that it [could] not be prevented from these quarters."[16] Muff went on to say that his informant had told him of a serious quarrel which had broken out between Habicht and Reschny, and for this reason Reschny had made his decision secretly in order to present Habicht with a fait accompli. What Muff did not say was that Reschny had removed the SA Obergruppe Austria from Habicht's jurisdiction, and that together with the Austrian Legion he had control over ten thousand well-trained men.[17]

In May, Baron Gustav Otto von Wächter, a thirty-three-year-old lawyer, son of a former defense minister, and in 1934 Habicht's representative in Austria, told an official of the German Foreign Ministry that pressure against the Austrian Nazis had recently become so great that if martial law were employed against them it would be difficult to prevent an insurrection. A revolt was all the more likely because Austrian Nazis had gained access to considerable quantities of explosives as a result of the Socialist uprising in February. Inasmuch as a rebellion was virtually inevitable (Wächter argued), it would be preferable to have an organized one rather than a spontaneous one that could be easily crushed. His pleas went unheeded.[18]

Wächter gave an even more candid description of conditions within the Austrian Nazi party in a second conversation with a German diplomat two days later. Extremist tendencies within the party, he said, were

> constantly on the increase; . . . uniformity of leadership was lacking.
> The SA did what it wanted. . . . The political leadership at the
> same time introduced measures which sometimes meant the exact

opposite. . . . Everyone supposed that a solution was being prepared and that, by his basic orders, the Führer desired to create the necessary peaceful and favorable atmosphere for the forthcoming negotiations. But when nothing followed in the meantime, and on the other hand the countermeasures of the Austrian administration grew more and more brutal and incisive from day to day, the radical elements moved afresh and came forward with the statement that the chancellor had issued his orders only for tactical reasons, but was inwardly in agreement with every manly act of opposition. . . . They were now working on this principle.[19]

In short, Wächter was saying that a psychological crisis was building up within the Austrian Nazi party during the spring and early summer of 1934. This situation was very reminiscent of the internal tension preceding Hitler's Beer Hall Putsch in 1923. Nazi "dynamism" (or "eagerness for power") could not be restrained indefinitely.

Radical members of the party, particularly in the paramilitary SA and SS formations, wanted action, and they wanted it soon. Their belonging to an outlawed, and from their point of view "persecuted," organization only enhanced their impatience. As mostly unemployed young men they had no desire, and saw no need, to wait for several years while the German evolutionary policy of subtle, subversive propaganda had time to work its course. They were either ignorant of or indifferent to the requirements of German foreign policy, and like the German SA after 1923, they had difficulty taking seriously Hitler's avowals of legality.[20] Their high hopes in the spring of 1933 for an early seizure of power had by now dissipated almost completely. After the crushing of the Socialist uprising in February, the Dollfuss regime appeared to be stronger than ever while the Nazi movement, as in Germany in the fall of 1932, appeared to be on the brink of disintegration.[21]

The latter fear was by no means imaginary. Relations between leaders of the impoverished SA and SS, and also between those two militant groups and the relatively well-heeled political organization, had long been bad, and were now growing even worse.[22] According to at least two German diplomats, the Austrian party was no longer growing in the early summer of 1934, and may even have been shrinking, at least in Vorarlberg. Nazi terrorism itself was driving some "fence-sitting" Austrians into the Dollfuss camp, and the closing of the Austro-German border to Nazi propaganda depressed the Austrian Nazis' morale.[23]

Feeling deserted by the German Foreign Ministry, and sometimes even by the exiled party leadership in Munich (though not by Hitler), the Austrian

Nazis, simplistically saw no other alternative beyond resignation and renunciation on the one hand, and the violent overthrow of the government on the other. Like the Beer Hall Putsch, therefore, the July Putsch was a sign of weakness, not strength.

Habicht, Reschny, and the Final Preparations

The question of who made the final decision to go ahead with the Putsch has never been clearly established. Later attempts by participants to blame others or (after 1938) to claim undue credit for the action have only obscured the issue. The evidence, however, points to Theo Habicht and Alfred Frauenfeld.

Since the beginning of 1934 at the latest, Habicht's position had been growing increasingly precarious. Reference has already been made to the quarrel between Habicht and Reschny, which induced the latter to plan a Putsch for March.[24] By January the Landesleiter found himself caught between the radical SA, which demanded more action from Habicht, and relatively moderate individuals like Walter Riehl and Alfred Frauenfeld. The two Austrians felt Habicht's policies were already too radical and preferred a strictly native leadership. To make matters worse, there were grumblings among party members about Habicht's allegedly "lavish" style of living. Many SA men and party intellectuals were also upset and depressed by the events surrounding the so-called Röhm Putsch. Even Hitler was unhappy about Habicht's leadership and the recent slow progress of the party in Austria.[25] In short, there was little time left to the state director. The SA was out of control and preparing a separate action, the moderates were disgruntled, and Hitler was impatient. If Habicht wished to hang on to his power he would quickly have to do something decisive.

The trouble was, such a "decisive" act was likely to run counter to the recently adopted German foreign policy of Gleichschaltung and peaceful penetration. It would represent the very kind of unwarranted German interference in domestic Austrian affairs that the German Foreign Office had repeatedly warned might provoke an international anti-German reaction. And it would come at a time when Germany was still militarily weak.

The only apparent way for Habicht to escape this dilemma was to make a Putsch appear to be a purely domestic revolt provoked by the repressive Dollfuss regime. Even so, Habicht hesitated to act until after the Venice meeting between Hitler and Mussolini in mid-June failed to have any effect on the Austrian chancellor.

The pretext Habicht was looking for came on 18 June 1934, when the Dollfuss government announced that the death penalty would no longer be restricted to cases involving martial law. This decree seemed to confirm Wächter's earlier argument that Dollfuss was hoping the execution of a Nazi would lead to a spontaneous uprising which the government could easily smash.[26]

Apparently sometime during the spring of 1934 Habicht put Baron von Wächter in charge of the political aspects of a prospective Putsch. The baron later claimed he had accepted the appointment only on the assumption that the action had been approved by Hitler's deputy, Rudolf Hess.[27] However, this contention seems more than dubious in view of Wächter's obvious effort to establish an alibi for the action when he spoke with two officials of the German Foreign Office in late May.

Wächter and Habicht had two precedents—one positive, the other negative—to use as lessons when planning the Putsch. In the summer of 1933 the Nazis had learned that force could be successfully used against the government when they freed the imprisoned Gauleiter of Tyrol-Vorarlberg, Franz Hofer.[28] But they had later learned from the Socialist uprising in February that Vienna and the government could not be seized from the outside. Only the capture of the government in its entirety seemed to hold the prospect of success.[29]

Nevertheless, the SA of Vienna and Lower Austria were completely excluded from the planning of the Putsch even though Vienna was destined to be the heart of the rebellion. Fridolin Glass, the leader of the SS Standarte Eighty-nine, which was supposed to capture the Dollfuss cabinet, saw the Putsch as an opportunity to weaken the Austrian SA decisively. Habicht's only connection with the SA was through Hermann Reschny, who, it was hoped, would lead an SA uprising in the federal provinces. But not surprisingly, Reschny refused to accept any second-class status in the Putsch. A successful Putsch, he feared, could only benefit his bitter rival, Habicht, as well as the SS. Once he received definite word of the final plans on 16 July he secretly relayed the information to the Austrian security forces. Reschny had been preparing his own plans for many months; however, his SA men would not be properly armed with smuggled-in weapons until September. Consequently, when the Putsch came many SA leaders were taken utterly by surprise.[30]

Habicht's hopes for success, like Hitler's in 1923, rested on the expectation, or at least the wish, that the army would join an armed uprising. Contacts with various high-ranking officers in the Austrian army were made before the Putsch. And certainly many Nazi sympathizers could be found in military ranks. Pro-Nazi soldiers had joined a Deutsche Soldatengewerkschaft (later called a Soldatenbund or German Soldiers' League). Some of these men were expelled from the army and proceeded to form the same SS Standarte Eighty-nine, which invaded the Ballhausplatz on 25 July.[31] Moreover, some Nazis believed (quite erroneously, as it turned out) that the reserve and retired officers of the Imperial and Royal Army were secretly pro-Nazi. In reality the Nazis were relatively successful only in recruiting that generation which had fought in the World War as young men.[32] But in any event Dollfuss had been careful to dismiss pro-Nazi officers from the army. As late as 5 June 1934 General Muff had warned the German Foreign Office that "today, and probably for a considerable time yet, the armed forces are still firmly in the hands of the government."[33]

Habicht also grossly underestimated the size of the Austrian army and the paramilitary formations that supported the government. According to his calculations the army had only 15,000 men; even adding the gendarmerie and paramilitary formations the regime, he believed, could count on only 44,000 troops. The German Foreign Ministry, on the other hand, estimated with far more accuracy that the Austrian government could rely on 22,000 men in the army and 74,000 armed supporters altogether.[34]

Somewhat more realistic and encouraging was Habicht's appraisal of the internal weaknesses of the Dollfuss government. He was correct in telling an officer of the German Legation in Vienna that sharp differences existed between Starhemberg and Fey, and between Starhemberg and Dollfuss. Habicht also pointed out that factionalism was rife within the Heimwehr as a whole. And, of course, Habicht knew he could count on the active support of the Nazis' armed ally, the Styrian Heimatschutz (now part of the SA), as well as the former governor of Styria and current ambassador to Italy, Anton Rintelen.[35] The latter was to be the new chancellor in a Nazi-dominated government which would hold new elections and later a plebiscite on the Anschluss question.

Habicht put the finishing touches on the Putsch plans in a meeting in Zürich with Fridolin Glass. The Austrian chancellor and his cabinet would be captured before Dollfuss had the opportunity to visit Mussolini in Italy, a visit that was expected to consolidate the chancellor's position. Habicht appears to have left other details to the illegal Nazi leaders inside Austria, above all to those in the Vienna SS.[36]

Course and Failure of the Putsch

The Putschists had three targets, which they hoped to capture simultaneously: the entire cabinet meeting at the Ballhausplatz in Vienna, the national radio station or "Ravag" (also in the capital), from which the revolution would be announced, and President Miklas, who was vacationing in Carinthia. In none of these aims were the rebels completely successful.

Although the Ravag was captured briefly by the Putschists, the Nazis broadcast only one quick message announcing the "resignation" of Dollfuss and his replacement by Anton Rintelen. This announcement was to be the signal for a mass uprising throughout the country. But the proclamation was too short and general to be fully effective.[37] Incredibly, the Nazis played records after their announcement. Nor were any helpful announcements made by German stations, much to the bitter disappointment of the Putschists in the provinces.[38]

At the Chancellery, the disguised rebels had little difficulty in overpowering the few (unarmed) guards, who mistook them for soldiers and policemen. After entering the building, they captured its 150 inhabitants, including part (but only part) of the cabinet. The chancellor was mortally wounded (under still mysterious circumstances, but possibly as he was trying to escape). But within a short time the Ballhausplatz was surrounded by members of the police and Heimwehr. The Putschists were forced to surrender after negotiating at length over a guaranteed free passage to the German frontier. The government withdrew the guarantee, however, after learning of the chancellor's death.[39]

Heavy fighting also took place in the Austrian provinces, especially in Styria and Carinthia. However, with the Putsch in Vienna already squelched, and with Hitler denouncing the revolt, the cause was lost. For a short time the Nazis (or to be more exact, 2,800 members of the former Styrian Heimatschutz) may have controlled as much as two-thirds of Styria outside the capital of Graz. In fact, the role played by the old Heimatschutz was so great that after the rebellion the *Völkischer Beobachter* and several other German newspapers claimed that the revolt had been nothing more than a clash between the Heimatschutz and the progovernment Austrian Heimwehr, into which a few Nazis had been inadvertently drawn.[40]

Still heavier fighting occurred in neighboring Carinthia, which, according to SA plans, was supposed to be the center of its separately coordinated rebellion. The SA in Carinthia suffered less from a lack of arms and training than the SA in any other province and was unique in enjoying considerable popular support. Nevertheless, because earlier plans had not called for an uprising until September, and a general alert for a Putsch was not issued until 23 July, the Putschists were caught unprepared. The fighting did not begin until 27 July, when it had already ended in Vienna and Styria. Elsewhere there was only light fighting in Salzburg and Upper Austria. In those two states, as in Styria and Carinthia, the Putschists were inadequately trained and poorly armed.[41]

The Austrian Legion, now located in southern Bavaria, was somewhat better prepared in these respects and was alerted for action on the twenty-fifth. However, its training was still insufficient, and it had lost many men in previous terror raids into Austria or through flight. Austrian Nazi leaders were therefore opposed to an invasion by the Legion and doubted whether the general population would respond favorably to such an action. Consequently, the Legion made only minor border raids into Austria before Hitler, fearing an armed intervention by Italy, Yugoslavia, and possibly Czechoslovakia, ordered the Legion to cease further activity.[42]

The poorly planned attempt to kidnap President Miklas, who was vacationing at the Wörthersee in Carinthia, was also foiled. The police, who were informed about the plot, arrested the three conspirators before they could even approach the president.[43]

The Putsch as a whole collapsed for a variety of reasons: poor strategy, decentralization of authority, insufficient preparations, and many others. But two general causes stand out: overconfidence and internal rivalries. Despite their pre-Putsch frustrations and their awareness that Dollfuss was growing stronger, not weaker, the Austrian Nazis, like the Führer in the middle of the Second World War, had fallen victim to their own propaganda. "Eighty percent" of the general population, they imagined, would support a revolution.[44] In reality, the Austrians remained largely passive during the uprising, and the Austrian army, far from joining it as Habicht had hoped, played an active role in its suppression.[45] The same was true of 52,820 well-armed and well-trained members of the Heimwehr and other paramilitary formations who took the lead in crushing the revolt. Nowhere, in fact, did any members of the executive or the Heimwehr refuse to obey orders.[46] It is little wonder, then, that the Nazi rebels felt betrayed by Habicht's promises of support from the Austrian executive.

Actually, the Putsch was doomed before it even began. The state police had learned of the plot from a Nazi informant, Johann Dobler, twenty-four hours before its scheduled implementation. Police incompetence prevented Dollfuss from hearing the news until a scant forty-five minutes before the rebels burst into the Ballhausplatz. But the chancellor still had enough time and good sense to order some of his cabinet members to return to their respective ministries. Much more inexplicable, from the Nazi point of view, was their ignoring the fact that Starhemberg (recently appointed vice-chancellor) was safely beyond their reach in Italy.[47]

The other overarching cause for the Putsch failure was the rivalries within the Nazi party, especially those between the SA and the SS. Bitterness between the two militant organizations had been greatly intensified by the Röhm Purge of 30 June, when SA leaders in Germany were summarily dragged from their beds in the middle of the night and shot. So embittered was the SA over these events that the leadership of the Austrian SA in Munich, as we have seen, tried to warn the government in Vienna about the Putsch plans of the SS; unfortunately these warnings were not taken seriously.[48]

We have already noted how the Austrian SA had Putsch plans of its own that it sought to keep secret from Habicht. As a consequence, when in the middle of the Putsch itself the SS tried to get the SA in Vienna and Lower Austria to march to the Ballhausplatz and relieve the besieged SS Standarte Eighty-nine occupying the Chancellery, the SA units refused to move. They may never have received the order or they may have simply refused to obey it.[49] In the provinces the situation was reversed with the SS refusing to assist the beleagered SA.

Although the Nazis' own internal problems were quite sufficient to ruin their hopes for success, the Putsch would likely have failed in any case. Mussolini, who was awaiting the arrival of his personal friend and protegé, Dollfuss, was infuriated by the news of the assassination. He immediately ordered four Italian divisions (approximately 48,000 men) to join the more than 50,000 soldiers already stationed near the Brenner Pass to guard against a possible invasion of Austria by either the Austrian Legion or the German army.

Hitler and the Putsch

Hitler would doubtless have been overjoyed had the Putsch succeeded; in fact, there are indications that he reacted favorably to the first optimistic reports about the action. But he was outraged by its failure. His mortification was made all the greater by the fact that world public opinion held him at the very least morally, and in many cases personally, responsible for the brutal murder of the Austrian chancellor.[50] There appeared to be an obvious parallel between the events of 30 June and those of 25 July. And Hitler himself had identified the Nazi party with the German state when he wished to accuse Dollfuss of poisoning Austro-German relations.[51]

Hitler's real reponsibility for the Putsch, either direct or indirect, has aroused a considerable controversy among historians. Gerhard Weinberg says, "It may be assumed that the coup was launched with the knowledge and at least the tacit approval of Hitler," because some individuals in the party headquarters in Munich and in the German Legation in Vienna knew about the plot in advance.[52]

Weinberg's opinion appears to be a minority one, however. The European historians Jens Petersen, Dieter Ross, and Gerhard Jagschtz have all accepted Hermann Göring's testimony at the Nuremberg trials that Hitler was essentially tricked by Habicht into supporting a type of Putsch which never occurred, namely one led by the Austrian army.[53] We also know that as late as 16 July Hitler told Neurath he was in "no hurry" with regard to the Austrian question.[54]

On the other hand, Hitler was far from being totally uninformed about developments in Austria prior to the Putsch. The German envoy to Austria, Kurt Rieth, had already warned Hitler about the possibilities of a Putsch and its dangerous consequences in February 1934. Hitler's nonchalant response to Rieth's report was simply to say that he doubted whether a Putsch could be prevented in the long run. The interview ended in typical fashion with Hitler giving Rieth no specific instruction.[55]

Rieth's memorandum reveals the extent of Hitler's wishful thinking. We have to assume that he felt he could avoid any responsibility for an explosion in Austria by merely refusing to take a position on Austrian Nazi activities. Possibly he felt that to speak out sharply against a conspiracy would only demoralize the party and provide propaganda ammunition for the Austrian government.

Hitler's indirect responsibility indeed lies in his reluctance to make firm decisions of any kind. Thus he allowed Germany's policy toward Austria to drift after 1933 without any centralized control. There had been at least four separate bodies trying to exercise some authority: party leaders in Austria, the Munich Landesleitung under Habicht, the Berlin Foreign Office under Neurath (which had been staunchly opposed to a Putsch and a premature Anschluss), and Hitler, who had given the Landesleitung a largely free hand. The result was Hitler's only major prewar diplomatic defeat and the total isolation of Germany.

To salvage what he could from the wreckage, Hitler did his best to dissociate himself from the Putsch. He ordered the immediate closing of the

German-Austrian border; any rebel caught crossing it was to be arrested and put in a concentration camp. When Franz von Papen saw Hitler in Bayreuth (where the chancellor was attending the Wagnerian festival) on the twenty-sixth the Führer was still "hysterical" over the recklessness of the Austrian party.[56]

Hitler chose Papen to be the new special German envoy to Vienna in hopes that the former diplomat and chancellor, current vice-chancellor, and practicing Roman Catholic would have the necessary experience and prestige to ingratiate himself with the highly suspicious Austrians.[57] However, Papen accepted the appointment only on several conditions. Among them were that (1) Habicht had to be dismissed from his office and the State Directorate in Munich had to be dissolved; (2) the Reich German party was to sever all relations with the Austrian NSDAP and to refrain from interfering in any way with the internal affairs of Austria; (3) the Austrian party would have to get along with only the moral and perhaps economic help of the Reich; and (4) the Anschluss question was to be resolved not by force but by "evolutionary" means.[58]

Papen also insisted that Austrian Nazi leaders responsible for the Putsch were not to be rewarded by other high positions in the party. The German press was to cease all aggressive attacks on the Austrian government. Cultural and economic ties between the two countries were to be encouraged and all rash actions, which might drive together members of the old Christian Social party and the Heimwehr, were to be avoided.[59]

To guarantee that the first of his demands was fulfilled, Papen insisted that Hitler summon Habicht to Bayreuth and dismiss him on the spot. The Führer, in a rare display of humility, agreed.[60] Several months later Habicht was reported living in a small town in the Harz Mountains of central Germany, forbidden to speak publicly or to wear a uniform. Even his visitors were closely monitored.[61]

Only three days after Habicht's dismissal Hitler ordered the dissolution of the Austrian Landesleitung in Munich. Its members were almost all demoted when not placed in concentration camps. At best, they received only decorative positions in Germany.[62]

Hitler, of course, had no more abandoned his ultimate objective of absorbing Austria into the Third Reich than he had given up the idea of attaining power in Germany after the Beer Hall fiasco in 1923. Just as there are remarkable parallels between the Munich and Vienna Putsches, so too is there a striking similarity in how Hitler changed his tactics after these disasters. In both 1924 and 1934 he came to realize that violent, almost romantic, adventures would lead nowhere.

Rudolf Hess made this point in a letter to Alfred Frauenfeld, who had briefly become the "dean" of the exiled Nazis: "Hitler and his colleagues realize how harsh this ruling [of nonintervention] is, but it is necessary for Germany and not least of all for the NSDAP in Austria. As you know, the Führer decided after November 1923 to follow a completely new and legal policy, a policy which he stuck to and which was later proven to be right and successful. Be assured that the same will be true of the new policy for National Socialism in Austria.[63]

Hitler's post-Putsch policy was not as sharp a reversal of form as it would at first seem. As early as March 1934 he had decided to pursue a policy of "peaceful penetration" in Austria, eschewing even direct propaganda attacks on the Austrian government. But he had made the fateful (and nearly fatal) mistake of allowing "the old leadership," that is, Habicht and the Landesleitung in Munich, to implement that policy. After realizing his mistake, he had the ability to exercise great patience in carrying out his new policy. He had waited nearly a decade to gain power after the Munich calamity. Now he was prepared to wait another four years or more before taking control of Austria.

This time the Great Powers were to be given no obvious grounds for accusing Germany of interfering in Austria's internal affairs. The Austrian Nazi party was to be permitted no major role in subverting the Austrian government. Instead, it would be an instrument in taking over the state once international relations became more favorable.[64]

Hitler was not bluffing. On 18 August, he issued an order that "neither party authorities nor anyone else [could] discuss, either on the wireless or in the press, questions concerning German-Austrian policy, unless agreement had been previously reached between the Reich propaganda minister and the present minister in Vienna, Herr von Papen."[65]

Hess, in the same letter quoted earlier, told Frauenfeld, who hoped to gain influence over Germany's Austrian policy, that

> by order of the Führer, the Reich German party must have nothing
> to do with the National Socialists in Austria. . . . The Führer's order
> is not merely a formality, but is definitely an order which must be
> obeyed unconditionally. Failure to obey this order will entail severe
> punishment, which, in cases where the interests of the German Reich
> are threatened, may even include imprisonment.
>
> It is simply and solely a matter for the National Socialists residing
> in Austria [to decide] where and in what form they should build anew
> a purely Austrian NSDAP.[66]

Eight years earlier, Adolf Hitler had parted company with Karl Schulz because the latter was not willing to be a part of a single Nazi party controlled from Munich. Now the Führer was insisting to one of his most loyal followers that the Austrian Nazis *had* to form their own independent party.

The July Putsch stands as a watershed between the beginning of rapid Austrian Nazi growth in 1930 and the Anschluss in 1938. In the years after the establishment of the Hitler Bewegung in 1926 and before the Nazi Putsch in 1934 Hitler had followed an ambivalent policy toward the Austrian party. On the one hand he considered the party to be simply one part of the Gesamtpartei and subordinated it to the Reichsleitung of the party headquarters in Munich. In so doing he made good relations between the Austrian government and the Austrian NSDAP the sine qua non of good relations between the German and Austrian governments. Yet, on the other hand, Hitler failed to establish tight control over the Austrian party either personally or through a German or party institution.

De facto, if not de jure, the Austrian Nazis made their own policies, which not even Habicht was always able to control. The lack of a centralized and effective leadership after Habicht's expulsion from Austria helped increase competition between the SA and the SS and accelerate the campaign of terror. The July Putsch was as much a last, desperate effort by Habicht to regain control of the Austrian Nazi party as it was an attempt to overthrow the Dollfuss regime.

For the first, but by no means the last time in his career, Hitler's unwillingness to give clear-cut responsibilities to a single person or agency to carry out a policy led to a near disaster. His appointment of Franz von Papen as special envoy to Austria was an attempt to clarify Germany's policy. And no longer was the Austrian Nazi party treated like an integral part of the Gesamtpartei. Only one thing did not change after the Putsch: Hitler's desire for the Gleichschaltung of his native land.

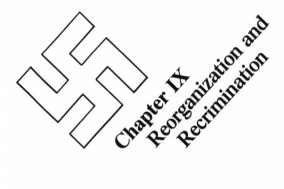

The Party in Ruins

Eight years after the formation of the Hitler Bewegung, and eighteen months after Hitler's rise to power in Germany, the Austrian Nazis found themselves virtually back where they had begun. In many ways, they were actually in worse shape than in 1926. Their longtime leaders were, almost without exception, dismissed or denounced, in detention camps or in German exile. Those party members who remained at large in Austria felt betrayed and abandoned, because they had been left without the orders or financial assistance that had previously come from Germany.[1] Many Austrian Nazis were so depressed after the Putsch that they predicted an Anschluss would not come for another five, ten, even twenty years.[2] Thousands of the party's rank and file had fled from Austria, most of them to Yugoslavia. By January 1935 the sum of Austrian refugees in Germany, counting those who had fled Austria both before and after the Putsch, may have reached forty-two thousand.[3]

Many Putschists who could not escape were arrested, most of them in Styria and Carinthia. Of those who were captured by Austrian authorities over six thousand were quickly tried by special courts, and more than five thousand were sent to Wöllersdorf.[4] Moreover, the disclosure of complete membership lists enabled police to suppress hitherto clandestine Nazi cells. Austrian authorities were also able to destroy—if only temporarily—the party's Political Organization. Between August 1934 and the middle of 1935 the party's leadership had to be completely rebuilt.

Financially, too, the party returned to its impoverished condition of the middle and late twenties. Hitler made it clear after the Putsch that he wanted all political connections between Reich and Austrian Nazis severed; this ruling included most financial ties. Although much is still unknown about the financing of the Austrian party, some illegal support did reach the Austrians after the Putsch, the disclaimers of Wilhelm Keppler, Hitler's economic adviser, and Franz von Papen notwithstanding. An Austrian Refugee Society (Fluchtlingshilfswerk) had existed in Germany before the revolt. It secretly continued to send financial assistance to the families of executed or arrested Nazis after July 1934. In 1935 alone the German Nazi party allocated some 9 million Reichsmarks for this purpose. In large measure this aid was intended to stop the flow of Nazi refugees streaming into Germany, where they were a burden on the government. But equally important was the goal of encouraging Austrian Nazis to remain in their homeland so they would be grateful for German support and be a nuisance to Vienna authorities.[5]

After August 1934 the Austrian Refugee Society was headed by a Reich German and sometime leader of the Austrian SS, Alfred Rodenbücher. By 1936 Rodenbücher's staff in Berlin had grown to some 260 men. The money was distributed in Austria by an illegal Hilfswerk that had existed since the outlawing of the party in 1933. Money was "laundered" in a variety of places—banks and organizations in Switzerland, Poland, Czechoslovakia, and Hungary. Especially important was an Austrian firm called Krentschker and Company, a commercial society which had its headquarters in Graz. Although the Austrian police worked feverishly to discover its identity, the company remained undetected by using middlemen. Not even the leader of the illegal Hilfswerk knew the name of this mysterious benefactor.[6]

The financial aid was ostensibly intended to reach the families of those *Parteigenossen* who had suffered a death or a crippling injury, or who languished in a jail or prison for their service to the party. The Hilfswerk also tried to help those who had lost their jobs or who needed legal advice.[7] Additional money was sent during the Christmas season.

The Hilfswerk's resources were distributed according to a precise formula devised in Berlin, which rewarded the provinces with the largest membership and the greatest willingness to obey. Thus Styria, even though having only the third-largest population in Austria, received 26.5 percent of the funds (2,190,800 Austrian Schillings or $246,157), followed by Vienna (20 percent) and Carinthia (18 percent). Lesser amounts were given in descending order to Lower Austria, Salzburg, Upper Austria, Tyrol, Vorarlberg, and the Burgenland. In all, 8,226,435 Schillings, worth $924,318, were disbursed [8]

Another 2,108,514 Schillings (or $236,912) were sent to various other Nazi organizations and pro-Nazi groups. Of this amount, the largest single portion (567,750 Schillings or $63,781) went to a legal Hilfswerk headed by an Upper

Austrian pan-German politician, Franz Langoth.[9] Chancellor Schuschnigg was aware of the existence of this group and even sanctioned it in December 1936, but never realized its true significance.

Although the Hilfswerk was supposed to eschew politics and have only a charitable purpose, it did not always adhere to its professed aims. Rodenbücher earmarked as much as 100,000 Marks a month in loans to pro-Nazi Austrian manufacturers and industrialists who had suffered because of their political beliefs. Still more money went to Nazi-oriented farmers and landowners who were harassed by the Schuschnigg government. A total of nearly 375,000 Schillings ($42,169) was given to the Austrian Landesleitung between 1934 and 1938. Still another special fund of 417,000 Schillings ($46,741) reached the Carinthian Nazi leader, Odilo Globocnik, on 10 March 1938 to aid in the military occupation of Austria. Although the Austrian authorities succeeded in arresting individual members of the illegal Hilfswerk, they never managed to break up the entire apparatus. Its operations were never even so much as interrupted.[10]

Within Austria itself the Nazis saw their fiscal resources nearly dry up after 1934. The giant steel company in northern Styria, the Alpine-Montan Gesellschaft, which had supported the Styrian Heimatschutz until 1933 and the Nazis thereafter, was purged of its Nazi directors by the government.[11] Even party members were for a time less than faithful in paying their dues. The party's subsequent lack of financial reserves helps explain why both the Austrian Security Directorate and Franz von Papen noted that the Nazis were relatively quiet in the year following the Putsch.[12] This situation made it all the easier for von Papen to prevent "radical elements . . . both in Germany and Austria, from pursuing any policy that would lead to international complications."[13]

On the first anniversary of the Putsch, the special envoy reported to Hitler that the Austrian NSDAP had dwindled "to a small but reliable nucleus. But ultimately the dynamism of even the most zealous fighters cannot but suffer under the almost total spiritual and material isolation from the Reich, and under the impossibility of obtaining orders from the Reich and from the Führer for conducting the internal opposition."[14]

Another German observer in Austria noted in December 1935 that the core of the movement, including the former members of the GVP, the anticlerical government officials and employees, as well as nationalistic students, had remained loyal to the party. But many fellow travelers, workers, and especially peasants in the provinces of Vorarlberg, Tyrol, and Salzburg had drifted away.[15]

Even more pessimistic was a report sent to the German Foreign Office in January by an unidentified member of the German Volksbund für das Deutschtum im Ausland (People's League for German Heritage Abroad) who was living in Vienna:

> The organization of the NSDAP is, with a few exceptions in the provinces, fully disintegrated. There is no solution. Two years of illegality, a reckless use of the best strength and unlimited activity by the ambitious and political dilettantes were too much for the most dedicated. . . . The party is no longer an instrument of power.
>
> There may be in the provinces some subgroups which are hardly weaker than in the period of the greatest flourishing, but there is lacking a unifying leadership apparatus. The police are well informed even about the heart of the organization so they can arrest the subleaders if danger threatens. Masses without leaders are no danger for the state.
>
> We are seeing that the most worthwhile and farsighted people are more and more turning away from the party.[16]

Although rank-and-file Nazis remained without effective leadership in the year following the Putsch, those who retained their freedom were still active. Taking their cue from the Communist underground, they built or rebuilt their organization so as to focus on the small cell, which could infiltrate any institution. They took particular care to make sure their local leaders were known only to their immediate subordinates and superiors. The carelessness of one individual was thus not permitted to endanger the whole organization.[17]

Ingenious code names were developed for prominent party officials. Prior to his fall from grace, Theo Habicht had been called "Flatterer," and (no doubt much to the delight of his enemies) the code name for Alfred Proksch was *Schweinskopf.* These tactics prevented security forces from discovering more than five or ten Nazis at any one time.[18]

Equally impossible to halt was Nazi penchant for making lists. *Parteigenossen* were required to analyze public opinion and to determine who among the civil servants, army officers, and businessmen were pro-Nazi, or at least politically neutral. With these names the Nazis would assure themselves of reliable supporters in key places once the takeover of Austria had been completed.[19]

Of more immediate use to the Nazis were secret spy reports describing the activities of the government's Fatherland Front, the police, gendarmerie, and army. Other reports dealt with the morale and activities of the party itself.

Spies even penetrated the Security Directorate of the federal chancellery.[20] Spying, in fact, was probably the chief occupation of the Nazi underground before the last few dramatic weeks preceding the Anschluss.

Spies for the Nazi movement were scattered throughout the entire Austrian bureaucracy. Secretaries to state ministers, assistants to police commissioners, underlings in Jewish-owned concerns, employees of regular news agencies, and so forth, were often dedicated Nazis who would carry what they had heard or read to central espionage offices, which in turn relayed the information to Germany. "Probably no conqueror in history was so well informed of an immense variety of details concerning his prospective victim as was Hitler."[21]

On the other hand, the value of all this data was substantially diminished before the Anschluss (but not later) by the wealth of information the Austrian Security Directorate had about even the most carefully guarded Nazi secrets. A major source of its knowledge was former Nazis, some of whom had been leading officials who had fled to Yugoslavia after the Putsch, moved to Germany, and finally returned to Austria.[22]

The Nazis were also active in front organizations operating under the guise of cultural, gymnastic, and social clubs. The Deutsche Turnerbund 1919 (German Gymnastic League 1919), Deutsche Schulverein Südmark (South German School Society), Deutsch-österreichische Volksbund (German-Austrian People's League) as well as the Volksbund für das Deutschtum im Ausland were four such groups which flourished both before and after the July Putsch and right up to the Anschluss.[23]

Still another front group was the Bund der Reichsdeutschen in Österreich (League of German Citizens in Austria). This League, with headquarters in Vienna since its foundation in 1919, had grown to include some twenty-seven thousand of the forty-thousand Germans living in Austria in 1934. By April 1935 the League had become a cover for the Nazis' Auslandsorganisation (Foreign Organization) or AO, headed by Ernst Wilhelm Bohle. Although membership was supposed to be confined to German citizens, Bohle began recruiting Austrians, a clear violation of Hitler's directive of August 1934 concerning nonintervention in Austrian affairs by German Nazis. The AO, which had a special Austrian Section in its Berlin offices, founded numerous *Reichsdeutsch* newspapers in Austria, which published Anschluss propaganda.[24]

Camouflaged within the League of German Citizens were various Nazi affiliations, such as the Hitler Jugend, a gymnastic section, a social club of the Deutsche Arbeitsfront (German Work Front) or DAF, and others. Because it was often impossible for the police to prove any direct link with the illegal

NSDAP it was difficult for the government to control the activities of the League and other Nazi front associations and their subgroups.[25]

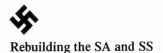

Rebuilding the SA and SS

Nazi suborganizations, including the staffs of the SA and SS, were supposed to be dissolved after the Putsch. The same order applied to the Austrian Legion as well as the Landesleitung and *Gauleitungen*.[26] In reality, all these institutions were secretly rebuilt within a few months.

As the party's oldest affiliate, the Austrian SA could trace its origins back to 1922 when it had been called the Ordnertruppen. The Austrian SS, as we have seen, was relatively new, having been founded in Vienna in 1929 by Alfred Frauenfeld. The Carinthian SS was inaugurated by the Reichsführer SS, Heinrich Himmler himself, in April 1930. Other units were founded in the various provincial capitals in 1931. But as late as June 1932 their total membership was still only six-hundred men.

The functions of the Austrian SA and SS before the party was outlawed in 1933 had been the same as in Germany. The SA was always described as the party's army and the SS as its police. More specifically, the partly armed SA was in charge of protecting meetings and displaying the party's might by marching into "enemy territory," such as industrial districts. Young men who enjoyed fighting, most of them the sons of industrial workers, tended to join the SA. Their love of brawling meant that the SA was involved in some of the early acts of terror in 1932–33. The SS, composed mainly of employees and state officials, was assigned duties that could only be done by individuals. Such tasks included protecting Nazi speakers and other party leaders.[27]

The SA and SS, like most other Nazi organizations, were autonomous. They had their own revenues and their own structures, which paralleled those of the party. However, their leaders had to be approved by the respective political leaders. A *Fachberater* (special advisor) served as a liaison between the party and the SA and SS (as well as between the party and all other Nazi affiliates). He saw to it that the orders of the party leaders were carried out, although the way in which the orders were fulfilled was supposed to be left to the SA. Members of the SA and SS were expected, but not required, to become members of the party as well.[28]

Neither the SA nor the SS had been seriously affected by the outlawing of the party. Unlike the Political Organization, they had been anticipating the prohibition and prepared for it. Both organizations were devastated, however, by the results of the Putsch.

It is extremely difficult to estimate the size of the SA after July 1934. In May 1933 the Austrian police believed that the SA had over 30,000 men, but the authorities tended to overestimate Nazi strength.[29] On the other hand, the Austrian SA leader from 1936 to 1938, Alfred Persche, estimated that the SA had 40,000 members after the Putsch, a catastrophic decline from the more than 100,000 members he claimed it had before the revolt.[30]

The SS, which was normally supposed to have only 10 percent of the membership of the SA, counted 9,450 men in its ranks just before the July Putsch. But by even the most optimistic accounting it was back to just 7,500 Black Shirts in 1938.[31] In 1935 there were another 4,600 refugee SS men stationed at Dachau (Bavaria).

The SS refugees, organized into the SS Sammelstelle, were housed together with the Austrian Legion in the Dachau camp. Both groups received military training from officers of the German army. According to one German observer, members of the Legion (who were automatically also members of the SA) formed an army, which was fully prepared to march in 1935, with first-class training and weapons.[32]

This status was a far cry from Hitler's earlier intentions for the Legion just after the Putsch. On 1 August 1934, Colonel Walther von Reichenau, chief of the Wehrmachtsamt, was told by Hitler to disband and disarm the Legion militarily and to transform it into a charitable organization called the Hilfswerk Nordwest. As such, it would care for Austrian refugees under the unimpeachable cover of the Red Cross. SA Obergruppenführer Hermann Reschny, the only member of the pre-Putsch Austrian Landesleitung to retain a major post, was put in charge of the Legion's metamorphosis.[33]

But only a few weeks later the SA chief of staff's special commissioner for Austria told an official in the German Foreign Office that Hitler did not want the Legion dissolved. The name *Hilfswerk Nordwest* was retained, however, as a cover. The Legion was to be transferred to the north in units of 500 to 600. This order was finally carried out in the fall of 1935 when the Legion was moved to the Rhineland area. But Reschny continued to hold meetings with SA leaders from Austria in clear violation of Hitler's decree forbidding interference by refugees in Austrian affairs.[34]

The Legion was therefore still very much in existence after July 1934 and continued to be a potential threat to Austria's independence. Its membership had grown from 4,500 in October 1933 to around 9,000 in December 1934. It was augmented in the latter month by refugees who had previously fled to Yugoslavia and then were transferred to Germany, where they were drafted into the Legion.[35] By 1938, however, its membership had fallen to only 3,000.[36]

Reschny lost his command over the SA in Austria itself. He was replaced first by a young Viennese, Johann Lukesch, and then in April 1935 by the thirty-two-year-old Styrian, Alfred Persche. A native of Split, in what later became Yugoslavia, Persche was arrested on twelve different occasions after joining the SA in 1930. Except for brief periods of imprisonment he remained in charge of the SA until February 1938.[37]

The SA in Austria led a fairly placid existence after the Putsch, partly because it was ordered to do so, and partly out of sheer necessity. An order from the SA leadership in June 1935 forbade the use of terror or arson. The attacks of 1933–34, the order pointed out, had not destroyed the regime. Instead it had cost the movement much popular sympathy, because taxes had to be raised to repair damaged public property.[38]

Hitler was evidently serious about enforcing his new, more peaceful policy toward Austria. German border officials were given strict instructions in 1935 to prevent the smuggling of explosives into Austria. Even the apartment of the former Tyrolean Gauleiter Franz Hofer, located in the border city of Füssen, was searched by the Gestapo for explosives; but none were found. In April 1936, Hermann Reschny, who still exercised considerable influence over the SA in Austria, was told that the Führer unequivocally prohibited the use of terror and would be compelled to take ruthless measures against instigators who disobeyed his command. And on 12 December 1936 Alfred Persche forbade the sale or purchase of arms by SA members as well as participation in public demonstrations. Those who belonged to terrorist groups would be expelled, he warned.[39]

Nevertheless, SA terror squads still existed after 1934, although their activity was directed more against Nazi "traitors" than against the non-Nazi population. The use of terror had to be limited if only because both the SA and the SS had lost most of their already insufficient supply of weapons after the Putsch. Their military training was also made hazardous by the Austrian security forces; exercises, limited to no more than seven men, had to be disguised as Sunday-afternoon picnics in the Vienna woods or in similar remote areas. Likewise, no roll calls or leadership conferences were held in public places in order to avoid police action.

In general, SA discipline declined after the Putsch. Many members failed to attend the secret meetings. Contributing to the debacle was the diminished status of the SA following the Röhm Purge, the defeat in the July Putsch, the frequent arrest of SA leaders, and probably the effectiveness of Austrian police aided by Nazi denunciations. With the exception of Styria, the condition of the SA in mid-1935 was so deplorable that members had to be admonished not to flee to Germany. Anyone doing so who could not prove that he was threatened by arrest was escorted back to the border by German authorities. Further, he was warned that another attempt might jeopardize his "right to take part in the final victory of the Austrian NSDAP."[40] Austrian officials were therefore probably justified in having no fear of a second Nazi Putsch between 1934 and 1936, despite constant rumors of a second Putsch attempt.[41]

The Austrian SS was equally quiet, but nevertheless significant, after 1934. Its principal occupation until 1938 was gathering information and sending it to Berlin. In apparent violation of Hitler's orders separating the German and Austrian parties, the SS, in contrast to the SA, still received German financial subsidies. Equally contrary to orders was the continued leadership of the Austrian SS by the German Alfred Rodenbücher. Rodenbücher, who was also responsible for dissolving the Austrian Landesleitung, was eventually replaced as SS leader by a Lower Austrian, Engineer Hiedler. Finally, in 1936, the SS was taken over by the infamous Upper Austrian Ernst Kaltenbrunner.

Born in 1903, Kaltenbrunner was the Roman Catholic son and grandson of lawyers, whose ancestors hailed from the same *Waldviertel* district as Adolf Hitler. The postwar inflation depleted the family's savings, but the young, six-foot seven-inch Kaltenbrunner still managed to work his way through law school in Graz, graduating in 1926. Once he had joined his father's law firm, disaster struck again in the form of the Great Depression. The economic crisis only strengthened Kaltenbrunner's extremist convictions, and he joined Prince Starhemberg's Heimwehr. Then in 1932 he became a member of both the Nazi party and the SS. Thereafter his rise in the SS can only be described as meteoric, especially after 1934. In large part, his success was simply the result of so many SS leaders' being removed by death or imprisonment. (Among his "achievements" as leader of the Austrian SS was persuading the young Adolf Eichmann, then a member of the Frontkämpfervereinigung in Linz, to join the SS.) Although Kaltenbrunner was already well known within the Austrian NSDAP by the end of 1937 his real fame began in 1938 with his role in the Anschluss. Later he gained far more notoriety as the successor of Reinhard Heydrich in leading the Nazi secret police (Reichssicherheitshauptamt or RSHA).[42]

Even under Kaltenbrunner's leadership the Austrian SS was far more controlled by SS authorities in Germany than it was by leaders of the Austrian Political Organization. With the Austrian SA frequently also following its own inclinations, one can scarcely talk about a single Austrian Nazi party. In reality there were at least three separate organizations, with major divisions existing within each one.

ERNST KALTENBRUNNER. *Leader of the Austrian SS, 1936–1938, and later chief of the Reichssicherheitshauptamt. DÖW.*

The Reinthaller Action

The disunity and temporary impotence of Nazi radicals following the abortive Putsch did at least provide moderates an opportunity to take over the party's leadership and to reach some kind of accommodation with the Austrian government. Such an agreement would mesh well with Hitler's policy of "peaceful penetration" of Austria and in fact had the Führer's blessing.[43] The man who undertook this task was Anton Reinthaller.

Most Nazi moderates like Reinthaller had previously belonged either to the Greater German People's party or to the Agricultural League until those two parties were absorbed by the Nazis after 1930. Born in 1895, Reinthaller had belonged to the Landbund until 1930, when he joined the NSDAP and became Gauleiter of Upper Austria. Habicht had made him the leader of the Agricultural Division of the Landesleitung in 1932; but differences with Habicht over the use of terror had led to Reinthaller's dismissal in just a matter of months. Nevertheless, Rudolf Hess appointed Reinthaller Landesbauernführer (State Peasant Leader) early in 1934, and the latter went on to establish an anti-Habicht-Proksch-Frauenfeld front within the party. After Habicht's negotiations failed in the winter of 1933–34, Reinthaller tried his own hand at a separate settlement with the government. These talks were abruptly interrupted, however, by the July Putsch.[44]

With the backing of the Viennese lawyer Arthur Seyss-Inquart, Gauleiter Hubert Klausner of Carinthia, Hermann Neubacher, Walter Riehl, and other Nazi moderates, Reinthaller resumed negotiations with Schuschnigg after the revolt as part of a "National Action." The chancellor, who was a regimental comrade of Reinthaller, welcomed the new discussions. He was eager to eliminate all ties between the Reich and the Austrian Nazi party. Schuschnigg was also anxious to broaden the very narrow base of his government. Papen was likewise delighted with these conversations, because they conformed nicely with his policy of internal pacification at a time when he was too distrusted by the Austrian government to carry out this maneuver himself.

An official in the German Legation in Vienna reported to Berlin in October 1934 that Reinthaller wanted to "regain [the Austrian Nazi party's] legal status while at the same time severing its connexion with the Party organization in the Reich. A new organization [called the Nationalsozialer Volksbund Österreich was] envisaged which [would] be strong and independent while adopting the National Socialist Party's programme as a basis. It [was] intended that all national circles, especially the former Pan-Germans [GVP] and the members of the Landbund, [should] range themselves around the present NSDAP Austria as the hard core of the movement."[45]

In addition, Reinthaller wanted the government to cease arresting Nazis and reserve positions in the federal and local governments for Nazis who would then belong to a legal National Unity List. Minor participants in the July Putsch would have to be released from prison, and Nazi armed formations (the SA and the SS) would have to be coordinated with Germany's. Finally, a plebiscite would be held to determine Austria's future fate. In other words, he wanted everything Habicht had demanded nine months before, and more. In exchange Nazi terror (which had already greatly abated) would end as would Germany's "thousand-Mark blockade."[46]

Although the negotiations continued sporadically as late as March 1936, they had, for all practical purposes, already failed by October 1934. Their demise had several causes: Schuschnigg correctly suspected the Nazis of using the National Action as a cover for reorganizing their party. He therefore insisted that Nazis enter the government's all-encompassing Fatherland Front, individually rather than en masse as demanded by Reinthaller. Moreover, Schuschnigg wanted each province to have its own National Action leader to facilitate this entry. This would, it was hoped, prevent the reestablishment of a strong, centralized Nazi leadership. Reinthaller realized that this demand alone would deprive the Nazis of any political influence, would leave the party without a leader, and would be unacceptable to nearly all Nazis.

The attempted reconciliation failed also because of opposition in Schuschnigg's cabinet, especially from Prince Starhemberg. The prince was no more willing to tolerate a Nazi-government agreement than he had been when Dollfuss made such a move in January of the previous year. In a meeting on 27 October between Schuschnigg and representatives of the National Action, the uninvited Heimwehr leader denounced the whole proceedings as a "swindle." It seems more likely, however, that he was still worried about the Heimwehr's being bargained out of existence, as indeed it would be two years later.[47]

These factors were only the surface causes of the failure, however. At bottom the issue was once again the disputed leadership of the Nazi party. The *Altkämpfer* (the "old fighters" who had joined the party before it was outlawed in 1933) and unemployed radicals did not consider it "suitable" for the upstart Reinthaller to be leading the party. They resented his appointment of former members of the GVP and Landbund to positions of local leadership. Reinthaller was seen as "a stupid fellow who [was] willing to sell out the party and [the] cause to the system."[48] They suspected Schuschnigg of using the negotiations to lessen Heimwehr pressure, to please Mussolini, and to find out information about the party. The Austrian SA also rejected negotiations for the same reasons.

Following the failure of the Reinthaller action, the party remained divided into two hostile factions: the moderates, who wanted peace and reconciliation with the government, and the radicals, who wanted to continue an aggressive policy toward the Schuschnigg regime. The "peace party," headed by Reinthaller, was backed by Göring and Hess, whereas the "war party," led by Josef Leopold, received encouragement from Goebbels, the SA chief Viktor Lutze, and the leader of the Auslandsorganisation, Ernst Bohle. Among the "hawks" were also Austrian Nazi exiles like Alfred Frauenfeld, Franz Hofer, and Hanns Rauter, who had converted to the NSDAP from the Styrian Heimatschutz. The hawkish exiles were led by the former Austrian SA leader Hermann Reschny.[49]

Hitler and Leadership Quarrels—Again

With the failure of the Reinthaller action the struggle for leadership within the Austrian Nazi party reached a new intensity. Gerhard Weinberg has concluded that "the history of the Austrian party from 1933 to 1938 is to a very large extent a tedious record of factional struggles, mutual betrayals, and endless recriminations."[50]

The German military attaché in Vienna, Wolfgang Muff, shrewdly observed that the Führerprinzip was simply not functioning well in Austria. The system worked only where there was a "superior personality" to lead the party. But this condition was prevented in Austria by the police. Muff attributed the breakdown of the Austrian Nazi hierarchy to Hitler. He warned in September 1934 that "the Austrian party might break apart if the leadership question was not settled soon and unequivocally by the Führer in a diplomatically discreet form."[51] Another German writer called the leadership question in Austria a "vicious circle." "The only undisputed leader is someone who has been legitimized by the Reich. But legitimization can only be obtained by someone who has proved himself a leader."[52]

The problem was now aggravated by Hitler's new policy of ostensible nonintervention in Austrian affairs. Whereas the chaotic leadership in the Austrian party during the late twenties had been caused largely by Hitler's indifference to Austria and preoccupation with attaining power in Germany, as well as his distaste for decision making, it now resulted from Hitler's fear of provoking a reaction by the anti-German Great Powers. At most, the

Austrian leaders might win Hitler's temporary and limited approval, as in the case of Reinthaller in the fall of 1934, or Josef Leopold two years later.[53]

The many contenders for the leadership frequently made secret trips to the Reich, seeking the Führer's blessing. But none of them ever received his unqualified support as sole leader of the Austrian party. Not even *Gauleiter* enjoyed undisputed authority. The struggle for control over the Landesleitung was simply repeated at the Gau level. In Styria, for example, there were sometimes as many as three different claimants for the title of Gauleiter. But a few kind words from Hitler or one of his principal lieutenants could enormously enhance the prestige of a Gauleiter or Landesleiter.[54]

The less than total authority of the various *Landesleiter* led to all kinds of complications. Many subleaders were reluctant to follow a more passive policy after July 1934. They were particularly opposed to giving their followers a mere intellectual (*geistig-weltanschaulich*) indoctrination. Another challenge to the authority of the state leaders came from Sudeten Nazis and former Austrian leaders who had been discredited and exiled after the July Putsch. Despite numerous complaints by Anton Reinthaller and Josef Leopold along with repeated chastisements by Rudolf Hess, former leaders like Alfred Frauenfeld and Alfred Proksch continued to dabble in the affairs of the Austrian party. This interference sometimes caused great confusion, as orders were sent into Austria via couriers that contradicted those of the Landesleiter.[55]

As mentioned above, the leadership crisis worsened in the winter of 1934–35 after the failure of the Reinthaller action. Reinthaller's alleged lack of negotiating skill cost him the confidence of the Austrian *Gauleiter*, who demanded his resignation. Reinthaller therefore reluctantly stepped down in favor of his friend Hermann Neubacher at the beginning of 1935.[56]

Like nearly all of the Austrian Nazi leaders, Neubacher, at forty-two, was still relatively young in 1935. During his university years he had been a member of one of the traditionally pan-German fraternities. After a stint as a highly decorated soldier in the World War, he had helped to found two postwar pan-German clubs in 1925.

However, the *Altkämpfer* rejected Neubacher as a mere newcomer in the party just as they had Reinthaller and Frauenfeld before him. This repudiation was all the more emphatic in Neubacher's case, because his position had not been legitimized by a German official. Moreover, he had long had good relations with the Austrian Social Democrats, whom he admired for their social reformism even though he rejected their Marxist internationalism.

Neubacher's leadership was challenged almost immediately by Josef Leopold, then still the Gauleiter of Lower Austria. Leopold and his supporters issued a kind of manifesto reproaching Neubacher for being a Catholic, having connections with Moscow, and having Marxist tendencies. Leopold was then chosen to be the new Landesleiter in a meeting of *Gauleiter* representatives held in December 1934. Ugly quarrels between the two rivals only worsened when Leopold was released from prison on 16 February. An uneasy compromise between the two men was finally arranged by the two Austrian *Gauleiter* when they met in Krems (Lower Austria) on 23 March. By the terms of their agreement, Neubacher recognized Leopold as the legitimate state leader, whereas Leopold promised to regard Neubacher as his "closest confidant," with whom he would consult on all important questions. Franz Schattenfroh, a one-time cavalry captain in the Austro-Hungarian army, editor of Nazi newspapers, and more recently a representative of Habicht, was to become the deputy Landesleiter as soon as he was out of prison.[57]

This awkward diarchy, so reminiscent of the Pfrimer-Steidle leadership of the Heimwehr between 1928 and 1931, was unworkable from the start. The two men had trouble even maintaining contact, because Leopold was closely watched by the police in his home town of Krems. That Neubacher enjoyed more freedom in Vienna only aroused Leopold's ire. As it turned out, the agreement had little practical effect except as a source of later arguments. Both Leopold and Neubacher were arrested and imprisoned again in June 1935 for distributing a propaganda pamphlet entitled, "For Austrian Freedom and Justice." They were not freed until July 1936.

With Austria's two principal Nazi leaders out of circulation, the party's leadership problem became even more hopelessly chaotic. The source of much confusion was a so-called testament that Leopold had left behind in case of his arrest. According to this document, Franz Schattenfroh, as Leopold's deputy, was to be his successor. But because Schattenfroh was now himself imprisoned, the testament provided that the party should be ruled by a directorate consisting of the *Gauleiter* of Vienna and Lower Austria together with the leaders of the Austrian SA and SS. This body would receive orders from Leopold via the latter's wife, who was allowed to visit him every two weeks. Thus Leopold would retain effective control over the party even while behind bars![58]

The *Gauleiter* from the Alpine states, left politically impotent by Leopold's testament, never accepted the testament's legitimacy. They had already come to view Leopold as an overbearing and dangerous sergeant and questioned his right to choose his own successor. Because Leopold had claimed the office of Landesleiter by virtue of his seniority, the Alpine *Gauleiter* reasoned that the second most senior Gauleiter, Major Klausner of Carinthia, ought to be the new de facto state leader.

Klausner, who had been born in the German-speaking South Tyrol in 1892, had been a front officer in the World War. He was severely wounded in the right arm during the conflict and was handicapped the rest of his life. He was one of the oldest members of the Nazi party, having joined in 1922. His career as a Nazi was hampered by his war injury. Even his friends did not regard him as sufficiently competent to be a Landesleiter, the real reason perhaps being his rumored alcoholism. The western *Gauleiter* therefore decided in July 1935 to make him a mere figurehead in a college of *Gauleiter*. In other words, the provincial leaders wanted to pay lip service to the Führerprinzip while reserving the right to dismiss a leader in whom they had no confidence.[59] One could say they wanted a "parliamentary dictatorship."

With the creation of this college of *Gauleiter* the Austrian Nazis not only reverted to the 1928 to 1931 period when a similar committee had existed in the party, but in a strange way they also repeated the fourteenth-century history of the papacy. This Nazi conciliar movement failed for the same reason as the Council of Pisa in 1409: the Nazi "pope," Leopold, and his hand-picked directorate, refused to step aside in favor of the college of *Gauleiter*. Just as there were two, and for a time three, popes in the early fifteenth century, so there were now two Nazi leadership groups, each claiming supremacy, although Leopold was still generally recognized as the de jure leader.

In general, the Alpine *Gauleiter* enjoyed somewhat more success than their eastern rivals, because fewer of their members were imprisoned. Within the western group two young men attained especial prominence during the first half of 1936 with Klausner's blessing. The two men, both Carinthians, were Dr. Friedrich Rainer, who became chief of the party's political staff, and Odilo Globocnik, who assumed the position of liaison officer between the Austrian party and the Reich.[60]

By March of 1936 Rainer and Globocnik were among the few Austrian leaders not in Wöllersdorf or German exile. The conditions of the party were so lamentable that they evoked nothing but disgust from German Nazis. When Rainer visited the German capital after Easter 1936 the Berlin offices of the party, the Foreign Ministry, and other government offices would have nothing to do with him. Hitler was unwilling to make any commitment concerning the party's political leadership or to give it any guidance.[61] In part this reception resulted from Hitler's nonintervention order, and in part because "everyone who came from Austria did nothing but squabble and insult, because no one could say what [he] wanted, because everyone had contempt for everyone else and called them idiots, etc."[62]

It is no wonder that the Austrian security officials claimed in 1935 that they had caused "great confusion" in Nazi ranks.[63] "Three-fourths" of the Nazis' time had to be devoted to defense against Austrian authorities.[64] It is equally easy to understand why the illegal Nazi press continued to devote itself to maintaining morale rather than to winning new converts.

The two years following the July Putsch therefore marked one of the lowest points in the history of the Austrian Nazi party. Thousands of *Parteigenossen* were in detention camps or had fled to Germany. Most of the already insufficient supply of weapons belonging to the SA and SS had been confiscated. Above all, the centralized and reasonably effective leadership of Theo Habicht was now over and most of the political, psychological, and financial ties to the Reich party had been broken by Hitler himself. The few Nazi leaders who remained in Austria constantly quarreled with each other when they were not imprisoned. The efforts by both moderate leaders like Reinthaller, and not so moderate individuals such as Leopold, to find a new, legal footing for the party had all been rejected by Chancellor Schuschnigg.

Nevertheless, the party and all its suborganizations were still functioning and their membership was substantial, and in fact slightly larger than before the Putsch. The party's eclipse had been caused in large measure by Germany's diplomatic isolation following the July uprising. And the Austrian government had been aided in its drive to suppress the Nazis by the military backing of Italy and the diplomatic support of Great Britain and France. Once this international constellation—so fortuitous for Vienna—changed, so too would the fortunes of the Austrian Nazi party.

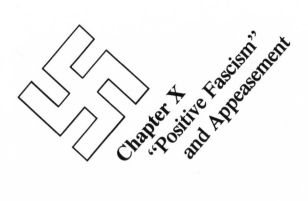

Chapter X
"Positive Fascism" and Appeasement

The Austrian government's nearly total suppression of overt Nazi activity was destined to be short-lived. The Ethiopian War, which began in October 1935, turned Italy from being a defender of Austrian independence into a partner of Nazi Germany. Encouraged by these international developments, the Austrian Nazis regained their confidence and momentum. The government of Kurt von Schuschnigg lacked both the internal strength and the external backing to crush the Nazis. Instead, it felt compelled to appease them. One method of doing this was a program that might be called "positive fascism," which was designed to imitate what appeared to be the more popular features of fascism in Germany and Italy. The other approach was the "Gentlemen's Agreement" with Germany concluded in July 1936. Of course, neither policy worked in the long run. But the short-term effects of each policy are not so easy to evaluate.

The Nazis' Neo-Renaissance

If domestic developments during most of 1935 gave the Austrian Nazis small cheer, the same could not be said of the news from abroad. While the employment rate in Austria continued its steady decline in 1934 from 79.8 percent of the 1929 level to 66.8 percent in 1935 and 64.6 percent in 1936, Germany's masses were rapidly gaining employment. The percentage of employed in 1934 (compared with the 1929 standard) was already 85.5. In 1935 it rose to 90.6 and then to 97.2 in 1936.[1] In January 1935 the Austrian Nazis were encouraged by the perfectly free League of Nations' plebiscite in the Saar district, where over 90 percent of the inhabitants voted to return to German rule. By March 1935 the monthly report of the Security

Directorate admitted that "while one couldn't speak of the masses being enthusiastic about National Socialism, the public was nevertheless growing lethargic toward the policies and undeniable dynamism of the Nazis."[2]

But what really turned the situation around for the Austrian Nazis was Mussolini's unquenchable thirst for empire and glory. With the legions of Austria's one-time protector bogged down in the mountains and deserts of Ethiopia, Austria stood defenseless before the growing might of Nazi Germany. Nor were the Western Democracies willing to fill the military breach. Their timidity was graphically illustrated by their insipid response to Hitler's reoccupation and remilitarization of the Rhineland in March 1936.

The impact of these developments on Austria's internal tug of war was both swift and profound. As late as May 1935 Styrian Nazis were attempting to organize a boycott of Italian imports. But the very next month they were encouraged by improving Italo-German relations, and by July they were confidently expecting to benefit from an Ethiopian War that had not yet even begun. In stark contrast, government loyalists were fearful already in September about possible damaging repercussions from the impending war; they became even gloomier following the Rhineland reoccupation the next March.[3]

The effects of the diplomatic revolution, together with an increase in Nazi spying activities, were soon reflected in the reports of the previously optimistic Austrian Security Directorate. In his detailed report dealing with the Austrian Nazi party dated 4 April 1936, Eduard Baar-Baarenfels observed that frequent acts of treason made it difficult to fight the Nazis. The Nazis had little reason to fear arrest because they could anticipate being rewarded with a job in Germany once they were released. Nazis were increasingly reluctant to betray their party for fear of being assassinated by the Nazi Sicherheitsdienst (Security Service), which was operating on Austrian soil, Baar-Baarenfels observed.[4] A month later he noted that even government supporters were unwilling to fight the Nazis, apprehensive that their businesses might be boycotted or they themselves murdered.[5]

Taking the Wind out of Nazi Sails:
The Dollfuss-Schuschnigg Dictatorship

The Austrian government responded to this renewed Nazi threat with a two-sided defense, neither aspect of which was new. The first of these policies was purely domestic: the development of a one-party dictatorship.

Chancellor Dollfuss had once remarked that what was "good and healthy" in National Socialism was already a part of his Christian Social party's program. Basically, what he and his successor, Kurt von Schuschnigg, did was to emphasize such "good and healthy" points by imitating German Nazism and Italian Fascism in hopes of "taking the wind out of the Nazis' sails."[6] The chancellors hoped an Austrian Nazi would no longer envy Germany if he could find the best features of Nazism in his native country.

Chancellor Dollfuss was already well advanced in fulfilling this policy of positive fascism by the time of his assassination. After the unexpected dissolution of Parliament in March 1933, further moves to the right by Dollfuss were caused not only by his desire to deflate the Nazis but also in large measure by extreme pressure placed on him by the Austrian Heimwehr and Benito Mussolini. The Heimwehr was eager to increase its own influence through the establishment of a dictatorship and the elimination of its hated opponents, the Socialists; meanwhile, Mussolini foolishly wanted Dollfuss to alienate the Western Powers and thus become more dependent on Italy.

In September of 1933 Dollfuss partially yielded to this coercion when he delivered a major speech in Vienna denouncing the social and economic weaknesses of liberalism, capitalism, and Marxism. There was nothing in this triad, at least as far as it went, with which even the most fanatic Nazi or Heimwehr man could disagree. After having rid himself of the Socialist opposition in February 1934, the chancellor, aping Hitler's pseudolegality, had a new authoritarian constitution confirmed by the Christian Social and Heimwehr members of the old Parliament on 30 April. This constitution (never fully implemented) provided for a highly centralized state with few powers either for the state parliaments or for the federal assembly, which represented seven fascist-style economic corporations. The latter could not initiate or even debate legislation. The federal president appointed the chancellor, who had sweeping emergency powers.[7]

Dollfuss and Schuschnigg were both careful to distinguish between Austria's "authoritarian system" and Germany's dictatorship. Postwar historians, especially in Austria during the Allied occupation, were equally reluctant to call the constitution of 1934 "fascist" for fear it would be equated with the systems of Fascist Italy, or still worse, Nazi Germany.[8] The difference with Germany, however, was more a matter of personalities and national traditions than clear-cut powers. Both the German and Austrian regimes suppressed democratic elections and political representation. Freedom of the press and of speech were abolished and detention camps were used to coerce political enemies.

Yet the differences were real enough, too. Most strikingly, there was no blanket persecution of religion in Austria. In fact, the Roman Catholic Church flourished during the Dollfuss-Schuschnigg era. Several historians have pointed out the distinctly temporary and defensive nature of the two regimes. According to these writers, neither chancellor had any desire to set up a permanent dictatorship. Instead, they saw their one-party rule as a kind of necessary evil until the twin challenges of Marxism and National Socialism could be contained.[9] There was no talk about making the new system last for a "thousand years."

Moreover, neither Dollfuss nor Schuschnigg fit the mold of a typical fascist or totalitarian dictator. Both men were sincere, practicing Catholics, although they were in no real sense clericalists. Neither had the slightest interest in military glory (even if Austria had had the capacity). Nor is there any evidence that they lusted for sheer power. Dollfuss resembled Hitler and Mussolini only in "coming from the people." But unlike them he never became aloof from the masses. Schuschnigg, on the other hand, by his birth, education, and personality, was very decidedly *not* one of the crowd. On the contrary, he was a well-born, well-educated, dignified gentleman. But unfortunately, his reserve—he rarely even smiled—and natural shyness made him appear cold and disdainful at a time when charisma was very much in vogue on the Continent. If his personality made him incapable of being a demagogue, it also prevented him from becoming a really popular leader.[10]

Chancellors Dollfuss and Schuschnigg clearly wanted a government strong enough to subdue Nazi radicals (and Socialists) but mild enough to appeal to the more moderate Nazis. Had economic conditions in Austria been healthier and international circumstances more favorable, perhaps they would have succeeded. As things were, however, the two dictators were anathema to genuine democrats, an outrage to Socialists, and merely pale imitations of real totalitarian dictators to hardened Nazis. Only Christian Socials and Heimwehr men were pleased with Dollfuss. And Schuschnigg managed to lose the support of even the Heimwehr in 1936. In short, Austria between 1933 and 1938 had a mild but unpopular semifascist dictatorship.

Hitler himself, of course, had nothing but contempt for the Austrian "system." On 9 February 1934 he explained his concept of totalitarianism [*Totalität*] to the German envoy to Austria at that time, Kurt Rieth. "It depended," the Führer said, "on a strong leadership personality whose authority can be trusted. . . . The government in Austria," he went on to say, "would be able to exercise authority only if it were based on the clearly expressed will of the people."[11]

Dollfuss and Schuschnigg were authentic anti-Nazis who did their best to revive an Austrian patriotism. Dollfuss, to be sure, had long been an

Anschluss partisan and remained one for a time even after Hitler's takeover in Germany. But he eventually perceived Hitler's irrationality and feared his anticlerical and totalitarian claims. And when Dollfuss switched from being a pro-Anschluss to a pro-Austrian and anti-Prussian, the conversion was genuine. Schuschnigg, on the other hand, though very much an Austrian patriot, could never quite rid himself of his pan-German sympathies. He often spoke of creating a "true Christian Germanism" as a bastion against the secular, pagan, ultranationalistic character of Nazism. In his book, *My Austria*, written in November 1937, Schuschnigg stressed the "Germanness" of both Austria and himself.

Neither Dollfuss nor Schuschnigg should be censured too severely for his pan-German proclivities. Most German-speaking Austrians had been aware of their Germanness since the rise of nationalism in the late monarchy. Even President Miklas repeatedly referred to the "German" character of Austria during patriotic ceremonies. The duty of the two chancellors, as Baar-Baarenfels saw it, was to convince the Austrian people that "the concept of Austria contained the idea of Germanism and that the fight against National Socialism was not directed against that Germanism."[12] It would not be easy.

The Fatherland Front

The idea of "Germanism" was in fact one of the major ideological pillars of the Fatherland Front or Vaterländische Front (VF), the concept of which Dollfuss announced in May 1933. This all-encompassing "umbrella" organization was created for the purpose of rendering the old political parties, including the chancellor's own Christian Social party, superfluous. Like the semifascist state parties in Hungary, Rumania, Yugoslavia, the Union Patriotica of Primo de Rivera in Spain, and the Uniao Nacional in Portugal, the Front was artificially created from "above" in sharp contrast with the true fascist parties of Italy and Germany, which conquered power for their leaders and supporters. The idea evidently originated with Prince Starhemberg, who became the Front's first Führer (his actual title). But it was Dollfuss who launched the Front shortly before his assassination. And it was during Schuschnigg's rule that it reached its maturity.

Superficially the organization looked impressive. Membership was widespread, reaching a peak of 3 million in November 1937.[13] But because the VF was a creature of the government, it never had the kind of spontaneous enthusiasm enjoyed by the fascist parties of Germany and Italy. And unlike the Fascists and Nazis the VF never commanded the state, but was commanded by it.

Membership in the Fatherland Front was all but compulsory. "Every kind of moral, social, and financial pressure was brought to bear on every Austrian to join."[14] The long-run value of this sort of pressure is extremely doubtful, as it simply led to closet Nazis joining the Front to protect their jobs. This phenomenon in turn seriously weakened the VF and provided the Nazis with still another camouflage for their activities.[15] Some Nazis even became VF functionaries. An example was the director of the University of Graz library, who tried to sabotage all efforts to resist the Nazis in the Styrian capital. Ultimately VF pressure tactics backfired as it became increasingly difficult for the government to identify its enemies.[16]

The only people who joined the Front without reservations were the former Christian Socials and the Legitimists. And they certainly would have supported Dollfuss and Schuschnigg even without the new organization. A popular anecdote of the mid-1930s told how "four Viennese men were sitting at a table in a café gossiping; all were wearing the Fatherland Front badge. After a little while two of them got up and left the café. One of the remaining two then said to the other: 'Do you think those two Nazis know we are Communists?' "[17]

Another well-known story dating from the same period described a visit Schuschnigg supposedly made to

> an industrial town to address one of the innumerable appeals of the Fatherland Front. Prior to the meeting he asked the local leader about the political orientation of the people.
>
> "Well" came the reply, "there is a little handful of Communists, perhaps two or three percent. The Nazis unfortunately are fairly strong; let's say twenty percent, perhaps twenty-five. Then, you know, the "Reds" were always well organized here. There is no doubt that sixty percent remain with them and possibly even. . . . "
>
> "My God!" interrupted Schuschnigg, "How many are in the Fatherland Front?" "Why everybody, Herr Kanzler—absolutely one hundred percent."[18]

The philosophy and policies of the Front were clearly designed to lessen the appeal of Nazism. Besides "Germanism" the VF exalted authority; and like the Nazis it denounced Marxism and liberalism and their progeny, the class struggle, democracy, capitalism, and individualism.[19]

On the other hand, the Front also rejected "exaggerated" racism, including racial anti-Semitism. But this policy did not prevent it from adopting the more traditional kind of cultural anti-Semitism popularized earlier by Karl Lueger, even though nearly all Jews were staunch supporters of the regime. Neither the leaders of the Front nor the leaders of the government were overtly anti-Semitic. Nonetheless they made no attempt to suppress anti-Semitism when it was expressed by others, as for example in the otherwise tightly controlled press. Without resorting to the fanfare employed by Nazi Germany, the Schuschnigg government quietly permitted the number of Jews in banking and the law and medical professions to be reduced by attrition in order to bring their numbers more into line with their percentage of Austria's total population. Large firms that depended on trade with Germany even dismissed their Jewish employees. The very few Jews in local, state, and federal governments were almost completely excluded. Thus, Walter Riehl's proposal, made early in the century, and repeated by nearly every other Austrian anti-Semite thereafter, to reduce "Jewish influence" drastically, was at least partially realized. Again, the transparent purpose of this comparatively "mild" form of anti-Semitism was to appease the country's moderate anti-Semites without totally alienating the government's important Jewish supporters.[20]

The insignia and organization of the Fatherland Front were also remarkably similar to those of the Nazis. Instead of a *Hakenkreuz* (crooked cross or traditional swastika) the VF had its *Kruckenkreuz* (untranslatable) a kind of double-sided swastika. The Kruckenkreuz had purportedly been used in ancient times by the Lombards and Visigoths on their coins and later on the shields of the medieval Crusaders. The Kruckenkreuz appeared on the Front's flags and on some of the national currency.

The Fatherland Front was organized on the hierarchical Führerprinzip. As in the Nazi party, the Führer was not elected but was simply "there." He named his own deputy, who appointed his subordinates and so on down to the lowest echelons of the organization. The Führer had unlimited power over the Front, whose members owed him unconditional obedience.[21]

The lowest level of the hierarchy was the "cell," which consisted of a leader and fifteen to thirty members. Among the cell leaders' duties was observing and reporting to the local police on the "enemies'" propaganda. They were also given explicit instructions to see that VF members attended all rallies and applauded at appropriate times! As with Nazi speakers, one had to take a special course and oral examination to become a cell leader.[22]

The Fatherland Front developed an array of subsidiary organizations similar to those of Fascist Italy and Nazi Germany. Many of these groups were worthwhile and apparently popular. Again, all of them were designed to reduce the lure of Nazism. The largest and most successful of these organizations was Neues Leben (New Life). It was obviously inspired by (though not a duplication of) Italy's Dopolavoro (After Work) and Germany's Kraft durch Freude (Strength through Joy).[23]

Founded in 1936, Neues Leben offered its members, who numbered some 500,000 by early 1938,[24] theater tickets at 40 to 50 percent discounts, reduced fares on the state railroads, and special ski holidays. It sponsored sporting events and prize contests for painting, photography, films, music, and patriotic plays. To reduce the high unemployment rate among talented young actors and actresses, traveling theater groups were established by Neues Leben and sent into remote rural areas. Special lectures and book and picture exhibits were also arranged and were well attended.[25]

The attitude of the Fatherland Front toward women likewise resembled that of Austria's northern and southern neighbors. To reverse the country's sharply declining birthrate, reputedly the lowest in Europe, laws were enacted against birth control. It was also unlawful for women to work if their husbands were employed. The VF's Mütterschutzwerk (Mothers' Aid Society) which was similar to the Nazis' Volkswohlfahrt (People's Welfare) gave payments to needy families having four or more children and provided homes for young, unmarried mothers. As in Germany there was also a Mother's Day on 12 May to honor motherhood.

The Fatherland Front, like the NSDAP, also had two paramilitary formations. The Frontmiliz was created in 1936 to replace three older militant groups, the Ostmärkische Sturmscharen, the Freiheitsbund, and the Heimwehr. The latter was dissolved by Schuschnigg in October of the same year. Far more disciplined than any of these older paramilitary groups was the Sturmkorps, an elite body founded in the summer of 1937. It was expected to have an ultimate membership of thirty to fifty thousand men between the ages of nineteen and thirty. But the sudden Anschluss in 1938 prevented this figure from ever being realized. In many ways the Sturmkorps was indistinguishable from the SS. Its dark blue uniforms closely resembled the black clothing worn by the SS. In place of the SS slogan, *Unsere Ehre heisst Treue* (Honor for us means Loyalty) the slogan of the Sturmkorps was *Unser Wille werde Gesetz* (Our Wishes shall be Law).[26] Nevertheless, any similarity between the SS and the Sturmkorps was denied by Austrian officials. Its purpose was to create a fighting spirit among the Austrian people and to maintain order.[27]

To complete the picture, the Front had, like its fascist neighbors, a youth organization called Österreichisches Jungvolk, a Winterhilfe (Winter Charity), a Sportfront, a Freiwilliger Arbeitsdienst (Voluntary Work Force), and a propaganda ministry. The latter helped organize huge rallies in the manner of Albert Speer in Germany.[28]

The VF also made a claim to "totality," which excluded all political (but not nonpolitical) opposition views.[29] The American historian William Sheridan Allen has concluded that the components of fascism in some countries "were engendered by the fashionability of the idea of apparent successes of the Italian and German regimes."[30]

The new face of Austria prompted Franz von Papen to write Hitler in July 1935 that "the Austrian regime in its struggle against the spiritual influence being exerted by Germany and its fear for its bread and butter [has] learned a great deal from the methods of German National Socialism. Interesting parallels would emerge if the imitations of National Socialist legislation in all spheres were ever analyzed."[31]

Even more revealing is a letter Hermann Göring wrote to Dr. Guido Schmidt, the Austrian secretary for foreign affairs, on 2 February 1937:

> I have heard many Austrians who tell me that they cannot understand it when the [Austrian] government on the one hand rejects everything which is National Socialist and says National Socialism is not for Austria, and on the other hand copies German National Socialism in its own state structure, that is to say the same forms, the same organizations, the same expressions, the same laws, the same methods, only with reversed insignia [*Vorzeichen*]. They say that in Austria one only has to substitute the Kruckenkreuz for the Hakenkreuz and the word patriotic [*vaterländisch*] for National Socialist in order to have in Austria the living mirror image of Germany.[32]

The July Agreement

The development of positive fascism was only one aspect of the government's anti-Nazi strategy. The other, more direct approach, was the use of negotiations with the "moderate" wing of the NSDAP. This policy had produced the talks with Anton Reinthaller.[33] The failure of Reinthaller's National action did not mean, however, that Chancellor Schuschnigg had given up all hope of reaching some sort of accommodation with the Nazis, both inside and outside Austria. In the long run his regime and the independence of Austria could only be preserved if the Austrian Nazis were somehow pacified, if their connections with Germany were permanently severed, and if normal commercial relations with Germany were resumed.

Schuschnigg was in no hurry to achieve this settlement, as Austria's diplomatic position continued to be strong during the first half of 1935. But by

October of the same year the outbreak of the Ethiopian War had completely reversed the roles of suitors and suppliants. Mussolini, peeved at the Western powers for allowing the League of Nations to enact economic sanction against Italy during the war, decided to throw in his lot with Hitler. But the price the Italian dictator had to pay was abandoning his Austrian protectorate. In March 1936 the Duce told Schuschnigg to bring about an internal peace, which meant in effect the elimination of the Nazis' bitter enemy, the Heimwehr. The next month he cut off his financial assistance to the HW.[34]

Although the road to an agreement with the Nazis was now wide open, the wisdom of Schuschnigg in dissolving the Heimwehr and removing Starhemberg as leader of the Fatherland Front is open to question. Whatever may be said about Starhemberg's character, he and his Heimwehr, along with the Ostmärkische Sturmscharen, were still the only militant anti-Nazis around in 1936.[35] The Heimwehr's role in suppressing the July Putsch had been crucial. Moreover, Schuschnigg's hope of absorbing the Heimwehr after its final dissolution in October 1936 proved illusory. The ex-HW members either became politically apathetic or else actually joined the Nazis or revolutionary Leftists.[36] Schuschnigg's already narrow base of popular support, estimated to be 30 percent at the end of 1935 by the Papal Nuncio in Vienna, was therefore reduced still further.[37]

The Nazis were elated by these developments, as the reports of the Austrian Security Directorate reveal. So optimistic were they that there were rumors in May 1936 about preparations for a new armed revolt in Styria and Carinthia. When the Heimwehr was about to be dissolved in September the Nazis made no effort to hide their *Schadenfreude* (malicious glee).[38]

With Austria diplomatically isolated by the summer of 1936, members of the Austrian government felt they had no choice but to reach some kind of understanding with Germany. An agreement would presumably retain their country's independence, if only temporarily. The Austrians were not so naive as to suppose that any agreement with Hitler would last indefinitely. But one should also keep in mind that Hitler's infidelity to treaties had not yet been firmly established. Schuschnigg, in particular, hoped that by conciliating the Nazi Führer he might buy two or three years of breathing time during which the balance of power might shift back in his favor. If this was appeasement, then the Austrians were at least in good company. Great Britain, Poland, and even the Vatican had already expressed confidence in Hitler's willingness to respect the sanctity of treaties he himself signed.

The negotiations, which finally resulted in the Austro-German Agreement of 11 July 1936, can be considered the climax of three years of discussions between the Nazis and the Austrian government. The participants varied from time to time, beginning with Habicht and Dollfuss and ending with von Papen and Schuschnigg. But the objectives remained remarkably the same: amnesty and equality of rights for Nazis and their representation in the Austrian government in exchange for the total end of terror, the resumption of normal diplomatic and economic relations between Germany and Austria, and a German promise to respect Austria's independence.

Many Austrians were still opposed to any deal with the Nazis in the summer of 1936. However, as Franz von Papen himself wrote to Hitler, these people, "Legitimists, Socialists [Heimwehr], fascists, and the democratic elements of Catholicism and liberalism, although all bitter enemies of German [and Austrian] National Socialism regard[ed] each other with almost greater hatred than they [did] the Third Reich."[39] It was a classic case, experienced earlier in Russia, Italy, and Germany, of the opponents of totalitarianism being unable to unite against a common foe.

The key sections of the *published* portion of the July Agreement declared that the German government recognized the "full sovereignty" of Austria and regarded "the question of Austrian National Socialism as an internal affair," which it would not seek to influence either "directly or indirectly." In return, Austria had to regard itself as a "German State." This was simply a polite way of saying that it had to avoid any anti-German alliance.[40] Because Austria had no anti-German links after the German-Italian rapprochement, this publicized section of the July Agreement was an apparent victory for Schuschnigg. The Austrian chancellor had long been convinced that he had nothing to fear from the Austrian Nazis as long as they were cut off from German aid and comfort.[41]

Far more insidious for Austria was the unpublished "Gentlemen's Agreement." Its ten articles essentially provided for a resumption of normal cultural and economic relations between the two countries. On the surface, nothing could have been more beneficial to Austria, which had long suffered from a drastically reduced tourist trade. But "tourists" could spread Nazi propaganda as was now also possible through the resumed sale of Reich German books and newspapers in Austria.[42]

Article IX of the Gentlemen's Agreement was more political—and controversial. It called on the Austrian chancellor to grant an amnesty to all political prisoners. When this promise was fulfilled two weeks later, it involved the release of 17,045 Nazis, including most of the *Gauleiter* and higher leaders of the SA and SS.[43]

The second part of this article provided that "for the purpose of promoting a real pacification," representatives of the "National Opposition" enjoying the chancellor's confidence would be included in the cabinet. This point was to cause endless disputes in the future. Schuschnigg interpreted "National Opposition" to include non-Nazi, pan-German nationalists, whereas the Nazis assumed it meant only party members. Schuschnigg himself later admitted that there simply was no non-Nazi National Opposition.[44]

The Austrian Nazis and the Agreement

According to Nazi historians, writing years after the event, "There was great joy on both sides of the [German-Austrian] border over the Agreement."[45] The contemporary reaction was a good deal less sanguine. To be sure, members of the party's moderate Reinthaller faction "hailed the Agreement from the very beginning."[46] Although they regretted its temporary renunciation of the Anschluss, the Agreement closely resembled the modus vivendi they had long desired.

Nazi radicals, on the other hand, were shocked and dismayed by the Agreement. As Papen later wrote to Hitler, "It was perhaps not easy psychologically for [the] Party . . . after three years of hard self-sacrificing struggle and endurance of all kinds, to see the Reich make its peace with the Schuschnigg government."[47] Some Nazis in Carinthia were so angry about the accord that they switched over to the Communist party.[48]

Illegal Austrian Nazi publications put on a brave front by telling their readers they should trust their leaders and maintain the party's strength and discipline. Just as there had been, for tactical reasons, periods of quiet between battles on the Austro-Italian Isonzo front in World War I, so too was such a pause necessary in 1936. Some comfort was taken from the fact that the Agreement forbade Austria to pursue an anti-German foreign policy. The illegal *Mitteilung* of the Austrian Nazi Landesleitung credited the party's struggle against the regime for making the Agreement possible.[49] But the Agreement's actual conclusion by German *diplomats* could not have been very pleasing to them. The most radical Nazis felt betrayed by the Agreement and its recognition of Austrian sovereignty. Still others thought that Hitler had agreed to the treaty only for the sake of appearances and did not take it seriously himself.[50]

As for Hitler, when Papen informed him by telephone about the signing of the treaty the Führer poured out a "stream of invectives" to the startled envoy. Papen later recalled, "He said that I had seduced him to make too far-reaching concessions in return for only platonic concessions, which the Austrian government would not live up to anyway. He was just being taken for a ride. He seemed extremely upset and out of sorts. The only answer that I could make was that my office was at his immediate disposal, if he found my accomplishments so poor."[51] Nevertheless, Hitler soon changed his mind when reports of favorable world reaction to the treaty began to reach the German capital. From an opponent of the Agreement he became a partisan.[52] And Papen, far from being dismissed, was promoted from special envoy to ambassador.

To make certain his new policy was followed in Austria, Hitler, possibly at the instigation of Papen, summoned Odilo Globocnik and Friedrich Rainer to his mountain retreat near Berchtesgaden. The meeting of 16 July took place in the presence of Josef Goebbels and Martin Bormann (Hitler's special deputy for personnel questions). The two Austrians were startled to hear an angry lecture by the Führer on the mistaken policy pursued by the party in Austria. There had to be an end to the eternal arguments. One had to fit oneself into the framework of the Fatherland Front. The National Socialist idea had to be absorbed before any other actions could be taken. He would prefer it if Josef Leopold were already the chancellor of Austria. But because he wasn't, one could only deal with realities.[53]

The startled Rainer could only stammer: "Mein Führer, our only task is to support you to execute your orders loyally until victory." Hitler replied: "You have to help yourself with all kinds of means."[54] The Führer went on to explain "clearly and in an ice-cold fashion" why he had concluded the treaty. "My foreign-policy actions cannot tolerate the burden of Austria. I am constantly receiving demarches from Paris and London and I must build a friendly relation with Italy and need time to enlarge the Wehrmacht. The German Wehrmacht must be the strongest in the world. I must build up the officer corps. I need two more years to make politics. For that length of time the party in Austria must maintain discipline."[55]

After Hitler had spoken for about twenty minutes, Rainer was finally able to interject: "Mein Führer, we are not those at whom you are angry. We [the Carinthian Nazis] have endeavored to follow a reasonable policy in Austria, but it is very difficult because we are forbidden and have no connections." Rainer added the pledge that he and Globocnik would influence the members of the party to conduct themselves as Hitler desired. At last, somewhat appeased, the Führer became friendlier and said: "After all, Austria is my own home country, and I will never forget my home country." But he still refused to order the Austrian party to be prepared for a German takeover of Austria.[56]

Hitler's instructions to the two Austrians reveal an all-too-seldom appreciated aspect of his foreign policy and perhaps even his character. His seemingly irrational behavior during the last four years of the Second World War has obscured his earlier cool calculations and extreme patience. Once convinced that a premature grab for Austria would run high international risks, he exercised a restraining influence on the far more restive and impetuous Austrian Nazis.

The Reich chancellor followed the same line with regard to Nazis in Danzig, the Memel territory of Lithuania, and in Yugoslavia. In each case Hitler's unwillingness to intervene caused disillusionment among his followers. When the Nazi leader in the Memelland was released from a Lithuanian prison in July 1938, he was told by Reich authorities "to impose a stricter and more unequivocal discipline than before on the young hotheads in the Memel territory who hoped to be able to force a quick and violent solution of the Memel problem."[57]

The July Agreement:
Its Impact on the Austrian Economy
and the Fatherland Front

The doubts of most Nazi radicals concerning the July Agreement were soon laid to rest by their own propaganda and by the actual consequences of the treaty. Hitler had already won so many diplomatic victories that it seemed probable to many early critics of the treaty that it too would have a favorable outcome. Austrian Nazis soon realized that the Reich wanted to use the illegal party to pressure the Austrian government into still closer relations with Germany.[58] The underground *Österreichischer Beobachter* pointed out how the Agreement ended Italy's role as an anti-German power. It also provided the Viennese with an opportunity to escape the Jewish domination of their city's culture. There would now be a flood of imported German films as well as concerts, lectures, and even sporting events having German performers.[59]

From a purely economic point of view, the July Agreement did have some real value for Austria. The resumption of trade between the two German-speaking countries led to a surplus of 2 million Schillings (or $224,716) in the federal treasury by the end of the year. Prospects for the Austrian economy in 1937 were the best in eight years. The rise in the price of foodstuffs and raw materials led to a modest improvement in the income of peasants and miners. Unemployment dropped from a high of 550–600,000 in 1936 to 401,000 in 1937. The index of production for heavy industrial goods (1929=100) increased from 74 in 1936 to 94 in 1937. On the other hand, the production of consumer goods failed to increase, and overall the Austrian recovery remained far behind that of Germany or Britain.[60] Nevertheless, the improvement may have induced a few former Socialists to take a more positive attitude toward the government.[61] If these trends could have continued for a few years, the Schuschnigg regime might have been able to establish a modicum of popular tolerance, if not enthusiasm.

As it was, the short-term consequences of the Agreement were more beneficial to Germany than to Austria. The revival of Austro-German tourism, for example, meant that Austrians could now travel to Germany for the first time since the imposition of the 1,000-Mark blockade. They actually took advantage of the open border in greater numbers than did the Germans. Those tourists from the Reich who did come to Austria were limited in the amount of money they could spend. And in any event, they were careful to seek out the inns of well-known pro-Nazis and avoided those of government supporters.[62] The relatively unrestricted travel also enormously reduced the previous difficulties that Austrian and German Nazis had had in communicating with one another.[63]

Friends of the Austrian government were also surprised and dubious about the July Agreement. But unlike the Nazis', their anxieties never entirely vanished. The government issued reassuring statements that the Agreement "in no way meant a change in direction" and was in the tradition of Dollfuss's efforts toward a reconciliation with Germany.[64] Although some of their worst fears were calmed, many members of the Fatherland Front remained convinced that the treaty was the first step on the road to Austria's Gleichschaltung,[65] as indeed it was.

Nazis now entered the Fatherland Front in ever-increasing numbers, and with Hitler's blessing. Membership became even less a proof of patriotism than before. The upshot was that government supporters hesitated to take any overt anti-Nazi action for fear of later Nazi reprisals. Even before the July Putsch it had not been easy to convict Nazis, because judges were either pro-Nazi themselves or were nervous about possible future Nazi revenge. The situation had improved for a time following the revolt when the government's internal and external position was strong. But the judicial process deteriorated once again after July 1936.[66]

By the fall of 1936 the Austrian Nazis felt bolder than ever. They were convinced that any attempt to suppress them would be construed in Berlin as a violation of the July Agreement. Even slightly anti-Nazi speeches could be so interpreted by German and Austrian Nazis. To avoid such charges, the government in Vienna severely limited the political activities of the VF, allowing just a few large demonstrations to prove that it was still alive. According to one Austrian diplomat, Martin Fuchs, only the Legitimists could still be considered militant anti-Nazis after the eleventh of July.[67]

Therefore, a kind of passivity and lethargy vis-à-vis stepped-up Nazi activities began to prevail in both government and VF circles. This change in mood was first clearly manifested on 29 July. On that day the Olympic torch passed through Vienna on its way from Greece to the site of the games in Berlin. A ceremony, held in Vienna's huge Heldenplatz in honor of this event and the departure of Austria's Olympic athletes, was turned into a wild demonstration by 30,000 spectators chanting "Heil Hitler" and "Heil Grossdeutschland." To one Heimwehr man who was also a policeman present at the fracas, Prince Starhemberg later remarked:

> "Well, you did not distinguish yourself the day before yesterday. Had you perhaps received instructions not to interfere?"
>
> He answered "Oh no . . . we had no special instructions. But after all, what are we to do? Can we tell? Before we know where we are, the Nazis will be in the government. How can we know if a Nazi will not be made minister for security? Then, anyone who has been too active against them . . . will pay for it. Besides, how can we know if the government really wants us to take drastic action?"
>
> That was the way it was in Austria. That's the way the overwhelming part of the Austrian civil service thought . . . and thousands of small functionaries in the Fatherland Front.[68]

Even allowing for Starhemberg's understandable bitterness over his ouster from the government and his penchant for exaggeration, there is still much truth in the above quotation. Yet Kurt von Schuschnigg perhaps came even closer to the truth when years later he wrote in his memoirs that "the real reason for all the difficulties was that Germany tacitly had an entirely different conception of the object of the agreement from that of Austria. For us it was the maintenance and for Germany the elimination of Austria as an entity."[69]

The deterioration of the Austrian party proved to be short-lived. The example of Germany's growing prosperity, together with Italy's inability and unwillingness to defend Austria's independence after the start of the Ethiopian War, began reviving the Austrian NSDAP toward the end of 1935. The Nazis' neo-Renaissance made it increasingly imperative for the Austrian government to meet their challenge by further developing some kind of counterideology and alternate political organization.

Part of the government's response was to revive the memory of Austria's imperial past and to stress the Catholic nature of the state—as distinct from the Protestantism and even paganism of Germany. But in warfare—and a virtual state of war existed between the Nazis and the Austrian government after 1933—there is a tendency for opponents to take on the characteristics of their enemies; witness the British and American terror-bombing of German and Japanese cities during World War II. Challenged by the dynamism and totalitarian ideology of the Nazi party, the Austrian government, in a desperate attempt to weaken the Nazis' popular appeal, became ever more like its hated rival.

However, the positive fascism of the Austrian government failed to increase its popularity significantly. Schuschnigg's lack of support, not only at home but abroad as well, finally induced him to make a deal with Nazi Germany in the hope of buying some time for Austria's independence. The July Agreement did include a formal German declaration recognizing Austrian sovereignty and it brought a slight improvement in Austria's dismal economy. It is doubtful, however, that the treaty even delayed the Anschluss. In reality, it increased contact between German and Austrian Nazis and facilitated the subversion of the country. So by the summer of 1936 the prospects of the Austrian Nazi party were radically improved from what they had been only a year before.

The nineteen-month period between the signing of the July Agreement in 1936 and the Hitler-Schuschnigg meeting at Berchtesgaden in February 1938 was marked by continued rivalries within the Austrian party and between it and the parent German party. The release and relative freedom of movement of Austrian Nazi leaders that resulted from the July Agreement intensified the rivalries, because the leaders could now compete more freely and with less fear of government interference.[1]

With Italian patronage of Austrian independence for all practical purposes a thing of the past, and with the July Agreement facilitating Germany's policy of peaceful penetration, the Anschluss, or at least the Gleichschaltung of Austria, once again seemed imminent. But the awareness that their long-sought goal was almost within reach only added to intraparty feuding. Each competing group wanted to get all the credit for implementing the Anschluss. To the victors would go the spoils—choice administrative positions—or so they hoped. Consequently, each of the rival Austrian factions tried to convince party authorities in Germany that its policy alone could result in a Nazi takeover. Their rivals' strategy was bound to end in disaster.[2]

It may well be that party leaders in the Reich encouraged these quarrels to prevent the emergence of a single, powerful Austrian leader. Nevertheless, given the aggressive and egotistical nature of the Austrian Nazi leaders, together with the disparities between their socioeconomic backgrounds, they doubtless would have quarreled even without encouragement from the Reich.

Still, there was a limit to how much disorder the German leaders would tolerate. Such concern was demonstrated in July 1937 when Hitler appointed his economic expert, Wilhelm Keppler, to supervise relations between the German and Austrian parties. Lacking any outside control, the volatile Ausrian Nazis might resort to a premature use of force as they had done in 1934, thus jolting the Great Powers out of their diplomatic-military lethargy. With the renewal of German intervention into the affairs of the Austrian party the Alpine and Danubian Nazis realized to their dismay that not only Austria's independence was at stake, but their own as well.

The Three-Sided Struggle for Power

The reintroduction of German supervision over the Austrian Nazi party in 1937 resulted from the bitter and prolonged three-sided struggle for the supremacy of the Austrian party. One group, consisting of Habicht, Proksch, Frauenfeld, and other former Austrian *Gauleiter*, counted mostly as a nuisance factor because its members had lost their jobs and most of their influence after the July Putsch. However, this setback did not prevent Frauenfeld and others from intriguing against Leopold.[3] According to some of the Nazis who had remained behind in Austria, the refugees were evening old scores with rivals.[4] Information they gave to the Austrian police led to frequent arrests and house searches.

The second and most important group between 1935 and the early part of 1938 was led by Josef Leopold. His deputy in 1936 was a physician from Saint-Pölten, Dr. Hugo Jury. When Jury joined Leopold's rivals in 1937, he was replaced by Leopold Tavs, a Sudeten-born biochemist, former city councilman, and after March 1937, the Gauleiter of Vienna. This faction was regarded by its rivals, and especially by Franz von Papen, as having dangerous and violence-prone radicals.[5] But by contrast, Austrian security forces considered Leopold a moderate in 1936. They thought he wanted nothing more than to attain power through a legalized Nazi party and negotiations with the Austrian government, much as the Nazis had done in Germany.[6]

The third Nazi faction, located in Carinthia, looked to the leadership of Hubert Klausner. The Carinthian Gauleiter favored a semilegal takeover and eschewed terror. This faction was supported by middle-class "Catholic Nationals" headed by the Viennese lawyer Arthur Seyss-Inquart. The Catholic Nationals were on good terms with Austrian heavy industry and high finance and likewise supported an evolutionary course that would leave their country with a measure of autonomy under a Nazi government.[7] Only a few Nazis, such as Walter Riehl and Anton Reinthaller, stood outside these three factions; but these men had little influence in the middle and late thirties.[8]

The Nazis' chronic factionalism was a godsend to the hard-pressed Austrian government, allowing it to play off one group against the others. Without this political windfall, Schuschnigg could hardly have kept the Nazis in hand as well as he did.

Josef Leopold: A Capsule Biography

Josef Leopold owed his prestige and popularity in large part to his being the only Gauleiter who did not flee from Austria when the party was outlawed in 1933. He was able to remain in Austria after the July Putsch for the simple reason that he was in prison during the attempted revolution. After the dissolution of the Landesleitung in 1934, thousands of his followers (Persche claims it was "several hundred thousand"), mostly in the eastern provinces, regarded him as their natural leader.[9]

Leopold's background was remarkably similar to Hitler's. Born just two months before the Führer (in February 1889) and in the same rural *Waldviertel* of Upper Austria, his ancestors had been peasants since at least 1789. "Only half educated and primitive in his thoughts and actions,"[10] for Leopold "everything was simple and clear."[11] Here again was an interesting parallel between Leopold and Hitler, both of whom were academic failures. Hitler dropped out of secondary school, and Leopold never passed the examination that would have made possible a career as a regular officer. These experiences may have contributed to the revulsion both men had toward intellectuals, even those within the party. Leopold's "simplicity," however, did not extend to material things. As Landesleiter he was fond of driving an automobile more luxurious than those of government officials. Hitler bought a huge Mercedes as soon as he was released from prison in 1925 and until 1933 insisted on passing every car on the highway.

Leopold, who fought in the Great War of 1914–18, was captured by the Russians in 1915 and sent to Siberia. After the Revolution he escaped and returned to his troops in 1918. Although his father had been an ardent follower of Georg von Schönerer for three decades, the younger Leopold, much to his chagrin in later years, briefly joined the Social Democratic party in December 1918. At the same time he became a lieutenant in the Marxist paramilitary Volkswehr.[12] This ideological detour proved short-lived and in fact was not uncommon for many Austrian and Sudeten Nazis.[13]

Leopold joined Walter Riehl's DNSAP in 1919, becoming the Ortsgruppenleiter of Krems in 1924 and a district leader in 1926. When the party split in the latter year, he joined the "right" faction and was rewarded by being

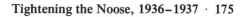

CAPTAIN JOSEF LEOPOLD. *Leader of the illegal Austrian Nazi party, 1935–1938. The date on his sleeve indicates the year he joined the Hitler Movement. Austrian National Library Picture Archive.*

made deputy Gauleiter of Lower Austria. The next year Hitler himself elevated Leopold to Gauleiter. For three years after the party was outlawed he spent more time in prison than out, being free only from 16 February to 21 June of 1935.

The Gauleiter's frequent imprisonment between June 1933 and July 1936 helped lead, as we have already seen, to a wide-ranging decentralization of the party's leadership. *Parteigenossen* throughout the country came to regard the central authorities as nothing more than mediators. In general, local leaders did whatever they wanted, just as they had done before 1931. SS leaders in particular, owing certainly in part to the rising fortunes of the SS in Germany, refused to take orders from the SA man Leopold. Anton Reinthaller was likewise reluctant to follow Leopold's orders.[14]

The Carinthian Nazis

Throughout the year and a half between January 1935 and July 1936, Josef Leopold, despite his imprisonment, continued to be, at least nominally, the federal leader of the Austrian Nazi party. But, as previously noted, Major Klausner acted as the de facto deputy leader and appointed two young fellow Carinthians, Dr. Friedrich Rainer and Odilo Globocnik, to take charge of the organization and political aspects of party activities. The two younger men, in fact, for a time became the real leaders of the party while Leopold, and for a time also Klausner, were in prison.

Rainer, born in 1903, was extraordinarily young to be a political leader, even by Nazi standards. He studied politics and jurisprudence at the University of Graz where he was awarded a doctorate in the latter subject. He joined the Nazi movement in 1930 and thereafter his influence rapidly increased in party affairs.[15]

Like so many leaders of the Austrian Nazi party, Globocnik, or "Globus" as his party friends called him, came from an area outside the territory that became the Austrian Republic in 1918. A native of Trieste (b. 1904), he was trained as a master builder before being granted citizenship in the Austrian Republic after the breakup of the monarchy. Globocnik was a determined and energetic man. In 1920, at the impressionable age of sixteen, he joined the Austrian Nazi party. Since 1934 he had been in charge of the "special service" of the Carinthian Gauleitung, which grew rapidly into an intelligence network. According to Rainer, the Carinthian Gau enjoyed a high prestige within the party because of its excellent organization. And even more important, it was free of the leadership quarrels that so debilitated the other *Gaue*.[16] When Leopold was finally released from the Wöllersdorf detention camp on 23 July 1936, Rainer and Globocnik were unenthusiastic about surrendering their influence within the party.[17] Alfred Persche experienced the same difficulties at this time when he tried to resume his leadership of the Austrian SA.[18]

Leopold won what turned out to be a largely empty victory on 31 July 1936, when Rainer and Globocnik met with the Landesleiter to assure him of their fidelity. Leopold modestly referred to himself as merely the federal president of a Rainer cabinet. His graciousness and sincerity may be doubted, however. The Landesleiter (correctly) suspected the two Carinthians of having ambitions of their own and of having secret ties with authorities in Germany. He also feared that they were trying to organize a Nazi opposition to him which would include the Styrian Gauleiter, Walter Rafelsberger. As a matter of fact, Rafelsberger did serve in Berlin as a contact man between the Carinthians and Joachim von Ribbentrop's Foreign Bureau as well as with the party chancellery in Munich. Consequently, in mid-September Leopold dismissed Rainer, Globocnik, and various other young party members without explanation.[19] Major Klausner's dismissal followed on 9 October.

Leopold's leadership was greatly enhanced by two important events in late January and early February 1937. On 24 January the Austrian Landesleitung, together with the *Gauleiter* and their deputies, met in Vienna and expressed their confidence in Leopold. But they coupled their approval with the wish that a reconciliation be achieved with the Nazi opposition (centered in Carinthia). Then, during a visit to Berlin at the end of the month, Heinrich Himmler placed the entire Austrian SS under Leopold's command. The only condition was that the Austrian SS remain subordinate to the Reichsführer SS in personnel matters. The Landesleiter's prestige and authority were further enhanced by two long and friendly conversations with Hermann Göring on the thirty-first and with Hitler himself on 1 February.[20]

A Conflict of Strategies

Behind the dispute between Leopold and his rivals lay a fundamental difference in strategy. Leopold's enemies, and even many historians, have labeled him a wild-eyed revolutionary ready and willing to use force to achieve his objectives.[21] In reality his strategy, at least until 1938, was relatively moderate (from the Nazi point of view).

Until that late date Leopold had sought to gain some kind of legal standing for the Austrian Nazi party, perhaps as a cultural union, or by incorporating the entire party as a bloc into the Fatherland Front. Such a role for the Nazis would soon lead to a coalition government and eventually to a Gleichschaltung following the German model. This result was possible, however, only if Germany avoided alarming the Schuschnigg regime by recognizing Austria's independence. Moreover, it would have to give complete freedom to the Austrian Nazi party to recruit new members, agitate, and carry out propaganda activities.[22]

It is likely that Leopold also believed any mass incorporation of the Nazi party in one form or another into the Fatherland Front would enhance his own position because he could rely on the support of the forty-thousand-man Austrian SA. Klausner, Rainer, Globocnik, and their faction, even though backed by the Austrian SS, had no such mass support and wanted to keep the illegal organization "as small as possible."[23] This difference in popularity may also explain Rainer's retrospective criticism of Leopold for his unwillingness to forego public fame.

In any event, the Carinthians regarded Leopold's plan for a "deal" with the Schuschnigg government as worthless and preferred to dissociate themselves from the party organization. Its only possible value might be in some kind of emergency. Rainer had decided sometime between the summer of 1935 and his meeting with Hitler at Berchtesgaden on 16 July 1936 that the only way the Austrian Nazis could achieve power was to enter the Schuschnigg government and the Fatherland Front on an individual basis. "An illegal party could never be a mass party."[24] Moreover, an enemy could not be fought from prison. His faith in the party had apparently been undermined by the success of government informers. He became even more disillusioned by the leadership quarrels, which had provoked the contempt of the German leaders he encountered in Berlin in the spring of 1936.

Rather than using the party to enter the government, Rainer preferred a more roundabout approach. This technique involved the use of bourgeois professionals like the military historian Edmund Glaise-Horstenau and Arthur Seyss-Inquart. Seyss, though not formally a member of the party, was a pan-German Catholic who enjoyed the confidence of both Hitler and Schuschnigg. Such individual efforts to enter the Austrian government, Rainer believed, could only be successful if accompanied by pressure from the outside by Berlin. Thus the only task of the Austrian party would be to spread the Nazi ideology among sympathetic elements of the Austrian population. It would renounce all acts of violence that might alarm foreign powers.[25]

The Carinthians could agree with Leopold that the presence of Nazis in the Austrian government would eventually bring about the country's Gleichschaltung. Austria would then remain a nominally independent Nazi state until such time as Germany, strengthened by its growing military power, could carry out an Anschluss. In other words, the Austrian party as a whole could do nothing decisive on its own and was therefore utterly dependent on Germany. This strategy, however, did not prevent individual Nazi leaders such as the Carinthians themselves from taking certain actions without consulting the Germans in advance. Leopold, for his part, agreed that "we need the Reich. Without the Reich we are lost." Yet he also believed that without the Austrian Nazi party, Germany "could do nothing."[26]

The differences between the two factions were not enormous. Both hoped to achieve a Gleichschaltung by having Nazis enter the Austrian government. Both were willing to adhere to the concept of gradual "peaceful penetration." They disagreed mainly over who should do the penetrating. The Carinthians saw Germany playing the key role, with individual Austrian Nazis assuming the status of minor actors. For Leopold and the SA, the Austrian Nazis as a whole would take the initiative, although they would also need occasional support from the Reich.

There is no doubt, however, that Rainer's interpretation was closer to that which Hitler and von Papen had in mind when the July Agreement was signed. Rainer and Globocnik managed to win limited support for this policy when they met with the *Gauleiter*, in Anif, just south of Salzburg, on 17 July following their conference with Hitler at the Berghof.[27] But the Anif gathering took place before Leopold and his followers were released from prison so that nothing permanent was achieved.

Whatever the differences between the Nazi leaders, it is important to note that none of them wanted Austria simply swallowed up in an expanded German Reich.[28] Therefore, to divide Austrians between "patriots" and "traitors," with the Schuschnigg supporters all in the first camp and the Nazis and pro-Nazis in the second, is as misleading as it is unfair. Virtually all Austrians wanted to see the preservation of at least some autonomy for their homeland. They envisaged an equal partnership between Germany and Austria and expected "Hitler, as an Austrian, would implement this conception."[29] Therefore, not even the most rabid and misguided of the Nazis thought of themselves as being in any sense traitors. They naively thought they could reconcile their loyalty to Austria with their loyalty to the party.

Leopold admitted on one occasion to Alfred Persche that the Austrian Nazis shared Schuschnigg's view that Austria had a special mission. Both he and Persche were equally convinced that Austrians could best lead other Austrians. He interpreted the Führer's order concerning noninterference in Austrian affairs by party offices in the Reich even more literally than Hitler intended.[30]

The Leopold-Schuschnigg Negotiations

Leopold thought he saw in Article IX of the secret Gentlemen's Agreement (attached to the July Agreement of 1936) an opportunity to bring himself into the Austrian government and the Nazi party into the Fatherland Front. The second section of that notorious clause, of course, had stipulated that "for the purpose of promoting a real pacification," representatives of the "National Opposition," enjoying the confidence of the chancellor and selected by him, were to be given political responsibility.[31]

This clause was a constant source of friction between the German and Austrian governments. If Schuschnigg were to acquiesce on this point and add genuine Nazis to the cabinet, he would risk a Gleichschaltung. To refuse, however, could easily be interpreted as a violation of the July Agreement, thus giving Germany a welcome pretext for using force.

However, the Agreement was silent about whole organizations being taken into the government; consequently, Leopold was wrong in expecting the legalization of the party. On the other hand, Kurt von Schuschnigg was naive in believing that there was a significant Austrian National Opposition distinct from the Nazi party. It is therefore not surprising that Leopold, the generally, if not universally, acknowledged leader of the Austrian Nazis, was indignant when neither he nor any of his entourage were appointed to the Schuschnigg cabinet.[32]

Leopold did not allow this snub to prevent him from seeking negotiations with the Austrian chancellor. His goal was to create a disguised Nazi organization called the Deutschsozialer Volksbund (German Social People's League) and then to incorporate it en masse into the Fatherland Front. Here was a resurrection of the many Nazi attempts to relegalize their party and slip it into a government body. Now that Habicht and Reinthaller had already tried and failed, it was Leopold's turn.

The Landesleiter faced several major obstacles in reaching any agreement with Schuschnigg. Not the least of the roadblocks was the enormous difference in social background between the two men. The uneducated son of a peasant, and a former low-ranking officer, Leopold was personally distasteful as a negotiating partner to the highly educated Schuschnigg, a member of an old officer family.[33]

There was another handicap. Just as the Heimwehr had blocked the Habicht-Dollfuss and Reinthaller-Schuschnigg negotiations, so too did parts of the Fatherland Front and the Nazi extremists object to renewed discussions. Members of the Fatherland Front no doubt saw visions of a new Trojan horse whereas some Nazis, at least in Styria, were afraid that Schuschnigg was only negotiating in order to expose and arrest the entire Nazi organization.[34] Franz von Papen also reported to Hitler that the *Gauleiter* and the SA saw little hope of success for the talks and were critical of the Landesleitung.[35]

Probably to avoid the charge of "selling out," Captain Leopold drew up a set of demands in January 1937, which were transmitted to the Austrian cabinet. These "minimum demands," in seven closely typed pages, would have gone far beyond the terms of the July Agreement in turning Austria into a completely Nazified state.

The terms included the following: an amnesty for prisoners convicted of "base crimes" if they had been committed "for clearly political motives" and a "recognition of the principle that National Socialist conviction and activity [had] no character hostile to the state or government"; all restrictions regarding the import of books and periodicals from Germany were to be dropped; a "solemn declaration in favor of common racial stock as the purpose of the political life of the state" was to be made as well as a "prohibition [declared] against the Jewish press"; new cabinet ministers were to be appointed "having the confidence of both sides"; a defensive alliance with the Reich "was to be concluded and a plebiscite [held] to determine the form of state and the Anschluss"; finally, in order to effect a permanent and real solution," the Deutschsozialer Volksbund had to be established with full freedom of action.[36] To facilitate the discussions leading to its creation within the Fatherland Front, a so-called Committee of Seven headed by Leopold was formed.

Schuschnigg met with Leopold himself for the first time on 11 February 1936 and worked out a compromise. Nothing was said about Leopold's extreme demands. The Landesleiter agreed to abandon, at least temporarily, the formation of the Volksbund and to take cognizance of the independence of Austria "for reasons of Realpolitik." Schuschnigg in turn promised to release another 145 imprisoned Nazis and to give a "sympathetic examination" of all officials and students dismissed for Nazi activities. And finally, he would protect from police action a permanent office in Vienna established by the Committee of Seven for the purpose of further pacification.[37] The latter would be, in effect, a grievance committee allowing Nazis to complain about alleged excesses committed by the police and the Fatherland Front. The Committee's offices on the Teinfaltstrasse in Vienna's central district became the illegal party's unofficial headquarters with orderlies even wearing party uniforms. The government tolerated this arrangement because the existence of the headquarters made it easier to monitor Nazi activities. Leopold, for his part, gained a de facto if not a de jure recognition for his Nazi activities.[38]

Leopold hoped to win still more favors from the Schuschnigg government through both internal and external pressure. Thus, the German foreign minister's visit to Vienna on 22–23 February 1937 was accompanied by gigantic demonstrations by perhaps as many as one hundred thousand Nazis. At the same time, Neurath took advantage of his visit to try (unsuccessfully) to coax Schuschnigg into conceding the Nazis' earlier demands.[39] Even the Italian foreign minister, Count Galeazzo Ciano, was asked by Leopold to intervene on behalf of the Austrian Nazis. But Ciano's efforts were rebuffed by the Austrian foreign minister, Guido Schmidt. Far from capitulating, Schuschnigg dismissed his pro-Nazi minister of security, Dr. Odo Neustädter-Stürmer, on 20 March.[40]

In fact, none of Leopold's moves in Austria in the early part of 1937 brought him any appreciable success. His willingness to negotiate with the Schuschnigg government and particularly his tactical recognition of Austrian independence appeared to confirm Nazi rumors that he had sold out the party's platform and committed treason. These sentiments led to mutinies in Styria and Vienna in February and April which, even though suppressed by Leopold, only undermined his prestige.[41]

Leopold's Committee of Seven was also less than a resounding success. A police raid in May 1937 uncovered memoranda of conversations between Austrian and Reich party leaders, including Hitler. There was also evidence of anti-Austrian propaganda from Austrian exiles, proof that antigovernment demonstrations had been ordered by the illegal party, and information about a courier service between the German and Austrian Nazis.[42] The whole affair could only have reduced still further Schuschnigg's meager confidence in Leopold's good faith and raised questions, even among Leopold's followers, about his intelligence in not destroying such incriminating material.

Leopold and His Enemies: Papen and Seyss-Inquart

Although Leopold managed to hang on to the leadership of the Austrian Nazi party until February 1938, his star began falling rapidly soon after his inconclusive negotiations with Schuschnigg in early 1937. The Nazis, as always, needed unqualified successes to maintain their morale and "dynamism." But Leopold lacked sufficient strength to compel the government to make the kind of concessions he needed. The Landesleiter's failures only encouraged his party rivals to accelerate their own efforts to reach an accord with the Austrian government outside the framework of the Nazi organization. In this connection, Franz von Papen and Arthur Seyss-Inquart began to play larger roles after the spring of 1937.

The immense differences in social status and religious and political outlooks between the plebeian Austrian, Leopold, and the aristocratic, Catholic diplomat from western Germany, Papen, were almost bound to cause conflicts eventually. To the German ambassador, Leopold was limited in his education, "stubborn and dogmatic in character—a typical, unintelligent noncommissioned officer."[43]

On the other hand, Papen described Seyss-Inquart as well known as a "conscientious, tolerant, and intelligent man whom no one believed capable of precipitating any wild adventure." The German ambassador saw it as his duty "to prevent radical elements in the Nazi party both in Germany and Austria from pursuing any policy which would be likely to lead to international complications." Leopold's only task was to win over the Austrian population to a pro-German policy. Therefore it was natural that Papen eventually threw his weight behind Seyss-Inquart and other middle-class moderates like Rainer and Reinthaller, in their struggle for supremacy within the party.[44]

Leopold had not begun his relations with Papen very auspiciously when he tried to block the then vice-chancellor's appointment as special envoy in 1934. To Leopold, Papen was "more a Catholic than a real Nazi,"[45] a description he also applied to Seyss-Inquart.

Seyss came from the same middle- to upper-class background as Papen, Klausner, Rainer, Globocnik, and Jury. Like so many of the Austrian Nazi leaders, he was a Sudeten German, born in Iglau (Jihlava) in 1892 and raised in Olmütz (Olomuec). As a Moravian he grew up in an atmosphere of only moderate German nationalism and relatively strong Catholicism, in stark contrast to the more passionately nationalistic and free-thinking Germans of neighboring Bohemia.[46]

Neither his restrained nationalism nor his Catholicism endeared him to a hard-line Nazi like Leopold. Nor could Leopold be pleased with Seyss-Inquart's toleration of Jews, his successful academic career, and his flourishing postwar legal practice in Vienna. Both Seyss-Inquart and Leopold fought in the World War, though even here was a major difference, because Seyss had been a distinguished officer.[47]

As a matter of fact, in social background, religion, and education, Seyss-Inquart was far closer to Schuschnigg, the anti-Nazi, than he was to Leopold. Both Seyss and Schuschnigg came from well-to-do families, both were practicing Catholics, both had been officers in the World War, both were lawyers, and both were moderate pan-Germans who hated violence. Seyss was also a personal friend of several members of the Schuschnigg government, including the secretary of the Fatherland Front, Guido Zernatto, as well as numerous former leaders of the Christian Social party.[48]

Seyss and Schuschnigg agreed that representatives of the National Opposition ought to enter the government on an individual basis. Most important of all, Seyss-Inquart was able to convince Schuschnigg, if Persche's account can be trusted, that he (Seyss) was both completely opposed to Leopold yet fully acceptable to the Reich party leadership.[49] It is no wonder then that the two men had confidence in each other and could collaborate whereas they both detested the uncouth Leopold.

The social differences between Seyss-Inquart and Leopold are of more than just passing interest; it was those very distinctions rather than political ideas and objectives that divided the two men. Both Seyss and Leopold wanted an Anschluss in which Austria would be assured a privileged autonomy. And concomitantly both wanted an independent Austrian Nazi movement which would be dependent on Hitler only for ideological guidance. But for political leadership within Austria the bourgeois Seyss preferred the same middle-class moderates as Papen, namely Rainer, Jury, and Neubacher, along with Reinthaller.[50]

Leopold was also infuriated by Seyss-Inquart's unwillingness to become a bona fide member of the party and his refusal to subordinate himself to Leopold's leadership. The Viennese lawyer did indeed hold himself aloof from the party apparatus. By so doing he could continue his profession untroubled by the police while maintaining good relations with the federal government. But it was this very freedom of movement that so embittered Leopold and Persche and other members of the SA who, especially before 1936, constantly ran the risk of imprisonment.

As one reads the letters and memoirs left by Leopold and his enemies—Papen, Seyss-Inquart, and the Carinthians—one cannot help becoming aware of their intense feelings of class consciousness and excessive provincial loyalties. For all the Nazi sloganeering about *Ein Reich* and *Ein Volk*, Leopold's rivals, like Alfred Proksch and the early Sudeten leaders of the Austrian Nazi party, were as good as foreigners. To a native of eastern Austria even the Carinthians were outsiders. By the same token, to his rivals, Leopold, the son of a wine-grower, was a typical, crude, lower-class member of the

Sturmabteilung. He was good perhaps for leading street demonstrations, but certainly not for holding high office, either inside or outside the party.

Even making allowances for the traditional class-consciousness and regionalism of Central Europe which Leopold, after all, did not invent, it still must be admitted that at least some of his troubles were self-inflicted. No less an authority than his friend and biographer, Alfred Persche, volunteered that it was not easy to get along with the Landesleiter, who was "very self-willed and had a strongly stamped personality."[51]

Under these circumstances, therefore, it is understandable that Leopold "showed a remarkable ability for making enemies."[52] Of course, he would alienate those people like the Carinthians, Klausner, Rainer, and Globocnik, whom he expelled or tried to expel from the party. Eventually he managed to add to his list of enemies the entire Austrian SS, Papen, Seyss-Inquart, and finally all the leading Reich Nazis: Göring, Himmler, Hess, and even Hitler himself.

But for this isolation Leopold was not entirely to blame. Persche was partly correct when he wrote that Leopold's predicament was caused by his refusal to submit to anyone except Hitler; he insisted on treating the Nazi hierarchy as equals.[53]

Leopold's Growing Isolation

In the late summer and early fall of 1936 Papen was briefly won over to Leopold's idea of the Austrian NSDAP entering the Fatherland Front as a block. Leopold even gained the approval of Rudolf Hess for the project.[54] But as early as 28 July 1936, the ambassador wrote to Hitler that the most important duty of the Austrian party leadership was to "keep still and wait."[55] For Papen, a strong and active illegal party could only interfere with the operation of the recently concluded July Agreement, which he regarded as his personal achievement. This viewpoint was essentially the same as that held by the Carinthians; but the activist and ambitious Landesleiter as well as most other Austrian Nazis could never reconcile themselves to such a passive, second-class role.

By January 1937, at the latest, Papen had become a sharp critic of Leopold, denouncing him to Hitler for his alleged interference in German-Austrian relations and his "obstructionism" in internal Austrian affairs. The ambassador repeated these criticisms to Schuschnigg and various Catholic leaders, thus hardening their already deep suspicions of the Landesleiter.[56]

Leopold lost all patience when Papen, at Schuschnigg's urging, began to support Seyss-Inquart as the representative of the National Opposition in still another attempt to pacify the Nazis. Papen's efforts in May 1937 to enlist Leopold's aid in this new action met a hostile reception. Leopold objected because the new agent of reconciliation, called the Volkspolitische Referat (National Political Office, or VPR), would bypass the Leopold-dominated Committee of Seven and would be led by Seyss, who was formally not even a member of the party. Worse yet, the VPR idea was backed by Rainer and Globocnik.[57]

Leopold's response to Papen's urgings was to terminate all social relations between the party and the German ambassador. Papen counterattacked a few days later by ordering members of the embassy to "break off all relations with Captain Leopold and his agents."[58]

The limit for Leopold was Seyss-Inquart's appointment to the Schuschnigg cabinet as councilor of state on 16 June 1937. In a meeting between the two men on 23 June, Leopold made his cooperation with Seyss conditional on the latter's subordination.[59] But Seyss was simply unwilling to assume this secondary role. The Viennese lawyer secretly tried to establish connections with the Austrian *Gauleiter* and SA leaders. How successful he was in these endeavors is impossible to determine. More useful were ties he forged with Papen, the elite Herren Club in Berlin, and the German Club in Vienna. Most beneficial of all were his relations with Reinthaller. Through the good offices of the latter he initiated a merger of the Nazi peasantry with the Catholic Peasant League, a step violently opposed by Leopold, who complained to Hitler that these moves violated a promise by Seyss not to form any separatist groups.[60]

But Hitler ignored this appeal, apparently preferring to give limited support to two rival leaders. By so doing he could play his old game of preventing the emergence of a single powerful leader outside his control. Moreover, he could throw his weight behind either the "respectable," "legal" Seyss-Inquart or the volatile and forceful Leopold, depending upon the needs of the moment.

The Ties that Bind:
Wilhelm Keppler and the Austrian Nazi Party

Seyss-Inquart's fortunes rose still higher, but those of Leopold plummeted correspondingly lower on 12 July 1937. On that day Hitler gave State Secretary Wilhelm Keppler the authority to handle relations between the

German and Austrian Nazis as well as responsibility for supervising the Fluchtlingshilfswerk and the Austrian Legion.[61]

A member of the party since 1927, Keppler had become Hitler's personal economic adviser in 1932. As one of the architects of the German Four-Year Plan he had established contact with Hermann Göring and kept the latter well informed about his activities in Austria. The state secretary also enjoyed the confidence of Martin Bormann. Likewise he was on good terms with the SS Reichsführer, Heinrich Himmler, who, like Göring, hoped to expand his personal power by using Keppler to gain control of Germany's Austrian policy.

Keppler first met Austrian Nazi leaders in his capacity as head of the Agricultural Department of the German Economic Ministry. By the end of 1936 he had already decided to support the "moderate" policy of the Carinthian Nazis in opposition to Leopold.[62] During the next summer, Keppler, on the recommendation of Odilo Globocnik, was named by Hitler to be chief of a mixed Austro-German commission to supervise the execution of the economic aspects of the July Agreement. At the same time he was supposed to carry out a survey of Austrian industries to facilitate their exploitation after an Anschluss. Finally, the Führer made Keppler his deputy to look after the party in Austria.[63]

Leopold did not help his own cause in a meeting with Keppler on 7 August. The state secretary informed the Landesleiter that Hitler had given him (Keppler) the right to lead party affairs in Austria. He added that the Führer would not attempt to solve the Austrian question before 1942. Leopold retorted by charging that Keppler's new position gave him no right to interfere in purely Austrian party matters. To do so would lead to the same kind of disaster that had occurred under Habicht.[64] A few days later the Landesleiter broke with the state secretary by forbidding party members to associate with either Keppler or Seyss-Inquart.[65]

Because Keppler and Seyss-Inquart, along with their fellow travelers, Rainer, Globocnik, Jury, and Reinthaller, were all members of the SS, the struggle in Austria now more than ever shaped up as one between the SS and the pro-Leopold SA. Persche regarded Keppler as a "gray eminence," and "a second Holstein."[66] He held the state secretary responsible for intriguing against Leopold and for eventually bringing about the "external" solution to the Anschluss question through the use of German force.[67]

Keppler's appointment revealed that German intervention, which according to Hitler's order of August 1934 was supposed to be nonexistent, was in reality on the upswing again. Persche's bitter allegation, that "99.9 percent" of the intrigues against Leopold originated in the Reich,"[68] was exaggerated, but still substantially true. What the SA leader neglected to say, however, was that every quarreling Nazi faction in Austria, including Leopold's, looked to the Reich for a benefactor.[69] The biggest prize of all, of course, was Adolf Hitler himself. Anyone enjoying the Führer's unconditional support had little to fear from his rivals. Leopold had journeyed to Berlin in March to obtain the Leader's blessing; he had returned with promises of money to succor the families of arrested Nazis and for the families of unemployed SA men.[70]

Next in the Nazi hierarchy after Hitler came his deputy, Rudolf Hess. Seyss-Inquart visited Hess, along with Göring, in early July, soliciting support for his extraparty strategy. Göring was noncommittal, but "Hess was most interested and cordial and said about as follows: 'You certainly have good intentions and I shall follow your work with interest. I regret you are not one of the old fighters.'"[71] According to Dietrich Orlow, the historian of the German Nazi party, Hess gave orders to Keppler in September to begin political preparations for the Anschluss.[72]

Leopold had good relations with Göring for a time and was able to pump considerable sums of money out of him, as the Luftwaffe chief later complained. But the Landesleiter managed to dry up the well by refusing to make Göring's Austrian brother-in-law, Franz Hueber, a leader in the SA. With that, Göring's subsidies abruptly stopped flowing. Leopold's relations with Hess, Goebbels, and Himmler were no better.[73]

Leopold's alienation of Himmler was perhaps his final downfall. Although Himmler had at least theoretically placed the Austrian SS under Leopold's command in January, he never fully relinquished his control. When Leopold expelled Globocnik, an honorary SS leader, from the party in August, the Reichsführer ordered the Carinthian retained.

The Ascendance of the Austrian SS

Himmler's action was only part of a larger effort to enhance the status of the Austrian SS at the expense of the SA. Adolf Hitler had put the obstreperous German SA severely in its place during the "night of the long knives" on 30 June 1934. The heavy-handed tactics of the SA had been useful in intimidating opponents during the years of struggle leading to Hitler's appointment as chancellor and even during the Gleichschaltung process in 1933. But once totalitarian power had been achieved and all internal enemies had been suppressed, the SA became more of a nuisance than a necessity. The

SA's call for a "second revolution" finally led to the Röhm Purge of 30 June 1934. The biggest victor to emerge from that massacre was Heinrich Himmler. His SS now became fully independent of the SA and replaced it as the most important militant auxiliary of the NSDAP.

The effects of the Purge, however, were confined largely, if not exclusively, to Germany. Even Alfred Persche did not learn the true causes and effects of the Purge until after the Anschluss. In Austria the SA continued to play the leading role in the fight against the government as it had since the outlawing of the party in June 1933.[74]

In leaving the Austrian SA undisturbed, Hitler was being more consistent than it might seem at first; the German SA had outlived its usefulness in 1934. But the *Kampfjahre* (fighting years) in Austria continued far beyond that year, and the SA still had an important role to play—important, but not exclusive. The fatal mistake of the Austrian SA, and of Leopold, was to imagine that they could or should seize power with little or no help from the Reich. Even more naive was their expectation that they would be allowed to retain power after a Machtergreifung.

Just as Leopold resented and resisted any outside interference, so too did Persche try to keep the Austrian SA entirely independent of German control. When in June 1937 the Austrian SS leader and German citizen Alfred Rodenbücher offered Persche a German subsidy, Persche curtly refused. Two months later Rodenbücher informed Persche that the Führer would soon subordinate the SA in Austria to the leader of the exiled Austrian SA, Hermann Reschny. Unlike Rodenbücher, Reschny was a native Austrian and had led the entire SA until after the July Putsch. But Persche told Rodenbücher that he would resign rather than subordinate himself to someone who was not at the scene of the day-to-day struggle. Shortly thereafter he expressed the same sentiments in a letter to Hitler.[75]

But worse things were in store for the SA. In late November Wilhelm Keppler informed Persche that Hitler needed two more years to solve the Austrian question. In the meantime, the Austrian Nazis were to do nothing unless ordered by Berlin. Persche replied that to carry out such a scheme would cause an SA revolt. The Austrian SA recognized Hitler's leadership in matters of Weltanschauung, but nothing else, as the Führer himself had directed after the July Putsch.[76] If anyone should try to dissolve the SA as a preparation for a German occupation of Austria, it would lead to a mutiny and an attempt by the SA to seize power by force.[77] Only Ernst Röhm (or perhaps Josef Leopold) would have dared make a statement like that.

While Leopold and Persche were losing their German patrons and the

Austrian SA was in danger of losing its independence, the Austrian SS was surging toward supremacy. Persche thought the SS was poorly organized in Austria and not good for anything except special tasks.[78] But this opinion was not shared by the Austrian police, who regarded the SS as the best organized of all Nazi formations.[79] Although the SA was still far larger than the SS in 1937, numbers counted for little in the fierce competition for superiority, as even Persche admitted. What really mattered was that the Austrian SS enjoyed the support of Keppler and Himmler.[80]

Its very smallness made the Austrian SS acceptable, curiously enough, to both the German and Austrian governments. For Hitler it was too weak to harbor ambitions of seizing power on its own—in sharp contrast to the Austrian SA. And like the German SS it had a tradition of fanatical loyalty to both Himmler and Hitler. To the Austrian government it appeared to be both less dangerous and more socially respectable than the ruffian SA, so much so in fact that Ernst Kaltenbrunner and his colleagues were given relative freedom of movement. By contrast, Persche and other SA leaders were hunted down and arrested by the Austrian police as late as 1938.[81]

Hitler and Leopold

Even before Keppler threatened the integrity of the SA, Leopold, in desperation, decided to appeal directly to Hitler to salvage his position as leader of the Austrian Nazi party. Such a straightforward approach had succeeded in February and March; perhaps it would work again.

In two long letters to the Führer written on 22 August and 8 September, Leopold outlined his version of the attempt by Keppler, Seyss-Inquart, Rainer, and others to undermine his authority as Landesleiter. The intrigue against him, he said, had caught the attention of the foreign press, further damaging his effectiveness. He complained that he was criticized from some quarters for being a wild radical and from others for going too slowly. Impossible rumors had been spread about him that had reached the "highest positions in the Reich." Altogether his opposition did not even add up to 100 men. Their only strength lay in their influence with the Austrian government and security forces on the one hand, and their success in gaining financial support from the Reich on the other.[82]

The Landesleiter promised not to depart "a hair's breadth" from Hitler's general Austrian policy, but insisted that he had to determine tactics for

Austrian domestic affairs himself. Otherwise another catastrophe could result. He concluded by asking to be kept informed of all discussions and agreements made between the German Foreign Office and the German Embassy in Vienna and the Austrian government. There is no evidence that Hitler even received these letters. At any rate, Leopold certainly achieved no satisfaction of his grievances.

Consequently, at the urging of the SA leaders, Leopold decided to go to Berlin to speak with Hitler personally. He might better have stayed at home. For one thing, Seyss-Inquart had written to Keppler on 18 August to complain about Leopold's references to Seyss-Inquart's colleagues, Rainer and Globocnik, as "traitors, scoundrels, and rogues."[83] Seyss made his continued work in the VPR dependent on the "clarification" of his relationship with Leopold.

Keppler told Martin Bormann (now the second man after Rudolf Hess in the party's headquarters) about this letter. Bormann, who on 30 September had advised Keppler to demand unconditional discipline from Leopold, reported back to Keppler that Hitler now considered the Austrian Nazi Political Organization to be less important than before. Any further violations of discipline might cause Leopold's recall.[84]

Keppler went so far as to prevent Leopold from meeting either Hitler or Foreign Minister Neurath. The official explanation for Hitler's not even having enough time to shake the Landesleiter's hand was Mussolini's state visit to Germany. The Reich chancellor was naturally not eager to emphasize his ties to the Austrian Nazi party at the very time he was courting the former defender of Austria's independence.

The best Leopold could do in Berlin was to gain an interview with Hermann Göring. But even that meeting took place in the presence of Wilhelm Keppler. After a lengthy discussion, the prime minister agreed to leave the leadership of the illegal party in Leopold's hands. However, the latter was not to interfere in the activities of Seyss-Inquart and his colleagues; on the contrary, they were to be supported. Those working for Seyss were to be given a leave of absence from the party. Furthermore, Leopold had to promise to maintain "strict discipline."[85]

Far from strengthening Leopold's position, the trip was still another triumph for Keppler and Seyss-Inquart. The Landesleiter had been snubbed and chastised. When ordered to go to Berlin in late November, he refused rather than subject himself to another such humiliation.[86]

Control of the party was rapidly slipping out of Leopold's hands. If he and his followers were ever to capture power and head off their SS rivals, they would have to do something drastic—and soon. The noose was tightening not only around Schuschnigg's neck, but around Leopold's as well.

The year and a half between July 1936 and January 1938 witnessed a sharp increase in the self-confidence of Austrian Nazis as well as in a renewed effort to work out some kind of accommodation with the government that would restore at least a disguised legality to the party. These efforts, however, attained only a very limited success.

The total numerical strength of the Nazis may have been equal to that of the government and its supporters, but the Nazis were simply too divided among themselves to achieve power on their own. The rivalry between the Austrian SA and SS, which had been vividly apparent during the July Putsch, resumed and even intensified after the July Agreement. And the Political Organization was split between Josef Leopold and his supporters in eastern Austria, and Klausner, Rainer, and Globocnik in the west.

These divisions were welcome, not only to the Schuschnigg government, but strangely enough to Adolf Hitler as well. By playing one faction off against the others Schuschnigg was able to seriously weaken his enemies and prop up his unpopular regime. The same divisions within the Austrian Nazi party, which Hitler never attempted to resolve, made it unlikely that the party would do anything rash before the Führer thought the time had come to complete the Gleichschaltung and ultimately the annexation of Austria.

Chapter XII
The Execution: Berchtesgaden and the Anschluss

So much has been written about the final weeks and days of the first Austrian Republic that the historian hesitates to embark on still another account. The story of Chancellor Schuschnigg's humiliating trip to Berchtesgaden, his ill-fated plebiscite, Göring's ultimata, and the German invasion on 12 March has been told in great, sometimes hour-by-hour detail. Yet in all accounts the Austrian Nazi party has never been treated as more than an incidental adjunct of German foreign policy. And little or no attempt has been made to demonstrate that the Austrian party sometimes followed independent goals contrary to those desired by German leaders, just as it had in earlier years.

In the four months between November 1937 and March 1938 most Austrian Nazis were no more willing to follow Hitler meekly than they had been in the days of Walter Riehl and Karl Schulz. On the contrary, just as in the diplomatic crisis preceding the First World War so too in 1938 it was frequently Austrians (in the latter case both Nazis and non-Nazis) who were forcing the pace of events with the Germans reacting to them.

Hitler, Leopold, and the Hossbach Conference

Adolf Hitler had largely ignored Austria since the July Agreement in 1936; domestic concerns and the Spanish Civil War absorbed his attention. But by November 1937 German rearmament was fairly well advanced and Hitler could now consider abandoning his restraint in foreign affairs. Anxiety about his health and fear of a premature death may have also induced him to speed up the realization of his foreign-policy objectives.[1]

On the fifth of November Hitler met with his top military advisers as well as his foreign minister, Neurath, in what has subsequently been called the Hossbach Conference. The prosecution at Nuremberg and most historians up to 1960 regarded this meeting at the Reich chancellery as Hitler's "blueprint" for a world war. The Anschluss of Austria "was part of a program declared to his own circle, and was the first step in the well-conceived and carefully planned campaign of aggression: Austria first, Czechoslovakia second, and Poland third."[2] Then in 1961 the British historian Alan J. P. Taylor, in his *Origins of the Second World War*, dismissed Hitler's exposition at the conference as "in large part day-dreaming, unrelated to what followed in real life."[3]

Few historians have accepted Taylor's thesis uncritically. Although admitting that the conference was no blueprint or accurate prophecy, most recent interpretations view the meeting as marking a definite turning point in Hitler's foreign-policy strategy.[4] The Führer had, on countless earlier occasions, spoken of the need for Lebensraum in the East. But now for the first time he got down to specific cases: Czechoslovakia and Austria would be his first conquests between 1943 and 1945 at the latest, but possibly much sooner.

Colonel Friedrich Hossbach, who recorded the minutes of the meeting, noted no surprise or objections from Göring or Admiral Erich Räder, the commander in chief of the navy. But Neurath, General Werner von Fritsch, commander in chief of the army, and Minister of War Werner von Blomberg were all thoroughly alarmed. Blomberg was especially upset, arguing that Germany's defenses in the west were of "very small value" in the event of a general war.

Blomberg's reaction to the Hossbach conference was by no means short-lived. Sometime toward the end of 1937, probably during a visit by Leopold to Berlin in late November, the German war minister met with the Landesleiter to discuss the Austrian situation. They soon discovered that they both resented Hitler's interference in "their" affairs (Austria and the Wehrmacht). And both wanted to prevent a German invasion of Austria and Czechoslovakia, which they feared would result in a hopeless multifront war for Germany.

When Blomberg told Leopold about the Hossbach conference and Hitler's deadline for war, Leopold was at once (perhaps conveniently) convinced that Hitler would not wait another four to six years before launching an attack. To avoid the catastrophic consequences of a new world war, the Austrian Nazis would have to settle the Austrian "question" through a fait accompli before Hitler had a chance to do it from the outside.[5] Judged against the backdrop of Leopold's later plans and activities, however, it is hard to believe that he was that worried about a world war. His primary concern was not how he could prevent a German invasion of Austria—however desirable a goal that might be—but how he could obtain power for himself.

To Blomberg's query of whether a peaceful takeover in Austria was possible, Leopold replied in the negative. Schuschnigg, he said, was convinced that he (Leopold) would soon be replaced by a "Catholic activist."[6] And the chancellor believed that if worse came to worst and Leopold was replaced by a Reich German, he (Schuschnigg) could still obtain better terms from a German than from Leopold.

The Landesleiter therefore insisted that his (Leopold's) only option was to proclaim a countergovernment in Linz, which would immediately reaffirm Austrian independence. No direct German intervention would be needed, because Leopold had already secured the allegiance of the Alpine commanders of the Austrian army. The real irony behind Leopold's plan, as he himself admitted to Blomberg, was this: its success depended on Hitler's covering Leopold's flank in case his countergovernment provoked an invasion by Hungary, Czechoslovakia, or possibly even Italy.[7]

Sometime in January or early February, Franz von Papen obtained a copy of a circular order from Leopold to his colleagues, asking them to be prepared to renew the fight (against the Austrian government) at any moment. But Leopold's hopes of disrupting the efforts of Papen and Seyss-Inquart toward an "evolutionary" settlement of the Austrian "problem" were soon to be shattered.

With Austria's former protector, Italy, heavily committed, first in Ethiopia and then in the Spanish Civil War, Vienna's international situation continued to deteriorate in the second half of 1936 and throughout 1937. During a grandiose state visit to Germany in September 1937, Mussolini formally recognized "Germany's special interests in Austria."[8] France, politically divided and in the worst phase of the Great Depression, was in no mood to aid even its eastern allies let alone neutral Austria. Great Britain was barely beginning to rearm in 1937–38 and regarded Germany's revisionist aims as largely justified.

Therefore when on 27 January 1938 Papen issued Schuschnigg an invitation authorized by Hitler himself to visit the Führer in Germany, the Austrian chancellor felt in no position to refuse. But before venturing to Germany Schuschnigg apparently wanted to strengthen his bargaining position by exposing the illegal activities of the Austrian Nazi party.

A good excuse for action arose with the publication of an interview which the Gauleiter of Vienna, Leopold Tavs, gave to a newspaper in Prague. Republished in Vienna's *Reichspost* on 25 January, it was an open challenge to the Austrian government. Tavs declared that Schuschnigg's police would not dare to prosecute the Austrian Nazis in the face of German retaliation. When the police raided the Nazis' office on the Teinfaltstrasse, what they found shocked even them.

Among various plans of action was a memorandum by Tavs asserting that the Nazis could not expect any further progress with Schuschnigg. The only solution, therefore, was the threat of an invasion by Germany followed by a Nazi government under Leopold.[9] One plan, reminiscent of an incident staged by the Germans at the outset of the Polish campaign in 1939, called for an attack on the German embassy and the murder of Papen by Austrian Nazis disguised as members of the Fatherland Front.[10]

Whether the so-called Tavs Plan was approved by German authorities has long been disputed. Tavs himself has claimed that "the people in Munich and Berlin didn't know anything about the . . . Plan."[11] In view of the growing disfavor in which illegal Austrian Nazis found themselves by the early part of 1938 it is unlikely that Hitler or his lieutenants even knew about the Plan let alone approved it. In any event, the Tavs papers revealed the desperate and reckless character of the Austrian Nazi movement at this juncture. Their discovery set in motion a chain reaction, which soon led to the demise of not only Tavs, but also Leopold and the rest of their cohorts.

Meanwhile Leopold's fate was rapidly being sealed by unrelated developments in Germany. On 26 January Leopold's co-conspirator Blomberg was dismissed as war minister following the revelation that his recent bride was a former prostitute. The news of Blomberg's dismissal was published in the German press on 4 February along with the announced resignation of Fritsch and Neurath, both of whom, like Blomberg, were opponents of Hitler's expansionist plans.

Blomberg's downfall wrecked Leopold's hopes for a countergovernment. In late January or very early February, Leopold told Persche to have "the SA ready to march in no less than two days and no more than fourteen," to protect the prospective Nazi government in Linz.[12] Shortly thereafter the Landesleiter announced his intentions to the Austrian *Gauleiter* at a two-day meeting on a Danube island near Vienna. By this time three or four Austrian generals of Alpine units as well as the Austrian SA were in a high state of readiness. The *Gauleiter* gave their enthusiastic approval to Leopold's plan. Then came the shocking news from Berlin.[13]

The Meeting at Berchtesgaden

As Leopold had feared, Schuschnigg began negotiating with Seyss-Inquart in early February. The chancellor hoped to reach an understanding with the National Opposition before meeting with Hitler. This tactic would presumably forestall the pressure he expected the Reichskanzler to exert. In exchange for Hitler's removing Leopold and his Landesleitung from Austria, Schuschnigg was prepared to appoint Seyss-Inquart as minister of public security and arbiter in cases involving the Nazi opposition. The chancellor could make this concession with relative equanimity because he was convinced that Seyss-Inquart and other Nazi moderates were independent of Berlin and basically on his side.[14]

Beyond this, Schuschnigg, through his negotiator, Zernatto, was willing to make still more far-reaching concessions. He would agree to a new amnesty for imprisoned Nazis and the appointment of a Nazi finance minister with four other Nazis holding high government offices. Point Seven of the agreement, called the "Ten Points (*Punktationen*) with Dr. Seyss-Inquart," declared that there were "certainly some important basic concepts of a nonparty-bound National Socialism which can be organically incorporated into a political ideology of the new Austria." After the necessary preconditions had been met, there could even be a military cooperation between Austria and Germany. Members of the National Opposition would also be permitted various athletic, educational, agricultural, and industrial clubs.[15]

Schuschnigg had in fact conceded the essentials of a Gleichschaltung with Germany even before his unhappy meeting with Hitler at Berchtesgaden. In Schuschnigg's defense, one should add that he considered the Punktationen to be *maximum* concessions. But Seyss-Inquart passed on the substance of the secret negotiations to Friedrich Rainer and other Nazis. They in turn forwarded the information to Hitler who used the Points as his *minimum* demands on Schuschnigg.[16]

The Ten Points proved to be the undoing not only of Schuschnigg but of Leopold as well. In an attempt to disrupt the Schuschnigg/Seyss-Inquart talks the Landesleiter ordered a wave of bombings and demonstrations, which led to the arrest of 400 Nazis. But such activities only served to solidify Leopold's enemies against him.

In a final effort to eliminate his rival, Seyss-Inquart sent the moderate Nazi and art historian Kajetan Mühlmann to Berchtesgaden ahead of Schuschnigg. Mühlmann was instructed to insist to Hitler and Keppler (who was also at

Hitler's mountain retreat) that Leopold and the Landesleitung be removed from Austria.

Seyss-Inquart got his way. Although neither Leopold nor the Austrian Landesleitung was specifically mentioned in the Berchtesgaden Protocol of 12 February, it did stipulate that "such persons whose further stay in Austria appears to be detrimental to relations between [Germany and Austria] shall, after an examination of each individual case and by agreement between the two Governments, be made to transfer their residence to the Reich."[17] Moreover, following the signing of the agreement, Hitler assured the downcast Austrian chancellor that he intended to demand Leopold's resignation as Landesleiter in the near future. Thus Leopold "would not be able any longer to really follow a line of conduct which was at absolute variance with the one now determined upon."[18]

Superficially, the terms of the Protocol did not go far beyond the Ten Points. In addition to reaffirming the amnesty of Nazis imprisoned in Austria, Schuschnigg agreed that Austrian Nazis should have the right to participate as individuals within the framework of the Fatherland Front and all other Austrian organizations. Seyss-Inquart was given the responsibility for implementing this measure.

In the Punktationen the chancellor had merely conceded that *moderate* Nazis could enter the Front, an important distinction not made in the Protocol. Likewise, Seyss-Inquart became not only the minister of the interior, as previously discussed, but was also named minister of security. The latter responsibility was watered down, however, when Schuschnigg increased the powers of Vienna Police President Michael Skubl. Finally, all economic discrimination against the Nazis was to end, and they were to be given equal access to military service. Wearing the swastika was also permitted in the Protocol, as was the Hitler salute. The party flag and uniform, however, remained forbidden.[19]

Many Austrian Nazis, the great majority of whom had no detailed knowledge of the agreement, were at first unhappy with it. They had had no opportunity to participate in the negotiations and resented that the agreement enhanced the position of Seyss-Inquart. But far more revealing of the real nature of the Berchtesgaden Protocol was the judgment of Hitler himself. Two weeks after the agreement had been signed he met with Leopold and his followers. The Führer characterized the Protocol as "so far-reaching that if completely carried out the Austrian problem would be solved automatically."[20]

What was even worse for Austria was the impression given by Schuschnigg that he had made the concessions only under pressure. It was natural for Austrian and German Nazis to assume that more coercion would net still more gains. The chancellor had also set a disastrous precedent by allowing the leader of a foreign country to dictate his selection of ministers.[21]

The meeting at Berchtesgaden and its immediate aftermath provided Leopold's enemies with an ideal opportunity to move in for the kill. When Hitler asked Mühlmann whether Schuschnigg could be trusted to respect a treaty, the professor replied in the affirmative. The chancellor would do so, however, only if Austria's independence were recognized and Leopold recalled. Two days later Papen himself repeated to Hitler Seyss-Inquart's demand for the removal of Leopold and Tavs.[22] In his *Memoirs* Papen remarked that he "was astonished at how willingly Hitler accepted this petition. [Papen could] only assume that Leopold was too much of a bull in a china shop, even for him."[23]

Taking no chances on Hitler's changing his mind, Seyss-Inquart hurried to Berlin on 17 February to argue his case before Leopold, scheduled to arrive in the German capital the next day, could defend himself. When Seyss saw Hitler, he demanded the removal of Leopold and his top associates to Germany. Only then would he agree to serve as arbiter between the German and Austrian governments in cases involving the Austrian Nazi party.[24]

In reality, the new policy, which Seyss-Inquart now proposed, was not entirely different from what Leopold's had been before 1938. Like Leopold, Schulz, and Riehl, Seyss insisted on the need for an independent leadership, not bound to the party in Germany. Hitler should be viewed in Austria as merely the founder, leader, and carrier of a political idea. But the implementation of that idea had to be adjusted to Austrian conditions. Where Seyss differed from Leopold's radical policies of February 1938 was in pointing out "the necessity of rendering the National Socialist activity lawful in the framework of Austrian contingencies" (thus reverting to a position Leopold himself had taken in 1937) and promising to "imprison the National Socialists who would show any illegal activity."[25]

Hitler approved of Seyss-Inquart's proposals while telling Seyss that "he was not quite sure that he [Seyss] would be able to carry out [these] plans in Austria."[26] Seyss-Inquart made a good impression on Hitler. The Führer especially liked the fact that Seyss (in contrast to Leopold) was "not too strong a man."[27]

The ultimate humiliation for Leopold was the desertion of several of his longtime associates, as well as most of the Austrian *Gauleiter* after the Berchtesgaden meeting. When Leopold called a conference of all the top Nazi leaders in Austria, Kaltenbrunner, Leopold's one-time deputy Dr. Hugo Jury, and Anton Reinthaller, refused even to attend. The *Gauleiter* of Lower Austria, Salzburg, and the Burgenland along with Alfred Persche reaffirmed their support of the Landesleiter. But the other Gau leaders all remained silent.[28]

When Leopold learned that Hitler had ordered him to appear in Berlin on 18 February, he made one last desperate attempt to assert his independence. On the 17th he authorized a circular order to the party calling for wide-ranging violence. Tavs, who had just been released from prison the day before by Schuschnigg's Berchtesgaden amnesty, gave instructions (never implemented) that the windows of the German embassy in Vienna be smashed. Other plans called for provoking Seyss-Inquart, now the minister of interior and security, into arresting Nazis and then branding him a traitor to the nationalist cause.[29]

Captain Leopold was now summoned to the chancellery in Berlin to receive the Führer's wrath. The recent actions of the federal leadership, Hitler fumed, had been "insane." "Such activities could have put him into the most painful and mortifying predicaments. . . . It was his unalterable decision to remove and replace Leopold."[30] Every attempt by the Landesleiter to defend himself was interrupted by Hitler. Leopold was ordered to stay completely out of Austrian politics. He and his immediate subordinates, including Tavs, would have to move to Germany.

A few days later (on 26 February), after Leopold and his colleagues had returned to Germany for good, Hitler was in better spirits. He treated the Austrians like honored guests at a special evening reception. They were assured that their removal was merely a small tactical necessity and that nothing would happen in Austria without Leopold's approval. Within a short time they would be able to return to their homeland. To keep him out of mischief, Hitler appointed Leopold to the staff of Rudolf Hess.[31] But there was no disguising the fact that these measures were Hitler's way of sugar-coating a bitter pill.

During Blomberg's last meeting with Hitler in January 1938 the Reich chancellor had promised him that he would be recalled in time of war. But that was the last time Blomberg ever saw Hitler, and the field marshal was forced to sit out the entire war. Leopold likewise never saw the Führer again in private and had to experience the Anschluss from his German exile under what amounted to house arrest. But Hitler's flattery and promises served their purpose; neither Leopold nor Blomberg offered any resistance to their dismissals.

So ended, for all practical purposes, the career of Captain Josef Leopold. However fanatical a Nazi he considered himself or was considered by others, he was in fact more of an Austrian than a Nazi. And it was this local pride which led him to commit one unforgivable sin: he had defied the Führer by attempting to build up a following of his own. Hitler could forgive anything except disobedience. Leopold thus met the same fate as his predecessors, Walter Riehl and Karl Schulz.

A Vacuum of Power: Hubert Klausner as Landesleiter

In the meantime Hitler, on the recommendation of Keppler and Seyss-Inquart, had appointed Major Klausner as the new Austrian Landesleiter on the very afternoon he sacked Leopold. Klausner was given specific instructions about how he was to change illegal activities into legal ones by following the "inspiring" example of Gauleiter Josef Bürckel in the Saar. Klausner was also ordered to cooperate with Seyss-Inquart, "who had no ambitions of any kind to lead the party." In particular, Klausner had to curb the activities of the radicals in order to facilitate the task of Seyss-Inquart. Seyss was to take orders from Klausner, but (in the usual confusing Nazi way) was directly responsible to Hitler within his own political sphere.[32]

According to Keppler, who had been ordered by Hitler to check up on the Austrian party every three or four weeks, Klausner did an excellent job in his new position as Landesleiter. The latter presumably enjoyed respect and "loyal cooperation everywhere."[33] Alfred Persche had a far different opinion of Klausner's effectiveness. Persche, who had just been replaced as leader of the SA by Johann Lukesch, on 22 February, described the latter as courteous but Klausner as downright insulting toward him.[34]

Persche related how, when Klausner summoned the SA-brigade leaders and *Gauleiter* to a meeting in Vienna on 10 March, no one greeted or cheered the new Landesleiter. And there was nothing but ridicule and curses for the temporizing policy of the new federal leadership. Moreover, the events of 20 February to 11 March also demonstrated that the Nazi Landesleitung was unable to maintain full control over the party, particularly in Styria.[35]

Few writers now believe that either Klausner or Seyss-Inquart was the real leader of the Austrian Nazis during the last weeks of the First Republic. Schuschnigg, in his most recent memoirs, sees Seyss-Inquart as "nothing but a figurehead," whereas Klausner "had no say-so."[36] Schuschnigg, Persche, and the Austrian historian Ludwig Jedlicka all consider Wilhelm Keppler, supported by his adjutant, Edmund Veesenmayer, a fellow German, to have been the chief manipulators.[37] Keppler's task was to "build golden bridges for Schuschnigg," that is, to convince the chancellor of the benefits of an Anschluss.[38] To make the job easier, Keppler told a meeting of Austrian Nazi leaders on 4 March that an acceleration of party activities was not in the interests of Germany.[39]

The truth is, however, that Keppler was hardly more effective than Klausner or Seyss-Inquart in controlling the Nazi radicals. It was Friedrich Rainer and Odilo Globocnik who, in Schuschnigg's words, "set about deliberately radicalizing the reorganized party over the head of Seyss-Inquart [and also Keppler]." Apparently no longer needing front men like Seyss, the program of the two young Carinthians in fact now scarcely differed from Leopold's: internal Austrian politics should be sharpened until there was a danger of civil war. At that point the Reich would be forced to intervene, but (presumably) would not actually invade Austrian territory.[40]

The Dam Bursts: Austrian Nazi Activities, 20 February–8 March

The dam holding back the Nazi flood developed its first leak in Styria, the longtime stronghold (*Hochburg*) of the party. Despite internal dissension and general dissatisfaction with their Gauleitung, the Styrian Nazis were brimming with confidence by the beginning of 1938. Party members were so well organized and numerous that Nazis in other states were actually jealous and eager to "catch up."[41] By the party's own (no doubt exaggerated) estimate, 80 percent of the capital city of Graz was sympathetic to the movement, while 90 percent of the municipal officials supported the party.[42] Even the commanding general of the Austrian army garrison in Graz estimated that at least 70 percent of the civil servants in the city were National Socialists.[43] Students at the University of Graz were so thoroughly Nazified that the half of the faculty who were anti-Nazi did not dare to criticize Hitler. Huge Nazi demonstrations on 19 February forced the temporary closing of both the university and the nearby technical institute.

Led by Armin Dadieu, a thirty-seven-year-old professor of physical chemistry, head of the Styrian section of the People's Political Office (VPR), and friend of Hermann Göring's brother-in-law, Franz Hueber, the Nazi party became increasingly aggressive during the last week in February and the first week of March. Especially helpful to the Nazi cause in Styria was the National Socialist Soldiers' Ring, a secret organization within the army and police, which in Graz amounted to about one-fourth of the garrison and the police.[44] Also aiding the Nazi cause were the freshly amnestied Nazis (including the former governor of Styria and July Putsch conspirator, Anton Rintelen).

This group, anxious to make up for lost time, was especially radical. The Styrians were determined to prevent any compromise solution advocated by the Nazi moderates. Like Leopold before them, and in clear violation of the Berchtesgaden Agreement, they were determined to provoke an armed uprising in which the government would be obliged to shoot Nazis, thus at last compelling Germany to intervene.[45]

The turning point for the Nazis of Styria and to a lesser extent the rest of Austria was Hitler's Reichstag speech of 20 February. In this, the first speech by Hitler ever broadcast in its entirety over the Austrian radio, Hitler mentioned that Germany could not ignore the fate of the "ten million Germans outside the Reich. . . . The constitutional separation of the Austrians and Sudeten Germans from the Reich [could] not lead to a complete denial of self-determination which had been formally guaranteed in President Wilson's Fourteen Points . . . Just as England [represented] its interests around the whole world so [would] the present-day Germany know how to take care of its much more limited interests."[46] In marked contrast to earlier addresses by Hitler, not a word was said about Austrian independence.

Hitler's scarcely veiled threat depressed supporters of the Fatherland Front and emboldened Nazi sympathizers in Graz to display the forbidden swastika flag. Schuschnigg's reply, delivered to the Austrian Parliament four days later, contained the assertion that Austria would go "up to here but no further" in fulfilling the Berchtesgaden Protocol. This defiance temporarily raised the morale of government loyalists, but only angered and further radicalized the Nazis.[47]

Sensing an imminent Anschluss, and therefore no longer fearing imprisonment, the 20,000 Nazis in Graz, listening to Schuschnigg's speech over loudspeakers in the city's main square, reacted by demanding that the pro-Nazi mayor, Hans Schmidt, hoist the swastika flag over the city hall and switch off the loudspeakers. The demands were promptly fulfilled. The next day every student at the University of Graz was wearing a swastika armband; people in public places not displaying the insignia were beaten up. In Graz, as elsewhere in Austria, the illegal greeting "Heil Hitler" was openly used and old Nazi marching songs were sung in the streets. One American journalist in the Styrian capital was shocked to see uniformed Nazis calmly cleaning a disassembled machine gun in a tavern.

Seyss-Inquart and Lukesch now joined Klausner and Keppler in trying to halt the runaway Styrian Nazi steamroller. But when Seyss-Inquart spoke in Graz on 1 March, his appearance merely touched off a Nazi demonstration of strength. Twenty thousand Nazis from all over Styria, including uniformed SA and SS men, greeted Seyss, who felt compelled to respond with the Nazi salute. After his return to Vienna he confided to his friend Guido Zernatto that he doubted whether his program could be enacted against the will of the party.[48]

Johann Lukesch was equally helpless to stem the Nazi tide. In order to accede to the wishes of Keppler and Seyss-Inquart for a nonviolent evolutionary Gleichschaltung, Lukesch was even willing to disband the SA for as long as two years. When he issued an order to this effect in late February, the response was exactly the opposite of what he had wanted: the tempo of illegal SA activity increased, especially in Styria. After one meeting between the Landesleitung and SA brigade staff leaders in Vienna, the Styrian representatives taunted: "The Landesleitung can lick our asses, we are going back to our men and march!"[49]

Lukesch made several trips to Styria in late February and early March to try to contain the radicals; but each time he only returned to Vienna inspired by the Styrians' enthusiasm. He described to Persche the many "Heil Hitlers" he had heard and swastika-bedecked vehicles he had seen. Although he had first believed in the program of Keppler, Seyss-Inquart, and Klausner, Lukesch finally concluded that their policy was hopeless; thereafter he allowed himself to be driven along by the course of events.[50]

Schuschnigg's Desperate Gamble

As early as the eighth of March, events in Styria, and only to a lesser extent in the rest of Austria, were threatening to outstrip the government's ability to control. Wilhelm Keppler, who made a tour of inspection throughout Austria between the third and sixth of March, noted in a memorandum that

> there is satisfaction [among Nazis] at the fact that the road for further progress is now clearly outlined. The various parades and demonstrations have taken place under surprisingly good discipline, and the joining of the Fatherland Front is understood. The expression "The New Fatherland Front" was coined as a contrast with the old Front. National Socialist demonstrations everywhere had five to ten times as many participants as the parades of the old system. . . .
>
> The *Volkspolitische Referat*, and the racial German labor union connected with it, will now be extended down to the single local groups, and the direct leaders of the Party are now to be firmly placed in it. The

Hitlerjugend has already to a great extent been incorporated in the
Youth Organization [Jungvolk] of the Fatherland Front and in many
parts of the country already controls it.[51]

The Styrian Nazis had succeeded in turning their province into a virtual
Nazi republic from the Semmering Pass to the Yugoslav border. In Graz,
which Hitler a few weeks later would call "the city of the people's revolution" (*Stadt der Volkserhebung*), Nazi leaders negotiated with representatives
of the federal government on 8 March over the participation of Nazis in the
provincial cabinet. When the federal authorities refused a demand for three
Nazi seats, thousands of Nazi demonstrators surrounded the building in which
the talks were being held and could be cleared away only through the combined efforts of policemen and soldiers. Although this show of strength had
succeeded in its immediate aim, it seemed to be only a question of time until
the Schuschnigg regime lost control of the situation and collapsed. It was on
account of this danger and the need to head off more Nazi demands that the
chancellor made one last gamble.[52]

Since the outlawing of their party in 1933, the Austrian Nazis had been
demanding a plebiscite on the Anschluss question, claiming that in any fair
vote they would get about 80 percent of the ballots.[53] As long as the position
of the Austrian government was strong, it had little to gain and much to lose
by any such poll. The Tyroleans and Salzburgers had voted overwhelmingly
in favor of an Anschluss in 1919 and the Saarlanders had favored a return to
the Reich by a ratio of nine to one in a plebiscite held in 1935.

Even if the Nazis had gained no more than the 41 percent they had garnered
in the Innsbruck election of April 1933, the Austrian government would have
been seriously embarrassed. By making their demands, the Nazis could pose
as the champions of freedom and self-determination, while, by refusing, the
government would look dictatorial and insecure. Moreover, if there should be
a vote purely on the Anschluss issue, the Nazis could expect to gain the votes
of many non-Nazis who simply wanted an end to their country's apparently
hopeless economic situation. American press representatives in Vienna estimated that the National Socialists would win 55 to 60 percent of the vote on
the question of Anschluss alone.[54]

These considerations made it obvious why neither Dollfuss nor Schuschnigg had been willing to take such a high risk. But by March 1938 the
situation had altered radically from what it had been only a few weeks before. To do nothing entailed the probability of at least a Gleichschaltung in
the near future. On the other hand, a progovernment vote would seriously
embarrass the Nazis and make any aggressive move by either the Austrian or

German Nazis appear to be a clear violation of their own principle of self-determination.

But as we have seen, to hold the plebiscite on the straightforward issue of a union with Germany would be very much to the Nazis' advantage. Therefore, the question put to the voters was whether they approved of the government's all-inclusive slogan, "for a free and German, independent and social, Christian and united Austria; for freedom and work, and for the equality of all who declare for race and fatherland."[55] Voting against such a question would be like an American rejecting the Stars and Stripes, apple pie, and motherhood. Even the Nazis would be attracted by the words *German*, *social*, *work*, and *race*. And if the vote should be positive, as expected, the words *free*, *independent*, *Christian*, *Austria*, and *Fatherland* could be interpreted to mean that the Austrian people had rejected the union with Germany.

Only the Legitimists, Jews, and Communists were ignored by the slogan. But the first two groups could be counted on to vote yes in any event, and the Communists were too few to matter. By choosing the positive approach of asking for approval of the regime rather than approval for an Anschluss, Schuschnigg expected to win 65 to 70 percent of the vote.[56]

In order to make a positive outcome even more likely the voting was to be held on 13 March, only four days after Schuschnigg announced the forthcoming plebiscite. Thus, the startled Nazis would have little or no opportunity to organize a response to the government's propaganda. The voting conditions, as they were originally announced on 10 March, were also blatantly unfair and undemocratic. The minimum voting age had earlier been set at twenty-four to exclude a large number of Nazi youths. Only yes ballots with patriotic red-white-red stripes on both sides were to be issued; those wishing to vote no had to bring their own paper (thus revealing their voting preference). "Good Austrians" were to be allowed to show their yes ballots, thereby making a truly secret vote impossible.[57] Registration procedures were also highly irregular and would not have prevented multiple voting.

Actually, Seyss-Inquart was able to persuade Schuschnigg to modify many of these voting regulations on 10 March, the same day they were announced; he was so pleased with the chancellor's concessions that he agreed to support the plebiscite. In the end, however, Schuschnigg's concessions to fair play could not alter the initial impression that the plebiscite was rigged. Far from making a Nazi takeover more difficult, therefore, the plebiscite gave Hitler a welcome pretext for intervention.

When the Austrian Nazi leaders first learned of the plebiscite through a spy in Zernatto's office, they were so taken aback that they were unsure how to respond. On only two issues could both moderates and radicals agree: the plebiscite was a breach of the Berchtesgaden Protocol, and word of the voting had to be quickly passed on to Berlin. It took the radicals little time to make up their minds in favor of an uprising. And even the moderates thought the vote was directed against them. They were afraid of the outcome, should the plebiscite actually take place.[58]

Hitler learned of Schuschnigg's decision even before the Austrian chancellor made his announcement. The news was related through Friedrich Rainer and then in more detail by Odilo Globocnik, who had flown to Berlin. Finding the news "absolutely incredible,"[59] however, he took no action until Wilhelm Keppler had returned from a fact-finding mission to Austria. When at last Keppler had confirmed the news, "Hitler responded as though someone had trodden on a painful corn. He had received no warning, and had made no preparations. It was clear to him that 'the evolutionary solution' was dead. He must either act or be humiliated."[60]

After Keppler's arrival Hitler made three decisions: he ordered General Wilhelm Keitel to work out plans for a possible invasion of Austria, he sent Globocnik back to Austria with instructions to give the party freedom of action, and he dictated a letter to Seyss-Inquart ordering him to persuade Schuschnigg to postpone the plebiscite and to change the voting arrangements. If the chancellor refused, an invasion would follow.[61]

The Nazis Unleashed: Austria's Final Day

The eleventh of March was the last and most hectic day of the First Republic's twenty-year history. When it began, Schuschnigg's plebiscite was just two days away and the government was still in control of the streets, at least outside Styria. By the day's end, however, Schuschnigg had been replaced by Seyss-Inquart, the Nazis were in complete command of thoroughfares and public buildings throughout the country, and the German army was poised to invade its southern neighbor.

Dramatic events succeeded each other at such a breathtaking rate that even now they are difficult for the historian to disentangle. It is helpful, however, to keep in mind that there were four major centers of activity: the federal chancellery on the Ballhausplatz in Vienna, the Reich chancellery in Berlin, the streets of Vienna, and the public avenues and buildings of other Austrian cities, especially those of the provincial capitals.

One might be tempted to assume that Seyss-Inquart, the Austrian Nazis, and the German leaders in Berlin were all coordinating their efforts to overthrow Schuschnigg, to find a pretext for a German invasion, and to annex Austria to Germany. But things were hardly that simple. Seyss-Inquart and the Austrian Nazis feared a German invasion nearly as much as Schuschnigg and President Miklas. And the Nazis in the streets were anxious to avoid the impression that Seyss-Inquart and German pressure were alone responsible for the Austrian chancellor's impending demise.

There is little point in recounting the well-known telephone conversations between Göring and Seyss-Inquart and the subsequent negotiations between the minister of security and Schuschnigg.[62] For years it was widely assumed that Seyss-Inquart was a "Trojan horse" who willingly carried out the orders of Berlin in order to subvert his own country's independence.[63] As early as 1939, however, Guido Zernatto described how Seyss "turned pale" after a phone call with Göring in which the minister president demanded the resignation of Schuschnigg. Seyss-Inquart's description of himself as nothing more than a "historical telephone girl" is basically correct.

At the Nuremberg Trials we also learned that it was Göring, not Hitler, who took the initiative after the Führer had instructed Seyss-Inquart to demand that Schuschnigg call off his plebiscite. Göring testified that just after the Austrian chancellor agreed to this first demand at 2:45 on the afternoon of 11 March, he (Göring) "had the instinctive feeling that the situation was now mobile and that now, finally, that possibility which we had long and ardently awaited was there—the possibility of bringing about a complete solution. And from that moment on I must take 100 percent responsibility for all further happenings because it was not the Fuehrer so much as I, myself, who set the pace and, even overruling the Fuehrer's misgivings, brought everything to its final development."[64] Göring saw the crisis as a heaven-sent opportunity to distract German opinion from the recent shakeup in the German government (involving Fritsch, Blomberg, Neurath, and Papen) and to ease the strain on the German economy by assimilating Austria's valuable gold reserves, raw materials, and badly needed manpower.[65]

Göring consequently told Seyss (at 3:05 P.M.) to insist on Schuschnigg's resignation and Seyss's own appointment as chancellor. Seyss objected strenuously to this new ultimatum but feared that its rejection and a German invasion would eliminate the last shred of Austrian independence. Moreover, as chancellor he would be in a better position to prevent a violent clash between Austrian Nazis and anti-Nazis, which the Germans could use as a pretext for an invasion.[66]

At 3:30 Schuschnigg resigned and by 7:30 in the evening the ex-chancellor joined Seyss and Police President Skubl in trying to persuade President Miklas to appoint the minister of interior and security as the new chancellor. Under

PROPAGANDA POSTER *for the Schuschnigg plebiscite of 13 March 1938 defaced by a swastika. DÖW.*

the circumstances, Seyss seemed to be the least of all possible evils: he was a Catholic, was opposed to violence, and was eager to form a government that included non-Nazis. If such a solution had occurred, many aspects of the Austrian Nazis' dream would have been fulfilled. (But of course, many Nazis would not have favored Seyss as chancellor.) It is also quite possible that had Seyss become the new chancellor at this point, there would have been no German invasion and no annexation, at least for the time being.

One person adamantly stood in the way of this course of action: President Miklas. The president's determined refusal to appoint Seyss-Inquart now appeared to jeopardize everyone's plans. Austrian Nazis and anti-Nazis alike feared the imminent invasion of their country. And the German Nazis faced the distasteful prospect of having to move without a convenient pretext. Hitler temporarily avoided making such a choice when Keppler passed on a false report from Vienna saying that Seyss-Inquart had been named chancellor.[67]

Meanwhile, rank-and-file Austrian Nazis had not been idle. During the previous twenty-four hours SA brigade leaders in the provinces, in defiance of the Landesleitung, had been struggling once more to "catch up" with the Styrians through demonstrations of their own. When Hitler's "freedom of action" order reached Vienna on the morning of the eleventh, it merely put the seal of approval on what was already an accomplished fact everywhere except in Vienna.[68] Only now, under the new orders from Hitler, did the Nazi leadership of Klausner abandon its inhibitions and imitate in Vienna the actions of subleaders in the federal states.

Major Klausner placed the responsibility for leading the "final political actions" in the hands of his two closest collaborators and fellow Carinthians, Rainer and Globocnik. At the same time the Landesleiter ordered that the government be presented with an ultimatum demanding a postponement in the plebiscite for three weeks.[69]

The Austrian Nazi leaders made no attempt to inform Seyss-Inquart of Hitler's unconditional support and were uninterested in Seyss's plan for a compromise "Black-Brown" (clerical-Nazi) coalition government. The minister of security was soon forced to confess to Zernatto that "he no longer controlled the course of affairs [did he ever?]; the weight of decision rested with the party."[70]

In the early afternoon of 11 March, Zernatto reported to Schuschnigg that SA and SS units had been gathering in parts of the Burgenland, Vienna, and Lower Austria since daybreak.[71] He might have added that there had been violent clashes the night before in Graz between Nazis and the government's paramilitary Sturmkorps. The situation was saved for the government only with the arrival of truckloads of soldiers, who occupied the thoroughfares and public squares thereby turning the Styrian capital into a veritable armed camp.

At 2:50 P.M. Rainer learned from Seyss-Inquart that Schuschnigg had called off the plebiscite. Rainer therefore implemented a contingency plan worked out the night before: great demonstrations were to be held throughout the country. In Vienna, Nazi street demonstrators became increasingly self-confident and aggressive as the day wore on. In the afternoon hours there was a kind of competition between Nazis and partisans of the Fatherland Front with the latter for a time apparently having the better of it.[72]

Ultimately the advantage lay with the Nazis. This was partly due no doubt to their better organization and enthusiasm. But to a large extent it was also a result of their self-confidence and the tolerant attitude of the Austrian police. Even during the early stages of the demonstrations in Vienna, the city's seven thousand policemen moved only timidly to quell disturbances. The progovernment demonstrators therefore had the distinct impression that the police were not on their side, a feeling which only added to their defeatism and boosted the morale of the Nazis.[73] In fact, fully 10 percent of the police were at first secretly, and by the end of the day more openly, pro-Nazi. The other 90 percent were simply neutral.[74]

By the late afternoon the SA and SS were marching in the larger provincial capitals of Graz, Salzburg, Linz, and Innsbruck; at 5:00 P.M. they began occupying a number of municipal and provincial government buildings. Increasingly they were joined by nervous fence sitters who had been waiting to see which way the political winds were blowing.[75]

The coup de grâce to the progovernment demonstrators was the radio announcement shortly past 6:00 stating that the plebiscite had been postponed. A second bulletin followed a few minutes later revealing that the Schuschnigg cabinet, except for Seyss-Inquart, had resigned.

At 7:00 in the evening, even though political power in the provinces was already largely in Nazi hands, Wilhelm Keppler still refused to sanction a seizure of power in Vienna. But the Austrian Nazi leaders were as indifferent to Keppler's views as they were to those of Seyss-Inquart. Only through a seizure of power could they forestall a German invasion and assure themselves the spoils of victory. This Machtergreifung would now be easy, because the Austrian government was under the mistaken impression that a German invasion was at hand.[76]

Schuschnigg made the Nazi takeover far easier by giving a radio address at 7:47 P.M. formally announcing his resignation and reviewing the day's events. In his brief but emotional speech, Schuschnigg mentioned the German ultimatum demanding his replacement as chancellor. He correctly pointed out the falsity of the German claim that there had been "workers' riots [and] that rivers of blood [had] flowed." His own rebuttal, however, that the government was in control of the situation was at best misleading and for many parts of Austria simply untrue.

Schuschnigg's assertion that "we are resolved not to spill German blood"[77] by forcefully resisting the German invasion ignored the fact that some of his top advisers, including the state secretary of defense and the state secretary of security, had warned him only a few hours earlier that resistance to an invasion would probably provoke an uprising within the police and the army.[78]

Shortly after this speech, Klausner discussed the situation with Lukesch, Kaltenbrunner, and other Nazi leaders in the office of Dr. Walter Pembauer, the head of the VPR. Lukesch informed the Landesleiter that his six thousand Viennese SA men would be ready to march within half an hour. Kaltenbrunner made the same pledge for his five hundred SS men in the capital. Thus reassured, Klausner ordered his SA and SS leaders to seize power in Vienna and the *Gauleiter* to complete the transfer of power in the provinces. Once more, no one bothered to inform Seyss-Inquart of this latest decision.[79]

Actually, little needed to be done in several of the provinces by this time (8:00 P.M.). In Graz the Nazis merely celebrated their already accomplished victory with a torchlight parade, which attracted an estimated sixty to seventy thousand screaming spectators. In Linz, Innsbruck, and Klagenfurt, SA and SS units demonstrated in public squares and occupied provincial parliament buildings, railroad stations, governors' offices, Fatherland Front headquarters, and newspaper offices. Later that evening, whenever a frantic local official called the Chancellery in Vienna, he was blandly misinformed by Globocnik, who was manning the switchboard, that the Nazis had already taken over the federal government.[80]

Meanwhile, in Vienna, Lukesch and his SA men had occupied the Ringstrasse, the broad avenue surrounding the central government district, and Kaltenbrunner's SS men had surrounded the Chancellery, virtually shutting it off from the outside world. Around 10:00 P.M. a special group of forty, seventeen- to twenty-two-year-old SS youths from the same 89th Standarte that had led the July Putsch began to enter the building. Armed, but without uniforms, save for their swastika armbands, they encountered no resistance from the guards. Elsewhere in Vienna, the Nazi flag was hoisted over the police headquarters at exactly 10:31 P.M.; an hour later members of the Nazifront German Gymnasts' Club, equipped with rifles, began their takeover of the huge neo-Gothic city hall. Now only the defiant president Wilhelm Miklas stood between the Austrian Nazis and total power.

Austria and the German Invasion

Schuschnigg's resignation and speech, together with the de facto seizure of power by the Austrian Nazis, left the Austrian and German Nazis working at cross-purposes during the evening hours of 11 March. Whereas the Austrian Nazis were happy to have the *threat* of a German invasion as a means of intimidating the Schuschnigg government into allowing a peaceful takeover, an *actual* invasion was quite another matter. The value of the threat was demonstrated when the president, acknowledging the Nazi takeover of the provinces, and receiving confirmed reports of the movement of German troops toward the Austrian border, finally gave in around midnight and appointed Seyss-Inquart chancellor. But the Austrian Nazis could only realize their dream of a Nazified but formally independent Austria if the German army stayed on its side of the Inn River.

A mere Gleichschaltung of Austria was no longer good enough for Göring, however. On 10 March he had instructed Keppler to carry a letter to Seyss-Inquart that contained the draft of a telegram the Austrian minister was to send to Germany. Seyss was supposed to beg for German troops to "restore order" in the Austrian cities. But Seyss refused to send this message. Keppler, once again in Vienna, was forced to phone Göring at 8:48 P.M. on the eleventh to inform him of Seyss's refusal. He added that "the SA and SS are marching through the streets, but things are very quiet here."[81] The Gauleiter of Upper Austria, August Eigruber, likewise testified years later in Nuremberg that "there was no necessity for the invasion because there was no unrest, at least there was no unrest in my district."[82] The lack of disturbances did not impress the Reich marshal in the least. He told Keppler: "show [Seyss] the telegram and tell him all we ask—in fact he doesn't need to send the telegram at all. All he needs to do is say: 'agreed.'"[83]

Contrary to the claims of the prosecution at Nuremberg, the telegram was finally sent to Berlin. However, the sender was not Seyss-Inquart but Keppler. The former, after having been repeatedly pestered by Keppler, had finally told the German emissary to do whatever he pleased about the telegram.[84] Therefore it was duly sent at 9:10 P.M. What significance this act may have had is revealed in the fact that twenty-five minutes earlier, at 8:45, Hitler had already ordered the Wehrmacht to march. After considerable cajoling, the Führer had finally accepted Göring's argument that Germany would lose face if it remained inactive after having issued an ultimatum. But the invasion may have also been directed against the Austrian Nazis themselves whose "dangerous" autonomist tendencies would have been increased by a takeover of the government in Vienna.[85]

The news was hardly welcome to the new chancellor in Vienna, Seyss-Inquart. With Austria now firmly under Nazi control, he did his best to stop the German invasion and the loss of Austrian autonomy. To emphasize the "Austrian" character of his new ministry, and to prevent domination by the German NSDAP, which he feared would follow from a purely Nazi cabinet, he attempted to form a coalition with non-Nazis. The effort was in defiance of instructions from Göring, who at 5:00 P.M. had ordered the formation of a cabinet composed solely of National Socialists. Göring had even specified the names of several individuals who were supposed to be appointed to various positions. Seyss-Inquart's exertions met with limited success. Guido Schmidt, for example, Schuschnigg's foreign minister, declined an invitation to join Seyss's cabinet.[86]

Meanwhile, at 2:10 on the morning of 12 March, General Muff, the German military attaché, acting on instructions from Seyss-Inquart, called Günther Altenburg, the Austrian desk officer in the German Foreign Ministry, asking that the German troops be halted at the border.[87] But ten minutes later Altenburg called back to say that the Führer had decided the invasion could no longer be stopped.[88] The Austrian Nazis' dream had lasted approximately six hours.

Hitler provided an ex post facto justification for the invasion in an interview on 13 March with Ward Price, a special correspondent of Britain's *Daily Mail*. The Reich chancellor claimed that if Schuschnigg had gone ahead with his plebiscite a civil war would have broken out and Austria would have become a "second Spain." More than two thousand Austrians had lost their lives in their struggle for freedom against a government which had the support of only 10 percent of the country's population. Hitler concluded the interview by inviting Price to return to Austria in four years to see how much things had improved.[89]

The history of the last month of the First Austrian Republic is full of paradoxes. At no time in all of Austria's history were its people more divided and filled with hatred toward each other. Rivalries between Nazi factions reached a peak at the same time that the enmity between the Nazis and the Austrian government was also reaching a climax. Yet strangely enough, beyond all the noisy demonstrations the Austrian people had far more in common than they realized. Even the most patriotic and anti-Nazi Austrians conceded that they were Germans—albeit a special kind. But at the same time, the most fanatical Nazis resisted the prospect of a German invasion and the total loss of their Austrian identity.

The quarrel within Austria, then, was not so much over whether the country should remain autonomous, but over who should rule it and how they should come to power. The Nazis all favored the policy of Gleichschaltung and at one time or another all preferred using an evolutionary process to achieve it. Josef Leopold merely abandoned this tactic when he was unable to reach an accommodation with the Schuschnigg government. Leopold's rivals, the Carinthian Nazis, were for a long time too numerically weak to contemplate the use of force. Their greater moderation was ultimately rewarded when Hubert Klausner replaced Leopold as Landesleiter in February 1938. But only four weeks later the Carinthians, with Hitler's approval, employed the same kind of force to seize power that they had denounced when Leopold used it.

Not until the Anschluss did the Austrian people finally discover just how much they had in common. For twenty years they had been asking themselves whether they were more German or Austrian. Only when their country's independence was a thing of the past would they finally realize the answer.

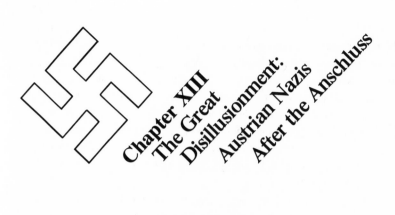

Popular Reactions to the Anschluss

Although neither Seyss-Inquart nor any of the Austrian Nazi leaders had wanted a German invasion, it was not immediately certain that such an invasion would entail the end of a nominally independent Austrian Nazi state. Nearly all historians now agree that not even Hitler had made up his mind about the future status of Austria until he was swept away by the enthusiasm of the crowds which greeted him and the German army and he realized that the Great Powers were not going to offer any armed resistance to the invasion. He may also have been influenced by Göring's plea to "go the whole hog" and annex Austria.[1]

Although there were instances of Nazis being transported from the provinces to Vienna to welcome Hitler, it would be a serious mistake to imagine that most of the enthusiasm was not genuine. Even many people who were normally indifferent to politics wildly greeted the Germans on 12–13 March.[2] A quarter of a million people crowded into the ancient capital's huge Heldenplatz to hear Hitler announce the "reunification" of Austria and Germany and another five hundred thousand to six hundred thousand spectators lined the Ringstrasse to cheer the Führer after the speech.[3]

This display of emotion does not mean that every Austrian wishing to catch a glimpse of the German chancellor and approving a union of the two countries necessarily accepted all of the Nazi ideology. Many were simply relieved that five years of almost constant civil strife and twenty years of economic misery were now at last (presumably) about to end. For all those groups which had felt neglected by the Dollfuss-Schuschnigg regime or by the Socialists' doctrine, Nazism appeared to offer the hope that many old bureaucratic structures and institutions would soon be removed.[4]

Contributing to the easy German takeover was the attitude of foreign countries and the churches of Austria. Despite the efforts of the pretender to the Austrian throne, Otto von Habsburg, to preserve at least the legal fiction of Austrian independence, the governments of Britain, France, and the United States accorded the Anschluss, not just a de facto, but instead a full de jure recognition even before the Nazi plebiscite of 10 April had confirmed Austria's change of status.[5] Both the Catholic and Protestant churches of Austria were eager to pledge their loyalty to the new order. On the very day of the invasion, 12 March, Protestants issued declarations of loyalty to the Nazi leadership, followed by a similar pronouncement by Cardinal Innitzer the next day. Innitzer went so far as to order church bells in Vienna rung when Hitler entered the city on 14 March.

The euphoria after the Anschluss lasted only a few weeks, and in some cases much less. By the fourteenth there were one hundred thousand German troops in Austria.[6] Following close behind them was a second army consisting of German administrators who were assigned to every branch of the civil service and even to the economy. Officially, they came only as advisers. But in reality they took charge of the highest offices from the very beginning.[7] Soon most Austrians felt like natives in a conquered colony. The German name for Austria, *Österreich*, was immediately replaced by the old Carolingian name, *Ostmark*, and the provinces of Upper and Lower Austria became *Ober-* and *Niederdonau* (Upper and Lower Danube) without the respective *Gauleiter* even being informed in advance. By 1942 even the word *Ostmark* had too much of a separatist ring to it and was replaced by the phrase "Alpine and Danube *Gaue*." The change in nomenclature was all the more galling when the Austrians noted that the Bavarians and people of other German states were allowed to keep their historic names.[8]

By the fall of 1938, the Germans had managed to alienate virtually every social and political group in Austria. The Catholic nationalists were indignant over the Nazis' virulent anticlericalism. Former members of the GVP did not care for the attacks on economic liberalism. Austrian Protestants, who had been among the Nazis' strongest supporters even before 1938, were antagonized by the nationalization of their private schools and the Nazis' attack on religion in general.[9] Peasants and industrial workers resented the growing shortages of food and consumer goods even before the outbreak of World War II.

The popularity of the Germans deteriorated so rapidly that already by June 1938, just three months after the Anschluss, a Gestapo report compiled in Innsbruck observed that only 15 percent of the Tyrolean population could be regarded as "absolutely reliable National Socialists." Another 30 percent of the people had joined the party for strictly opportunistic reasons. Ten to 20

ADOLF HITLER *reviews the German army in Vienna just after the Anschluss. Arthur Seyss-Inquart is on the extreme right side of the picture. To Hitler's immediate right is Reichsführer SS Heinrich Himmler. DÖW.*

percent were "occasional supporters" and the remaining 30 to 40 percent were "open or hidden opponents of the movement." Other secret public-opinion reports for Vienna revealed substantially the same attitudes.[10]

The Disappointing Spoils of Victory

Of all the Austrians none were more disillusioned by the Anschluss than some of the leading Nazis themselves. Only seven days after the German invasion the American chargé in Austria sent this perceptive dispatch to Washington:

> Seyss-Inquart himself was duped by the German tactics. He had
> no idea that the independence of Austria would be extinguished.
> He foresaw a National Socialist Austria with himself as Chancellor. . . .
> My impression is that the German Government and National Socialist
> Party in Germany took over Austria by a series of surprise moves
> which the local National Socialist leaders were obliged to accept with

the best grace they could. Rumors have it that disillusionment in Austrian Nazi circles has not been long in coming. The "plums" are going to the German Party comrades.[11]

The Austrian Nazis discovered just who was in charge already before daybreak on 12 March, well before German troops arrived in Vienna. When Reichsführer SS Heinrich Himmler landed at Vienna's Aspern airfield at 4:30 A.M., he immediately replaced Seyss-Inquart's choice for state secretary of security, Michael Skubl, with the Austrian SS leader, Ernst Kaltenbrunner. But even Kaltenbrunner, though an SS man, was not fully trusted by Himmler's nominal subordinate and head of the State Police (Gestapo), Reinhard Heydrich. Heydrich put Kaltenbrunner as well as Seyss-Inquart and his circle under constant surveillance beginning on 13 March.[12]

What little regard Himmler had for Odilo Globocnik and Friedrich Rainer was revealed when the two Austrian Nazi leaders, who had come to the airport to greet the Reichsführer, were left standing with no means to return to the city. So discouraged were Globocnik and Rainer that a few days later they, along with Major Klausner, flew to Berlin to persuade Hitler that they had played an important role in the takeover of Austria.[13]

Their efforts were only partly successful. To be sure, Kaltenbrunner became the Austrian minister of security in Seyss-Inquart's cabinet and remained in charge of the police in the Ostmark for the next three years. Major Klausner became the education minister and Dr. Jury and Anton Reinthaller also received cabinet posts as did Franz Hueber, who became minister of justice. But other Austrian Nazi leaders, including Rainer, Globocnik, Leopold, and Persche, were left out of Seyss-Inquart's forty-hour government. Alfred Frauenfeld, whose popularity was feared by Hitler, was even forbidden to return to his native Vienna.[14]

Although some Austrian Nazis were bitterly disappointed by the Anschluss, it would be grossly inaccurate to say that the majority of the *Parteigenossen* were left empty-handed. Lesser Nazis benefited from the "Aryanization" of Jewish businesses and the civil service. Many Austrian Nazi leaders did get important positions outside Seyss-Inquart's cabinet. All of the new *Gauleiter* were Austrians. Globocnik became the Gauleiter of Vienna, albeit for only a year. He was later to gain far more notoriety as the man who directed the extermination of the Polish Jews, before he committed suicide in June 1945.[15] Dr. Jury was named Gauleiter of the Lower Danube. Rainer became the leader of Gau Salzburg, and Carinthia was headed by Hubert Klausner, to name but a few of the more prominent *Gauleiter*. Klausner also became the deputy of Josef Bürckel, who was named "Reichskommissar for the Reunification of the Ostmark with the Reich" on 23 April 1938. Bürckel became the real ruler of the Ostmark until the middle of 1940, because Hitler, as usual, could not be bothered with day-to-day operations in Austria. As for Klausner, his career ended with his sudden death in 1939.[16]

Even though all of the new *Gauleiter* of the Ostmark were Austrians and *Altkämpfer*, with the exception of Klausner, none of them had ever held a national office in the Austrian Nazi party; and none at all had ever defied Hitler's leadership.[17] Even Klausner was replaced as Landesleiter of the Austrian NSDAP by Bürckel immediately after the Anschluss.

Vienna was the only Gau after 1939 to be led by a German from the Altreich. But even there the great majority of the subleaders were mostly Austrians, often native Viennese. Only about eleven hundred members of the Vienna municipal employees were ever dismissed by the Germans or just 4.5 percent of the total employed. Of those who were fired, about half were Jewish. The Nazis simply did not have enough experienced administrators to afford a wholesale purge. Most Austrian officials cooperated with the German carpetbaggers, fearing that if they did not their jobs would be in jeopardy. Nevertheless, the Germans never fully trusted them.[18]

A close examination of the Austrian *Gauleiter* reveals that six of the seven were members of the SS. Only one, the Gauleiter of Upper Austria, August Eigruber, had been a follower of the SA man and former Landesleiter Josef Leopold; and none at all had been an émigré.[19] Instead of becoming the chancellor of an *angesschlossen* Austria, Captain Leopold did not even remain the Gauleiter of his native province. Alfred Persche observed that Hitler did not give Leopold or himself the slightest sign of recognition or thanks during a ceremony at the Vienna Rathaus on 14 March. For Persche, this was the most bitter day of his life.[20]

Leopold later complained to Persche that his whole staff was being treated like criminals. When the former SA leader asked the Hauptmann what explanation or reproach Hitler had offered for this treatment, Leopold tearfully replied that the Führer had said nothing to him at all.[21] Obviously, the former Landesleiter had still not learned that one did not challenge the authority of the Leader with impunity.

Leopold spent the next three years of his life working in a back room of the party chancellery in Munich, lacking any real power or responsibility. In order to escape this dreary existence he volunteered to fight on the Russian front, where he died as a lieutenant colonel (Oberstleutnant) on 24 June 1941, just two days after the start of the German invasion. For his part, Persche had seen so much Byzantine intrigue and lack of consideration among high party officials that he had no desire to remain a party leader after 1938.[22]

Those Austrian Nazi leaders who had tried to follow an independent policy of one kind or another were given jobs, if at all, outside of the Ostmark after the Anschluss. Leopold's former deputy, Franz Schattenfroh, became the director of a minor department in the German Foreign Ministry. Anton Rintelen, the would-be Nazi successor of Dollfuss, was simply ignored when the spoils were divided. Theo Habicht was also not permitted to return to Austria and was killed on the Russian front in 1944.[23]

Another former Austrian Nazi leader who had once challenged Hitler's supremacy, Dr. Walter Riehl, was arrested after the Anschluss but was soon released. His appeal to be reinstated in the party was rejected by a party court, however, because of the anti-Hitlerian tone adopted by the *Deutsche Arbeiter-Presse* during his renewed editorship in 1934–35.[24] Riehl survived the war and lived in Vienna until his death in 1957.

Alfred Frauenfeld was comparatively fortunate, being appointed to the German Reichstag. During the war he became the Generalkommissar for the Crimea. In this capacity he dreamed of transferring to the Crimea the Volga Germans, some South Tyroleans, and even German Russians who had emigrated to the United States. After the war Frauenfeld was arrested on the charge of plotting to overthrow the Bonn government in 1953. He died in Hamburg in 1977.

Hermann Neubacher momentarily became the popular mayor of Vienna after the Anschluss; but his prominence declined rapidly after the Nazi plebiscite in April when the Austro-German union was formally ratified.[25] He was dismissed in March 1940, possibly in part because of his willingness to aid Jews, but more likely because neither Hitler nor Bürckel wanted a truly popular Austrian Nazi leader.[26] After the war he worked for the municipal government of Addis Ababa in Ethiopia; he died in 1961.[27] Anton Reinthaller, the peasant leader and minister of agriculture in Seyss-Inquart's ephemeral cabinet, was the only Austrian Nazi leader to pursue a political career inside Austria after the war. In 1955 he founded a small right-wing party called the Freiheitspartei and died in 1959.[28]

As for Seyss-Inquart, he was apparently forced to agree to the Anschluss law, which united Austria and Germany on 13 March 1938, something he had certainly not desired. His request to Hitler, that Austria retain a measure of administrative autonomy, was in practice ignored as Austria was just as thoroughly dominated after 1938 by Berlin and the party's headquarters in Munich as was the rest of the Greater German Reich. Seyss himself was named by Hitler to be the Reichsstatthalter (governor) of the Ostmark from the Anschluss until 1 May 1939. But in reality he was increasingly subordinate to Josef Bürckel.[29] Seyss-Inquart and his Land government were allowed to linger on with steadily diminishing powers until March 1940 when the government was abolished altogether. By that time Seyss had been made governor of Poland, and finally, from 1940 to 1945, Reichskommissar of the Netherlands. Tried at Nuremberg, he was acquitted of the charge of conspiring to prepare an aggressive war, but was convicted as a war criminal for his activities in Holland. He was hanged in 1946.[30]

Chapter XIV
Hitler and the
Forgotten Nazis

La Plus ça change, la plus ça même chose (the more things change the more they stay the same). One could hardly find a better example of this proverb than in the history of Austrian pan-Germanism and National Socialism. From the formulation of the Linz Program in 1882 until the Anschluss fifty-six years later, most of the basic goals, leadership problems, ideology, and social composition of the proto-Nazis, Nazis, and near Nazis remained remarkably consistent even during very different political circumstances.

As early as Austria's expulsion from the German Confederation (Deutsche Bund) in 1866, a union (or reunion) with Germany became the fundamental policy of the Austrian pan-Germans. Yet, however anti-Habsburg, anti-Catholic, antiliberal, or antidemocratic they might be, they nevertheless clung to the idea of a special autonomous position for German-Austria in a Greater German Reich. To this program the postwar Austrian Nazis added the idea of preserving the autonomy of their party within the Gesamtpartei.

But neither the German Imperial government during the First World War[1] nor Adolf Hitler after it displayed any sympathy for these objectives. Hitler was as contemptuous of an independent Austrian Nazi party as he was of Austrian independence itself. He went out of his way to display this attitude in opposing Walter Riehl at the Interstate Nazi meeting in Salzburg in 1923, in his "conversations" with Karl Schulz in 1925–26, at the Weimar party congress in 1926, and in his policy toward the South Tyrol. His humiliating treatment of Schulz in Munich in 1925 was virtually a dress rehearsal for his performance against Chancellor Kurt von Schuschnigg at Berchtesgaden thirteen years later.

Hitler shackled the Austrian Nazis' hopes for autonomy by refusing to appoint a strong leader with unambiguous powers. He could hardly have imagined that Friedrich Jankovic, Heinrich Schmidt, or even Hans Krebs could have provided the Austrian Nazis with the firm leadership they were demanding. Although Theo Habicht was a more effective leader, his powers were diluted by those of Alfred Proksch.

Despite Hitler's unwillingness to support or even permit a strong, autonomous Austrian party, the Austrians nonetheless managed to assert themselves, as became painfully evident to Hitler in July 1934. The disastrous Putsch forced the Führer to grant the Austrian Nazis the independence they had long desired, but without most of the financial support they needed to become a major force in Austrian politics. And Hitler did nothing to resolve the leadership quarrels in Austria, refusing to give his unqualified support to any of the rival leaders.

The Austrian Nazis at last had an opportunity to flex their muscles in February 1938 after Hitler decided to speed up the Gleichschaltung of Austria. But even then the Austrians were to be disappointed. Hoping for a mere *threat* of a German invasion, they got instead the real thing. The entrance of German troops extinguished their hopes for a Nazified but autonomous Austrian state.

When it came to uniting behind a single leader, the Austrian Nazis and proto-Nazis were their own worst enemies. Even though they had subscribed to the Führerprinzip ever since the time of Georg von Schönerer, they remained divided into a confusing number of parties, clubs, and leagues, which often fought each other with more fanaticism than they did their common enemies. Schönerer's insistence on blind obedience alienated even his most loyal supporters. Riehl in 1923 and Schulz three years later proved to be too moderate to retain the support of young Hitler advocates. Jankovic was too old and incompetent, Schmidt too bland, and Krebs too preoccupied with Sudeten affairs to be able to provide the party with capable leadership. The Sudeten-born Alfred Proksch was regarded as little better than a foreigner.

Theo Habicht was a considerable improvement as a party leader; but even he was handicapped by his unfamiliarity with Austrian politics, his impulsiveness, and his German citizenship. Following the ill-conceived July Putsch, Anton Reinthaller and Hermann Neubacher lacked sufficient seniority in the party and were too willing to compromise with the hated Schuschnigg regime to suit the *Altkämpfer*. Josef Leopold had a strong following among the SA but was considered far too plebeian by the middle-class SS. Worst of all, his determination to seize power on his own, by force if necessary, eventually cost him the backing of Hitler. Hubert Klausner did not enjoy much respect outside SS circles and his native Carinthia, whereas Arthur Seyss-Inquart was distrusted by many Austrian Nazis because of his Sudeten birth and nonmembership in the party.

Thus, for all their talk about "ein Reich, ein Volk, ein Führer," the Austrian Nazis remained dogmatically parochial and class conscious, traits shared by many of their countrymen. Rarely did a Nazi, or for that matter a Heimwehr leader, attract much of a following outside his home province. If there was an exception it was Theo Habicht, who was, significantly enough, a Reich German. Yet the Austrians resented being dictated to by "outsiders" from either Germany or the Sudetenland, a fact that became especially obvious after the Anschluss.

Austria between the wars is a classic example of the importance of a talented and charismatic leader to the success of a fascist movement. The conditions that gave rise to fascism in other countries existed in abundance in this Alpine state. A sense of betrayal stemming from the Treaty of Saint-Germain, despair over the economic future of the country, an impoverished and underemployed middle class, fear of a powerful Marxist party, hatred and envy of wealthy Jews, and a rebellious and unemployed youth. Yet no single fascist leader, inside or outside the Nazi party, was able fully to exploit the situation. None was even able to attract a group of fanatically loyal lieutenants in the manner of Hitler or Mussolini. Far from uniting their country, as they claimed they would do, the fascist leaders could not even unite their own party.

Although the Austrian Nazis failed miserably in standing behind a common leader—other than the distant and preoccupied Hitler—they had considerably more success in pledging their allegiance to a common ideology. For example, the Anschluss issue had long been a feature of pan-Germans and Nazis. To be sure, the DAP did not jump on the Anschluss bandwagon until 1918 and the Nazis had anything but a monopoly on the Anschluss idea before 1933.

Anti-Semitism was another unifying bond of all right-wing groups in Austria. Dating back to the Middle Ages, it acquired "modern," "racial" characteristics in Austria after 1867 and was part of Schönerer's Linz Program. The dislocations of the World War and the postwar inflation served to intensify anti-Jewish feelings. The ideology was particularly strong among university-aged students who, not surprisingly, became the hard core of the Austrian Nazi party.

The idea of a *Volksgemeinschaft* (people's community) was already part of the prewar program of the Deutsche Arbeiterpartei, and territorial expansion was, in a sense, found in the Linz Program of 1882. Extremism, opposition to the international aspects and "Jewish" character of Marxism, and anti-liberalism were already well developed in the programs of Schönerer and the prewar DAP as well as in the postwar Austrian Nazis. They all saw compromise as a sellout.

All these common ideological denominators may be a little deceiving, however. Austrian Nazi literature seldom gives the impression that ideology was taken all that seriously by its adherents. Actions were always far more highly regarded than words. Seizing power, by almost any means, was the supreme goal. And such an aim could more easily be realized through charismatic leadership than by even the most refined and sophisticated ideology, or so it was believed. The high percentage of young people in the Austrian Nazi party as well as their heterogeneous social and political backgrounds, may help account for this relative indifference to ideology.[2]

Only the Schulz Nazis showed a real interest in ideology. But they may well be the exception which proves the rule; for it is doubtful whether they can really even be considered Nazis, at least in the orthodox "Hitlerian" sense of the word. And in any event their preoccupation with ideology eventually made them more a historical curiosity than a real force in Austrian, let alone Central European politics.

The theme of continuity is also very much apparent in the social composition of pan-Germanism and Nazism. Young people, especially students, supported Georg von Schönerer in the 1880s just as ardently as their grandchildren were to idealize Adolf Hitler in the 1930s. The high unemployment rate of the Depression, particularly in the professions, only heightened the desperation and fanaticism of the later generation.

Groups that felt threatened by the Industrial Revolution and Jewish competition were also likely candidates for right-wing extremism, both before and after the World War: small businessmen, professional people such as lawyers and doctors, and above all, teachers. Civil servants, either unemployed or underemployed after the disintegration of the Habsburg Monarchy, were ready to join any organization that promised to unite Austria with Germany, thus creating more civil-service opportunities.

Protestants, especially recent converts, although small in absolute numbers, flocked to the ranks of Schönerer and Hitler to an extent out of proportion to their tiny percentage of Austria's population. The ostentatious Catholicism of the old regime and the governments of Dollfuss and Schuschnigg only enhanced their sense of alienation.

Geographically, the ethnic borderlands such as Styria and Carinthia, with their long history of national conflict, and provincial capitals, with their high percentage of civil servants, students, and professional people, consistently provided the nucleus of the pan-German, Nazi, and Heimwehr fascist ranks, especially their leadership.

Only in two areas can a significant shift in the composition of right-wing Austrian organizations be noted between the 1880s and the 1930s. Trade unionists (frequently railroad, and telephone and telegraph employees) made up an important element of the pan-German movement, particularly in the DAP and the DNSAP from the beginning of the twentieth century until the early 1920s. Thereafter, however, they began to decline, if not in absolute terms, then at least relatively. When the Austrian Nazis split in 1925–26, the trade unionists remained loyal to Karl Schulz, thus leaving the Hitlerian Nazis with a younger, more professional, and academic membership.

The other major change in the social composition of right-wing groups involved peasants. Long discriminated against by franchise laws, they voted at first for Karl Lueger's Christian Social party. This affiliation continued after the war, although peasants often belonged simultaneously to Heimwehr units. With the catastrophic economic conditions of the Depression, however, along with the German boycott of Austrian products and the prospects of new markets in a Greater German Reich, the peasants began shifting their support over to the Nazis.

The most important leitmotiv in our story has been Hitler's ambition to absorb Austria into his Third Reich. From the start of his political career in 1919, or at any rate from his writing of *Mein Kampf* in 1924 until the Anschluss itself in 1938, he never lost sight of his ultimate objective. This fact is all the more remarkable in view of the changing international circumstances that sometimes forced him to alter his tactics. Austria, in fact, provides an outstanding example of the basic characteristics of Hitler's overall foreign policy: "consistency of aim with complete opportunism in method and tactics."[3]

Although Hitler declared the necessity of Austria's "returning to the Reich" in the very first sentence of *Mein Kampf*, he never allowed the Anschluss question to distract him from what he regarded as more important, or at least more pressing issues. His first aim, as far as Austria was concerned, was to gain control over the Austrian Nazi party, even though this involved splitting the party into two almost equal parts. Nor did the sensibilities of Austrians, both Nazis and non-Nazis, prevent him from renouncing the South Tyrol in exchange for winning the friendship of Mussolini and Fascist Italy. Even after his rise to power, Hitler kept Austria on the "back burner" while he consolidated his power in Germany and built up the Wehrmacht.

The image of Hitler foaming at the mouth and impulsively attacking countries indiscriminately may have some validity for the years between 1941 and 1945. But it would distort the truth to apply this image to his handling of the Austrian question. On the contrary, he was able to exercise considerable restraint, flexibility, and above all, patience in realizing his long-range goal. Indeed, one of his most important difficulties was curbing the reckless enthusiasm of some of his followers, not only in Austria, but also in such places as the Sudetenland,[4] Danzig, Yugoslavia, and the Memelland.

The relative ease of the Gleichschaltung process in Germany in 1933–34 misled Hitler and the Austrian Nazis into pursuing a rapid takeover in Austria, which was seen as a domestic problem that could be solved with the usual Nazi combination of terror, promises, and bombastic electoral campaigns. The refusal of Engelbert Dollfuss to surrender to Nazi intimidation and the Austrian chancellor's abolition of elections, and slightly later the Nazi party itself, forced Hitler to adopt a new approach. On 26 May 1933 he launched his "thousand-Mark blockade," accompanied by propaganda attacks on the Austrian government, which originated from German territory. International indignation aroused by Habicht's radio speeches merely caused Hitler to switch to more subtle—and more insidious—propaganda in February 1934. His attempt to call off the terror campaign in Austria, however, proved disastrously ineffective.

More drastic changes were required in Hitler's Austrian policy following the July Putsch fiasco. Theo Habicht and his Landesleitung were both sacrificed to appease an outraged world public opinion. Hitler now reverted to the same politics of legality he had used with such success in German domestic affairs after 1925. So abrupt did his change of tactics appear that Austrian Nazis felt depressed and abandoned by their Führer. But Hitler was merely making a virtue out of a necessity, renouncing for the moment something that he lacked the power to seize by force.

The July Agreement of 1936, although not initiated by Hitler, can be regarded as a continuation of the same policy of patience and ostensive legality. Once again most Austrian Nazis felt betrayed and deserted, and once again Hitler had to assure them, through Friedrich Rainer and Odilo Globocnik, to have faith and patience.

Hitler had several ways of influencing the Austrian Nazis after 1934 (when they were officially independent), even though his control was far from absolute. His new German envoy to Austria, Franz von Papen, kept a watchful eye on Nazi activities as did the German economic expert Wilhelm Keppler, after July 1937. Further control was maintained through the Hilfswerk, whose subsidies to Austrian Gaue could be increased or decreased according to their degree of cooperation. Finally, Hitler could exercise substantial influence over events by giving or withholding his blessings to moderate or radical Austrian leaders, depending on the needs of the moment and their willingness to follow his commands.

After 1933, when Hitler altered his policy of directly annexing Austria in favor of the more subtle goal of Gleichschaltung, he was extremely reluctant to revert to his original aim. To be sure, he decided to speed up the process at the so-called Hossbach conference in November 1937; the actual acceleration began with his famous meeting with Schuschnigg at Berchtesgaden in February 1938. In all likelihood he expected it to be several months, if not years, before Austria became a fully Nazified state. Yet it was his threatening speech to the Reichstag of 20 February that (probably inadvertently) encouraged Styrian and later other Austrian Nazis to take matters into their own hands. Hitler probably did not realize that he had helped set in motion a chain reaction which would reach its climax only with the annexation of Austria just three weeks later.

Although Hitler did not directly intervene in the drama unfolding in Austria between 20 February and 9 March, he did expect Arthur Seyss-Inquart and Wilhelm Keppler to restrain the more rambunctious Nazis in order to avoid the kind of trouble that might necessitate a German invasion. Only when Schuschnigg announced his luckless plebiscite on the ninth did Hitler feel compelled to "unleash" his Austrian followers at a time when many of them had long since unleased themselves. But even then his intention was simply to force Schuschnigg to call off his vote, not to invade, and certainly not to annex Austria. It was Hermann Göring rather than Hitler who played the leading role in ousting Schuschnigg and engineering the German invasion. And it may have been Göring, once again, who helped persuade Hitler to discard his inhibitions and carry out the Anschluss on 13 March.

Thus Hitler's role in the Anschluss spectacle was far more passive than has commonly been supposed. His genius lay not in the day-to-day direction of Austrian Nazi affairs, in which he never had a hand, nor even after the Anschluss, in providing inspiring propaganda. Rather it was in curbing the enthusiasm of his Austrian *Parteigenossen* until the international constellation made a "peaceful" Anschluss possible.

On the other hand, the significance of the Austrian Nazis in bringing about the Anschluss has heretofore been either ignored or underestimated. They refused merely to await their "liberation." Yet it is doubtful whether they could have seized power, even for the few hours that they did, without the intimidating presence of German troops on the Austrian frontier.

After 1938, the Austrian Nazis were quickly forgotten. Hitler and the German Nazis refused to give them credit for the Anschluss; and to postwar Austrians their memory was an embarrassment they were anxious to eradicate from history. The perverted idealism and misdirected energy of the Austrian Nazis were wasted for a cause in which they were among the first to be disillusioned. Their story, which is tragic in its own way, shows the ineffectiveness of the fascist Führerprinzip in overcoming a country's deep historical divisions, especially when the scene is void of any competent Führer.

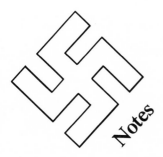

Notes

Preface

1. Alfred Persche, "Hauptmann Leopold," DÖW, #1460.
2. Legal judgment by Alfons Gorbach, ibid., pp. 3–5.
3. For the latest contribution to this debate see Gilbert Allardyce, "What Fascism Is Not."
4. Ernst Nolte, *Three Faces of Fascism*, p. 456.
5. Juan Linz, "Some Notes Toward a Comparative Study of Fascism in Sociological Historical Perspective," p. 13; Zeev Sternhell, "Fascist Ideology," p. 347.
6. R. John Rath, "The First Austrian Republic," p. 179.
7. For further details on the "leadership principle" see my article "Fascism and the *Führerprinzip*."

Chapter I

1. Friedrich Funder, *From Empire to Republic*, p. 218.
2. Karl Stadler, *The Birth of the Austrian Republic, 1918–1921*, p. 149.
3. Leo Pasvolsky, *Economic Nationalism of the Danubian States*, p. 95.
4. Ibid., p. 149.
5. Lajos Kerekes, "Wirtschaftliche und soziale Lage Österreichs nach dem Zerfall der Doppelmonarchie," p. 89.
6. Julius Braunthal, *The Tragedy of Austria*, pp. 37–38.
7. Kurt von Schuschnigg, *The Brutal Takeover*, p. 37.
8. Braunthal, *Tragedy of Austria*, p. 43.
9. Kerekes, "Wirtschaftliche Lage Österreichs," p. 87.
10. David Mitrany, *The Effects of the War on Southeastern Europe*, p. 174.
11. Herbert Hoover, *The Memoirs of Herbert Hoover*, 1:395.
12. *The World Almanac and Book of Facts*, 1929, p. 588; C. A. Macartney and A. W. Palmer, *Independent Eastern Europe*, p. 201.
13. Norbert Schausberger, *Der Griff nach Österreich*, pp. 81–87.
14. See Gerard Silberstein, *The Troubled Alliance*.
15. Alfred Low, *The Anschluss Movement, 1918–1919 and the Paris Peace Conference*, p. 4. See also Duane Myers, "Berlin *versus* Vienna." Myers points out that immediately after the collapse of Austria-Hungary the Anschluss movement was

stronger in Austria than in Germany, where diplomats feared Allied retaliation if they pushed an Anschluss program prematurely (pp. 154, 175).

16. David Strong, *Austria (October 1918–March 1919)*, p. 294.

17. Low, *Anschluss Movement*, p. 314.

18. Ibid., pp. 452–53, 458–59.

19. Charles Seymour and Harold B. Whiteman, Jr., eds., *Letters from the Paris Peace Conference*, p. 268.

20. Schausberger, *Griff nach Österreich*, pp. 39, 64, 79; letters of Wedel to the AA, 29 Jan. 1919, 7 Apr. 1919, NA, T-120, R. 5416/K287904, K287932.

21. Schausberger, *Griff nach Österreich*, pp. 102, 103.

22. *Deutsche Grenzwacht*, 6 May 1921.

23. Malcolm Bullock, *Austria 1918–1938*, p. 175.

24. Aurel Kolnai, "The Problem of Austrian Nationhood," p. 303.

25. Eric Kollman, "The Austrian Presidency, 1918–1958," p. 92.

26. Adam Wandruszka, "Die Krise des Parlamentarismus, 1897 und 1933," p. 77.

27. Mary MacDonald, *The Republic of Austria, 1918–1934*, pp. 43–44.

28. Klemens von Klemperer, *Ignaz Seipel*, p. 227; Alfred Diament, *Austrian Catholics and the First Austrian Republic*, pp. 78–80, 120.

29. William Hubbard, "Politics and Society in the Central European City," pp. 36–38, 43; Franz Borkenau, *Austria and After*, p. 160.

30. Adam Wandruszka, "Österreichs politische Struktur," p. 430; Kurt Shell, *The Transformation of Austrian Socialism*, pp. 3–4.

31. C. A. Macartney, *The Social Revolution in Austria*, p. 142.

32. Francis Carsten, "Interpretations of Fascism," p. 420.

33. Klemens von Klemperer, "Chancellor Seipel and the Crisis of Democracy in Austria," p. 470; Adolf Hitler, *Mein Kampf*, pp. 47–50.

34. Charles Gulick, *Austria from Habsburg to Hitler*, 1:751.

Chapter II

1. Paul Molisch, *Geschichte der deutschnationalen Bewegung in Österreich von ihren Anfängen bis zum Zerfall der Monarchie*, p. 141; Peter Pulzer, *The Rise of Political Anti-Semitism in Germany and Austria*, p. 7.

2. Pulzer, *Anti-Semitism*, p. 10.

3. Leo Goldhammer, *Die Juden Wiens*, p. 9; Franz Borkenau, *Austria and After*, p. 95.

4. *The World Almanac and Book of Facts*, 1929, p. 588.

5. Goldhammer, *Juden Wiens*, pp. 39–40; William Jenks, *Vienna and the Young Hitler*, p. 120.

6. Hugo Gold, *Geschichte der Juden in Wien*, p. 36.

7. Henry Steed, *The Hapsburg Monarchy*, p. 184. See also Robert Schwarz, "Antisemitism and Socialism in Austria, 1918–1962," p. 446.

8. Arthur May, *The Hapsburg Monarchy, 1867–1914*, p. 177.

9. Pulzer, *Anti-Semitism*, p. 294.

10. Herbert Rosenkranz, "The Anschluss and the Tragedy of Austrian Jewry, 1938–1945," p. 480.

11. Pulzer, *Anti-Semitism*, pp. 248, 328; Karl Stadler, *Austria*, pp. 138–39.

12. Andrew Whiteside, "Austria," pp. 310–11.

13. Ibid., pp. 312–13.

14. Karl Wache, "Land und Volk," p. 33; Hugo Hantsch, *Die Geschichte*

Österreichs, 2:445; Albert Fuchs, *Geistige Strömungen in Österreich, 1867–1918*, p. 182.

15. Quoted in Pulzer, *Anti-Semitism*, p. 153.

16. Francis Carsten, *The Rise of Fascism*, p. 34; Fuchs, *Geistige Strömungen*, p. 296, n. 10.

17. Andrew Whiteside, *The Socialism of Fools*, p. 304.

18. Ibid., p. 113.

19. Ibid., pp. 3, 308.

20. Ibid., pp. 6, 264, 280.

21. F. L. Carsten, *Fascist Movements in Austria*, p. 19; Whiteside, *Socialism of Fools*, pp. 43, 311; Pulzer, *Anti-Semitism*, pp. 279, 281.

22. Although Schönerer's followers had long been known as pan-Germans (Alldeutschen) it was not until 1901 that they officially took that name. See Fuchs, *Geistige Strömungen*, p. 295.

23. Whiteside, *Socialism of Fools*, pp. 217, 316.

24. Molisch, *Geschichte der deutschnationalen Bewegung*, pp. 110–11, 153.

25. C. A. Macartney, *The Habsburg Monarchy, 1790–1918*, pp. 654–55.

26. Pulzer, *Anti-Semitism*, p. 207.

27. Carsten, *Fascist Movements*, p. 21; Molisch, *Geschichte der deutschnationalen Bewegung*, p. 157.

28. Whiteside, *Socialism of Fools*, p. 263.

29. Ibid., pp. 241, 282.

30. Werner Barth, "Germany and the Anschluss," pp. 126–27.

31. *Das Hakenkreuz*, March–April 1926, p. 35; Hans Völz, *Daten der Geschichte der NSDAP*, p. 6; Carsten, *Fascist Movements*, p. 33.

32. Rudolf Brandstötter, "Dr. Walter Riehl und die nationalsozialistische Bewegung in Österreich," pp. 49, 86, 109–10, 115; Andrew Whiteside, "The Deutsche Arbeiterpartei, 1904–1918," p. 5.

33. Andrew Whiteside, "Reply to the Above Comments," p. 16.

34. Both quotations are from M. W. Fodor, *Plot and Counterplot in Central Europe*, p. 163.

35. *Das Hakenkreuz*, Mar.–Apr. 1926, p. 36; Brandstötter, "Riehl," p. 54.

36. Juan Linz, "Some Notes Toward a Comparative Study of Fascism in Sociological Historical Perspective," p. 30.

37. *Austrian National Socialism before 1918*, p. 115.

38. Brandstötter, "Riehl," pp. 12–17.

39. Whiteside, "Deutsche Arbeiterpartei," p. 9.

40. Brandstötter, "Riehl," pp. 119–20, 133, 137–38.

41. Alois Ciller, *Deutscher Sozialismus in den Sudetenländer und der Ostmark*, pp. 136–37, 139.

42. Max Kele, "The Evolution of Austrian National Socialism from an Indigenous Party to an Appendage of Hitler's Movement," p. 3.

43. "Deutsche Arbeiterpartei," p. 3.

44. Kele, "Evolution," p. 3.

45. Whiteside, *Austrian National Socialism*, p. 121.

46. Quoted in Georg Franz-Willing, *Die Hitlerbewegung*, 1:95. Emphasis by Franz-Willing.

47. For similarities between Hitler and Riehl see Linzer *Vkst*, 20 Aug. 1923, p. 1; Alexander Schilling, *Dr. Walter Riehl und die Geschichte des National Sozialismus*, pp. 96, 352; Hitler, *Mein Kampf*, p. 79; Ciller, *Deutscher Sozialismus*, p. 139; Brandstötter, "Riehl," p. 19.

48. For the differences between Hitler and Riehl see Hitler, *Mein Kampf*, p. 102; Schilling, *Walter Riehl*, p. 85; Brandstötter, "Riehl," pp. 13, 215–16.
49. *DAP*, 21 Aug. 1920, p. 2.
50. Ibid., 17 Jan. 1920, p. 3; Konrad Heiden, *Geschichte des Nationalsozialismus*, p. 33.
51. Werner Maser, *Die Frühgeschichte der NSDAP*, p. 243.
52. 4 June 1921, p. 1.
53. Heiden, *Geschichte des Nationalsozialismus*, p. 34.
54. 16 Oct. 1920, p. 1.
55. *DAP*, 25 Aug. 1923, p. 1.
56. Müller to the Organisationsleitung der NSDAP in Munich, 21 Apr. 1927, Slg. Sch. 305 2:3–4.
57. Ludwig Jedlicka, "Die Anfänge des Rechtsradikalismus in Österreich (1919–1925)," p. 98.
58. Gerhard Botz, "Aspects of the Social Structure of Austrian National Socialism (1918–1939)," pp. 2–3.
59. *DAP*, 16 Oct. 1920, p. 1.
60. Ibid., 1 Jan. 1920, p. 1; Müller to the RL, 27 Apr. 1927, Slg. Sch., 305 2:1–3.
61. Evan Bukey, "The Nazi Party in Linz, Austria, 1919–1939," p. 2.
62. Botz, "Social Structure of Austrian National Socialism," p. 5.
63. Kele, "Evolution," p. 5.
64. Brandstötter, "Riehl," pp. 159, 162.
65. Franz Pisecky, *Tirol-Vorarlberg*, p. 8.
66. Schilling, *Walter Riehl*, pp. 239, 308, 331, 336; Max Kele, *Nazis and Workers*, p. 34.

Chapter III

1. *NSM*, Apr.–June 1928, p. 25.
2. *DAP*, 7 Jan. 1933, p. 3.
3. Ibid., 11 Aug. 1923, p. 1.
4. Report by Walter Riehl on the November 1930 election, Slg. Sch., 305 2:3.
5. Ibid.
6. The Ordnertruppen had been founded in 1922. At the Salzburg meeting in 1923 its name was changed to the Vaterländische Schutzbund (and in 1926 to the Sturmabteilung or SA). See the *DAP* for 18 Aug. 1923, p. 1.
7. Alexander Schilling, *Dr. Walter Riehl und die Geschichte des Nationalsozialismus*, pp. 342–45.
8. Linzer *Vkst*, 22 Aug. 1923, pp. 1–2; F. L. Carsten, *Fascist Movements in Austria*, p. 81.
9. *DAP*, 25 Aug. 1923, p. 2. Although Walter Riehl would never again dominate the Austrian Nazi party, he remained a figure of considerable importance down to at least 1933. This status did not, however, prevent his erstwhile subordinates from expelling him from the party in 1924, allegedly because of "antiparty activities," but more likely because of a letter he wrote to Hitler asking him to restore order in the party. He and two hundred of his Viennese followers then formed their own "Dr. Riehl Bund" in June 1924 (later called the Deutschsozialer Verein). The next year this tiny group concluded Riehl's long-desired coalition with the GVP. Riehl was also active for a time in the paramilitary "Front Fighters' Association" (Frontkämpfervereinigung) before rejoining the Austrian Nazi party in 1930. See *DAP*, 12 July 1924, p. 1; *Die Stunde*, 25

Apr. 1924, TA, NS-Innere Konflikte; Rudolf Brandstötter, "Dr. Walter Riehl und die nationalsozialistische Bewegung in Österreich," pp. 218, 222.

10. Riehl to Anton Funk with a copy sent to Hitler, 24 Aug. 1923, NA, T–84, R. 5/3971–74.

11. Open letter to Rudolf Jung, n.d., ibid./3970–80.

12. *DAP*, 17 Nov. 1923, p. 3.

13. Ibid., 21 Aug. 1926, p. 1; circular letter of the Ortsgruppe Knittelfeld (Styria), written by Hans Blumauer, Simon Pleschka, and Peter Zelling, 29 Oct. 1926, Slg. Sch., 305 folder 2; Willi Frischauer, *The Rise and Fall of Hermann Goering*, p. 43. Hitler himself considered fleeing to Austria, but was arrested before he could do so. See John Toland, *Adolf Hitler*, p. 237.

14. *DAP*, 21 Aug. 1926, p. 1; Leo Haubenberger, ed., *Nationalsozialistische Jahrbuch*, p. 101.

15. *DAP*, 6 June 1924, p. 2.

16. Ibid., 19 July 1924, p. 1.

17. The Austrian authorities argued that Hitler had given up his citizenship rights when he fought in the German army in World War I. See Geoffrey Pridham, *Hitler's Rise to Power*, p. 34.

18. Brandstötter, "Riehl," p. 227.

19. Jeremy Noakes, *The Nazi Party in Lower Saxony, 1921–1933*, p. 56.

20. P. 516.

21. *Mein Kampf*, p. 514.

22. Quoted in Karl Bracher, *The German Dictatorship*, p. 137.

23. Ibid., p. 135.

24. P. 344.

25. See Andrew Whiteside, *Austrian National Socialism before 1918; DAP*, 22 Feb. 1919, p. 1.

26. *DAP*, 22 Feb. 1919, p. 1; 29 Dec. 1919, p. 2.

27. Gerhard Botz, "Faschismus und Lohnabhängige in der Ersten Republik," p. 114.

28. Gerhard Botz, "Aspects of the Social Structure of Austrian National Socialism (1918–1939)," pp. 5, 6, 8, 10.

29. Raimund Haintz, "Die NSDAP," p. 252.

30. *DAP*, 7 Jan. 1933, p. 4.

31. Schilling, *Walter Riehl*, pp. 308, 326, 331, 363. Johann Auer, "Antisemitische Strömungen in Wien, 1921–1923," pp. 25–27.

32. Max Kele, "The Evolution of Austrian National Socialism from an Indigenous Party to an Appendage of Hitler's Movement," p. 7.

33. Josef Müller to the RL, 21 Apr. 1927, Slg. Sch., 305 2:2.

34. *DAP*, 21 Aug. 1926, p. 1.

35. Müller to the RL, 21 Apr. 1927, Slg. Sch., 305 2:2. Hitler spoke at one of these rallies. See Johann Auerl, "Zwei Aufenthalte Hitlers in Wien," p. 207.

36. Haintz, "NSDAP," p. 251; Carsten, *Fascist Movements*, p. 144.

37. Haintz, "NSDAP," p. 253.

38. *DAP*, 13 Feb. 1926, p. 3.

39. Brandstötter, "Riehl," p. 228.

40. Ludwig Jedlicka, "Die Anfänge des Rechtsradikalismus in Österreich (1918–1925)," p. 108.

41. Alois Adler, *Die historischen Fakten des Nationalsozialismus in Österreich*, p. 24; Gordon Shepherd, *The Austrian Odyssey*, p. 120; Personalfrageboden, BDC, PA, Hermann Reschny folder.

42. *DAP*, 7 Jan. 1933, p. 4.

43. Telegram from Neurath to the state secretary, 20 Nov. 1927, NA, T-120, R. 2832/E450743. Neurath's account seems plausible because Mussolini gave money to the Austrian Heimwehr after 1928 to support its Putsch plans. The Heimwehr, in return, had to promise to treat the South Tyrol as an "internal question" when it came to power. See Lajos Kerekes, "Akten zu den geheimen Verbindungen zwischen der Bethlen-Regierung und der österreichischen Heimwehrbewegung," pp. 301, 317.

44. *Der Nationalsozialist*, 10 Jan. 1923, p. 1.

45. P. 629.

46. Haintz, "NSDAP," p. 260.

47. *DAP*, 21 Aug. 1926, p. 1.

48. Brandstötter, "Riehl," p. 236. Hitler's rough treatment of Schulz and his references to power and subordination anticipated by four years a similar showdown with Otto Strasser who, like Schulz, was a Nazi "leftist." See Joachim Fest, *Hitler*, pp. 278–81, and Max Kele, *Nazis and Workers*, pp. 156–60.

49. *DAP*, 21 Aug. 1926, pp. 1–2; 28 Aug. 1926, p. 1.

50. Franz Sumetinger to Hitler, 22 Feb. 1931, BDC, PK, Alfred Proksch folder, p. 6.

51. Joseph Nyomarkay, "Factionalism in the National Socialist German Workers' Party, 1925–26," p. 34.

52. *DAP*, 4 Sept. 1926, p. 1; circular letter of the Ortsgruppe Knittelfeld, written by Blumauer, Pleschko, and Zellnig, 29 Oct. 1926, Slg. Sch., 305 2:4.

53. Haintz, "NSDAP," p. 262; *DAP*, 30 Apr. 1927, p. 2; Hans Völz, *Daten der Geschichte der NSDAP*, pp. 107–108.

54. Carsten, *Fascist Movements*, p. 153. Membership was highest in Lower Austria (1,214) led by Josef Leopold, followed by Styria (958), Vienna (900), Upper Austria (687), Carinthia (475), Salzburg (120), and the Tyrol (112). See Norbert Schausberger, *Der Griff nach Österreich*, p. 225.

55. Völz, *Daten*, p. 107. In 1932 Salzburg became a separate Gau again (ibid.).

56. Circular letter of Schmidt, 26 Oct. 1926, Slg. Sch., 305 2:6.

57. *Tgb*, 14 Oct. 1926, p. 2.

58. Excerpt from the *A-Z*, 23 June 1928, TA, folder NS-Innere Konflikte.

59. *DAP*, 9 July 1927, pp. 1–2.

60. P. 1.

61. The Lower Austrian Gauleitung to the LL in Linz, 18 Jan. 1930; Frauenfeld to the RL, 27 Jan. 1930; the Vorarlberg Gauleitung to the RL, 10 Jan. 1930, Slg. Sch., 305 folder 2.

62. Proksch to the USCHLA of the NSDAP in Munich, 10 Mar. 1931, BDC, PK, Proksch folder, p. 18.

63. *DAP*, 11 Mar. 1930, p. 2.

64. Schilling, *Walter Riehl*, p. 88.

65. *Tgb*, 10 Nov. 1930, p. 1.

66. 10 Jan., 1931, p. 1.

67. *DAP*, 26 June 1928, p. 1; 16 March 1929, p. 1; 21 June 1930, p. 1; 27 June 1930, p. 1.

68. Ibid., 13 Sept. 1930, p. 1.

69. 7 July 1933, p. 1.

70. 25 May 1934, p. 2.

71. Lebenslauf, BDC, PK, Walter Gattermayer folder, p. 4.

Chapter IV

1. Hereafter, unless otherwise noted, terms like "the party," "NSDAP," or "Nazis" will refer only to the Hitler Bewegung (HB) of the Austrian Nazi party.

2. "Notes of the Hungarian government agent concerning his conversation with the Heimwehr leader Pabst," 25 Jan. 1931, in Lajos Kerekes, "Akten zu den geheimen Verbindungen zwischen der Bethlen-Regierung und der österreichischen Heim-wehrbewegung," p. 338.

3. NSDAP circular letter, 31 May 1927, Slg. Sch., 305 2:2; letter from the LL Österreich to the RL, 20 Dec. 1926, NA, T-580, R. 63.

4. Edward Peterson, *The Limits of Hitler's Power*, pp. 4, 15, 431, 433; Dietrich Orlow, *The History of the Nazi Party, 1919–1933*, p. 151; NSDAP circular letter, 31 May 1927, Slg. Sch., 305 2:2. On Hitler's laziness and indecisiveness see also Albert Speer, *Inside the Third Reich*, pp. 185–86.

5. Alan Cassels, "Janus," p. 80. For similar views see Andrew Whiteside, "Austria," p. 333, and Jürgen Gehl, *Austria, Germany, and the Anschluss, 1931–38*, p. 54.

6. Unidentified writer in Innsbruck to the RL, 27 Sept. 1930, Slg. Sch. 305 folder 1.

7. Proksch to the USCHLA of the NSDAP in Munich, 10 Mar. 1931, BDC, PK, Proksch folder, p. 3.

8. Proksch to the RL, 22 Mar. 1930, Slg. Sch., 305 folder 1.

9. Proksch to the RL, 31 Jan. 1929, ibid.; anonymous article, "Hitler oder Schulzpartei," mid-1932?, Slg. Sch., 302 folder 1; Krebs to Strasser, 16 Apr. 1929, Slg. Sch., 305 folder 1.

10. Proksch to the RL, 22 Mar. 1930, Slg. Sch., 305 folder 1.

11. Letter to Strasser, 16 Apr. 1929, ibid.

12. "Exposé" by Leo Haubenberger, 30 Mar. 1930, Slg. Sch., 305 folder 2.

13. Memorandum on the development of the party crisis in Austria by HJ leader Pischtiak sent to Strasser, n.d., NA, T-580, R. 63.

14. Proksch to the USCHLA of the NSDAP in Munich, 10 Mar. 1931, BDC, PK, Proksch folder, pp. 2–3; excerpt from the Leipziger *Tagespost*, 11 Mar. 1930, TA, Proksch folder.

15. "Hitler oder Schulzpartei," Slg. Sch., 302 1:1–4.

16. Franz Inwihling to Strasser, 20 Aug. 1930, ibid., folder 1.

17. Interrogation of August Eigruber, 3 Nov. 1945, NA, NI, pp. 7–8.

18. Ibid., p. 8.

19. Ibid., p. 10.

20. Quoted in Jeremy Noakes, *The Nazi Party in Lower Saxony, 1921–1933*, p. 161.

21. Dietrich Orlow, *The History of the Nazi Party, 1933–1945*, p. 8; Peterson, *Hitler's Power*, p. 8.

22. Noakes, *Nazi Party in Lower Saxony*, p. 161.

23. "Exposé" by Leo Haubenberger, 30 Mar. 1930, Slg. Sch., 305 2:2–3.

24. Franz Morari to Strasser, 10 Mar. 1930, Slg. Sch., folder 1.

25. Excerpt from the Munziger *Archiv*, 20 Sept. 1934, TA, Frauenfeld folder; Juan Linz, "Some Notes Toward a Comparative Study of Top Fascist Leaders," p. 10.

26. Autobiography of A. E. Frauenfeld, AVA, NS Parteistellen K. 14; Frauenfeld's curriculum vitae (sent to Gregor Strasser in Munich on 20 Feb. 1930), NA, T-580, R. 63.

27. Party order of Hitler, 7 Apr. 1927, Slg. Sch., 305 folder 1.

28. Interrogation of Frauenfeld, 26 May 1945, essay by Frauenfeld, "Rise of Nazism in Vienna," NA, NI, p. 1; Friedrich Scheu, *Der Weg ins Ungewisse*, p. 100.

29. *Der Kampfruf*, 17 Sept. 1932, p. 8.

30. Interview in Vienna. Eduard Frauenfeld became the Gaupropagandaleiter of Vienna and during World War II was known as the "Goebbels of Vienna."

31. Rudolf Neck, "Simmering—16. Oktober 1932," p. 99.

32. G. E. R. Gedye, *Fallen Bastions*, pp. 69–70; A. E. Frauenfeld, "Der Aufstieg des Gaues Wien der N.S.D.A.P." pp. 281–82.

33. Frauenfeld to Strasser, 22 Mar. 1930, Slg. Sch., 305 folder 2; excerpt from the Frankfurter *Zeitung*, 9 Dec. 1932; Slg. Sch., 302 folder 1.

34. Franz Sumetinger to Hitler, 24 Feb. 1931, BDC, PK, Proksch folder, p. 1.

35. NSDAP circular letter, 31 May 1927, Slg. Sch., 305 folder 2.

36. Circular letter to party members from Ernst Sopper, 22 Mar. 1931, ibid.; Strasser to Sopper, 24 Mar. 1931, ibid.

37. Proksch to the Landes USCHLA in Linz, 15 Apr. 1931, AVA, K. 14. For an excellent account of Nazi party justice see Donald McKale, *The Nazi Party Courts*, especially pp. 2, 3, 5, 23.

38. Frauenfeld to Strasser, 27 Jan. 1932, Slg. Sch., 305 folder 2; anonymous article, "Hitler oder Schulzpartei," Slg. Sch., 302 1:5.

39. Anonymous, "Hitler oder Schulzpartei," Slg. Sch., 302 1:3, 8, 10.

40. Unsigned report, 30 July 1931, PAAA, 3/K468971–72; Peter Katzenstein, *Disjoined Partners*, p. 136. For example, the Landesinspekteur between 1931 and 1934, Theo Habicht, was a German as was the Gauleiter of Carinthia, Hans vom Kothen, as well as a number of SA and SS leaders. See Gerhard Jagschitz, "Zur Struktur der NSDAP vor dem Juliputsch," p. 4; Richard Moschner, *Kärnten*, p. 21.

41. Orlow, *Nazi Party, 1919–1933*, p. 118.

42. "The Union of Austrian Industrialists" (Hauptverband der Industriellen Österreichs) explicitly rejected aid to the Nazis in 1923. See *DAP*, 16 June 1923, p. 3.

43. Derda Robert and Ernst Graber to Friedrich Jankovic, 14 Sept. 1926, NA, T-580, R. 63.

44. *Beiträge zur Vorgeschichte und Geschichte der Julirevolte*, p. 4; Rudolf Brandstötter, "Dr. Walter Riehl und die nationalsozialistische Bewegung in Österreich," p. 270.

45. Raimund Haintz, "Die NSDAP," p. 259.

46. Heinrich Schmidt to Strasser, 8 Sept. 1928, Slg. Sch., 305 folder 2.

47. Haintz, "NSDAP," p. 265.

48. Gauparteitag in Linz, 16 Mar. 1930, Slg. Sch. 305 2:4.

49. Landesleitung Österreichs der NSDAP (Hitlerbewegung), ed., *Das Dienstbuch der NSDAP* p. 50. See also, Z. A. B. Zeman, *Nazi Propaganda*, p. 18. For a description of the leading newspaper of the entire Nazi party, which was also read by Austrian Nazis, see Roland Layton, Jr., "The *Völkischer Beobachter, 1920–1933*," especially pp. 370–72.

50. For example, Alfred Frauenfeld was the editor of *Der Kampfruf*, Alfred Proksch edited *Die Volksstimme*, and Walter Oberhaidacher published *Der Kampf*; see also Geoffrey Pridham, *Hitler's Rise to Power*, p. 253.

51. Karl Jung, "Die Völkische Presse in Österreich," pp. 345–46.

52. R. W. Rothschild, *Austria's Economic Development between the Two Wars*, p. 52.

53. Julius Braunthal, *The Tragedy of Austria*, pp. 113–14.

54. Bernt Hagtvet, "The Theory of Mass Society and the Dissolution of Parliamentary Democracy," p. 28.

55. Guido Zernatto, *Die Wahrheit über Österreich*, p. 66; memorandum by Eduard Baar-Baarenfels, "Information about the present condition of the National Socialist

Movement in Austria," 4 Apr. 1936, *Schmidt-Prozess*, p. 468; Alfred Persche, "Die Aktion Hudal," DÖW, #5116/1, 2:234; Alfred Persche, "Hauptmann Leopold," DÖW, #1460, p. 246.

56. Report on the November elections [of 1930] by Walter Riehl, Slg. Sch., 305 folder 1.

57. *Steirische Gaunachrichten der NSDAP*, 10 Jan. 1931, p. 2; anonymous letter to the Finanz und Parteiverwaltung z. Hd. Reichsleiter Meiler, 14 Dec. 1938, Slg. Sch., 303 folder 1.

58. Ernst Starhemberg, *Memoiren*, p. 85; Franz Winkler, *Die Diktatur in Österreich*, p. 31; Franz Langoth, *Kampf um Österreich*, p. 83.

59. Winkler, *Diktatur in Österreich*, pp. 31–32.

60. Starhemberg, *Memoiren*, pp. 88, 89, 94.

61. Exposé by Leo Haubenberger sent to the RL, 3 Mar. 1930, Slg. Sch., 305 1:4.

62. *Tgb*, 10 Nov. 1930, p. 1. The Nazis did by far the best in the Alpine provinces of Upper Austria, Salzburg, Tyrol, and Vorarlberg where their total vote leaped from 1,196 to 19,139. They also enjoyed a substantial increase in Lower Austria from 8,692 to 34,335. Elsewhere their vote followed or trailed the national average. See the report on the domestic political situation by Lerchenfeld, 31 Dec. 1930, NA, T-120, R. 4494/K231317. The Nazi vote in 1930 may have been hurt slightly by the constitutional reform of 1929, which raised the voting age from twenty to twenty-one.

63. *Vkst*, 15 Nov. 1930, p. 1.

64. Report on the November elections [of 1930] by Walter Riehl, Slg. Sch., 305 1:1.

65. The German Consul in Klagenfurt (Hans) to the AA, 28 Oct. 1930, NA, T-120, R. 2832/E450782.

66. Report on the domestic political situation by Lerchenfeld, 31 Dec. 1930, NA, T-120, R. 4494/K231320–29.

Chapter V

1. *Between Hitler and Mussolini*, p. 69. Habicht's association with the Communist party after World War I was never denied by the Nazis. See Gerhard Jagschitz, *Der Putsch*, p. 24.

2. *Memoiren*, p. 223.

3. Memorandum by Franz von Papen, 3 May 1945, *Schmidt-Prozess*, p. 348; two unidentified documents written in Oct. 1933, NA, T-120, R. 2836/E45373–74.

4. Excerpt from *Der Morgen*, 29 Aug. 1932, TA, NS–Führung.

5. Dietrich Orlow, *The History of the Nazi Party, 1919–1933*, p. 294; Gerhard Jagschitz, "Bundeskanzler Dollfuss und der Juli 1934," p. 152.

6. Habicht to Strasser, 2 Apr. 1932, Slg. Sch., 305 folder 1; Landesleitung Österreichs der NSDAP (Hitlerbewegung), *Das Dienstbuch der NSDAP*, preface.

7. *Dienstbuch*, preface, pp. 12, 14, 19, 21–22.

8. "Notes of the Hungarian government agent concerning his conversations with the Heimwehr leader Pabst," 25 Jan. 1931, in Lajos Kerekes, "Akten zu den geheimen Verbindungen zwischen der Bethlen-Regierung und der österreichischen Heimwehrbewegung," p. 338.

9. Preface. See also Habicht to Strasser, 2 Apr. 1932, Slg. Sch., 305 folder 1.

10. *Vkst*, 22 Apr. 1931, p. 1, 22 Aug. 1931, p. 7.

11. *Der Kampf*, 31 Dec. 1931, p. 7.

12. F. L. Carsten, *Fascist Movements in Austria*, p. 199.

13. Juan Linz, "Some Notes Toward a Comparative Study of Fascism in Sociological Historical Perspective," pp. 29–30. For more detailed accounts of the Austrian Heimwehr see C. Earl Edmondson, *The Heimwehr and Austrian Politics, 1918–1936*; Ludwig Jedlicka, "The Austrian Heimwehr"; Reinhart Kondert, "The Rise and Early History of the Austrian 'Heimwehr' Movement"; Sepp Kogelnik, ed., *Österreichisches Heimatschutz-Jahrbuch 1933*; Herbert Müller, "Heimatschutzbewegung, Heimatwehr, Heimwehr, Heimatbund, Heimatblock-Partei."

14. Charles Gulick, *Austria from Habsburg to Hitler*, 1:7–8; *New York Times*, 2 Dec. 1928, p. 4; C. A. Macartney, "The Armed Formations in Austria," p. 627; essay on the Austrian Heimwehr by G. R. Hoffmann, 23 Aug. 1929, NA, T-120, R. 2833/E451048. Veterans of the World War played a crucial role in the development of fascist movements all over Europe.

15. Ludger Rape, "Die österreichische Heimwehr und ihre Beziehungen zur bayerischen Rechten zwischen 1920 und 1923," pp. 533, 535.

16. For a complete history of the Frontkämpfervereinigung see Ingeborg Messerer, "Die Frontkämpfervereinigung Deutsch-Österreichs," especially pp. 21, 44, 60, and 118.

17. See above, pp. 13–14.

18. Memorandum on the development of the party crisis in Austria (by HJ leader Pischtiak), n.d., NA, T-580, R. 63, p. 3.

19. Interview with Karl Maria Stepan; interview with Walter Pfrimer.

20. C. Earl Edmondson, "Early Heimwehr Aims and Activities," p. 129.

21. Letter, illegible signature, from Klagenfurt to the AA, 18 June 1929, NA, T-120, R. 4494/K230827.

22. Bruce Pauley, *Hahnenschwanz und Hakenkreuz*, pp. 73–74.

23. Proksch to the USCHLA of the NSDAP in Munich, 10 Mar. 1931, BDC, PA, Proksch folder.

24. Pauley, *Hahnenschwanz und Hakenkreuz*, pp. 117–20, 127; Egon Berger-Waldenegg, "Ungedruckte Erinnerungen des ehemaligen österreichischen Aussenministers und Gesandten in Rom," pp. 308, 317; James Diehl, *Paramilitary Politics in Weimar Germany*, p. 283.

25. Konstantin Kammerhofer to Siegfried Uiberreither, 30 July 1940, Landesgericht für Strafsachen, Kammerhofer-Prozess, pp. 227, 253.

26. Gerhard Botz, "Faschismus und Lohnabhängige in der Ersten Republic," p. 106.

27. *Der Kampf*, 28 Nov. 1931, p. 1.

28. Ibid., 7 Nov. 1931, p. 1.

29. *Mein Kampf*, p. 516.

30. *Steirische Gaunachrichten der NSDAP*, 16 Nov. 1931, pp. 3–4, 19 Nov. 1931, p. 1.

31. *Vkst*, 31 Oct. 1931, p. 2, 20 Aug. 1932, p. 4.

32. *Steirische Gaunachrichten*, 2 Jan. 1932, p. 2; *Der Panther*, 16 Jan. 1932, p. 15.

33. This *völkisch* rivalry was not unique. The Stahlhelm, which had earlier joined the German Nazis in the "Harzburg Front," had also dropped out of their alliance. "At the end of 1932 it was often impossible to determine who was hated more by Röhm's storm troopers and Goebbels's propagandists, the 'Marxists' or the Stahlhelmer." See Volker Berghahn, *Der Stahlhelm*, p. 243.

34. *OH-Z*, 11 Mar. 1933, p. 2, 17 June 1933, p. 1.

35. *Der Panther*, 26 Mar. 1932, p. 7; *Steirische Gaunachrichten*, 2 Feb. 1932, p. 5.

36. *OH-Z*, 11 Mar. 1933, p. 2.

37. *Vkst*, 14 May 1933, p. 5; Habicht's general plan for the parliamentary campaign, part 1, "The Situation," Slg. Sch., 305 1:2.

38. *Vkst*, 14 May, 1933, p. 5.

39. Elections to the Parliament in Austria. Results for the various parties, Linz, 4 May 1932, HI, NS–HA, R. 33, folder 635.

40. Gerhard Botz, "Aspects of the Social Structure of Austrian National Socialism (1918–1939)," p. 14.

41. Elections to the Parliament in Austria. Results for the various parties, Linz, 4 May 1932, HI, NS-HA, R. 33 folder 635.

42. Koppel Pinson and Klaus Epstein, *Modern Germany*, pp. 603 and 604.

43. Walter Simon, "The Political Parties of Austria," p. 294.

44. Ibid.; *Dienstbuch*, preface.

45. Pinson and Epstein, *Modern Germany*, p. 603.

46. Simon, "Political Parties," p. 294; Botz, "Social Structure of Austrian National Socialism," p. 14.

47. Rieth to the AA, 12 Oct. 1932, NA, T-120, R. 2832/E450793.

48. Report by Lerchenfeld on the domestic political situation, 31 Dec. 1930, NA, T-120, R. 4494/K231328. For comparisons with Germany see Diehl, *Paramilitary Politics*, p. 283.

49. Zeev Sternhell, "Fascist Ideology," p. 320.

50. Anton Rintelen, *Erinnerungen an Österreichs Weg*, pp. 73–74. My emphasis.

51. Anonymous, membership list drawn up in 1938, Slg. Sch., 303 folder 1.

52. *Der Panther*, 20 May 1933, p. 2.

53. Wladimir von Hartlieb, *Parole: Das Reich!*, pp. 28–29.

54. *Der Panther*, 14 Jan. 1933, p. 1, 20 May 1933, p. 2. Sometime toward the end of 1933 or the beginning of 1934 Arthur Seyss-Inquart, at that time still a member of the Heimatschutz, advised Kammerhofer to copy Pfrimer's example and join the NSDAP. See Wolfgang Rosar, *Deutsche Gemeinschaft*, p. 60.

55. Kammerhofer to Rodenbücher, 15 Jan. 1935, Kammerhofer-Prozess, p. 259; *Landbund-Stimmen*, 27 Apr. 1933, p. 2.

56. *Vkst*, 5 May 1933, p. 5. For further information on the GVP see Isabella Ackerl, "Die Grossdeutsche Volkspartei," especially pp. 69–70, 97, 105, 312, 314, and Karl Jung, "Die Grossdeutsche Volkspartei," especially pp. 176–77, 179, 414–15.

57. Isabella Ackerl, "Das Kampfbündnis der Nationalsozialistischen Deutschen Arbeiterpartei mit der Grossdeutschen Volkspartei vom 15. Mai 1933," pp. 5 and 6.

58. Ibid., pp. 7–8, 23.

59. *Vkst*, 5 May 1933, p. 5.

60. "Minister Rieth to State Secretary Bülow," 22 Feb. 1933, *DGFP*, C 1:52–53; Franz Langoth, *Kampf um Österreich*, p. 102.

61. Ackerl, "Kampfbündnis," pp. 18, 20, 24.

62. Report concerning the transfer of the Landbund and the Grünen Front to the NSDAP, etc., Gendarmerieabteilungskommando, Wels, 26 Aug. 1934, DÖW, #6155.

63. Political report by Prince Erbach, German Legation, Vienna, to the foreign minister, 29 Aug. 1934, NA, T-120, R. 3395/E605512. For additional information on the Landbund see Angela Feldman, "Landbund für Österreich," and Ursula Benedikt, "Vinzenz Schumy, 1878–1962."

Chapter VI

1. "Memorandum by an Official of Department II," 20 May 1933, *DGFP*, C 1:474–75.
2. Weinberg, *The Foreign Policy of Hitler's Germany*, pp. 87, 106; Petersen, *Hitler-Mussolini*, p. 135; John Heineman, *Hitler's First Foreign Minister*, p. 104.
3. An exception was Vorarlberg, the province bordering on democratic Switzerland, where the Nazis gained only 10.5 percent of the vote in November 1932. The 8,033 votes did represent more than a tenfold increase since November 1930, however. See Hans Völz, *Daten der Geschichte der NSDAP*, p. 110.
4. Gerhard Jagschitz, *Der Putsch*, p. 28; Ernst Hoor, *Österreich 1918–1938*, p. 59; Hans Huebmer, *Österreich 1933–1938*, p. 30.
5. Report, "Impressions of the Revolution in Austria from 12–15 February and Its Consequences," NA, 77, R. 900/5652691.
6. Pp. 480–81.
7. *Der Kampf*, 14 Mar. 1931, p. 7.
8. Landesleitung Österreichs der NSDAP (Hitlerbewegung), *Das Dienstbuch der NSDAP (Hitlerbewegung)*, p. 198.
9. Ibid., pp. 44–45.
10. Ibid., p. 46.
11. Ibid., p. 49; Geoffrey Pridham, *Hitler's Rise to Power*, p. 101.
12. *Steirische Gaunachrichten der NSDAP*, 24 Feb. 1933, p. 2; *Dienstbuch*, pp. 190–91.
13. *Steirische Gaunachrichten*, 10 Feb. 1931, p. 1; *Dienstbuch*, p. 181.
14. *Steirische Gaunachrichten*, 10 Feb. 1931, p. 1; *Dienstbuch*, p. 182.
15. See, for example, *Arbeiterwille*, 27 Sept. 1931, p. 11, and *Tgb*, 6 Oct. 1931, p. 5.
16. *Tagespost*, 5 May 1932 (P.M.), p. 4.
17. Habicht's Election Plan, Slg. Sch., 305 folder 1.
18. *Vkst*, 30 Apr. 1933, p. 5. Compared to the last local election in 1931, the Nazis picked up 8,000 new votes; 4,000 came from the GVP, another 2,000 from the SDP, and 500 from the CSP. The Nazis undoubtedly also benefited from the abstention of the HW, which had gained nearly 3,500 votes in 1930 (ibid.).
19. *Der Vormarsch*, 2 June 1933, p. 2.
20. Wladimir von Hartlieb, *Parole: Das Reich!*, p. 37.
21. Habicht's General Election Plan, part VII, Communal Politics, Slg. Sch., 305 folder 1.
22. Ibid., part I, The Situation.
23. Juan Linz, "Some Notes Toward a Comparative Study of Top Fascist Leaders," p. 1.
24. NA, T-175, R. 451/2966867–916.
25. Gerhard Jagschitz, "Die Jugend des Bundeskanzlers Dr. Engelbert Dollfuss," p. 114; Linz, "Notes," p. 81.
26. Ernst Starhemberg, *Memoiren*, p. 308; Alfred Persche, "Die Aktion Hudal," DÖW, # 5116/1, 2:234; Arnold J. Toynbee, ed., *Survey of International Affairs*, 1933, pp. 133–34; Impressions of Austria by Braun von Sturm, Sept. 1936, NA, T-120, R. 5415/K287562.
27. Otto Reich von Rohrwig, *Der Freiheitskampf der Ostmark-Deutschen von St. Germain bis Adolf Hitler*, p. 93. The former Gauleiter of Vienna Leopold Tavs said that 50 percent of the Nazis were under the age of thirty. Many of the older Nazis were no doubt far less active than the younger ones, however.

28. "Training for Citizenship, 'Authoritarian' Austrian Style," p. 145; letter from Rath to the author.

29. Peter Merkl, *Political Violence under the Swastika*, pp. 258, 712.

30. Richard Moschner, *Kärnten*, pp. 35–36; *Dienstbuch*, p. 117.

31. Memorandum by Eduard Baar-Baarenfels, "Information over the Present Condition of the National Socialist Movement in Austria," 4 Apr. 1936, *Schmidt-Prozess*, p. 468. Hereafter referred to as Baar-Baarenfels's memorandum. Persche, "Aktion Hudal," 2:234.

32. John Haag, "Blood on the Ringstrasse," p. 32.

33. Peter Pulzer, *The Rise of Political Anti-Semitism in Germany and Austria*, pp. 11–14.

34. Baar-Baarenfels's memorandum, p. 468.

35. See above, p. 18.

36. *Der Kampfruf*, 3 Feb. 1931, p. 1.

37. *Der Panther*, 17 June 1933, pp. 2–3; interview with Walter Strzygowski.

38. Rath, "Training for Citizenship," p. 145.

39. Interview with Eduard Frauenfeld.

40. Riehl to Proksch, 26 Apr. 1932, Slg. Sch., 305 2:1. See also Walter Simon, "The Political Parties of Austria," p. 325. The German Nazi party experienced a similar growth in its membership coming from the intelligentsia. See Michael Kater, "The Social Composition of the Nazi Party's Membership, 1925–1945," p. 5, or his larger study, "Quantifizierung und NS-Geschichte," pp. 453–84.

41. Riehl to Proksch, 26 Apr. 1932, Slg. Sch., 305 2:1; Franz Borkenau, *Austria and After*, p. 234.

42. Riehl to Proksch, 26 Apr. 1932, Slg. Sch., 305, folder 1; Gerhard Botz, "Faschismus und Lohnabhängige in der Ersten Republik," p. 115; Joseph Buttinger, *Am Beispiel Österreichs*, p. 493.

43. Lajos Kerekes, "Wirtschaftliche und soziale Lage Österreichs nach dem Zerfall der Doppelmonarchie," p. 93.

44. Gerhard Botz, *Wien vom "Anschluss" zum Krieg*, p. 218; Evan Bukey, "The Nazi Party in Linz, Austria, 1919–1939," p. 10.

45. Jagschitz, *Der Putsch*, pp. 37–38; Wolfgang Rosar, *Deutsche Gemeinschaft*, p. 345.

46. Simon, "Political Parties," pp. 182, 184, 321.

47. P. 134.

48. Raimund Haintz, "Die NSDAP," p. 272. This trend also occurred in Germany during the same period. See Bernt Hagtvet, "The Theory of Mass Society and the Dissolution of Parliamentary Democracy," p. 28, and Botz, "Faschismus und Lohnabhängige," p. 119.

49. Unpublished document assembled for the government's *Rot-Weiss-Rot Buch*, report from Carinthia, Gendarmeriepostenkommando Gnessau, 27 May 1946, DÖW, #8350.

50. Jagschitz, *Der Putsch*, p. 26; Everhard Holtmann, "Zwischen 'Blutschuld' und 'Befriedung,'" p. 14.

51. Imgard Bärnthaler, *Die Vaterländische Front*, p. 179; Simon, "Political Parties," p. 206.

52. Bärnthaler, *Die VF*, p. 179. See also Helene Grilliet, *Eine Französin Erlebt Grossdeutschland*, p. 19.

53. Simon "Political Parties," p. 318.

54. Diestel to Dr. Lammers, 16 Aug. 1934, NA, T-120, R. 3393/E605763.

55. Peter Merkl, "The Nazis of the Abel Collection," pp. 25–26.

56. *Schmidt-Prozess*, p. 467.
57. Persche, "Hauptmann Leopold," pp. 4–5; Botz, "Faschismus und Lohnabhän-gige," p. 115. Persche does not define his term *Arbeiter*. Presumably he is talking about railroad and postal workers and the like.
58. *Dienstbuch*, preface, and pp. 48, 129.
59. *Vkst*, 30 Apr. 1933, p. 5.
60. Simon, "Political Parties," p. 330; Gerhard Botz, *Gewalt in der Politik*, p. 196, n. 35.
61. Botz, *Wien vom "Anschluss" zum Krieg*, p. 218.
62. Austria, Political Situation (no name), 2 June 1934, NA, T-120, R. 900/5652945.
63. Interview with Eduard Frauenfeld and Leopold Tavs; interview with Herbert Steiner.
64. Report on the situation in Austria as of 5 Jan. 1936 (by an unidentified official of the Volksbund für das Deutschtum im Ausland), NA, T-120, R. 2837/E453296.
65. Erika Weinzierl-Fischer, "Österreichs Katholiken und der Nationalsozialismus," 18:429, 432, 434, 438.
66. Friedrich Heer, *Gottes erste Liebe*, pp. 363–65.
67. Sylvia Maderegger, *Die Juden im österreichischen Ständestaat 1934–1938*, p. 138.
68. Weinzierl-Fischer, "Österreichs Katholiken," 18:432.
69. Maderegger, *Juden im österreichischen Ständestaat*, pp. 135 and 203; Heer, *Gottes erste Liebe*, p. 364.
70. Weinzierl-Fischer, "Österreichs Katholiken," 20:501.
71. Report on the discussion held on 17 Nov. 1932 by Hans Eibl, NA, T-580, R. 63, pp. 1–2.
72. Eibl to the Fürstenbischof, n.d., ibid.
73. Weinzierl-Fischer, "Österreichs Katholiken," 20:506–507.
74. Essay on the HW by G. R. Hoffmann of the German legation in Vienna and sent to the AA, 23 Aug. 1929, NA, T-120, R. 2833/E451048–49.
75. *Fascist Movements in Austria*, p. 283.
76. For the best study of the Nazi attitude toward women see Jill Stephenson, *Women in Nazi Society*.
77. Heinz Cohrs, "Das Innere Gefüge der N.S.D.A.P. Österreichs," pp. 301–302.
78. Habicht's Election Plan, "The Task," Slg. Sch., 305 folder 1, p. 1.
79. Letter to Josefine Schwanke, 28 Apr. 1932, NA, T-120, R. 63.
80. Bukey, "Nazi Party in Linz," pp. 5–6.
81. Herbert Tingsten, *Political Behavior*, p. 71.
82. Botz, *Wien vom "Anschluss" zum Krieg*, pp. 218, 220.
83. Letter of John Haag to the author, 16 Nov. 1978. For comparisons with Nazi Germany see Stephenson, *Women in Nazi Society*, p. 193.

Chapter VII

1. *Steirische Gaunachrichten der NSDAP*, 30 May 1933, p. 1.
2. Hans Völz, *Daten der Geschichte der NSDAP*, p. 112.
3. *Beiträge zur Vorgeschichte und Geschichte der Julirevolte*, p. 5.
4. Gerhard Botz, *Gewalt in der Politik*, pp. 190–91, 196, 201–202.
5. Gerhard Jagschitz, "Zur Struktur der NSDAP vor dem Juliputsch 1934," p. 13;

Rieth to the AA, 18 June 1933, NA, T-120, R. 3394/E606622–23; "Minister Rieth to State Secretary Bülow," 12 June 1934, *DGFP*, C 2:900–901.

6. Mary Ball, *Post-War German-Austrian Relations*, p. 200; Clyde Kendrick, "Austria under the Chancellorship of Engelbert Dollfuss," pp. 99–100.

7. Oswald Dutch, *Thus Died Austria*, p. 53.

8. Note by Hüffer, 6 June 1934, NA, T–120, R. 2838/E453400; Political report by Hüffer, 21 June 1934, ibid./E453474.

9. "The Minister in Austria [Messersmith] to the Secretary of State," 12 June 1934, *FRUS,* 1934, pp. 26–27.

10. Gerhard Jagschitz, *Der Putsch*, p. 42.

11. Max Dachauer, *Das Ende Österreich*, p. 202.

12. Rudolf Brandstötter, "Dr. Walter Riehl und die nationalsozialistische Bewegung in Österreich," p. 270.

13. *Arbeiterwille*, 21 June 1933 (P.M.), p. 2; the German Consul in Klagenfurt (Nahm) to the AA, 21 Aug. 1933, NA, T-120, R. 4633/K283290.

14. Ostenburg report on the domestic political situation in Austria, 1 Oct. 1933, NA, T-120, R. 2836/E452562.

15. The German Consul in Klagenfurt (Nahm) to the AA, 2 June 1934, ibid., R. 3394/E606692; "report on my discussions with Reich German National Socialists imprisoned on 13 June 1933" (written by Broick), ibid./E606638.

16. Jagschitz, "Struktur der NSDAP," p. 8.

17. *Memoiren*, pp. 137–38.

18. Wladimir von Hartlieb, *Parole: Das Reich!*, p. 211.

19. Memorandum by Hüffer concerning the Austrian question, 5 Apr. 1934, NA, T-120, R. 2836/E452766. But many Nazis were treated leniently by judges who feared reprisals in the event of a Nazi takeover. See Kendrick, "Austria under Dollfuss," p. 271.

20. Styrian Provincial School Board, 14 May 1935, HI, NS-HA, R. 33, folder 642; the German Consul in Klagenfurt (Nahm) to the AA, 21 Aug. 1933, NA, T-120, R. 4633/K283287; Wolfgang Neugebauer, "Politische Justiz in Österreich, 1934–1945," p. 177.

21. Felix Kreissler, *Von der Revolution zur Annexion*, p. 210.

22. Interrogation of August Eigruber, 3 Nov. 1945, NA, NI, pp. 3, 5.

23. Gerhard Jagschitz, "Die Anhaltelager in Österreich (1933–1938)," p. 147.

24. Everhard Holtmann, "Zwischen 'Blutschuld' und 'Befriedung,'" p. 14. This view is disputed, however, by Arnold Toynbee, ed., in *Survey of International Affairs,* 1934, p. 484.

25. Jagschitz, "Anhaltelager," pp. 130, 141, 147.

26. *Fallen Bastions*, p. 156.

27. Jagschitz, "Anhaltelager," p. 139.

28. Interview in Vienna.

29. "Extracts from the Minutes of the Conference of Ministers," 26 May 1933, *DGFP*, C 1:488–90; Gustav Otruba, "Hitlers 'Tausend-Mark-Sperre' und Österreichs Fremdenverkehr 1933," p. 153.

30. Otruba, " 'Tausand-Mark-Sperre,' " p. 115.

31. *Statistisches Handbuch* 1933, pp. 42, 45.

32. The German Consul in Klagenfurt (Nahm) to the AA, 22 June 1933, NA, T-120, R. 4494/K231635.

33. "Memorandum by an Official of Department II [Hüffer]," 19 Apr. 1934, *DGFP*, C 2:757.

34. "Memorandum by an Official of the Economic Department (Ulrich)," 4 Apr. 1934, ibid., p. 789.

35. Friedrich Hertz, *The Economic Problems of the Danubian States*, p. 147. For a more complete comparison see Hertz's table cited above, p. 64. Significantly, 1936 was also the last year of the German economic blockade.

36. Norbert Schausberger, *Der Griff nach Österreich*, p. 473 and "Ökonomisch-politische Interdependenzen im Sommer 1936," p. 292; Peter Katzenstein, *Disjoined Partners*, p. 157.

37. See, for example, the illegal *ÖB* for Mar. 1937, p. 4, and 29 Aug. 1937, pp. 7–8.

38. Memorandum by Eduard Baar-Baarenfels, "Information on the present condition of the National Socialist Movement in Austria," 4 Apr. 1936, *Schmidt-Prozess*, pp. 469–71. Hereafter referred to as Baar-Baarenfels's memorandum.

39. [Abw.] Austria, Political Situation (no name given), 22 Apr. 1934, NA, T-77, R. 900/5652948.

40. See above, p. 112.

41. *Beiträge zur Julirevolte*, p. 27; AA, Answer to the note delivered by the Austrian envoy on the 17th of this month, 31 Jan. 1934, NA, T-120, R. 3394/E606495.

42. *Beiträge zur Julirevolte*, pp. 28–30.

43. Unpublished reports of the gendarmerie to the provincial gendarmerie command in Salzburg assembled for the *Rot-Weiss-Rot Buch*, 28 May 1946, DÖW, #8349.

44. Copy of an SA order sent by von Papen to the AA, 22 June 1935, NA, T-120, R. 2837/E453081.

45. Note (by Heeren), 31 July 1933, ibid., R. 2838/E453737–47.

46. Draft of a letter by the state secretary to the Reichsminister, 31 July 1933, ibid./E453749–52.

47. Memorandum by Neurath of his conversation with Hitler, 14 Aug. 1933, ibid./E453847.

48. Political report by the German ambassador to Italy, Hassel, 22 Feb. 1934, ibid./E453998.

49. Köpke to Rieth, 15 Mar. 1934, NA, T-120, R. 2832/E450915.

50. "Memorandum by the Director of Department II," 16 Mar. 1934, *DGFP*, C 2:616.

51. Baar-Baarenfels's memorandum, *Schmidt-Prozess*, p. 472.

52. Memorandum by Theo Habicht on his meeting of 14–15 Apr. in Zürich with Vice–Chancellor A. D. Winkler, NA, T-120, R. 2836/E452784.

53. Rieth to the AA, 9 Sept. 1933, NA, T-120, R. 5415/K287235.

54. Rieth to the AA, 12 Dec. 1933, ibid./K287243; Papen to the AA, 8 May 1935, ibid./K287372; Bade to the German Legation in Vienna, 24 June 1936, ibid./K287497.

55. Jagschitz, "Struktur der NSDAP," pp. 10–11; report of Graf Revertera concerning Nazi activities, 1933–38, n.d., DÖW, #2162, p. 9.

56. News Service, n.d., AVA, NS-Parteistellen, K. 12; Dachauer, *Das Ende Österreich*, pp. 217–18.

57. Dachauer, *Das Ende Österreich*, p. 218; Hans Schopper, *Presse im Kampf*, p. 299; *ÖB*, 28 July 1936.

58. Gerd Rühle, *Das Grossdeutsche Reich*, p. 218.

59. Jagschitz, "Struktur der NSDAP," p. 11; Jagschitz, *Der Putsch*, pp. 40–41; unpublished documents assembled for the *Rot-Weiss-Rot Buch*, gendarmerie report from Oberwart, Burgenland, 30 May 1946, DÖW, #8339, p. 2.

60. Schopper, *Presse im Kampf*, p. 300.

61. Gustav Spann, "Die Illegale Flugschriftpropaganda der österreichischen NSDAP von Juliputsch 1934 bis zum Juliabkommen 1936," pp. 188–89.

62. Karl-Rudolf Hübener, "Illegale österreichische Presse von 1933 bis 1938," p. 61; *Der Rote Adler*, 19 June 1934; *Der Kampfruf*, June 1935; *ÖB*, 19 June 1937, p. 1.

63. Boleek to the RL (Propagandaleitung), Munich, 1 Dec. 1930, Slg. Sch., 305 folder 1.

64. *Der Kampf*, 2 Apr. 1933, p. 1.

65. W. Förster to Neurath (late July 1935), NA, T-120, R. 2837/E453191.

66. Baar-Baarenfels's memorandum, p. 471.

67. MLB, May 1935, pp. 7–8.

68. Isabella Ackerl, "Das Kampfbündnis der Nationalsozialistischen Deutschen Arbeiterpartei mit der Grossdeutschen Volkspartei vom 15. Mai 1933," p. 13; Ralf Koerner, *So haben sie es damals gemacht*, pp. 135–37, 141, 192; Action Program of the Austrian Nazi party, Aug. 1935, NA, T-120, R. 2837/E453198.

69. On the subject of Austrian Nazi humor see *Humor der Illegalen*, especially pp. 48, 9, and 47 for the anecdotes related.

70. Mitzi Hartmann [pseud.], *Austria Still Lives*, p. 222; Carl Friedrich and Zbigniew Brzezinski, *Totalitarian Dictatorship and Autocracy*, p. 135.

71. MLB, Mar. 1935, p. 1, and Oct. 1935, p. 2; Baar-Baarenfels's memorandum, p. 470.

72. W. Förster to Neurath (late July 1935), NA, T-120, R. 2837/E45189–90.

73. Friedrich and Brzezinski, *Totalitarian Dictatorship*, p. 131.

74. MLB, Mar. 1935, p. 1.

Chapter VIII

1. Jens Petersen, *Hitler-Mussolini*, p. 284; note (by Kurt Rieth) on a conversation with the Reichskanzler, 10 Feb. 1934, NA, T-120, R. 2836/E452473.

2. The German Consul in Linz (Langen) to Habicht, 11 Oct. 1933, NA, T-120, R. 3394/E606705.

3. "Memorandum by an Official of Department II," 30 Oct. 1933, *DGFP*, C 2:55.

4. *Beiträge zur Vorgeschichte und Geschichte der Julirevolte*, p. 47.

5. The German Consul in Linz (Langen), 26 Sept. 1933, NA, T-120, R. 2833/E451532.

6. "Memorandum by an Official of Department II," 30 Dec. 1933, *DGFP*, C 2:290–91.

7. Ernst Starhemberg, *Memoiren*, pp. 155–56.

8. Memorandum by von Renthe-Fink, 2 Jan. 1934, NA, T-120, R. 2889/E454159.

9. Habicht to Hüffer, 18 June 1934, NA, T-120, R. 2836/E452883.

10. "The Director of Department II to the Minister in Austria," 15 Mar. 1934, *DGFP*, C 2:615.

11. "Memorandum by the State Secretary," 9 Apr. 1934, ibid., p. 730.

12. "Memorandum by the Director of Department II," 16 Mar. 1934, ibid., p. 616.

13. Hüffer to Neurath, 21 Oct. 1933, NA, T-120, R. 2889/E45095.

14. "The Minister in Austria to the Secretary of State," 12 June 1934, *FRUS*, 1934, 2:26–27.

15. Gerhard Jagschitz, *Der Putsch*, p. 153.

16. "The Chargé d'Affaires in Austria to the Foreign Ministry," 21 Jan. 1934, *DGFP*, C 2:437–38.

17. Jagschitz, *Der Putsch*, p. 69; Norbert Schausberger, *Der Griff nach Österreich*, p. 286.

18. "Memorandum by the Deputy Director of Department II," 29 May 1934, *DGFP*, C 2:852.

19. Report by Köpke to Neurath, 31 May 1934, NA, T-120, R. 2838/E453423–24.

20. "The Chargé d'Affaires in Austria to the Foreign Ministry [Muff]," 30 Aug. 1934, *DGFP*, C 2:372–73.

21. Austria, Political Situation (no name), 2 June 1934, NA, T-120, R. 900/5652947; Dieter Ross, *Hitler und Dollfuss*, p. 235.

22. The leader of Sturmbahn I/21, Vienna. Quarterly report, Apr.–June 1932, 30 June 1932, AVA, SA, K. 19; Hellmuth Auerbach, "Eine nationalsozialistische Stimme zum Wiener Putsch," p. 202; report of Reichsamtleiter, Vienna, 3 Aug. 1938, Slg. Sch., 302 2:5–6.

23. Dr. Siebert to Minister President Ludwig Siebert, 21 June 1934, NA, T-120, R. 2838/E453503; political report by Hassel (Rome), 28 June 1934, ibid./E453493; letter by an unidentified individual to the AA received 5 July 1934, ibid./E453501.

24. See above, p. 126.

25. Jagschitz, *Der Putsch*, p. 80.

26. Wladimir von Hartlieb, *Parole: Das Reich!*, pp. 206, 212, 222; report on the NS uprising of 25 July 1934 in Vienna by Dr. Rudolf Weydenhammer, HI, NA-HA, R. 33, folder 634, p. 15.

27. NA, T-175, R. 32/2-539840-41.

28. Report on the NS uprising of 25 July 1934 in Vienna by Dr. Rudolf Weydenhammer, HI, NS-HA, R. 33, folder 634, p. 2.

29. Hartlieb, *Das Reich*, p. 222.

30. Gerhard Jagschitz, "Zur Struktur der NSDAP vor dem Juliputsch 1934," pp. 17–18; Jagschitz, *Der Putsch*, pp. 138–39; Franz Langoth, *Kampf um Österreich*, p. 314.

31. The military and air attaché in Vienna to the Oberkommando des Heeres in Berlin, 21 Dec. 1937, NA, T-78, R. 456/643545.

32. Report by the military attaché in Vienna (Muff), 7 Dec. 1933, NA, T-120, R. 2695/E414230.

33. "The Legation in Austria to the Foreign Ministry," 26 July 1934, *DGFP*, C 3:256, footnote 3; Austria, Political Situation (no name), 2 June 1934, NA, T-77, R. 900/5652947.

34. Report by V. L. R. von Renthe-Fink, Berlin, 15 Feb. 1934, NA, T-120, R. 3393/E605383–84.

35. "Memorandum by Rudolf Weydenhammer," 7–8 Mar. 1934, *DGFP*, C 2:576. As the Austrian ambassador to Rome, Rintelen had been doing everything in his power to disrupt Austro-Italian relations and had kept Habicht informed about the details of the numerous trips Dollfuss made to Italy (ibid., pp. 575–77).

36. Andrew Whiteside, "Austria," p. 347.

37. *Beiträge zur Julirevolte*, pp. 84–87; Jagschitz, *Der Putsch*, p. 114.

38. Report by a Gestapo agent on the situation in Austria, late Aug. 1934, NA, T-120, R. 2889/E454322–24.

39. "The Minister in Austria to the Foreign Ministry," 26 July 1934, *DGFP*, C 3:246–48.

40. Hans Rauter, opinion on the statement of Oberhaidacher, 24 Nov. 1937, Slg. Sch., 277.

41. Jagschitz, *Der Putsch*, p. 157, 161–62; Richard Moschner, *Kärnten*, p. 28.

42. Jagschitz, *Der Putsch*, p. 183; G. E. R. Gedye, *Fallen Bastions*, p. 122; Johann Messinger, *The Death of Dollfuss*, pp. 107–9.

43. *Beiträge zur Julirevolte*, pp. 80–82; Walter Maas, *Assassination in Vienna*, p. 97.

44. Otto Reich von Rohrwig, *Der Freiheitskampf der Ostmark-Deutschen von St. Germain bis Adolf Hitler*, p. 192; report by Gilbert In der Maur, Vienna, 16 Feb. 1934, NA, T-120, R. 2832/E450901.

45. *Die Juli-Revolte*, 1934.

46. Anonymous report on the July Putsch, 31 July 1934, sent to the AA on 2 Aug. 1934, NA, T-120, R. 3393/E605508–509.

47. "The Head of the Volksbund für das Deutschtum im Ausland to the Foreign Ministry," 2 Aug. 1934, *DGFP*, C 2:286.

48. *Die Erhebung der österreichischen Nationalsozialisten im Juli 1934*, p. 8.

49. NA, T-175, R. 32/2-539856–61; Ross, *Hitler und Dollfuss*, p. 216.

50. Franz von Papen, *Der Wahrheit eine Gasse*, p. 381; Jürgen Gehl, *Austria, Germany, and the Anschluss, 1931–38*, p. 101.

51. Jagschitz, "Struktur der NSDAP," p. 15; report on the Austrian *Braunbuch*, Wehrmacht Office, Berlin, 10 Oct. 1934, NA, T-77, R. 900/5653690.

52. *The Foreign Policy of Hitler's Germany*, pp. 103–4.

53. Petersen, *Hitler-Mussolini*, p. 338; Ross, *Hitler und Dollfuss*, p. 236; Göring's testimony, 11 Mar. 1946, IMT, 9:102.

54. Köpke to Hassel, 16 July 1934, NA, T-120, R. 2889/E454309.

55. Note (by Rieth) over a conversation with the Reichskanzler, 10 Feb. 1934, NA, T-120, R. 2836/E452732. Cf. Edward Peterson, *The Limits of Hitler's Power*, p. 15.

56. Papen, *Wahrheit*, p. 381.

57. Theodor Eschenburg, "Franz von Papen," pp. 154–56, 161.

58. Papen, *Wahrheit*, p. 383; guiding principles (of Franz von Papen) for Germany's future policy toward Austria, 19 Aug. 1934, NA, T-120, R. 2833/E451092.

59. Guiding principles (of Papen) for Germany's future policy toward Austria, 19 Aug. 1934, NA, T-120, R. 2833/E451090–92. This second group of demands was not mentioned by Papen in his memoirs.

60. Franz von Papen, *Memoirs*, p. 341. Although Göring as well as Papen took credit for Habicht's dismissal it should be recalled that Hitler had been unhappy with the Landesleiter for some time. See also John Heineman, *Hitler's First Foreign Minister*, p. 107.

61. Anonymous report in the confidence of the German legation in Vienna, 22 Jan. 1935, NA, T-120, R. 2892/E455615.

62. Guiding principles (of Papen) for Germany's future policy toward Austria, 19 Aug. 1934, NA, T-120, R. 2833/E451093. Frauenfeld, for example, received a position in the Reichstheaterkammer.

63. "The Führer's Deputy, Hess, to Herr Frauenfeld," 21 Aug. 1934, *DGFP*, C 3:353.

64. Gehl, *Austria, Germany, and the Anschluss*, p. 102.

65. "The Führer and Chancellor to Ministers Hess and Goebbels, Herr von Papen and the Office of the Secret State Police," 8 Aug. 1934, *DGFP*, C 3:299.

66. "The Führer's Deputy, Hess, to Herr Frauenfeld," 21 Aug. 1934, ibid./352.

Chapter IX

1. Report by W. Heinzmann, 30 Oct. 1935, and given to Hitler on 28 Dec. 1935, NA, T-120, R. 2837/E453288.
2. *IdVF*, 23 Aug. 1934; speech by Friedrich Rainer in Klagenfurt, Carinthia, 11 Mar. 1942, before Nazi leaders concerning National Socialism in Austria from the July rebellion in 1934 to the seizure of power on 11 Mar. 1938, IMT, #4005-PS, 34:6. Hereafter referred to as Rainer's speech.
3. Report by a man in the confidence of the German legation in Vienna, 22 Jan. 1935, NA, T-120, R. 2892/E453616.
4. Everhard Holtmann, "Zwischen 'Blutschuld' und 'Befriedung,'" pp. 4, 7, 8.
5. Karl Stuhlpfarrer, "Zum Problem der deutschen Penetration Österreichs," p. 317; Maurice Williams, "German Nazis and Austrian Relief," p. 4.
6. Maurice Williams, "Delusions of 'Grandeur,'" p. 14; Stuhlpfarrer, "Deutsche Penetration Österreichs," p. 317; interrogation of Friedrich Rainer, 15 Nov. 1945, NA, NI, p. 19.
7. Williams, "Delusions of 'Grandeur,'" p. 14.
8. Stuhlpfarrer, "Deutsche Penetration Österreichs," p. 318.
9. Ibid., pp. 318–19.
10. Ibid.
11. *Der Heimatschützer*, 28 Apr. 1934, p. 1; *IdVF*, 20 Nov. 1934, pp. 10–12.
12. MLB, Nov. 1935, p. 4; Franz von Papen, *Memoirs*, p. 353.
13. Papen, *Memoirs*, p. 347.
14. "The Minister in Austria to the Führer and Chancellor," 27 July 1935, *DGFP*, C 4:500.
15. The Political Situation in Austria (no name), 12 Dec. 1935, NA, T-78, R. 455/6433134.
16. Report is dated 15 Jan. 1936, NA, T-120, R. 2837/E453294–95.
17. Robert Schwarz, "The Austrian Nazi Movement (1918–1973)," p. 34; Max Dachauer, *Das Ende Österreich*, pp. 214–15; *Der Kampf*, 19 June 1934, p. 1; Richard Moschner, *Kärnten*, p. 17.
18. Report of Count Revertera, n.d., DÖW, #2162, p. 4; Dachauer, *Ende Österreich*, p. 215.
19. MLB, Mar. 1935, p. 6.
20. Report of Count Revertera, n.d., DÖW, #2162, p. 11.
21. Schwarz, "Austrian Nazi Movement," p. 35, 60–61.
22. German Consulate in Graz to the AA, 18 June 1935, NA, T-120, R. 2892/E455767,–82.
23. Guido Zernatto, *Die Wahrheit über Österreich*, pp. 152–53; Hans Bleyer-Härtl, *Ringen um Reich und Recht*, p. 138.
24. Donald McKale, *The Swastika Outside Germany*, pp. 79–80, 107.
25. Ibid., p. 107; Christine Fessl, "Die Innenpolitische Entwicklung in Österreich in den Jahren 1934 bis 1938," p. 45.
26. Renthe-Fink to the German embassy in London, Aug. 1934, NA, T-120, R. 2836/E452915; Gerhard Jagschitz, *Der Putsch*, p. 182.
27. Landesleitung Österreichs der NSDAP (Hitlerbewegung), *Das Dienstbuch der NSDAP*, pp. 13, 105–106, 113. Hereafter referred to as *Dienstbuch*. Zernatto, *Wahrheit*, p. 68; Gerhard Botz, "Faschismus und Lohnabhängige in der Ersten Republik," p. 120.
28. *Dienstbuch*, pp. 62–63; Dietrich Orlow, *The History of the Nazi Party, 1919–1933*, p. 101.

29. F. L. Carsten, *Fascist Movements in Austria*, pp. 197, 253.

30. Alfred Persche, "Hauptmann Leopold," DÖW, #1460, p. 142. See also Hans Schopper, *Niederdonau*, p. 44.

31. Gerhard Jagschitz, "Zur Struktur der NSDAP vor dem Juliputsch 1934," p. 10; testimony of Ernst Kaltenbrunner, IMT, 14:34. Persche placed the size of the Austrian SS in 1937 at only "two to three thousand," but he was a hostile witness. See "Hauptmann Leopold," p. 29.

32. Report by a man in the confidence of the German legation in Vienna, 22 Jan. 1935, NA, T-120, R. 2892/E455616–17.

33. Altenburg to Köpke, 29 Dec. 1934, NA, T-120, R. 3395/E606969–70.

34. "Memorandum by an Official of Department II," 29 Nov. 1934, *DGFP*, C 3:668; "Memorandum by an Official of Department II," 29 Aug. 1934, ibid.:369–70; "The State Secretary to the Führer's Deputy," 23 Nov. 1934, ibid.:662–63.

35. Osterburg report on the domestic situation in Austria, 11 Oct. 1933, NA, T-120, R. 2836/E452562.

36. Anonymous letter to the RL, 29 Jan. 1938, NA, T-120, R. 751/345205.

37. Persche, "Hauptmann Leopold," pp. 7, 166, 185; Frageboden, BDC, PK, Alfred Persche folder. Unidentified newspaper clipping of 2 Apr. 1938.

38. Copy of an SA order sent by Papen to the AA, 22 June 1935, NA, T-120, R. 2837/E453079–80.

39. SA order (Obergruppe Austria) to all brigades and for further distribution to all of the SA, Nov. 1936, DÖW, #6115.

40. Copy of an SA order sent by von Papen to the AA, 22 June 1935, NA, T-120, R. 2837/E453082.

41. MLB, May 1935, p. 4, and Nov. 1935, p. 7.

42. Robert Houston, "Ernst Kaltenbrunner," especially pp. 5, 10–11, 15, 17, 21; Gideon Hausner, *Justice in Jerusalem*, p. 30.

43. Gerhard Jagschitz, "Zwischen Befriedung und Konfrontation," pp. 162–63.

44. "The Chargé d'Affaires in Austria to the Foreign Ministry," 18 Oct. 1934, *DGFP*, C 3:499–500; *IdVF*, 21 Sept. 1934, p. 17.

45. "The Chargé d'Affaires in Austria to the Foreign Ministry," 18 Oct. 1934, *DGFP*, C 3:500.

46. *IdVF*, 12 Oct. 1934, pp. 2–16; the reconciliation action of Reinthaller written by Dr. Harold Hipfiner, 18 Aug. 1938, HI, NS-HA, R. 33, folder 642, pp. 1–3.

47. Ernst Starhemberg, *Memoiren*, p. 212; Barbara Berger, "Ernst Rüdiger Fürst Starhemberg," pp. 146–61.

48. Conversation between Friedrich Rainer and Dr. Siegfried Uiberreither, 8 July 1945, NA, NI, p. 2. See also Rainer to Bürckel, 6 July 1939, *NCA*, #812-PS, 3:500.

49. Anonymous report in a letter of Prince Erbach sent to the AA, 2 Mar. 1935, NA, T-120, R. 2499/E371924; McKale, *Swastika Outside Germany*, p. 107.

50. *The Foreign Policy of Hitler's Germany*, p. 88.

51. Report by Muff on the Austrian Situation, 10 Sept. 1934, NA, T-120, R. 2695/E414397.

52. Anonymous article written in Vienna on 11 Mar. 1935, "Notes concerning the Political Situation in Austria," ibid./E453008.

53. The German consul in Linz (Langen) to the AA, 30 Aug. 1934, ibid., R. 3394/E606189; Franz Langoth, *Kampf um Österreich*, p. 100; Wolfgang Rosar, *Deutsche Gemeinschaft*, p. 113.

54. Affidavit by Arthur Seyss-Inquart, "The Austrian Question," *NCA*, #3254, 5:964.

55. The German consul in Linz (Langen) to the AA, 30 Aug. 1934, NA, T-120, R.

3394/E606189; report by Reinthaller, n.d., ibid./E606196.

56. Report by the military attaché in Vienna (Muff), "The Crisis of the Führerprinzip in the Austrian NSDAP," 28 Aug. 1935, ibid., R. 2837/E453230–31.

57. Papen to Hitler, 4 Apr. 1935, *Schmidt-Prozess*, p. 389; report of the Federal Police Directory, Vienna, to the Security Directorate in Vienna concerning the action against Johann Amann, etc., 8 Apr. 1936, DÖW, #6014.

58. Report by Muff, "The Crisis of the Führerprinzip in the Austrian NSDAP," 28 Aug. 1935, NA, T-120, R. 2837/E453232.

59. Ibid./E453232,-36.

60. Rainer to Bürckel, 6 July 1939, *NCA*, #812-PS, 3:391; Ulrich Eichstädt, *Von Dollfuss zu Hitler*, p. 76; Rosar, *Deutsche Gemeinschaft*, p. 89.

61. Testimony of Friedrich Rainer, 15 Nov. 1945, NA, NI, p. 20; unidentified newspaper clipping, BDC, SS-Führer, Hubert Klausner folder.

62. Rainer's speech, IMT, #4005-PS, 34:14.

63. MLB, Sept. 1935, pp. 3, 6.

64. Report concerning the activity of the NS lawyers of Austria, 10 Oct. 1936, DÖW, #6036, p. 1.

Chapter X

1. All figures are from Friedrich Hertz, *The Economic Problems of the Danubian States*, p. 147.

2. MLB, Mar. 1935, p. 1.

3. Ibid., May 1935, p. 2, June 1935, p. 2, July 1935, p. 2, Sept. 1935, p. 16, Mar. 1936, p. 1.

4. *Schmidt-Prozess*, pp. 468–69, 473. Hereafter referred to as Baar-Baarenfels's memorandum.

5. MLB, May 1936, p. 6.

6. Adam Wandruszka, "Österreichs politische Struktur," p. 339. On the nature of the Dollfuss regime see also Heinrich Busshoff, *Das Dollfuss-Regime in Österreich in geistesgeschichtlicher Perspektive unter besonderer Berücksichtigung der "Schöneren Zukunft" und "Reichspost,"* especially p. 297.

7. R. John Rath, "Authoritarian Austria," pp. 26–27; Karl-Rudolf Hübener, "Illegale österreichische Presse von 1933 bis 1938," pp. 576, 589.

8. Grete Klingenstein, "Bermerkungen zum Problem des Faschismus in Österreich," pp. 4–5. For an apology of the new constitution see Ernst Hoor, *Österreich, 1918–1938*, p. 111.

9. Ernst Nolte, *Die Krise des liberalen Systems und die faschistischen Bewegungen*, p. 306; Robert Ingrim, *Der Griff nach Österreich*, p. 80; Ralf Koerner, *So haben sie es damals gemacht*, p. 141. According to Nolte, Latvia and Lithuania also developed authoritarian regimes as a defense against fascist movements (*Krise*, p. 280).

10. Mitzi Hartmann (pseud.), *Austria Still Lives*, p. 19; Hans Kohn, "AEIOU," pp. 524–25.

11. Memorandum by Kurt Rieth of a conversation with Hitler in Berlin, 10 Feb. 1934, NA, T-120, R. 2889/E454209.

12. Baar-Baarenfels's memorandum, p. 474.

13. Guido Zernatto, *Die Wahrheit über Österreich*, p. 94.

14. Quoted in Charles Gulick, *Austria from Habsburg to Hitler*, 2:1485.

15. Unpublished documents assembled for the *Rot-Weiss-Rot Buch*, Burgenland,

short report of the Landeshauptmann, 30 May 1946, DÖW, #8339, p. 1. See also Stefan Zweig, *The World of Yesterday*, p. 403.

16. Hans Frisch, *Die Gewaltherrschaft in Österreich*, p. 38.

17. Malcolm Bullock, *Austria, 1918–1938*, p. 272.

18. Quoted in Gulick, *Habsburg to Hitler*, 2:1486. This anecdote may have been borrowed from Fascist Italy, as an identical story was popular there. See Alan Cassels, *Fascism*, p. 71.

19. Vaterländische Front, Bundeswerbeleitung, *Richtlinien zur Führerausbildung*, p. ix.

20. On anti-Semitism in the VF and the Austrian government see especially VF *Führerausbildung*, p. 48; Karl Stadler, *Austria*, p. 140; Martin Fuchs, *Showdown in Vienna*, pp. 71–72, 221, and Sylvia Maderegger, *Die Juden im österreichischen Ständestaat 1934–1938*, pp. 115–16, 197, 224, 241, 266–67.

21. Imgard Bärnthaler, *Die Vaterländische Front*, pp. 56, 58.

22. Vaterländische Front, Bundespropagandaleitung, *Richtlinien für den Zellenleiter, Zellenvertrauensmann und Nachtrichtenmann*, pp. 3–4, 6, 8.

23. Bärnthaler, *Die VF*, p. 189; Hartmann, *Austria Still Lives*, pp. 188–89.

24. Zernatto, *Wahrheit*, pp. 91–92. For comparisons with the Kraft durch Freude program in Germany see Richard Grunberger, *The 12-Year Reich*, pp. 216–17.

25. Diverse circular letters of the VF LL, DÖW, #7544, 7548; Zernatto, *Wahrheit*, pp. 91–93.

26. Alfred Persche, "Hauptmann Leopold," DÖW, #1460, p. 248.

27. Reinhold Lorenz, *Der Staat wider Willen*, p. 139; Bärnthaler, *Die VF*, p. 58.

28. Letter of Prinz zu Erbach, Vienna, 10 May 1935 (destination unknown), NA, T-120, R. 2837/E453021–22; Kurt von Schuschnigg, *My Austria*, p. 256. For a picture of a VF rally see *Stimme der Heimat*, Feb. 1936, p. 1.

29. Bärnthaler, *Die VF*, pp. 173–77.

30. "The Appeal of Fascism and the Problem of National Disintegration," p. 62.

31. "The Minister in Austria to the Führer and Chancellor," 27 July 1935, *DGFP*, C 1:500.

32. *Schmidt-Prozess*, p. 307.

33. See above, pp. 148–50.

34. Jens Petersen, *Hitler-Mussolini*, pp. 482–83.

35. Zernatto, *Wahrheit*, p. 168.

36. Ernst Starhemberg, *Memoiren*, pp. 186–87; MLB, Oct. 1936, p. 18; Ludwig Jedlicka, "Ernst Rüdiger Fürst Starhemberg und die politische Entwicklung in Österreich im Fruhjahr 1938."

37. F. L. Carsten, *Fascist Movements in Austria*, pp. 275, 278–79.

38. MLB, May 1936, pp. 5–6, Sept. 1936, pp. 15–16.

39. Papen to Hitler, 21 Aug. 1936, *Schmidt-Prozess*, p. 407.

40. "Text of the German-Austrian Communique," 11 July 1936, *DGFP*, D 1:281–82.

41. Kurt von Schuschnigg, *The Brutal Takeover*, p. 172.

42. G. E. R. Gedye, *Betrayal in Central Europe*, pp. 188–89; testimony of Eduard Baar-Baarenfels, *Schmidt-Prozess* pp. 320–22.

43. "The German Ambassador in Austria to the German Foreign Ministry," 23 July 1936, *DGFP*, D 1:302.

44. *Brutal Takeover*, p. 154; Alois Adler, *Die historischen Fakten des Nationalsozialismus in Österreich*, p. 5.

45. Otto Reich von Rohrwig, *Der Freiheitskampf der Ostmark-Deutschen von St.*

Germain bis Adolf Hitler, p. 367. See also Max Dachauer, *Das Ende Österreich*, p. 232 and *ÖB*, Jan. 1938, p. 2.

46. Testimony of Richard Schmitz, *Schmidt-Prozess*, p. 192.

47. "The German Ambassador in Austria [Papen] to the Führer and Chancellor," 12 Jan. 1937, *DGFP*, D 1:368.

48. Report from Carinthia concerning the reception of the German-Austrian Agreement, n.d., in *Vom Justizpalast zum Heldenplatz*, ed. Ludwig Jedlicka and Rudolf Neck, doc. #65, p. 452.

49. *Mitteilung der Landespresse Amtes*, 10 July 1936, pp. 1, 2.

50. Jürgen Gehl, *Austria, Germany, and the Anschluss, 1931–38*, p. 148.

51. Memorandum by Franz von Papen, *NCA*, Supplement A, #3300-PS, 467–68.

52. Franz von Papen, *Der Wahrheit eine Gasse*, pp. 419–20.

53. Conversation between Friedrich Rainer and Siegfried Uiberreither, 8 July 1945, NA, NI, p. 6; testimony of Friedrich Rainer, 15 Nov. 1945, ibid., p. 24.

54. Conversation between Friedrich Rainer and Siegfried Uiberreither, 8 July 1945, ibid., p. 6.

55. Speech by Friedrich Rainer in Klagenfurt, Carinthia, 11 Mar. 1942, before Nazi leaders concerning National Socialism in Austria from the July rebellion in 1934 to the seizure of power of 11 Mar. 1934, IMT, #4005-PS, 34:16.

56. Testimony of Friedrich Rainer, 15 Nov. 1945, NA, NI, p. 26.

57. Norman Rich, *Hitler's War Aims*, 1:119–20. See also Herbert Levine, *Hitler's Free City*, p. 52.

58. Document of the Security Directorate concerning the Nazi Movement in Austria after the July Agreement, 24 July 1936, DÖW, #6524, p. 1.

59. MLB, 27 July 1936, pp. 2, 4; 29 Sept. 1936, p. 4.

60. Norbert Schausberger, *Der Griff nach Österreich*, pp. 479, 497.

61. Report of the military and air attaché concerning Styria sent to the Oberkommando des Heeres in Berlin, Vienna, 12 Dec. 1937, NA, T-78, R. 456/6434540,-42; excerpt from the *Wirtschafts-Zeitung des Pester Lloyd*, 2 Apr. 1937, ibid./6434594.

62. "Professor Franz Wehefsich to Dr. Altenburg of the German Foreign Ministry," Berlin, 10 Sept. 1936, *DGFP*, D 1:296.

63. MLB, Sept. 1936, p. 1; Oct. 1936, p. 2; Nov. 1936, p. 1.

64. *Stimme der Heimat*, Aug. 1936, p. 1.

65. MLB, Aug. 1936, p. 14.

66. Affidavit of George Messersmith, *NCA*, #1760-PS, 4:321–22.

67. *Showdown in Vienna*, pp. 62, 237.

68. *Memoiren*, pp. 275–76.

69. *Brutal Takeover*, p. 153.

Chapter XI

1. Maurice Williams, "Delusions of 'Grandeur,'" p. 8.

2. Papen to Hitler, 14 Jan. 1937, *Schmidt-Prozess*, p. 414; Alfred Persche, "Hauptmann Leopold," DÖW, #1460, p. 49.

3. Gerhard Botz, "Aspects of the Social Structure of Austrian National Socialism (1918–1939)," p. 21; Papen to Hitler, 4 Apr. 1935, *Schmidt-Prozess*, p. 389.

4. Report by anonymous official in the German legation in Vienna, 2 Mar. 1935, NA, T-120, R. 2892/E455611.

5. Franz von Papen, *Memoirs*, p. 385.

6. MLB, Feb. 1936, pp. 1–2.

7. Botz, "Social Structure of Austrian National Socialism," p. 21.

8. *IdVF*, 19 Oct. 1934, p. 13; MLB, Feb. 1936, p. 2.

9. Persche, "Hauptmann Leopold," p. 233.

10. Guido Zernatto, *Die Wahrheit über Österreich*, p. 164.

11. Persche, "Hauptmann Leopold," p. 3.

12. Excerpt from the Linzer *Volksblatt*, 22 May 1937, TA, Josef Leopold folder; *Deutsch-österreichische Tages-Zeitung*, 3 July 1932, ibid. Even here there are parallels with Hitler who, while still in the German army for a short time after the war, took orders from the revolutionary left. See Joachim Fest, *Hitler*, p. 84.

13. Peter Merkl, *Political Violence under the Swastika*, p. 109.

14. Persche, "Hauptmann Leopold," pp. 42–44; Ludwig Jedlicka, "Gauleiter Josef Leopold (1889–1941)," pp. 148–49.

15. Dieter Wagner and Gerhard Tomkowitz, *Anschluss*, p. 21; interrogation of Friedrich Rainer, 6 Nov. 1945, NA, NI, p. 1.

16. Radomír Luža, *Austro-German Relations in the Anschluss Era*, p. 30; speech by Friedrich Rainer in Klagenfurt, Carinthia, 11 Mar. 1942, before Nazi leaders concerning National Socialism in Austria from the July rebellion in 1934 to the seizure of power on 11 Mar. 1934, IMT, #4005-PS, 34:11. Hereafter referred to as Rainer's speech.

17. "Memorandum [by Altenburg]," 22 Sept. 1936, *DGFP*, D 1:299.

18. Persche, "Hauptmann Leopold," pp. 19, 26.

19. "Memorandum [by Altenburg]," 22 Sept. 1936, *DGFP*, D 1:299.

20. Wolfgang Rosar, *Deutsche Gemeinschaft*, pp. 111, 113.

21. See, for example, Extracts from the Closing Statement for the Defendant Keppler, "Ministries Case," 14:141; Kurt von Schuschnigg, *The Brutal Takeover*, p. 209; Andrew Whiteside, "Austria," p. 355; Leopold to Hitler, 20 Aug. 1937, DÖW, #5001, p. 13.

22. Papen to Hitler, 17 May 1935, NA, T-120, R. 2832/E450958–59; Gerhard Jagschitz, "Zwischen Befriedung und Konfrontation," p. 184.

23. Persche, "Hauptmann Leopold," pp. 142–44; testimony of Friedrich Rainer, 15 Nov. 1945, NA, NI, pp. 12–13.

24. Anonymous report from the files of Richard Riedl, NA, T-84, R. 16/44254.

25. Rainer's speech, 34:6, 13–14, 18; Rosar, *Deutsche Gemeinschaft*, pp. 98, 108; Persche, "Hauptmann Leopold," p. 47.

26. Persche, "Hauptmann Leopold," p. 135.

27. Rainer to Bürckel, 6 July 1939, *NCA*, #812-PS, 3:587–96; Rainer's speech, 34:17.

28. This generalization applies to moderates like Hermann Neubacher as well as to the SS leader, Ernst Kaltenbrunner. See the intermediate interrogation report of Hermann Neubacher, 29 Jan. 1946, NA, NI, pp. 36, 37.

29. Interrogation of Alfred Frauenfeld, 9 July 1947, ibid., p. 2.

30. Persche, "Hauptmann Leopold," p. 135; Jürgen Gehl, *Austria, Germany, and the Anschluss, 1931–38*, p. 149.

31. "The German-Austrian Agreement of July 11, 1936," *DGFP*, D 1:281.

32. Leopold to Hitler, 22 Aug. 1937, DÖW, #5001, p. 4; Zernatto, *Wahrheit*, p. 165.

33. Christine Fessl, "Die Innenpolitische Entwicklung in Österreich in den Jahren 1934 bis 1938," p. 47.

34. Report by the German consul in Graz (Drubba) to the German embassy in Vienna, 25 Mar. 1937, PAAA, folder 9, no. 22.

35. Letter of 14 Jan. 1937, *Schmidt-Prozess*, p. 414.

36. Affidavit, 28 August 1945 of George S. Messersmith. Detailed history of Nazi Preparations for the Incorporation of Austria in the German Reich, IMT, #1760-PS, 38:283–90.

37. "The German Ambassador in Austria [Papen] to the Fuehrer and Chancellor," 13 Feb. 1937, *DGFP*, D 1:391–92; Martin Fuchs, *Showdown in Vienna*, pp. 49–50.

38. Papen, *Memoirs*, p. 395; Martin Fuchs, *Showdown in Vienna*, p. 56; William Leavey, "Hitler's Envoy 'Extraordinary,'" p. 80.

39. Whiteside, "Austria," p. 357.

40. Schuschnigg, *Brutal Takeover*, p. 173.

41. The German Consul in Graz to Herr von Stein in Vienna, 9 Feb. 1933, PAAA, folder 9; Schiller to Herren Chef W. A., 4 Apr. 1937, NA, T-77, R. 901/5529295.

42. "The German Ambassador to Austria [Papen] Temporarily in Berlin, to the Feuhrer and Chancellor," 12 May 1937, *DGFP*, D 1:420.

43. Papen, *Memoirs*, p. 384.

44. Papen, *Wahrheit*, pp. 445, 392, 395. The anonymous author of a report in the files of Richard Riedl did not, however, believe that Papen had been helpful to Rainer or Globocnik. He even accused Papen of stabbing the SS faction in the back and being passive toward the goals of German foreign policy. See NA, T-84, R. 16/44259, and Leavey, "Hitler's Envoy 'Extraordinary,'" p. 89.

45. Alfred Persche, "Die Aktion Hudal," 2:245.

46. Personal declaration, BDC, PA, Seyss-Inquart folder; Rosar, *Deutsche Gemeinschaft*, pp. 22–24. See also Bruce Pauley, *The Habsburg Legacy, 1867–1939*, pp. 17–18, 29.

47. Personal declaration, BDC, PA, Seyss-Inquart folder.

48. John Leopold, "Arthur von Seyss-Inquart and the Austrian Anschluss," p. 40; Rainer to Bürckel, 6 July 1939, *NCA*, #812-PS, 3:59.

49. "Aktion Hudal," 2:244.

50. Seyss-Inquart's views in his essay "The Austrian Question," *NCA*, #3254-PS, 5:966–67, 970–71. For Leopold's opinions see Persche, "Hauptmann Leopold," pp. 220–21.

51. "Hauptmann Leopold," p. 172.

52. Gehl, *Austria, Germany, and the Anschluss*, p. 149.

53. Persche, "Hauptmann Leopold," pp. 22, 173.

54. Rosar, *Deutsche Gemeinschaft*, p. 101.

55. *DGFP*, D 1:291.

56. Persche, "Aktion Hudal," 2:246.

57. Rosar, *Deutsche Gemeinschaft*, p. 141; Gehl, *Austria, Germany, and the Anschluss*, p. 155; anonymous report from the files of Richard Riedl, NA, T-84, R. 16/44258.

58. "The German Ambassador in Austria [Papen] to the German Foreign Ministry," 5 June 1937, *DGFP*, D 1:429.

59. Gehl, *Austria, Germany, and the Anschluss*, p. 155.

60. Persche, "Aktion Hudal," 2:244; Papen, *Memoirs*, p. 295; Leopold to Hitler, 22 Aug. 1937, DÖW, #5001, p. 1.

61. Anonymous note to the leader of Hauptamt V, Lingg, 13 Dec. 1937, NA, T-120, R. 751/345237.

62. Rainer's speech, IMT, #4005-PS, 34:19.

63. Rainer to Bürckel, 6 July 1939, NCA, #812-PS, 3:392; interrogation of Friedrich Rainer, 11 July 1946, Keppler's Austrian Mission, NA, NI, p. 2.

64. Notes of Hauptmann Leopold of 7 Aug. 1937, DÖW, #5053, pp. 4–6.

65. "Memorandum" (taken from a file of Keppler's papers), *DGFP*, D 1:464.

66. Friedrich von Holstein (1837–1909) was a relatively unknown counselor in the German Foreign Office who, among other things, secretly used his position to worsen relations between Austria-Hungary and Russia, and helped to poison Wilhelm II's attitude toward Bismarck. See Hajo Holborn, *A History of Modern Germany*, 3:247, 299.

67. "Hauptmann Leopold," p. 219 and (from the same manuscript) Judgment of Dr. H. A. Kraus.

68. "Hauptmann Leopold," p. 186.

69. Ibid., p. 245; Zernatto, *Wahrheit*, p. 165.

70. Persche, "Hauptmann Leopold," p. 133.

71. Seyss-Inquart, "The Austrian Question, 1934–1938," NCA, #3254-PS, *NCA*, 5:968.

72. *The History of the Nazi Party, 1933–1945*, p. 235.

73. Persche, "Aktion Hudal," 2:247–48.

74. *IdVF*, 21 Sept. 1934, p. 1.

75. Persche, "Hauptmann Leopold," pp. 167–68, 178, 191.

76. Ibid., pp. 220–21.

77. Persche, "Aktion Hudal," 2:269.

78. Ibid.; Persche, "Hauptmann Leopold," p. 29.

79. Reports and observation notes of various political and police offices over terrorist activities of the illegal NSDAP in 1935. Report, "Building of the Illegal SA and SS," DÖW, #7314.

80. "Aktion Hudal," 2:244.

81. Ibid., p. 235.

82. Letters of Leopold to Hitler, 22 Aug. and 8 Sept. 1937, DÖW, #5001.

83. Jedlicka, "Josef Leopold," p. 150.

84. "Memorandum of a Conversation with Reichsleiter Martin Bormann on September 30 [apparently written by Keppler]," *DGFP*, D 1:462.

85. "Memorandum [by Keppler] of Call on Minister President Goering in the Company of Landesleiter Leopold on October 8, 1937," ibid.:469.

86. Persche, "Hauptmann Leopold," p. 210.

Chapter XII

1. Werner Maser, *Hitler*, pp. 212–13, 234.

2. Judgment: Introduction, Count One: Crimes against Peace, "The Ministries Case," 14:330–31.

3. P. 129.

4. See, for example, Keith Eubank, *The Origins of World War II*, pp. 81–84; Alan Bullock, "Hitler and the Origins of the Second World War," pp. 229–31.

5. Alfred Persche, "Die Aktion Hudal," DÖW, #5116/1, 2:252, 268.

6. Ibid., p. 253.

7. Ibid., pp. 253–54.

8. Norbert Schausberger, *Der Griff nach Österreich*, pp. 417–18.

9. "The Chargé in Austria [Wiley] to the Secretary of State," 29 Jan. 1938, *FRUS*, 1938, 1:386; Gunther Edlinger, "Friedrich Funder und die 'Reichspost' in ihrer Stellungnahme zur Politik des Nationalsozialismus gegenüber Österreich von 1930 bis zum Anschluss 1938," p. 129.

10. Guido Zernatto, *Die Wahrheit über Österreich*, pp. 182–85; Andrew Whiteside, "Austria," p. 357.

11. Interview in Vienna. Tavs went on to say that the purpose of the Plan was to put pressure on the Schuschnigg government to reopen negotiations with the illegal Nazis.

12. Alfred Persche, "Hauptmann Leopold," DÖW, #1460, p. 257.

13. Persche, "Aktion Hudal," 2:255–56.

14. "Undated Report," DGFP, D 1:512–13; Gordon Brook-Shepherd, The Anschluss, p. 35.

15. Keppler to Ribbentrop, 7 Feb. 1938, "Ministries Case," 12:711.

16. Kurt von Schuschnigg, The Brutal Takeover, p. 182.

17. "Protocol of the Conference of February 12, 1938," DGFP, D 1:516.

18. Extracts from the Testimony of Keppler, "Ministries Case," 12:764.

19. "Protocol of the Conference of February 12, 1938," DGFP, D 1:516; testimony of Friedrich Rainer, 15 Nov. 1945, NA, NI, p. 21.

20. "Memorandum from the files of Dr. Keppler," DGFP, D 1:548.

21. Jürgen Gehl, Austria, Germany, and the Anschluss, 1931–38, p. 176; Brook-Shepherd, The Anschluss, pp. 62–65.

22. "The German Ambassador in Austria [Papen] to the German Foreign Ministry," 14 Feb. 1938, DGFP, D 1:519.

23. P. 404.

24. Seyss-Inquart, "The Austrian Question," NCA, #3254, 5:974; Gehl, Austria, Germany, and the Anschluss, p. 181.

25. Seyss-Inquart, "The Austrian Question," NCA, #3254-PS, 5:974.

26. Ibid., pp. 974–76.

27. "Memorandum (by Keppler) of the Reception by the Fuehrer on the Afternoon of February 21, 1938 in the Presence of Field Marshal Göring," DGFP, D 1:540. (Hereafter referred to as "Memorandum Keppler.")

28. Persche, "Hauptmann Leopold," pp. 261–63.

29. "Report on the Austrian Situation up to February 18, 7 p.m. [by Vessenmayer]," DGFP, D 1:534.

30. "Memorandum Keppler," ibid., pp. 539–40.

31. Persche, "Hauptmann Leopold," p. 266.

32. "Memorandum Keppler," D 1:540–41; Rainer to Bürckel, 6 July 1939, NCA, #812-PS, 3:593; Zernatto, Wahrheit, p. 240.

33. "Memorandum of Trip to Vienna, March 3 to 6, 1938 [from the files of Dr. Keppler]," DGFP, D 1:559.

34. Persche, "Hauptmann Leopold," pp. 267–68, 279.

35. Ibid., pp. 274, 277–78; Dieter Wagner and Gerhard Tomkowitz, Anschluss, p. 62; Zernatto, Wahrheit, pp. 250–51.

36. Brutal Takeover, p. 205.

37. Ibid., p. 239; Persche, "Hauptmann Leopold," p. 340; Ludwig Jedlicka, "Gauleiter Josef Leopold (1889–1941)," p. 153.

38. Interrogation of August Eigruber, 3 Nov. 1945, NA, NI, p. 13.

39. Ulrich Eichstädt, Von Dollfuss zu Hitler, pp. 337–38.

40. Schuschnigg, Brutal Takeover, p. 239; Zernatto, Wahrheit, p. 249; Wolfgang Rosar, Deutsche Gemeinschaft, pp. 185–86.

41. "Memorandum of Trip to Vienna, March 3 to 6, 1938 [from the files of Dr. Keppler]," DGFP, D 1:559.

42. Ibid.; Wladimir Hartlieb, Parole: Das Reich!, p. 493.

43. F. L. Carsten, Fascist Movements in Austria, p. 321.

44. The military and air attaché in Vienna to the 3 Abteilung Attachegruppé, Berlin, 12 Dec. 1937, NA, T-78, R. 456/6434545.

45. Persche, "Hauptmann Leopold," p. 272; Zernatto, *Wahrheit*, pp. 249–51; interrogation of Siegfried Uiberreither, 1 Apr. 1946, NA, NI, pp. 4–5.

46. Zernatto, *Wahrheit*, p. 235; Schuschnigg, *Brutal Takeover*, p. 235. The quotation is from a speech by Hitler contained in the draft of an unidentified speech, n.d., NA, T-580, R. 61, p. 4.

47. John Leopold, "Arthur von Seyss-Inquart and the Austrian Anschluss," p. 83; Seyss-Inquart, "The Austrian Question," NCA, #3254-PS, 5:597.

48. Zernatto, *Wahrheit*, p. 254.

49. Persche, "Hauptmann Leopold," p. 277; Persche, "Aktion Hudal," 2:279–81.

50. Persche, "Hauptmann Leopold," pp. 273–74.

51. N.d., *DGFP*, D 1:559.

52. Brook-Shepherd, *The Anschluss*, p. 107. Schuschnigg himself admitted that the plebiscite was an "act of desperation" (*Brutal Takeover*, p. 258).

53. Speech by Theo Habicht given on 9 Aug. 1933, NA, T-120, R. 2838/E45384; Reinhold Lorenz, *Der Staat wider Willen*, p. 247; "Mitteilung des Landespresse Amtes," 19 June 1936, p. 3.

54. "The Ambassador in Germany [Wilson] to the Secretary of State," 30 Mar. 1938, *FRUS*, 1938, 1:469.

55. Quoted in Gordon Shepherd, *The Austrian Odyssey*, p. 128.

56. Hans Mikoletzky, *Österreichische Zeitgeschichte vom Ende der Monarchie bis zum Abschluss des Staatsvertrages*, p. 378. Later, the ex-chancellor lowered this estimate to 65–70 percent (*Brutal Takeover*, p. 271).

57. On the original voting conditions see Shepherd, *Austrian Odyssey*, pp. 128–29, and Rosar, *Deutsche Gemeinschaft*, p. 251.

58. Zernatto, *Wahrheit*, pp. 179, 283.

59. Extracts from the Testimony of Defendent Keppler, "Ministries Case," 12:768.

60. Taylor, *Origins*, p. 143.

61. Gehl, *Austria, Germany, and the Anschluss*, pp. 186–87; H. A. Schmitt, "End of the First Republic," p. 299.

62. For a translation of the transcript of these conversations see "Ministries Case," 12:718–31.

63. Opening Statements by the Prosecution, ibid., p. 151; Leopold, "Arthur von Seyss-Inquart," p. 2.

64. Göring's testimony, IMT, 9:333.

65. John Heineman, *Hitler's First Foreign Minister*, p. 173; Radomír Luža, *Austro-German Relations in the Anschluss Era*, p. 51.

66. Seyss-Inquart, "The Austrian Question," *NCA*, #3254-PS, 5:982.

67. Gehl, *Austria, Germany, and the Anschluss*, p. 190.

68. Persche, "Hauptmann Leopold," p. 279.

69. Rainer to Bürckel, 6 July 1939, *NCA*, #812-PS, 3:595.

70. Zernatto, *Wahrheit*, p. 303.

71. Otto Reich von Rohrwig, *Der Freiheitskampf der Ostmark-Deutschen von St. Germain bis Adolf Hitler*, p. 433; Oswald Dutch, *Thus Died Austria*, pp. 198–99.

72. This was the opinion of Guido Zernatto who, as secretary of the Front, was hardly the most objective possible observer. See his *Wahrheit*, p. 242.

73. Ibid., pp. 234, 274.

74. Seyss-Inquart, "The Austrian Question," *NCA*, #3254-PS, 5:984; Wagner and Tomkowitz, *Anschluss*, p. 161.

75. Walter Pembauer, *Im letzten Kampf um Österreich*, pp. 175, 177; Zernatto, *Wahrheit*, p. 242; Eugene Lennhoff, *The Last Five Hours of Austria*, p. 205.

76. Gehl, *Austria, Germany, and the Anschluss*, p. 192; anonymous report from the files of Richard Riedl, NA, T-84, R. 16/44269–70.

77. Wagner and Tomkowitz, *Anschluss*, p. 132.

78. Zernatto, *Wahrheit*, p. 310. On the other hand, Brook-Shepherd asserts that only 5 percent of the army consisted of Nazi sympathizers (*The Anschluss*, p. 167).

79. Rainer to Bürckel, 6 July 1939, *NCA*, #812-PS, 3:596.

80. Wagner and Tomkowitz, *Anschluss*, p. 158.

81. Transcript of Telephone Conversation between Göring and Keppler, Berlin-Vienna, 11 Mar. 1938, 20:48–20:54, "Ministries Case," 12:729.

82. Interrogation of August Eigruber, 3 Nov. 1945, NA, NI, p. 17.

83. Transcript of Telephone Conversation between Göring and Keppler, Berlin-Vienna, 11 Mar. 1938, 20:48–20:54, "Ministries Case," 12:729.

84. On the controversy about the telegram see Extracts from the Closing Statements for the Defendent Keppler, ibid., 14:133; Seyss-Inquart, "The Austrian Question," *NCA*, #3254-PS, 5:583; Dutch, *Thus Died Austria*, p. 214; Leopold, "Arthur von Seyss-Inquart," pp. 97–98.

85. Wagner and Tomkowitz, *Anschluss*, pp. 139, 141–42; Luža, *Austro-German Relations*, p. 47.

86. Rosar, *Deutsche Gemeinschaft*, p. 230.

87. "Minute [by Altenburg]," 12 Mar. 1938, *DGFP*, D 1:585.

88. Wagner and Tomkowitz, *Anschluss*, p. 172.

89. Hans Völz, *et al.*, eds., *Dokumente der deutschen Politik, 1933–1938*, vol. 6, Part 1, p. 152.

Chapter XIII

1. Jürgen Gehl, *Austria, Germany, and the Anschluss*, p. 194; Dieter Wagner and Gerhard Tomkowitz, *Anschluss*, p. 206; John Toland, *Adolf Hitler*, p. 618.

2. Wolfgang Rosar, *Deutsche Gemeinschaft*, p. 306.

3. Seyss-Inquart, "The Austrian Question," *NCA*, #3254-PS, 5:989.

4. Radomír Luža, *Austro-German Relations in the Anschluss Era*, p. 57.

5. Wagner and Tomkowitz, *Anschluss*, p. 208; Karl Stadler, *Austria*, p. 150; Extracts from Closing Statements of Defendent Keppler, "Ministries Case," 14:145.

6. "The Chargé in Austria [Wiley] to the Secretary of State," 14 Mar. 1938, *FRUS*, 1938, 1:445.

7. Alfred Persche, "Hauptmann Leopold," DÖW, #1460, p. 349.

8. Ibid.; Stadler, *Austria*, pp. 182–83.

9. Harry Slapnicka, *Oberösterreich*, p. 198.

10. The quotations are from Shepherd, *The Austrian Odyssey*, pp. 135–36.

11. *FRUS*, 1938, 1:457.

12. Sworn statement of SS-Sturmbannführer Dr. Wilhelm Hoettl about SS-Sturmbannführer Eichmann, DÖW, #5051, pp. 16–17. Heydrich's distrust was not limited to Kaltenbrunner and Seyss-Inquart. He also kept a file on Himmler and even Hitler. See Joachim Fest, *The Face of the Third Reich*, p. 102.

13. Rainer to Bürckel, 7 July 1939, *NCA*, #812-PS, 3:587.

14. Persche, "Hauptmann Leopold," p. 288; Alfred Frauenfeld, "Rise of Nazism in Austria," interrogation of Frauenfeld, 26 May 1946, NA, NI, p. 2; Luža, *Austro-German Relations*, p. 92.

15. Gitta Sereny, *Into that Darkness*, pp. 102, 162–63.

16. John Bernbaum, "Nazi Control in Austria," p. 230.

17. Ibid., pp. 229, 234.

18. Letter from an Ortsgruppenleiter to the NSDAP Kreisleitung, Feldbach, 16 June 1940, DÖW, #8346, unpublished documents assembled for the *Rot-Weiss-Rot Buch*.

19. Persche, "Hauptmann Leopold," p. 345; interrogation of August Eigruber, 3 Nov. 1945, NA, NI, p. 7.

20. Persche, "Hauptmann Leopold," pp. 295–96.

21. Ibid., pp. 368–69.

22. Persche, "Hauptmann Leopold," p. 350.

23. Ernst Starhemberg, *Memoiren*, p. 334.

24. NSDAP Gaugericht, 19 Dec. 1939, BDC, PK, Walter Riehl folder, p. 1.

25. Harry Ritter, "Hermann Neubacher and the Austrian *Anschluss* Movement, 1918–40," p. 381.

26. Luža, *Austro-German Relations*, p. 92.

27. Starhemberg, *Memoiren*, p. 338.

28. Max Riedlsperger, *The Lingering Shadow of Nazism*, pp. 150–51, 163.

29. Interrogation of Siegfried Uiberreither, 1 Apr. 1946, NA, NI, p. 7.

30. Bradley Smith, *Reaching Judgment at Nuremberg*, pp. 213–15.

Chapter XIV

1. Gerard Silberstein, *The Troubled Alliance*.

2. Andrew Whiteside, "Austria," p. 360.

3. Alan Bullock, "Hitler and the Origins of the Second World War," p. 222, also pp. 225, 231–32.

4. Ronald Smelser, *The Sudeten Problem, 1933–1938*, p. 55.

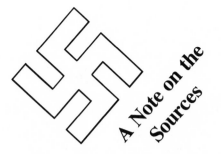

The sources for the study of Austrian National Socialism are scattered among a large number of archives, libraries, and institutes in Austria, Germany, and the United States. Probably the most important documentary collection is in microfilm at the National Archives in Washington, D.C.: the *World War II Collection of Seized Enemy Records*. Of these, the most frequently cited in this study are *The Records of the German Foreign Ministry* which contain reasonably objective reports by German diplomats in Austria on various activities of the Austrian Nazi party as well as other fascist groups, especially between 1930 and 1936. The more important of these documents have been translated and published by the United States Government Printing Office in the series *Documents on German Foreign Policy, 1918–1945*, *(DGFP)*, Series C, volumes I–V, and Series D, volume I.

By far the best primary source on the Austrian Nazi party for the late 1920s is the so-called Schumacher Sammlung (Slg. Sch.) at the Bundesarchiv in Koblenz, Germany. The letters of this collection exchanged between the Austrian Landesleitung and the Reichsleitung in Munich richly illustrate the many internecine quarrels of the early Austrian party.

The Dokumentationsarchiv des österreichischen Widerstandes (DÖW) in Vienna contains many original and reproduced documents relevant to the Austrian Nazi party. Especially helpful are the monthly situation reports (Monatliche Lageberichte, MLB) of the Austrian Security Directorate for the period after 1934, and two unpublished manuscripts by Alfred Persche: his 363-page "Hauptmann Leopold," and the less useful 450-page story of the "Aktion Hudal." Both accounts were written shortly after World War II. As the leader of the SA from 1936 to early 1938, Persche was an eyewitness to much of the intraparty intrigue and he presents vivid portrayals of the leading Nazi personalities. Although he clearly favored the Leopold faction, most of his more important observations have been confirmed by other sources. (See Ludwig Jedlicka, "Gauleiter Josef Leopold (1889–1941)," p. 161n.)

Some of the reports of the Austrian Security Directorate as well as sworn testimony and Austrian and German diplomatic correspondence can be found in *Der Hochverratsprozess gegen Dr. Guido Schmidt vor dem Wiener Volksgericht (Schmidt-prozess)*. Still another rich repository of documents for the Austrian Nazi party is the Allgemeines Verwaltungsarchiv (AVA) in Vienna.

Much biographical information on leading Austrian Nazis can be found in the Berlin Document Center (BDC) and in the *Records of the United States Nuremberg War Crimes Trials Interrogations, 1946–1949* (NI). These records have been indexed by the National Archives Trust Fund Board, but no distinction has been made between Germans and Austrians.

Newspapers are nearly as important for a study of Austrian National Socialism as documents. Clippings from all the major Austrian newspapers of the interwar years are carefully indexed by name and subject in the *Tagblatt* archive of the Arbeiterkammer in Vienna. The Austrian National Library has complete files of all the Austrian newspapers. Especially useful for this study was the *Deutsche Arbeiter-Presse (DAP)*, particularly for the years between 1919 and the party split in 1926. The Linzer *Volksstimme (Vkst*, after 1926 simply *Die Volksstimme*) was the leading Nazi journal between 1923 and 1933. The *Steirische Gaunachrichten der NSDAP*, though only a small, mimeographed newsletter, reveals much detailed Nazi strategy for the years 1931 to 1933. The illegal *Österreichischer Beobachter (ÖB)* tells a great deal about Nazi propaganda themes between 1934 and 1938.

Turning to secondary sources, two well-known surveys of Nazi history in general are Karl D. Bracher, *The German Dictatorship*, and Joachim C. Fest, *Hitler*. Karl Stadler's *Austria* is an overview of twentieth-century Austrian history from a distinctly Socialist point of view. An older, but still useful, survey is Heinrich Benedikt, ed., *Geschichte der Republik Österreich*, a portion of which was published later under the same title by Walter Goldinger.

An excellent, brief introduction to Austrian fascism is Andrew G. Whiteside's article, "Austria." A longer work that exploits the Austrian provincial archives is F. L. Carsten, *Fascist Movements in Austria*. Two Nazi works of a general nature are Karl Wache, ed., *Deutscher Geist in Österreich*, which is a collection of propagandistic articles by leading Austrian Nazis, and Hans Völz, *Daten der Geschichte der NSDAP*, which lists important dates and statistics.

On the origins of Austrian anti-Semitism and National Socialism see Peter G. J. Pulzer, *The Rise of Political Anti-Semitism in Germany and Austria*, and two books by Andrew G. Whiteside, *Austrian National Socialism before 1918* and *The Socialism of Fools*. An early Nazi work on the same subjects is Paul Molisch, *Geschichte der deutschnationalen Bewegung in Oesterreich von ihren Anfängen bis zum Zerfall der Monarchie*.

The early postwar years of the Austrian Nazis are covered in Max H. Kele's unpublished paper, "The Evolution of Austrian National Socialism from an Indigenous Party to an Appendage of Hitler's Movement," and the dissertation by Rudolf Brandstötter, "Dr. Walter Riehl und die nationalsozialistische Bewegung in Österreich." An early biography of Riehl is Alexander Schilling, *Dr. Walter Riehl und die Geschichte des Nationalsozialismus*. The strange love-hate relationship between the Styrian Heimatschutz and the Austrian Nazi party is explored in my *Hahnenschwanz und Hakenkreuz*. Additional, firsthand information can be found in the self-serving *Memoiren* of Ernst Rüdiger Starhemberg.

The organization and tactics of the Austrian Nazi party can best be seen in *Das Dienstbuch der NSDAP (Hitlerbewegung)* edited by the Landesleitung Österreichs der NSDAP with the special assistance of Theo Habicht. Information on the social composition of the Austrian party can be found in two articles by Gerhard Botz: "Faschismus und Lohnabhängige in der Ersten Republik" and his unpublished paper, "Aspects of the Social Structure of Austrian National Socialism (1918–1938)." Botz is also preparing a book-length study on the same subject. Erika Weinzierl-Fischer describes the Nazi appeal for Austrian Catholics in "Österreichs Katholiken und der Nationalsozialismus." A narrow but scholarly study of Austrian Nazi membership is Evan Bukey's unpublished work, "The Nazi Party in Linz, Austria, 1919–1939." An older but still useful study is Walter B. Simon's dissertation, "The Political Parties of Austria."

Gerhard Jagschitz has written several excellent articles related to the Austrian Nazis. His book, *Der Putsch*, is by far the best study of the July (1934) revolt. A collection of articles about the July Agreement of 1936 was published in 1977 by the Wissenschaftliche Kommission des Theodor-Körner Stiftungsfonds entitled *Das Abkommen von 1936*. Considerable information on the same topic as well as the Austrian Nazi party is found in Franz von Papen's autobiography, *Der Wahrheit eine Gasse* (translated as *Memoirs*).

Alfred Persche's manuscript, "Hauptmann Leopold," cited earlier, is the most revealing inside account of the years between 1936 and 1938. Covering the same years from the opposite side of the political fence is Kurt von Schuschnigg's memoirs, *The Brutal Takeover*. A far more objective account of the pre-Anschluss years is Wolfgang Rosar, *Deutsche Gemeinschaft*. Dieter Wagner and Gerhard Tomkowitz give an hour-by-hour narration of the German takeover in *Anschluss*. Radomír Luža provides some facts on the Austrian Nazis after the Anschluss in *Austro-German Relations in the Anschluss Era*. The aftermath of Austrian National Socialism is described in *The Lingering Shadow of Nazism* by Max Riedlsperger.

The posthumous memoirs of Alfred Frauenfeld (*Und trage keine Reu': Von Wiener Gauleiter zum Generalkommissar der Krim: Erinnerungen und Aufzeichnungen*. Leoni am Starnberger See: Druffel-Verlag, 1978) were published too late for extensive use in the text of this book. Frauenfeld's account, however, although containing numerous interesting and sometimes humorous anecdotes, adds little of substance to the information already cited in this book.

Frauenfeld maintains that Prince Starhemberg refused to enter a Nazi-Heimwehr coalition in the fall of 1930 only because he feared the government would force him to pay his overdue real estate taxes if he made common cause with the Nazis.

Frauenfeld also reveals that Gregor Strasser wanted to make him the Landesleiter in 1931, but chose Theo Habicht instead, owing to the jealousies his appointment would have aroused among the other Austrian *Gauleiter*.

The most interesting contention of Frauenfeld is his claim that Hitler was kept informed of the plans for the July Putsch by Frauenfeld and Habicht. Frauenfeld does not explain exactly what Hitler was told, however. Nor does Frauenfeld's assertion contradict the argument made in chapter eight that Hitler's role in the July Putsch was essentially passive. By not taking an active part in its planning he hoped to exploit the Putsch if it succeeded and dissociate himself from it if it failed. According to Frauenfeld, Hitler had made an agreement with Mussolini in June 1934 that neither man would interfere in Austrian affairs. In his account of the Putsch, Frauenfeld, over forty years after the event, is still anxious to show that he had not disobeyed the Führer's orders.

Bibliography

Documents and Manuscripts

Allgemeines Verwaltungsarchiv (AVA) (General Administrative Archive), Vienna.
NS Parteistellen, Information über des Gegner-Heimatschutz, carton 12.
NS Parteistellen, Organisation, Prozesse, carton 14.
SA, carton 19.
Berger-Waldenegg, Egon Baron. "Ungedruckte Erinnerungen des ehemaligen öster-
reichischen Aussenministers und Gesandten in Rom." Unpublished MS at the
Institut für Zeitgeschichte, Vienna (n.d.).
Berlin Document Center (BDC)
Nationalsozialistische Kartei. Personalakten (PA)
Fritz Lahr, Josef Leopold, Thomas Kozich, Johann Lukesch, Hermann Reschny,
Wolfgang Scholz, Arthur Seyss-Inquart, Leopold Tavs.
Parteikanzlei-Konrespondenz (PK)
Walter Gattermayer, Alfred Proksch, Walter Riehl.
SS-Führer
Hubert Klausner.
Bundesarchiv (Federal Archives), Koblenz, West Germany.
Sammlung Schumacher (Slg. Sch.).
277 Akten über den Anschluss des Steirischen Heimatschutz an die NSDAP.
302 Folder 1. Korrespondenz der Landesleitung Österreich der NSDAP, ab
1933–34.
303 Folder 1. Auflösung der NSDAP in Österreich und Wiederstehung in 1938.
305 Folders 1 and 2. Korrespondenz der Landesleitung der NSDAP in Österreich
mit den einzelnen Ortsgruppen sowie der Reichsleitung in München.
Dokumentationsarchiv des österreichischen Widerstandes (DÖW) (Documentation
Archive of the Austrian Resistance), Vienna. The following documents were
used in this study:
00087; 2162; 5001; 5053; 6014; 6036; 6115; 6155; 6184a; 6524; 7314; 7544;
7548; 8339; 8346; 8349; 8350; 8398.
Those documents not fully cited in the footnotes are:
1460 Alfred Persche, "Hauptmann Leopold: Der Abschnitt 1936–1938 der
Geschichte der nationalsozialistischen Machtergreifung in Österreich."
Unpublished MS (n.d.).
5116/1 Alfred Persche, "Die Aktion Hudal: Das letzte Aufgebot des Abend-
landes." 2 vols. Unpublished MS (n.d.).

6184a Monatliche Lageberichte/(MBL) des BKA/General Direktion für das
öffentliche Sicherheit (Monthly Situation Reports of the Austrian Security
Directorate), Vienna. December 1934–January 1938.

*Die Erhebung der österreichischen Nationalsozialisten im Juli 1934 (Akten der
Historischen Kommission des Reichsführers SS).* Arranged by Herbert Steiner.
Vienna, Frankfurt, and Zürich: Europa Verlag, 1965.

*Der Hochverratsprozess gegen Dr. Guido Schmidt vor dem Wiener Volksgericht: Die
gerichtliche Protokolle mit den Zeugenaussagen, unveröffentlichte Dokumenten,
sämtlichen Briefen und Geheimakten (Schmidt-Prozess).* Vienna: Verlag für der
österreichischen Staatsdrückerei, 1947.

International Military Tribunal. *Trials of the Major War Criminals before the International Military Tribunal* (IMT)
    Documents in Evidence, vols. 9, 34, 38, Nuremberg: International Military
    Tribunal, 1947–49.
    Case 11, "The Ministries Case." vols. 12, 14. Nuremberg: International Military
    Tribunal, October 1946–April 1949.

Kerekes, Lajos. "Akten zu den geheimen Verbindungen zwischen der Bethlen-
Regierung und der österreichischen Heimwehrbewegung." *Acta Historica* 11
(1965):299–339.

Landesgericht für Strafsachen (Provincial Court for Criminal Cases), Graz, Austria.
Kammerhofer-Prozess, 1949.

National Archives (NA), Washington, D.C.
World War II Collection of Seized Enemy Records.
    1. Records filmed at Alexandria, Virginia.
    Microcopy T-77. Reichswehr Ministry, reel 900.
    Microcopy T-78. Reichswehr Ministry, reels 455, 456.
    Microcopy T-84. Reichskommissar für die Wiedervereinigung Österreich mit
    dem Deutschen Reich, reels 5, 16.
    Microcopy T-175. Reichsführer SS and Chief of the German Police, reels 32,
    451.
    Microcopy T-580. Schumacher Material (Bundesarchiv, Koblenz, Germany),
    reels 61, 63.
    2. Records filmed at Whaddon Hall Bucks., England.
    Microcopy T-120. German Foreign Ministry Secret Documents, 1937–38,
    reel 751.
    Microcopy T-120, 1920–36, reels 1499, 2695, 2832, 2833, 2836, 2837, 2838,
    2889, 2892, 3393, 3394, 3395, 4494, 4633, 5415, 5416.

National Archives Trust Fund Board, *Records of the United States Nuremberg
War Crimes Trials Interrogations, 1946–1949* (NI). Washington, D.C.: National
Archives and Records Service General Service Administration, 1977. Record group
238. Materials relating to:
    Eigruber, August. 3 November 1945.
    Frauenfeld, Alfred. 26 May 1945, 9 July 1947.
    Neubacher, Hermann. 29 January 1946.
    Rainer, Friedrich. 8 July 1945, 3 November 1945, 6 November 1945,
    15 November 1945, 11 July 1946.
    Uiberreither, Siegfried. 8 July 1945, 1 April 1946.

Office of the United States Chief of Council for the Prosecution of Axis Criminality.
Nazi Conspiracy and Aggression (NCA). Washington, D.C.: U.S. Government
Printing Office, 1946. Supplement A and vols. 3, 4, 5.

Politisches Archiv des Auswärtiges Amt (PAAA) (Political Archives, Foreign Office),
Bonn, Germany.

Vienna Legation: Geiheimakten betreffend: Nationalismus, Faschismus, Heimwehr, Stahlhelm, Monarchismus, usw. von 1923 bis 1934, folders 3, 9.

Schumy, Vinzenz. "Ungedrukte Erinnerungen." Institut für Zeitgeschichte, Vienna. Unpublished MS written in 1938 and revised about 1960.

Stanford University. Hoover Institution Microfilm Collection. NSDAP Hauptarchiv (HI, NS-HA), Stanford, Calif. The Hoover Institution guide to the collection is *NSDAP: Guide to the Hoover Institution Microfilm Collection*, compiled by Grete Heinz and Agnes Peterson (Stanford, Calif.: The Hoover Institution on War, Revolution, and Peace, Stanford University, 1964).

Reel 33, folders 634, 635, 642

Tagblatt Archive (TA). This clippings collection originally assembled for the now-defunct *Neues Wiener Tagblatt* newspaper is located in the Arbeiterkammer in Vienna. The folders used in this study are:

Frauenfeld, Alfred

Leopold, Josef

NS-Führung

NS-Innere Konflikte

United States Department of State. *Documents on German Foreign Policy, 1918–1945 (DGFP)*. Series C, vols. 1, 2, 3, 4. Series D, vol. 1. Washington, D.C.: U.S. Government Printing Office, 1949–59.

————. *Foreign Relations of the United States: Diplomatic Papers*, 1934, vol. 2, 1938, vol. 1 (*FRUS*). Washington, D.C.: U.S. Government Printing Office, 1900.

Völz, Hans, *et al.*, eds. *Dokumente der deutschen Politik, 1933–1938*, vol. 6, part 1, 1938. Berlin: Junker und Dunnhaupt, 1939.

Newspapers and Periodicals

Arbeiterwille (Graz), 27 September 1931, 21 June 1933.

Arbeiter-Zeitung (*A–Z*, Vienna), 23 June 1928.

Deutsche Arbeiter-Presse: Nationalsozialistisches Wochenblatt (*DAP*, Vienna), 22 February 1919–25 May 1934.

Deutsche Grenzwacht (Radkersburg, Styria), 6 May 1921.

Deutsch-Österreichische Tages-Zeitung (Vienna), 3 July 1932.

Frankfurter *Zeitung*, 9 December 1932.

Das Hakenkreuz: Zeitschrift für völkische Politik, Wirtschaft und Kultur (Vienna), March–April 1926.

Der Heimatschützer (Vienna), 28 April 1934.

Informationsdienst der Vaterländische Front (*IdVF*, Vienna), 23 August 1934–20 November 1934.

Der Kampf (Graz), 14 March 1931–2 April 1933; 19 June 1934.

Der Kampfruf (Vienna), 3 February 1931–17 September 1932; June 1935.

Landbund-Stimmen (Graz), 27 April 1933.

Leipziger *Tagespost*, 11 March 1941.

Linzer *Volksblatt*, 22 May 1937.

Linzer *Volksstimme* (*Vkst*), 20 August 1923–25 September 1926. (Thereafter known as *Die Volksstimme*.)

Mitteilungen der Landespresse Amtes (illegal newsletter of the Landesleitung Österreich der NSDAP), 19 June 1936, 10 July 1936.

Der Morgen (Vienna), 29 August 1932.

Munzinger *Archiv*, 20 September 1934.

Der Nationalsozialist: Kampfblatt der Nationalsozialistischen Bewegung in Tirol

und Vorarlberg (Innsbruck), 10 January 1923.
Nationalsozialistische Monatshefte (*NSM*, Vienna), April–June 1928.
New York Times, 2 December 1928.
Österreichische Heimatschutz-Zeitung (*OH–Z*, Vienna), 11 March 1933.
Der Österreichischer Beobachter: Organ der N.S.D.A.P. in Österreich (*ÖB*), 28 July
    1936–January 1938 (mimeographed).
Der Panther (Judenburg, Styria), 16 January 1932–17 June 1933.
Pester Lloyd (Budapest), 2 April 1937.
Der Rote Adler: Kampfblatt der NSDAP für Tirol und Vorarlberg (Innsbruck),
    19 June 1934.
"Steirische Gaunachrichten der NSDAP" (Graz), 10 January 1931–30 May 1933
    (mimeographed).
Stimme der Heimat (Vienna), February 1936–September/October 1937.
Die Stunde (Vienna), 25 April 1924.
Der Tagblatt (*Tgb*, Graz), 14 October 1926, 10 November 1930, 6 October 1931.
Tagespost (Graz), 5 May 1932.
Die Volksstimme: Kampfblatt der Nationalsozialistischen Arbeiterpartei (*Hitler-
    bewegung*) (*Vkst*, Linz), 19 March 1927–14 May 1933.
Der Vormarsch: NS Nachrichtenblatt (Klagenfurt), 2 June 1933.

Interviews and Personal Correspondence with the Author

Frauenfeld, Eduard. Interview in Vienna, 17 July 1974.
Haag, John. Letter to the author, 16 November 1978.
Pfrimer, Walter. Interview in Judenburg (Styria), 2 July 1964.
Rath, R. John. Letter to the author, 26 July 1976.
Steiner, Herbert. Interview in Vienna, 18 July 1974.
Stepan, Karl Maria. Interview in Graz, 30 June 1964.
Strzygowski, Walter. Interview in Lincoln, Nebraska, 15 October 1960.
Tavs, Leopold. Interview in Vienna, 17 July 1974.

General

(Books, Articles in Journals and Books,
Theses and Dissertations)

Ackerl, Isabella. "Die Grossdeutsche Volkspartei." Ph.D. dissertation, University of
    Vienna, 1967.
_____. "Das Kampfbündnis der Nationalsozialistischen Deutschen Arbeiterpartei
    mit der Grossdeutschen Volkspartei vom 15. Mai 1933." Wissenschaftliche
    Kommission, "Das Jahr 1934. 25. Juli 1934."
Adler, Alois. *Die Historischen Fakten des Nationalsozialismus in Österreich.*
    Leibnitz: Retzhof, VBH Retzhof, 1968.
Allardyce, Gilbert. "What Fascism Is Not: Thoughts on the Deflation of a Concept."
    American Historical Review 84 (April 1979): 367–98.
Allen, William Sheridan. "The Appeal of Fascism and the Problem of National
    Disintegration." In Henry A. Turner, Jr., ed., *Reappraisals of Fascism.* New
    York: New Viewpoints, 1975: 44–68.
Auer, Johann. "Antisemitische Strömungen in Wien, 1921–1923." *Österreich in
    Geschichte und Literatur* 10 (1966): 23–27.

_____. "Zwei Aufenthalte Hitlers in Wien." *Vierteljahrshefte für Zeitgeschichte* 14 (April 1966): 207–208.

Auerbach, Hellmuth. "Eine nationalsozialistische Stimme zum Wiener Putsch vom 15. Juli 1934." *Vierteljahrshefte für Zeitgeschichte* 12 (1964): 201–18.

Ball, Mary Margaret. *Post-War German-Austrian Relations.* Stanford, Cal.: Stanford University Press, 1937.

Bärnthaler, Imgard. *Die Vaterländische Front: Geschichte und Organisation.* Vienna, Frankfurt, and Zürich: Europa Verlag, 1971.

Barth, Werner. "Germany and the Anschluss." Ph.D. dissertation, University of Texas, 1954.

Beiträge zur Vorgeschichte und Geschichte der Julirevolte. Vienna: Bundeskommissariat für Heimatdienst, 1934.

Benedikt, Heinrich, ed. *Geschichte der Republik Österreich.* Vienna: Verlag für Geschichte und Politik, 1954.

Benedikt, Ursula. "Vinzenz Schumy, 1878–1962: Eine politische Biographie." Ph.D. dissertation, University of Vienna, 1966.

Berger, Barbara. "Ernst Rüdiger Fürst Starhemberg: Versuch einer Biographie." Ph.D. dissertation, University of Vienna, 1967.

Berghahn, Volker R. *Der Stahlhelm: Bund der Frontsoldaten, 1918–1935.* Düsseldorf: Droste Verlag, 1966.

Bernbaum, John A. "Nazi Control in Austria: The Creation of the Ostmark, 1918–1940." Ph.D. dissertation, University of Maryland, 1972.

Bleyer-Härtl, Hans. *Ringen um Reich und Recht: Zwei Jahrzenten politischer Anwalt in Österreich.* Berlin: Kolk, 1939.

Borkenau, Franz. *Austria and After.* London: Faber & Faber, 1938.

Botz, Gerhard. "Aspects of the Social Structure of Austrian National Socialism (1918–1939)." Unpublished paper prepared for the Bergen (Norway) Conference on Comparative European Nazism/Fascism, June 1974.

_____. "Faschismus und Lohnabhängige in der Ersten Republik: Zur 'sozialen Basis' und propagandistischen Orientierung von Heimwehr und Nationalsozialismus." *Österreich in Geschichte und Literatur* 21 (March–April 1977): 102–28.

_____. *Gewalt in der Politik: Attentate, Zusammenstösse, Putschversuche, Unruhen in Österreich, 1918–1934.* Munich: Wilhelm Fink Verlag, 1976.

_____. *Wien vom "Anschluss" zum Krieg: Nationalsozialistische Machtübernahme und politisch-soziale Umgestaltung am Beispiel der Stadt Wien, 1938–39.* Vienna and Munich: Jugend und Volk, 1978.

Bracher, Karl D. *The German Dictatorship: The Origins, Structure, and Effects of National Socialism.* Translated by Jean Steinberg. New York and Washington, D.C.: Frederick Praeger, 1970.

Brandstötter, Rudolf. "Dr. Walter Riehl und die nationalsozialistische Bewegung in Österreich." Ph.D. dissertation, University of Vienna, 1970.

Braunthal, Julius. *The Tragedy of Austria.* London: V. Gollancz, 1938.

Brook-Shepherd, Gordon. *The Anschluss.* Philadelphia and New York: J. B. Lippincott, 1963. [See also Shepherd, Gordon.]

Bukey, Evan B. "The Nazi Party in Linz, Austria, 1919–1939: A Sociological Perspective." Unpublished paper prepared for the Western Association for German Studies, Tempe, Arizona, October 1977.

Bullock, Alan. "Hitler and the Origins of the Second World War." *Nazism and the Third Reich.* Edited by Henry A. Turner, Jr. New York: Quadrangle Books, 1972: 219–46.

_____. *Hitler: A Study in Tyranny.* New York: Bantam Books, 1961.

Bullock, Malcolm. *Austria 1918–1938: A Story of Failure*. London: Macmillan & Co., 1939.

Bundeskommissariat für Heimatdienst. *Beiträge zur Vorgeschichte und Geschichte der Julirevolte*. Vienna, 1934.

Busshoff, Heinrich. *Das Dollfuss-Regime in Österreich in geistesgeschichtlicher Perspektive unter besonderer Berücksichtigung der "Schöneren Zukunft" und "Reichspost."* Berlin: Duncker & Humblot, 1968.

Buttinger, Joseph. *Am Beispiel Österreichs: Ein geschichtlicher Beitrag zur Krise der sozialistischen Bewegung*. Cologne: Kiepenheuer & Witsch, 1953.

Carsten, F. L. *Fascist Movements in Austria: From Schönerer to Hitler*. Sage Studies in 20th Century History. Edited by Walter Laqueur and George L. Mosse. London and Beverly Hills, Cal.: Sage Publications, 1977.

Carsten, Francis L. "Interpretations of Fascism." *Fascism: A Reader's Guide: Analyses, Interpretations, Bibliography*. Berkeley and Los Angeles: University of California Press, 1976: 515–34.

———. *The Rise of Fascism*. Berkeley and Los Angeles: University of California Press, 1971.

Cassels, Alan. *Fascism*. New York: Thomas Y. Crowell Co., 1975.

———. "Janus: The Two Faces of Fascism." *Reappraisals of Fascism*. Edited by Henry A. Turner, Jr. New York: New Viewpoints, 1975: 69–92.

Ciller, Alois. *Deutscher Sozialismus in den Sudetenländer und der Ostmark*. Hamburg: Hanseatische Verlagsanstalt, 1939.

Cohrs, Heinz. "Das Innere Gefüge der N.S.D.A.P. Österreichs." *Deutscher Geist in Österreich*. Edited by Karl Wache. Dornbirn and Vorarlberg: C. Bruton-Verlag, 1933: 287–306.

Dachauer, Max. *Das Ende Österreich*. Berlin: Vaterländischer Verlag, C. A. Weller, 1939.

Diamant, Alfred. *Austrian Catholics and the First Austrian Republic: Democracy, Capitalism and the Social Order, 1918–1934*. Princeton, N.J.: Princeton University Press, 1960.

Diehl, James M. *Paramilitary Politics in Weimar Germany*. Bloomington and London: Indiana University Press, 1977.

Dutch, Oswald [Otto Deutsch]. *Thus Died Austria*. London: Edward Arnold & Co., 1938.

Edlinger, Günther. "Friedrich Funder und die 'Reichspost' in ihrer Stellungnahme zur Politik des Nationalsozialismus gegenüber Österreich von 1930 bis zum Anschluss 1938." Ph.D. dissertation, University of Vienna, 1964.

Edmondson, C. Earl. "Early Heimwehr Aims and Activities." *Austrian History Yearbook* 8 (1972): 105–47.

———. *The Heimwehr and Austrian Politics, 1918–1936*. Athens, Ga.: University of Georgia Press, 1978.

Eichstädt, Ulrich. *Von Dollfuss zu Hitler: Geschichte des Anschlusses Österreichs*. Wiesbaden: Franz Steiner Verlag, 1955.

Eschenburg, Theodor. "Franz von Papen." *Vierteljahrshefte für Zeitgeschichte* 1 (1953): 153–69.

Eubank, Keith. *The Origins of World War II*. New York: Thomas Y. Crowell Co., 1969.

Feldman, Angela. "Landbund für Österreich: Ideologie, Organisation, Politik." Ph.D. dissertation, University of Vienna, 1967.

Fessl, Christine. "Die Innenpolitische Entwicklung in Österreich in den Jahren 1934 bis 1938." Ph.D. dissertation, University of Vienna, 1967.

Fest, Joachim C. *The Face of the Third Reich: Portraits of the Nazi Leadership*.

Translated by Michael Bullock. New York: Pantheon Books, 1970.

_____. *Hitler*. New York: Vintage, 1975.

Fodor, M. W. *Plot and Counterplot in Central Europe*. London: Harper & Brothers, 1939.

Fraenkel, Josef. *The Jews of Austria: Essays on their Life, History and Destruction*. London: Vallentine, Mitchell, 1967.

Franz-Willing, Georg. *Die Hitlerbewegung: Der Ursprung, 1919–1922*. Hamburg and Berlin: R. von Decker's Verlag G. Schenck, 1962.

Frauenfeld, A. E. "Der Aufstieg des Gaues Wien der N.S.D.A.P." *Deutscher Geist in Österreich*. Edited by Karl Wache. Dornbirn: C. Bruton Verlag, 1933: 281–305.

Friedrich, Carl J.; and Brzezinski, Zbigniew K. *Totalitarian Dictatorship and Autocracy*. 2nd ed. New York, Washington, D.C., and London: Frederick A. Praeger, 1966.

Frisch, Hans. *Die Gewaltherrschaft in Österreich, 1933 bis 1938: Eine staatsrechtliche Untersuchung*. Leipzig and Vienna: Günther, 1938.

Frischauer, Willi. *The Rise and Fall of Hermann Goering*. New York: Ballantine Books, 1951.

Fuchs, Albert. *Geistige Strömungen in Österreich, 1867–1918*. Vienna: Globus Verlag, 1949.

Fuchs, Martin. *Showdown in Vienna*. New York: G. P. Putnam's Sons, 1939.

Funder, Friedrich. *From Empire to Republic: An Austrian Editor Reviews Momentous Years*. New York: Albert Unger, 1964.

Gasselich, Anton. "Landbund für Österreich." *Deutscher Geist in Österreich*. Edited by Karl Wache. Dornbirn: C. Bruton Verlag, 1933: 227–40.

Gedye, G. E. R. *Fallen Bastions (Betrayal in Central Europe)*. London: Harper & Brothers, 1939.

Gehl, Jürgen. *Austria, Germany, and the Anschluss, 1931–38*. London: Oxford University Press, 1963.

Gold, Hugo. *Geschichte der Juden in Wien: Ein Gedenkbuch*. Tel Aviv: Olamenu, 1966.

Goldhammer, Leo. *Die Juden Wiens: Eine statistische Studie*. Vienna: Löwit, 1927.

Goldinger, Walter. *Geschichte der Republik Österreich*. Vienna: Verlag für Geschichte und Politik, 1962.

Grilliet, Helene. *Eine Französin Erlebt Grossdeutschland*. Graz: Ulrich Moser Verlag, 1938.

Grunberger, Richard. *The 12-Year Reich: A Social History of Nazi Germany*. New York: Ballantine Books, 1972.

Gulick, Charles A. *Austria from Habsburg to Hitler*, 2 vols. Vol. 1, *Labor's Workshop of Democracy*. Vol. 2, *Fascism's Subversion of Democracy*. Berkeley and Los Angeles: University of California Press, 1948.

Haag, John. "Blood on the Ringstrasse: Vienna's Students, 1918–33." *The Wiener Library Bulletin* 29 (1976): 29–34.

Hagtvet, Bernt. "The Theory of Mass Society and the Dissolution of Parliamentary Democracy: A Reappraisal with Respect to the Weimar Case." Unpublished paper prepared for the Bergen (Norway) Conference on Comparative European Nazism/Fascism, June 1974.

Haintz, Raimund. "Die Nationalsozialistische Deutsche Arbeiterpartei (N.S.D.A.P.)." *Deutscher Geist in Österreich*. Edited by Karl Wache. Dornbirn: C. Bruton Verlag, 1933: 251–80.

Hantsch, Hugo. *Die Geschichte Österreichs*. Vol. 2, *1648–1918*. Graz: Verlag Styria, 1953.

Hartlieb Wladimir von. *Parole: Das Reich! Historische Darstellung der politischen*

Entwicklung in Österreich von März 1933 bis März 1938. Vienna: Adolf Luser Verlag, 1939.

Hartmann, Mitzi [pseud.]. *Austria Still Lives.* London: Michael Joseph, 1938.

Haubenberger, Leo. *Nationalsozialistische Jahrbuch.* Vienna: Verlag der Völkischen Buchhandlung, 1926.

Hausner, Gideon. *Justice in Jerusalem.* New York: Harper & Row, 1966.

Heer, Friedrich. *Gottes erste Liebe: 2000 Jahre Judentum und Christentum; Genesis des österreichischen Katholiken Adolf Hitler.* Munich: Bechtle, 1967.

Heiden, Konrad. *Geschichte des Nationsozialismus: Die Karriere einer Idee.* Berlin: Rowohlt, 1932.

Heineman, John L. *Hitler's First Foreign Minister: Constantin Freiherr von Neurath, Diplomat and Statesman.* Los Angeles and London: University of California Press, 1979.

Hertz, Friedrich. *The Economic Problems of the Danubian States: A Study in Economic Nationalism.* London: V. Gollancz, 1947.

Hitler, Adolf. *Mein Kampf.* Translated by Ralph Mannheim. Boston: Houghton Mifflin, 1943. Originally published in 1927.

Holborn, Hajo. *A History of Modern Germany.* Vol. 3, *1840–1945.* New York: Alfred A. Knopf, 1969.

Holtmann, Everhard. "Zwischen 'Blutschuld' und 'Befriedung': Autoritäre Julijustiz." Unpublished paper prepared for the Wissenschaftliche Kommission. Tagung am 8. Oktober 1974. "Das Jahr 1934. 25. Juli 1934."

Hoor, Ernst. *Österreich 1918–1938: Staat ohne Nation, Republik ohne Republikaner.* Vienna and Munich: Österreichischer Bundesverlag für Unterricht, Wissenschaft, und Kunst, 1966.

Hoover, Herbert. *The Memoirs of Herbert Hoover.* Vol. 1, *Years of Adventure, 1874–1920.* New York: Macmillan Co., 1951.

Houston, W. Robert. "Ernst Kaltenbrunner: A Study of an Austrian SS and Police Leader." Ph.D. dissertation, Rice University, 1972.

Hubbard, William H. "Politics and Society in the Central European City: Graz, Austria, 1861–1918." *Canadian Journal of History* 5 (March 1970): 25–45.

Hübener, Karl-Rudolf. "Illegale österreichische Presse von 1933 bis 1938." Ph.D. dissertation, University of Vienna, 1969.

Huebmer, Hans. *Österreich 1933–1938: Der Abwehrkampf eines Volkes.* Vienna: Österreichischer Verlag, 1949.

Humor der Illegalen: Österreichische Anekdoten und Witze aus der Verbotszeit. Vienna: Verlag Faber, 1938.

Ingrim, Robert [Franz Klein]. *Der Griff nach Österreich.* Zürich: Europa Verlag, 1938.

Jagschitz, Gerhard. "Die Anhaltelager in Österreich (1933–1938)." *Vom Justizpalast zum Heldenplatz.* Edited by Ludwig Jedlicka and Rudolf Neck. Vienna: Druck und Verlag der Österreichischen Staatsdruckerei, 1975: 128–51.

———. "Zwischen Befriedung und Konfrontation: Zur Lage der NSDAP in Österreich 1934 bis 1936." *Das Juliabkommen von 1936.* Edited by the Wissenschaftliche Kommission. Vienna: Verlag für Geschichte und Politik, 1977: 156–87.

———. "Bundeskanzler Dollfuss und der Juli 1934." *Österreich 1927 bis 1938.* Edited by the Wissenschaftliche Kommission. Vienna: Verlag für Geschichte und Politik, 1973: 150–60.

———. "Faschismus und Nationalsozialismus in Österreich bis 1945." *Fascism and Europe: An International Symposium.* Edited by the Institute of History, Czechoslovak Academy of Sciences, August 1969: 66–83.

———. "Die Jugend des Bundeskanzlers Dr. Engelbert Dollfuss: Ein Beitrag zur geistig-politischen Situation der sogenannten Kriegsgenerations des 1. Welt-krieges." Ph.D. dissertation, University of Vienna, 1967.

_____. *Der Putsch: Die Nationalsozialisten 1934 in Österreich.* Graz, Vienna, and Cologne: Verlag Styria, 1976.

_____. "Zur Struktur der NSDAP vor dem Juliputsch 1934." Unpublished paper prepared for the Wissenschaftliche Kommission. Tagung am 8. Oktober 1974. "Das Jahr 1934. 25. Juli 1934."

Jedlicka, Ludwig. *Vom alten zum Neuen Österreich: Fallstudien zur österreichischen Zeitgeschichte, 1900–1975.* St. Pölten: Niederösterreichisches Pressehaus, 1975.

_____. "Die Anfänge des Rechtsradikalismus in Österreich (1918–1925)." *Wissenschaft und Weltbild* 24, no. 2 (Vienna, 1971): 96–110.

_____. "The Austrian Heimwehr." *Journal of Contemporary History* 1, no. 1 (1966): 127–44.

_____. "Ernst Rüdiger Fürst Starhemberg und die politische Entwicklung in Österreich im Fruhjahr 1938." *Österreich und Europa: Festgabe für Hugo Hantsch zum 70. Geburtstag.* Graz, Vienna, and Cologne: Verlag Styria, 1965: 547–64.

_____. "Gauleiter Josef Leopold (1889–1941)." *Geschichte und Gesellschaft: Festschrift für Karl R. Stadler.* Edited by Gerhard Botz, Hans Hautmann, and Helmut Konrad. Vienna: Europa Verlag, 1974: 143–61.

Jedlicka, Ludwig; and Neck, Rudolf, eds. *Vom Justizpalast zum Heldenplatz: Studien und Dokumentationen, 1927 bis 1938.* Vienna: Druck und Verlag der österreichischen Staatsdruckerei, 1975.

Jenks, William Allen. *Vienna and the Young Hitler.* New York: Columbia University Press, 1960.

Die Juli-Revolte 1934: Das Eingreifen des österreichischen Bundesheeres zu ihrer Niederwerfung. Vienna: Im Auftrag des Bundesministeriums für Landesverteidigung gedruckt, 1936.

Jung, Karl. "Die Grossdeutsche Volkspartei." *Deutscher Geist in Österreich.* Edited by Karl Wache. Dornbirn: C. Bruton Verlag, 1933: 173–226.

_____. "Die Völkische Presse in Österreich." *Deutscher Geist in Österreich.* Edited by Karl Wache. Dornbirn: C. Bruton Verlag, 1933: 345–52.

Kater, Michael H. "Quantifizierung und NS-Geschichte: Methodologische Überlegungen über Grenzen und Möglichkeiten einer EDV-Analyse der NDSAP-sozialstruktur von 1925 bis 1945." *Geschichte und Gesellschaft* 3 (1977): 453–84.

_____. "The Social Composition of the Nazi Party's Membership, 1925–1945: An Exercise in Descriptive Statistics." Unpublished paper prepared for the American Historical Association, Dallas, Texas, December 1977.

Katzenstein, Peter J. *Disjoined Partners: Austria and Germany since 1815.* Berkeley and Los Angeles: University of California Press, 1976.

Kele, Max H. "The Evolution of Austrian National Socialism from an Indigenous Party to an Appendage of Hitler's Movement." Unpublished paper prepared for the Southern Historical Association convention, New Orleans, La., November 1977.

_____. *Nazis and Workers: National Socialist Appeals to German Labor.* Chapel Hill, N.C.: University of North Carolina Press, 1972.

Kendrick, Clyde K. "Austria under the Chancellorship of Engelbert Dollfuss." Ph.D. dissertation, Georgetown University, 1958.

Kerekes, Lajos. "Die 'Weisse Allianz': Bayrisch-österreichisch-ungarische Projekte gegen die Regierung Renner im Jahre 1920." *Österreichische Ostheft* 7 (1965): 353–66.

_____. "Wirtschaftliche und soziale Lage Österreichs nach dem Zerfall der Doppelmonarchie." *Beiträge zur Zeitgeschichte.* Edited by Rudolf Neck and Adam Wandruszka. St. Pölten: Verlag Niederösterreichisches Pressehaus, 1976: 81–94.

Kleinwächter, Friedrich. *Von Schönbrunn bis St. Germain: Die Entstehung der Republik Österreich.* Graz: Verlag Styria, 1964.

Klemperer, Klemens von. "Chancellor Seipel and the Crisis of Democracy in Austria." *Journal of Central European Affairs* 22 (January 1963): 468–78.

———. *Ignaz Seipel: Christian Statesman in a Time of Crisis.* Princeton, N.J.: Princeton University Press, 1972.

Klingenstein, Grete. "Bemerkungen zum Problem des Faschismus in Österreich." *Österreich in Geschichte und Literatur* 14 (January–February 1970): 1–13.

Koerner, Ralf R. *So haben sie es damals gemacht: Die Propaganda Vorbereitungen zum Österreich-Anschluss durch das Hitler-Regime, 1933 bis 1938.* Vienna: Gesellschaft zur Föderung wissenschaftlicher Forschung, 1958.

Kogelnik, Sepp, ed. *Österreichisches Heimatschutz-Jahrbuch 1933.* Graz: Landesleitung des Heimatschutzverbandes Steiermark, 1934.

Kohn, Hans. "AEIOU: Some Reflections on the Meaning and Mission of Austria." *Journal of Modern History* 11 (December 1939): 513–27.

Kollmann, Eric C. "The Austrian Presidency, 1918–1958." *Austrian History Yearbook* 1 (1966): 90–117.

Kolnai, Aurel. "The Problem of Austrian Nationhood." *Journal of Central European Affairs* 2 (October 1942): 290–309.

Kondert, Reinhart. "The Rise and Early History of the Austrian 'Heimwehr' Movement." Ph.D. dissertation, Rice University, 1971.

Kreissler, Felix. *Von der Revolution zur Annexion: Österreich 1918 bis 1938.* Vienna, Frankfurt, and Zürich: Europa Verlag, 1970.

Landesleitung Österreichs der NSDAP (Hitlerbewegung). *Das Dienstbuch der NSDAP: Österreichs Hitlerbewegung.* Linz, 1932.

Langoth, Franz. *Kampf um Österreich: Erinnerungen eines Politikers.* Wels: Verlag Welsermühl, 1951.

Laqueur, Walter, ed. *Fascism: A Reader's Guide: Analyses, Interpretations, Bibliography.* Berkeley and Los Angeles: University of California Press, 1976.

Layton, Roland V., Jr. "The *Völkischer Beobachter,* 1920–1933: The Nazi Party Newspaper in the Weimar Era." *Central European History* 3 (December 1970): 353–82.

Leavey, William J. "Hitler's Envoy 'Extraordinary'—Franz von Papen: Ambassador to Austria, 1934–1938 and Turkey, 1939–1944." Ph.D. dissertation, St. John's University, 1968.

Lennhoff, Eugene. *The Last Five Hours of Austria.* London: Rich & Lowan, 1939.

Leopold, John A. "Arthur von Seyss-Inquart and the Austrian Anschluss." M.A. thesis, Catholic University, 1964.

Levine, Herbert S. *Hitler's Free City: A History of the Nazi Party in Danzig, 1925–39.* Chicago and London: University of Chicago Press, 1973.

Linz, Juan J. "Some Notes Toward a Comparative Study of Fascism in Sociological Historical Perspective." *Fascism: A Reader's Guide.* Edited by Walter Laqueur. Berkeley and Los Angeles: University of California Press, 1976: 3–121.

———. "Some Notes Toward a Comparative Study of Top Fascist Leaders." Unpublished paper prepared for the Bergen (Norway) Conference on Comparative European Nazism/Fascism, June 1974.

Lorenz, Reinhold. *Der Staat wider Willen: Österreich 1918–38.* Berlin: Junker und Dünnhaupt Verlag, 1941.

Low, Alfred D. *The Anschluss Movement, 1918–1919 and the Paris Peace Conference.* Philadelphia: American Philosophical Society, 1974.

Luža, Radomír. *Austro-German Relations in the Anschluss Era*. Princeton, N.J.: Princeton University Press, 1975.

Maas, Walter B. *Assassination in Vienna*. New York: Charles Scribner's Sons, 1972.

Macartney, C. A. "The Armed Formations in Austria." *International Affairs* (London, November 1929): 618–32.

———. *The Habsburg Monarchy, 1790–1918*. New York: Macmillan Co., 1969.

———. *The Social Revolution in Austria*. Cambridge: Cambridge University Press, 1926.

Macartney, C. A.; and Palmer, A. W. *Independent Eastern Europe: A History*. London: St. Martin's Press, 1966.

MacDonald, Mary. *The Republic of Austria, 1918–1934: A Study in the Failure of a Democratic Government*. London: Oxford University Press, 1946.

McKale, Donald M. *The Nazi Party Courts: Hitler's Management of Conflict in His Movement, 1921–1945*. Lawrence, Manhattan, and Wichita: University Press of Kansas, 1974.

———. *The Swastika Outside Germany*. Kent, Ohio: Kent State University Press, 1977.

Maderegger, Sylvia. *Die Juden im österreichischen Ständestaat 1934–1938*. Vienna and Salzburg: Geyer-Edition, 1973.

Maser, Werner. *Die Frühgeschichte der NSDAP: Hitlers Weg bis 1924*. Frankfurt am Main and Bonn: Athenäum Verlag, 1965.

———. *Hitler: Legend Myth & Reality*. New York: Harper & Row, 1971.

May, Arthur J. *The Hapsburg Monarchy, 1867–1914*. Cambridge, Mass.: Harvard University Press, 1961.

Merkl, Peter H. "The Nazis of the Abel Collection: Why They Joined." Unpublished paper prepared for the Bergen (Norway) Conference on Comparative European Nazism/Fascism, June 1974.

———. *Political Violence under the Swastika: 581 Early Nazis*. Princeton, N.J.: Princeton University Press, 1975.

Messerer, Ingeborg. "Die Frontkämpfervereinigung Deutsch-Österreichs: Ein Beitrag zur Geschichte der Wehrverbände in der Republik Österreich." Ph.D. dissertation, University of Vienna, 1964.

Messinger, Johann, trans. *The Death of Dollfuss*. London: Denis Archer, 1935.

Mikoletzky, Hans L. *Österreichische Zeitgeschichte vom Ende der Monarchie bis zum Abschluss des Staatsvertrages*. Vienna: Österreichischer Bundesverlag, 1962.

Mitrany, David. *The Effects of the War on Southeastern Europe*. New Haven, Conn.: Yale University Press, 1936.

Molisch, Paul. *Geschichte der deutschnationalen Bewegung in Oesterreich von ihren Anfängen bis zum Zerfall der Monarchie*. Jena: Gustav Fischer, 1926.

Moschner, Richard. *Kärnten: Grenzland im Süden*. Die deutschen Gaue seit der Machtergreifung. Edited by Paul Meier-Benneckenstein. Berlin: Junker und Dünnhaupt Verlag, 1940.

Müller, Herbert. "Heimatschutzbewegung, Heimatwehr, Heimwehr, Heimatbund, Heimatblock-Partei." *Deutscher Geist in Österreich*. Edited by Karl Wache. Dornbirn: C. Bruton Verlag, 1933: 241–49.

Myers, Duane P. "Berlin *versus* Vienna: Disagreement about *Anschluss* in the Winter of 1918–1919." *Central European History* 4 (1972): 150–75.

Neck, Rudolf. "Simmering—16. Oktober 1932 (Symptom und Auftakt der österreichische Tragödie)." *Beiträge zur Zeitgeschichte*. Edited by Rudolf Neck and Adam Wandruszka. St. Pölten: Verlag Niederösterreichisches Pressehaus, 1976: 95–112.

Neck, Rudolf; and Wandruszka, Adam, eds. *Beiträge zur Zeitgeschichte: Festschrift Ludwig Jedlicka zum 60. Geburtstag*. St. Pölten: Verlag Niederösterreichisches Pressehaus, 1976.

Neugebauer, Wolfgang. "Politische Justiz in Österreich, 1934–1945." *Jüstiz und Zeitgeschichte*. Edited by Erika Weinzerl-Fischer and Karl R. Stadler. Salzburg: Ludwig Boltzmann-Instituts für Geschichte der Gesellschaftswissenschaften, 1977: 169–209.

Noakes, Jeremy. *The Nazi Party in Lower Saxony, 1921–1933*. London: Oxford University Press, 1971.

Nolte, Ernst. *Die Krise des liberalen Systems und die faschistischen Bewegungen*. Munich: R. Piper & Co. Verlag, 1968.

———. *Three Faces of Fascism: Action Francaise, Italian Fascism, National Socialism*. New York, Chicago, and San Francisco: Holt, Rinehart, and Winston, 1966.

Nyomarkay, Joseph. "Factionalism in the National Socialist German Workers' Party, 1925–26: The Myth and Reality of the 'Northern Opposition.'" *Nazism and the Third Reich*. Edited by Henry A. Turner, Jr. New York: Quadrangle Books, 1972: 21–44.

Orlow, Dietrich. *The History of the Nazi Party, 1919–1933*. Pittsburgh: University of Pittsburgh Press, 1969.

———. *The History of the Nazi Party, 1933–1945*. Pittsburgh: University of Pittsburgh Press, 1975.

Otruba, Gustav. "Hitlers 'Tausend-Mark-Sperre' und Österreichs Fremdenverkehr 1933." *Beiträge zur Zeitgeschichte*. Edited by Rudolf Neck and Adam Wandruszka. St. Pölten: Verlag Niederösterreichisches Pressehaus, 1976: 113–62.

Papen, Franz von. *Memoirs*. Translated by Brian Connelly. London: A. Deutsch, 1962.

———. *Der Wahrheit eine Gasse*. Munich: Paul List Verlag, 1952.

Pasvolsky, Leo. *Economic Nationalism of the Danubian States*. New York: Macmillan Co., 1928.

Pauley, Bruce F. "Fascism and the *Führerprinzip*: The Austrian Example." *Central European History* 12 (September 1979): 272–96.

———. *The Habsburg Legacy, 1867–1939*. New York: Holt, Rinehart, and Winston, 1972.

———. *Hahnenschwanz und Hakenkreuz: Steirischer Heimatschutz und österreichischer Nationalsozialismus, 1918–1934*. Vienna, Frankfurt, and Zürich: Europa Verlag, 1972.

Pembauer, Walter. *Im letzten Kampf um Österreich*. Vienna: Johannes-Günther Verlag, 1939.

Petersen, Jens. *Hitler-Mussolini: Die Entstehung der Achse Berlin-Rom, 1933–1936*. Tübingen: Max Niemeyer Verlag, 1973.

Peterson, Edward N. *The Limits of Hitler's Power*. Princeton, N.J.: Princeton University Press, 1969.

Pinson, Koppel S.; and Epstein, Klaus. *Modern Germany: Its History and Civilization*. 4th ed. New York and London: Macmillan Co., 1966.

Pisecky, Franz. *Tirol-Vorarlberg*. Die deutschen Gauen seit der Machtergreifung. Edited by Paul Meier-Benneckenstein. Berlin: Junker und Dünnhaupt Verlag, 1940.

Pridham, Geoffrey. *Hitler's Rise to Power: The Nazi Movement in Bavaria, 1923–1933*. New York: Harper Torchbooks, 1973.

Pulzer, Peter G. J. *The Rise of Political Anti-Semitism in Germany and Austria*. New York, London, and Sydney: John Wiley & Sons, 1964.

Rape, Ludger. "Die österreichische Heimwehr und ihre Beziehungen zur bayerischen Rechten zwischen 1920 und 1923." Ph.D. dissertation, University of Vienna, 1969.

Rath, R. John. "Authoritarian Austria." *Native Fascism in the Successor States.* Edited by Peter F. Sugar. Santa Barbara, Cal.: ABC Clio, 1971: 24–43.

_____. "The First Austrian Republic—Totalitarian, Fascist, Authoritarian, or What?" *Beiträge zur Zeitgeschichte.* Edited by Rudolf Neck and Adam Wandruszka. St. Pölten: Verlag Niederösterreichisches Pressehaus, 1976: 163–88.

_____. "Training for Citizenship, 'Authoritarian' Austrian Style." *Journal of Central European Affairs* 3 (July 1943): 121–46.

Reich von Rohrwig, Otto. *Der Freiheitskampf der Ostmark-Deutschen von St. Germain bis Adolf Hitler.* Graz: Leopold Stocker Verlag, 1939.

Rich, Norman. *Hitler's War Aims.* Vol. 1. *Ideology, the Nazi State, and the Course of Expansion.* New York: W. W. Norton, 1973.

Riedlsperger, Max. *The Lingering Shadow of Nazism: The Austrian Independent Party Movement Since 1945.* New York: Columbia University Press, 1978.

Rintelen, Anton. *Erinnerungen an Österreichs Weg.* Munich: Verlag F. Bruckmann, 1942.

Ritter, Harry R. "Hermann Neubacher and the Austrian *Anschluss* Movement, 1918–40." *Central European History* 8 (December 1975): 348–69.

Rogger, Hans; and Weber, Eugen. *The European Right: A Historical Profile.* Berkeley and Los Angeles: University of California Press, 1966.

Rosar, Wolfgang. *Deutsche Gemeinschaft: Seyss-Inquart und der Anschluss.* Vienna, Frankfurt, and Zürich: Europa Verlag, 1971.

Rosenkranz, Herbert. "The Anschluss and the Tragedy of Austrian Jewry, 1938–1945." *The Jews of Austria.* Edited by Josef Fraenkel. London: Vallentine, Mitchell, 1967: 479–545.

Ross, Dieter. *Hitler und Dollfuss: Die deutsche Österreich Politik, 1933–1934.* Hamburger Beiträge zur Zeitgeschichte, no. 3. Hamburg: Leibnitz, 1966.

Rothschild, K. W. *Austria's Economic Development between the Two Wars.* London: Frederick Muller, 1947.

Rühle, Gerd. *Das Grossdeutsche Reich: Die österreichischer Kampfjahre, 1918–38.* Berlin: Hummelverlag, 1940.

Schausberger, Norbert. *Der Griff nach Österreich: Der Anschluss.* Vienna and Munich: Jugend und Volk Verlag, 1978.

_____. "Ökonomisch-politische Interdependenzen im Sommer 1936." *Das Juliabkommen von 1936.* Edited by the Wissenschaftliche Kommission. Vienna: Verlag für Geschichte und Politik, 1977: 280–98.

Scheu, Friedrich. *Der Weg ins Ungewisse: Österreichs Schicksalskurve 1919–1938.* Vienna, Munich, and Zürich: Verlag Fritz Molden, 1972.

Schilling, Alexander. *Dr. Walter Riehl und die Geschichte des Nationalsozialismus. Mit einem Anhang: Hitler in Österreich.* Leipzig: Forum Verlag, 1933.

Schmitt, H. A. "End of the First Republic." *Southwestern Social Science Quarterly* 39 (March 1959): 291–306.

Schopper, Hans. *Niederdonau. Die deutschen Gauen seit der Machtergreifung.* Edited by Paul Meier-Benneckenstein. Berlin: Junker und Dünnhaupt Verlag, 1940.

_____. *Presse im Kampf: Geschichte der Presse während der Kampfjahre der NSDAP (1933–1938) in Österreich.* Brno: Rudolf M. Rohrer, 1942.

Schuschnigg, Kurt von. *The Brutal Takeover.* Translated by Richard Barry. London: Weidenfeld & Nicolson, 1969.

_____. *My Austria.* New York: Alfred A. Knopf, 1946.

Schwarz, Robert. "Antisemitism and Socialism in Austria, 1918–62." *The Jews of*

Austria. Edited by Joseph Fraenkel. London: Vallantine, Mitchell, 1967: 445–66.

————. "The Austrian Nazi Movement (1918–1973)." Unpublished MS, Florida Atlantic University, 1974.

Sereny, Gitta. *Into that Darkness: From Mercy Killing to Mass Murder*. New York, St. Louis, and San Francisco: McGraw-Hill Book Co., 1974.

Seton-Watson, R. W. *German, Slav, and Magyar*. New York: Howard Fertig, 1968. Originally published in 1916.

Seymour, Charles; and Whiteman, Harold B., Jr., eds. *Letters from the Paris Peace Conference*. New Haven, Conn.: Yale University Press, 1965.

Shell, Kurt L. *The Transformation of Austrian Socialism*. State University of New York Press, 1962.

Shepherd, Gordon. *The Austrian Odyssey*. London: Macmillan & Co., 1957. [See also Brook-Shepherd, Gordon.]

Silberstein, Gerard E. *The Troubled Alliance: German-Austrian Relations, 1914–17*. Lexington, Ky.: The University Press of Kentucky, 1970.

Simon, Walter B. "The Political Parties of Austria." Ph.D. dissertation, Columbia University, 1957.

Slapnicka, Harry. *Oberösterreich: Zwischen Bürgerkrieg und Anschluss (1927–1938)*. Linz: Oberösterreichischer Landesverlag, 1975.

Smelser, Ronald M. *The Sudeten Problem, 1933–1938: Volkstumspolitik and the Formulation of Nazi Foreign Policy*. Middletown, Conn.: Wesleyan University Press, 1975.

Smith, Bradley F. *Reaching Judgment at Nuremberg*. New York and Scarborough, Ont.: New American Library, 1927.

Spann, Gustav. "Die Illegale Flugschriftpropaganda der österreichischen NSDAP vom Juliputsch 1934 bis Juliabkommen 1936." *Das Juliabkommen von 1936*. Edited by the Wissenschaftliche Kommission. Vienna: Verlag für Geschichte und Politik, 1977: 188–97.

Speer, Albert. *Inside the Third Reich*. New York: Avon Books, 1970.

Stadler, Karl R. *Austria*. New York and Washington, D.C.: Praeger Publishers, 1971.

————. *The Birth of the Austrian Republic, 1918–1921*. Leyden: A. W. Sijthoff, 1966.

Starhemberg, Ernst Rüdiger. *Between Hitler and Mussolini*. London: Hodder & Stoughton; New York: The Cooperation Publishing Co., 1942.

————. *Memoiren*. Vienna and Munich: Amalthea Verlag, 1971.

Statistisches Handbuch 1933. Graz, 1934.

Steed, Henry W. *The Hapsburg Monarchy*. New York: Charles Scribner's Sons, 1913.

Stephenson, Jill. *Women in Nazi Society*. New York: Barnes & Noble, 1975.

Sternhell, Zeev. "Fascist Ideology." *Fascism: A Reader's Guide*. Edited by Walter Laqueur. Berkeley and Los Angeles: University of California Press, 1976: 315–76.

Strong, David F. *Austria (October 1918–March 1919): Transition from Empire to Republic*. New York: Columbia University Press, 1939.

Stuhlpfarrer, Karl. "Zum Problem der deutschen Penetration Österreichs." *Das Juliabkommen von 1936*. Edited by the Wissenschaftliche Kommission. Vienna: Verlag für Geschichte und Politik, 1977: 313–27.

Sugar, Peter F., ed. *Native Fascism in the Successor States, 1918–1945*. Santa Barbara, Cal.: ABC Clio, 1971.

Taylor, A. J. P. *The Origins of the Second World War*. 2nd ed. Greenwich, Conn.: Fawcett Publications, 1966.

Tingsten, Herbert. *Political Behavior: Studies in Election Statistics*. New York:

Arno Press, 1975. Originally published in 1937.

Toland, John. *Adolf Hitler*. New York: Ballantine Books, 1976.

Toynbee, Arnold J., *et al.*, eds. *Survey of International Affairs, 1933–1934*. Oxford: Oxford University Press, 1934–1935.

Turner, Henry A., Jr., ed. *Nazism and the Third Reich*. New York: Quadrangle Books, 1972.

———. *Reappraisals of Fascism*. New York: New Viewpoints, 1975.

Vaterländische Front. Bundeswerbeleitung. *Richtlinien zur Führerausbildung*. 2nd ed. Vienna: Vaterländische Front, 1935.

———. Bundespropagandaleitung. *Richtlinien für den Zellenleiter, Zellenvertrauensmann und Nachtrichtenmann*. Vienna: Vaterländische Front, 1935.

Völz, Hans. *Daten der Geschichte der NSDAP*. 11th ed. Berlin and Leipzig: Junker und Dünnhaupt Verlag, 1943.

Wache, Karl, ed. *Deutscher Geist in Österreich: Ein Handbuch des völkischen Lebens der Ostmark*. Dornbirn: C. Bruton-Verlag, 1933.

———. "Land und Volk: Ursprung und Werdegang." *Deutscher Geist in Österreich*. Edited by Karl Wache. Dornbirn: C. Bruton-Verlag, 1933: 9–69.

Wagner, Dieter; and Tomkowitz, Gerhard. *Anschluss: The Week That Hitler Seized Vienna*. Translated by Geoffrey Strachan. New York: St. Martin's Press, 1971.

Wandruszka, Adam. "Die Krise des Parlamentarismus 1897 und 1933: Gedanken zum Demokratieverständnis Österreich." *Beiträge zur Zeitgeschichte*. Edited by Rudolf Neck and Adam Wandruszka. St. Pölten: Verlag Niederösterreichisches Pressehaus, 1976: 61–80.

———. "Österreichs politische Struktur." *Geschichte der Republik Österreich*. Edited by Heinrich Benedikt. Vienna: Verlag für Geschichte und Politik, 1954: 289–485.

Weinberg, Gerhard. *The Foreign Policy of Hitler's Germany: Diplomatic Revolution in Europe, 1933–36*. Chicago: University of Chicago Press, 1970.

Weinzierl-Fischer, Erika. "Österreichs Katholiken und der Nationalsozialismus." *Wort und Wahrheit* 18 (1963): 417–39, 493–526; 20 (1965): 777–805.

Whiteside, Andrew G. "Austria." *The European Right: A Historical Profile*. Edited by Hans Rogger and Eugen Weber. Berkeley and Los Angeles: University of California Press, 1966: 308–63.

———. *Austrian National Socialism before 1918*. The Hague: Martinus Nujhoff, 1962.

———. "The Deutsche Arbeiterpartei, 1904–1918: A Contribution to the Origins of Fascism." *Austrian History Newsletter*, no. 4 (1963): 3–14.

———. "Reply to the Above Comments" [made by Robert A. Kann on Whiteside's article, "The Deutsche Arbeiterpartei"]. *Austrian History Newsletter*, no. 4 (1963): 16.

———. *The Socialism of Fools: Georg von Schönerer and Austrian Pan-Germanism*. Berkeley and Los Angeles: University of California Press, 1975.

Williams, Maurice. "Delusions of 'Grandeur': The Austrian National Socialists." Unpublished paper prepared for the Western Association for German Studies convention, Tempe, Arizona, October 1977.

———. "German Nazis and Austrian Relief: The Third Reich's *Hilfswerk* in Austria." Unpublished paper prepared for the Western Association for German Studies convention, Snowbird, Utah, October 1978.

Winkler, Franz. *Die Diktatur in Österreich*. Zürich: Orell Füssli, 1935.

Wissenschaftliche Kommission. Vol. 4. *Das Juliabkommen von 1936*. Vienna: Verlag für Geschichte und Politik, 1977.

The World Almanac and Book of Facts, 1929. New York: American Heritage Press, Workman Publishing Co., Facsimile Edition, 1971.

Zeman, Z. A. B. *Nazi Propaganda*. London: Oxford University Press, 1964.

Zernatto, Guido. *Die Wahrheit über Osterreich*. New York and Toronto: Longman's Green & Co., 1939.

Zweig, Stefan. *The World of Yesterday*. New York: Viking Press, 1943.